Animals, Man and Treescapes

The interactions between grazing animals, people and wooded landscapes.

Landscape Archaeology and Ecology, Volume 9, 2011
(b/w version)

Edited by Ian D. Rotherham and Christine Handley

Edited by Ian D. Rotherham and Christine Handley

ISSN 1354-0262
ISBN 978-1-904098-25-6

Published by:
Wildtrack Publishing, Venture House,
103 Arundel Street, Sheffield S1 2NT

Typeset and processed by Christine Handley

Supported by:
Biodiversity and Landscape History Research Institute.
Sheffield Hallam University.
HEC Associates Ltd.
South Yorkshire Biodiversity Research Group.
The Forest History Society.
Society for Landscape Studies
Landscape Conservation Forum.

Sponsored by:
British Ecology Society.

© Wildtrack Publishing and the individual authors 2011.

All rights reserved. No part of this publication may be reproduced or transmitted in any form or by any means, electronic or mechanical, including photocopying, recording, or any information storage or retrieval system, without permission in writing from the publisher.

Contents

Animals, Man & Treescapes – perceptions of the past in the present   1
Ian D. Rotherham

Encouraging the use of stock to enhance woodland biodiversity: a new web-based toolbox   33
Helen M. Armstrong, Bob Black, Kate Holl, Nick Mainprize, Lucy Sumsion and
Richard Thompson

Man, Swine and Miradal   45
Hans Baeté

*Continuity and Change: Fluctuations in Woodland Cover, Arable and Pasture in Prehistoric
and Modern times: Cycles of intensive land-use and abandonment*   48
Graham Bathe, Ben Lennon and Jonathan Spencer

The Perception of Trees and Forested Environments in Iceland   69
Adriana Binimelis Sáez

*EU-FIRESMART, Forest and Land Management Options to Prevent Unwanted Forest Fires:
SWOT Analyses in Agroforestry Systems*   84
Caroline Boström, Maria Julia Yagüe, Carmen Hernando, Rosa Planelles, Armando Buffoni,
Rosario Alves, Marielle Jappiot and Jesús San Miguel

*Wild Cattle – Wilder Valley: Sharing experiences from introducing extensive cattle grazing
to a Lakeland valley*   91
Gareth Browning and John Gorst

Re-wilding trees for ancients of the future   109
Jill Butler

Woodland grazing with cattle – the effects of twenty-five years grazing   116
Rita Merete Buttenschøn and J. Buttenschøn

The future potential of wood pastures   122
Iris Glimmerveen

Impact of the reintroduction of wild boar into the Forest of Dean, UK   137
Martin Goulding

Knepp Castle Estate Wildland Project   140
Charles Burrell, Bt. and Theresa Greenaway

Observations on the Knepp Castle Wildland Project   154
Ted Green

Observations on trees and grazing refuges in the west of Scotland   163
Richard Gulliver

Juniper Re-establishment Project - Isle of Islay, Argyll, Scotland   186
Richard and Mavis Gulliver

Re-wilding the Landscape: Some Observations on Landscape History   190
Della Hooke

Smuggling and surviving in the uplands: a landscape builder of grazing and cattle on the Portuguese and Spanish Borders in the nineteenth century   205
Cristina Joanaz de Melo

Woods, Trees and Animals: a South Yorkshire Historical Perspective   226
Melvyn Jones

What was the pre-Neolithic landscape like and is it a relevant template for modern conservation?   237
Keith J. Kirby

Impacts of herbivory on vegetation dynamics in the New Forest   242
Adrian Newton

Legacies of livestock grazing in the forest structure of Valonia oak landscapes in the Eastern Mediterranean   243
Tobias Plieninger, Harald Schaich and Thanasis Kizos

Creation of open woodlands through pasture: Genesis, relevance as biotopes, value in the landscape and in nature conservation in Southwest-Germany   261
Mattias Rupp

Palaeoecological records of woodland history during recent centuries of grazing and management examples from Glen Affric, Scotland and Ribblesdale, north Yorkshire   278
Helen Shaw and Ian Whyte

Treescapes: Trees, Animals, Landscape and 'Treetime'   282
Luke Steer

*Worldviews in Transition: The Impact of Exotic Plants and Animals on Iron Age/
Romano-British landscapes* 296
Naomi Sykes

Integrating Trees into Modern Agriculture 317
Michael J. Townsend

Can't see the trees for the forest 326
Frans Vera

*Yarncliff Wood at Hathersage: initial assessment of the impacts of sixty years of sheep
exclosure on an upland Pennine ancient wood* 328
Ondřej Vild and Ian D. Rotherham

Animals, Man & Treescapes – perceptions of the past in the present

Ian D. Rotherham
Sheffield Hallam University

Summary

The ongoing debates and discussions around the 'Vera Hypothesis' of the origins of north-western European landscapes (Vera, 2000) have stimulated academics and others to view the evidence afresh. In particular, it seems worthwhile to attempt to place the hypothesis into a framework of historic timelines of wooded environments and to consider its relationship to the cultural landscapes from medieval times onwards. Researchers have noted how ancient parks, originating in medieval or earlier times, provide unique insights into the once great primeval savannahs across much of north-western Europe. Certainly, their remarkable biodiversities provide evidence of such potential lineage. These landscapes present palimpsests of ecology and archaeology that reflect their economically driven origins over 800-1,200 years. Indeed, Since Oliver Rackham's seminal works *Ancient Woodland* (1980) and *The History of the Countryside* (1986), it has been accepted that wood-pasture was once the most abundant type of wooded landscape in north-western Europe. In essence, wood-pasture is a system of land management where trees are grown, and grazing by large herbivores (domesticated, semi-domesticated, wild, or a combination of stock), is permitted. Wood-pasture in England is well documented for over one thousand years, and the *Domesday Book* (1086) probably records a landscape dominated by the practice. It has been suggested that wood-pasture was an ancient system of management that developed in a multi-functional landscape where woodland was plentiful and where there was little need for formal coppice. The latter is a more intensive and rigorously managed system, intended to ensure vital supplies of wood and timber in a resource-limited landscape (Fowler, 2002; Hayman, 2003; Perlin, 1989). Pasture-woodland is the older system and in many ways more 'natural'. Significantly, most livestock, wild or domesticated, take leaf fodder or browse if offered. This is in preference to grazing (Vera, 2000). These systems of land management, their ecologies and economics, were described by Rotherham (2007a, b). This paper reports recent research that seeks to embed the Vera ideas within a framework of historic cultural ecology (Rotherham, 2011a).

There is considerable interest in the idea of either 'ancient' woods or 'old growth' forest (e.g. Rackham, 1976, 1980, 1986, 2007; Peterken, 1981, 1996) and in relating this to contemporary management. However, many approaches to wooded landscapes are fundamentally flawed by the absence of an understanding of the historic context of the sites and of their ecologies. Recent research in the UK and across Europe seeks to address these issues and to provide a robust interrogation of forest and woodland dynamics that can better inform contemporary management and conservation. This paper develops ideas presented by Rotherham (2011) as the evidence base for these assertions. That book chapter also provided a model into which historical and ecological information can be placed in order to critically assess issues of woodland antiquity and ecological continuity. These studies seek to integrate problems of cultural severance (Rotherham, 2008, 2011b) in wooded landscapes, with the potential for both dynamic change in ecology and the contradictions of long-term spatial stability too.

The progress reported so far, represents an attempt to reconcile to ideas of scholars such as Frans Vera (Vera, 2000), of an open savannah-like primeval landscape with dynamically fluid patches of high forest in Europe, with mediaeval and contemporary woodland in countries like England. A key idea to emerge from the studies is that of the Act of Commons or Statute of Merton representing a watershed in the spatial fixing of 'woods' in their landscape context. These named woods are today marked out and identifiable by so-called botanical indicators. Examples to test the ideas were taken from wooded landscapes in England in order to relate known historic time-lines to demonstrate changes in ecology, in woodland structure, and in pedology (Rotherham, 2011a). The methodology described (Rotherham, 2011a) helps to facilitate an improved understanding of woodland landscape history but it also informs future management and conservation strategies for forest and woodland areas. It attempts to place wooded landscapes in a wider context of historically grazed ecosystems.

Introduction

There is still a debate about the nature of this primeval landscape across north-western Europe. The discussions centred on the seminal work of Frans Vera (2000), have helped to clarify how the early landscape might have looked and perhaps aid the understanding of how their biodiversity relates to that which we see today. Our vision now is not one of wall-to-wall forest, but of plains or savannah that are more open with a rich diversity of other landscape and ecological components too, including woodland. Much of this variation would be related to basic environmental factors like climate and water-logging, but a key factor identified by Vera is the importance alongside these of large grazing herbivores. Not everyone agrees with Vera's hypothesis, but the argument is compelling and a refined version of his original vision has a considerable body of supporting evidence. Issues of upland / lowland variation and interactions also need to be built into the Vera ideas and these were discussed at the meetings held in Sheffield in 2005 and 2007 (Rotherham (Ed.), 2005, 2007c).

Figure 1. Chillingham Park Wild Cattle.

Figure 2. Fallow deer at dawn. Photograph: Paul Hobson.

I suggest that the European landscape had vast expanses of wetland, marsh, fen and peat bog with extensive coastal wetlands too. Dense woodland and thickets would grow up in the protection of rings of prickly Blackthorn and Bramble and here would be the plants and animals that characterise our so-called 'ancient woodlands' today; the Bluebell (*Hyacinthoides non-scripta*), Dog's Mercury (*Mercurialis perennis*), Wood Anemone (*Anemone nemorosa*), and Yellow Archangel (*Galeobdolon luteum*) for example. Outside the prickly halos of the thorns was a wide-open savannah with heath, grassland and giant old trees such as Pedunculate Oak (*Quercus robur*), which grew to ages of a thousand years or more before collapsing into oblivion. A further powerful driver of succession and change in this landscape would be pre-human fire caused by lightning strikes, taking out the great trees in the open plain. Further north and into the upland zones there would be a change to landscape dominated by great and similarly ancient Scots Pines (*Pinus sylvestris*), and again a strong influence of natural, lightning-related fires. Mountain zones would have large areas of disturbance through natural landslip and erosion areas, and all the great rivers would include sometimes-vast floodlands and meandering patterns of erosion and deposition in an ever-changing yet stable landscape. Much of this environment would have limited amounts of available nutrients, especially nitrogen and phosphorus, and this too had a great influence on associated biodiversity. Localised areas such as mountain downwash zones and alluvial fans had higher nutrient levels, and the whole landscape experienced abundant micro-disturbance through natural process, but only limited macro-disturbance. Erosion and deposition areas, animal-related disturbance, fire, successional, and life-cycle related changes, such as the collapse of ancient trees were the key to the ecological dynamics. This landscape provided a template for a richly diverse fauna and flora with regionally district ecologies related to broad climatic influences and localised geological and topographic factors. This was the landscape, the ecology and the biodiversity upon which the footprint of human activity was stamped with increasing effect over the following five to six thousand years.

Human colonisation of the north-western European landscape brought about a gradual, though sometimes abrupt conversion. From the template of savannah and forest, human activities created a 'cultural landscape' of wood, forest, meadow, field, pasture, heath, common, fen and bog. The habitats and species associations of the original landscape found their niches within the emerging cultural ecology of the medieval period. The evidence for this lineage is extensive and complex, but some simple ecological observations point the way. Several key aspects of grassland ecological diversity suggest a long-standing evolution of communities and complexity in ecosystems with a significant presence in the primeval landscapes. Firstly, we have a rich biodiversity of flowering plants and of invertebrates associated with pastures, meadows and heaths. Secondly, these communities include many species with complex mutualistic relationships between the plants and a range of fungi but especially the vesicular-arbuscular mycorrhizae. These interactions include multiples of interconnections between fungi and various plant individuals and species. Finally, there are incredibly complex interrelationships evolved such as between the Large Blue Butterfly and the ants that play host to the butterfly larvae. It is clear that all these examples suggest long-term stability on open communities in the early European landscape and the evolution of intimate and complex interrelationships. However, it is not suggested that this landscape was static and unchanging. These were extensive mosaics of inter-connected ecosystems with dynamic stability but at the same time fluid and changing. The natural dynamics of water and land, of lightning strike fires, and of Vera's herbivores would ensure that disturbance and successional change were key drivers in this ancient and evolving ecology. These impacts were mimicked and mirrored in the effects of human usage of the cultural landscape.

However, most of the earlier subsistence landscapes were swept away by the tide of improvement and the parallel revolutions in industry and in agriculture, triggered by revolutions in industry and agriculture. Rising human populations and urbanisation drove much of the change. Therefore, from the 1700s onwards the European landscape and its ecologies were changed forever. Habitats and communities that had ebbed and flowed in the pre-industrial environment struggled to adapt to eutrophication and macro-disturbance. In a little over two hundred years, the extensive and seamless savannah landscapes of Frans Vera were reduced to isolated fragments in a sea of inhospitable anthropogenic conditions. In contemporary landscapes, almost all the original template has been erased and eroded, and in the environments of urban-dwelling, of industry, and intensive farming and forestry, it can be hard to see the past through the present. The massive landscape transformations of the last three hundred years have changed much almost beyond recognition. Yet the ecology is sometimes surprisingly persistent; sometimes retaining an almost desperate hold as species persist in tiny relict areas or move to new sites as opportunity arises. I suggest that as humanity changed the early European landscape and its ecology, some of the complexity evolved in Vera's wide-open spaces between the dense forests and extensive wet woodlands, survived and adapted. Over countless centuries these animals, plants, and fungi, and those of the wooded zones, became the ecologies of the cultural landscape of the early medieval period. In the absence of petrochemically driven power and inorganic fertilisers, the species and communities dovetailed into niches in habitats similar to those in which they had evolved. The extensive heaths, commons, meadows, sheep walk, fens, bogs, woods, and forests were ideal analogues of their origins.

Today, we can see the shadows and imprints of this ancient ecology in the modern landscape. Old meadows and pastures, ancient heaths, medieval coppice woods, and similar features bear testimony to this remarkable lineage. Ancient parks are the most visibly obvious remnants of formerly extensive grazed wooded landscapes. However, even where deer parks survive (and this is rare), they do so as unique landscapes separated in time and function from their origins. In many cases, these areas reflect the landscapes of the time and place they were imparked, and changes of economic function and ecology over a long lifespan. When created, carved out of a working medieval or earlier landscape, their ecologies were driven by multi-functional systems of economic utilisation. Over time, as purpose changed so did ecology, each new phase incorporating, preserving, or removing, and modifying those that preceded it. It is argued by Frans Vera (Vera, 2000), Ted Green and others, that some of these great parks are landscapes that originate in medieval or earlier times, and give unique insights into the former extensive primeval savannahs of north-western Europe.

These observations provide a starting point for further investigation. In particular, medieval parks are of great interest since they, like the primeval savannah, were landscapes that mixed trees and grazing or browsing mammals. It is suggested that parks were one facet of a landscape complex that included wood pasture, wooded commons, forests, perhaps as relicts of what was probably in prehistory a great wooded savannah across much of north-western Europe. In both origins and ecology, parks are essentially a form of 'pasture-woodland', related to forests, heaths, moors, and some commons, with grazing animals and variable tree cover (Rotherham, 2007a, b). Aside from the obvious external enclosure, these landscapes were often essentially unenclosed grazing lands. In considering their ecology, it is important to establish origins and relationships to other wildlife habitats, and to recognise too, the range from areas of only a few hectares to massive sites extending over many kilometres of unenclosed ground. In the two centuries following the Norman Conquest, numbers of parks in England increased dramatically to perhaps 3,000, with possibly fifty in Wales, and eighty in Scotland. From the early thirteenth century, a royal licence was technically necessary to create a park in areas of royal forest; though Cummins (1988) notes that in both England and Scotland baronial parks were sometimes created without licence. Where documents survive, they provide invaluable reference materials for a now vanished age, giving insight into landscape and ecology. The average English medieval park was around fifty hectares but size varied considerably. The date of establishment, the area enclosed, the functions of the park and the interplay between enclosed and unenclosed areas all influenced the ecology of these landscapes (Jones, 1996; Jones *et al.*, 1996; Rotherham, 2007a, b). As lands were imparked, at the same time other areas were set aside as 'woods', and for other uses by the Lord or by the commoners. The interactions between these various landscape components, and the implications of legal recognition and of enclosure, are central to the theme of this research.

Ancient wooded landscapes

In Britain, it is generally accepted that there are two broad distinctions in 'ancient woodland' landscapes. Firstly, there are coppice woods, often managed since the medieval period as simple coppice, or more frequently 'coppice-with-standards'. These sites often have relatively few large trees, but possess strikingly rich and sometimes diverse ground floras. Secondly, there are parklands, which may have historic links back to their use as medieval parks. These areas generally have poorer ground floras due to grazing livestock, and are frequently notable for massive and ancient trees, chiefly 'pollards'. Sometimes the park may have no ancient trees, but often this is because they have been removed for financial reasons at some time in the site's long history. Many of these landscapes, both ancient coppice and mediaeval parklands, have significant evidence of human impacts and settlements within them (see Beswick and Rotherham, 1993). I suggest here that reality is more complex and that these are two clearly identifiable types within a broad complex of wooded landscapes.

Research over the last twenty years has demonstrated that many assumptions about these wooded landscapes are incorrect or naïve in their interpretation. Researchers such as Paul Harding stimulated interests in British pasture-woodlands, and both Frans Vera and Ted Green have challenged many accepted 'truths' of woodland history. Together, the new approaches help to place park and other grazed landscapes in their wider ecological context. Indeed, parks were juxtaposed with, but different from, medieval coppice woods, although the bigger parks often included 'woods' within them. The surving landscapes present unique resources for conservation and provide rich insights into ecological history (Rollins, 2003). As part of this process, research by scholars such as Keith Alexander and Roger Key has transformed the understanding of the importance of parks for invertebrates. Ted Green has awakened interest in ancient tree fungi and with Jill Butler and Helen Read especially, has emphasized the significance of the trees themselves. In northern Britain, Chris Smout (2003), and others, have transformed our knowledge of Scottish woods and the Caledonian Pine Forests and palaeo-ecologists such as Paul Buckland have closed the knowledge gaps about linking these landscapes and their ecologies to prehistoric and medieval periods. All this work helps to establish a new vision of the wooded landscape and its unique heritage value.

To further develop the context of our current studies it is important to note the seminal and influential writings of authorities like Oliver Rackham (1976 and 1986), George Peterken (1981 and 1996), and Donald Pigott (1993). Together these forge coherent visions of woodland landscape ecology, with parks and other grazed areas representing an important component. However, it is of significance that for many years medieval parks were not considered 'ancient woodland' by conservation agencies. They were in effect the 'Cinderellas' of nature conservation. Now, and from a broader 'woodland' perspective, it is possible to assess the historical ecology of medieval parks and other grazed wooded areas and place them in their landscape context. Parks have trees (usually but not always), and large (and sometimes smaller) grazing mammals, and to survive trees need protection. Some parkland trees are ornamental and others are managed 'working' trees, with fundamental differences in species and structures associated with these different functions. Taigel and Williamson (1993) and Bettey (1993) give useful introductions to the complexities of these landscapes. Such historical contributions are important since ecologists must understand history and historians the ecosystem. The potential of cross-fertilisation is considerable and Rackham (2004) provides an eloquent exposition on the evolution of park landscapes and of their trees in particular. Muir (2005) is a particularly accessible account of recent developments. In this paper however, I suggest that the interpretation of these landscapes may require re-visiting in order to appreciate more fully the complexities of the resource. In particular, I suggest that there were extensive and often-grazed wooded landscapes remaining at the time of the early medieval period, and that these linked backwards in time to Vera's primeval environment. However, and importantly, when manorial coppice 'woods' were enclosed, either triggered by or more likely reflected in, the Statute of Merton, much of this wooded landscape resource remained unenclosed and importantly for research purposes, unnamed. Not enclosed or named in the manorial records, these wooded landscapes were in the wider commons, including fens, moors, heaths and wastes.

The palimpsests of wooded landscapes

It is important to consider the known ecology of both parks and woods in order to begin to unravel these complex relationships. The difficulty in differentiating medieval parks from other imparked areas and from other associated grazing landscapes was noted by Rotherham (2007a, b). There can be major differences of opinion and hence difficulties in defining exactly what a park was or is. Furthermore, they share features with other unenclosed grazed landscapes that have trees and woods, such as chases, forests, moors, heaths, commons and some fens. An additional complication is that many parks 'took in' significant elements of earlier landscapes when they were enclosed often from 'waste' or 'forest'. In some cases, park management has allowed parts of this ancient ecology to survive. In other cases, parks include ecology and features from specific periods of active management (with specific ends and outcomes), from subsequent times of abandonment, or changed use. Each phase preserves, modifies, or removes earlier ecology and these working landscapes evolved over a thousand years or more. To understand today's ecology requires awareness of changes through pulses and periods of both management and neglect.

Ecological research has often failed to differentiate between contrasting parkland origins and histories, and for many ecologists a park is a park. However, the reality is very different and consequently the study of parkland ecology in often not set within a reliable historical framework. Furthermore, there is little hard information on the ecology of these landscapes in previous periods when they were working parks. Assumptions today are often made retrospectively based on modern observations, or information is gleaned from material such as household and estate accounts. The complexity of park occurrence and presentation in the landscape, both today and in the past, is well illustrated by Squires and Humphrey (1986), investigating and mapping in detail the parks of the former Charnwood Forest, Leicestershire. To understand the historical ecology of parks, it is essential to appreciate their form and function, and the changes over time. In many cases, only a fragment of the earlier landscape is visible today, and sometimes these fragments remain unrecognised. Even where a park survives with proven continuity to earlier periods, management today differs from that in the past.

Cantor (Squires and Humphrey, 1986) noted medieval parks were important features in their landscapes. He noted that medieval parks differed in character from modern counterparts that are affected by eighteenth-, nineteenth-, or even twentieth-century park creation and management. Cantor observed that medieval parks were very different from today's parks and were often areas of rough, uncultivated landscape, usually wooded, and frequently on the edge of manors away from cultivation (Cantor and Hatherly, 1979). Owned by the lord of the manor, these lands were managed as hunting parks, stocked with deer and other game, and provided food and sport in varying balance. Our vision of a working medieval park should be set in a landscape of open field, waste, common, heath, bog and fen, woodland, and royal forest. The ecologies of these different components were inexorably linked and intimately intertwined and form a complex of 'wooded landscapes' or 'treescapes'.

The extensive medieval landscapes, which included parks, provided hunting, foodstuffs, and both wood and timber for building and fuel. Alongside their deer, medieval parks contained wild boar, hares, rabbits, game birds, fish in fishponds, and grazing for cattle and sheep. For some, such as Bradgate Park, pannage (feeding pigs on acorns) from the oaks provided revenue in rents. Medieval parks generally had large areas of heath or grassland (called launds or plains) dotted with trees, along with woods (called holts or coppices, and if for holly (*Ilex aquifolium*) hollins). The launds provided food for animals in summer, and the hollins, provided it through the winter. Parks may have held and maintained deer (fallow (*Dama dama*) and red (*Cervus elaphus*)) for the table and the hunt. In the latter case, this sometimes involved release beyond the park pale and into the chase beyond (Whitehead, 1964 and 1980). Cummins (1988) discusses the size of parks and the differences between smaller baronial parks with semi-domesticated animals, and the much larger royal parks. Some parks extended over many miles. Woodstock (Oxon.) for example, had a perimeter of seven miles and permitted hunting on a grand scale; others were much smaller and some little more than deer paddocks. Their ecologies were similarly varied with larger parks taking in and maintaining more of the earlier wilderness or waste and its associated ecology. Hunting in the parks, the forest, and the chase, and the ecologies of these different areas were also closely associated.

Solitary trees in the launds were pollarded (high coppice), and some shredded (branches removed from the tall, main stem). The only new tree growth outside the woods took place in the protection of thickets of hawthorn (*Crataegus monogyna*), holly, and bramble (*Rubus fruticosus* agg.). There were special woods called holly hags or hollins where holly cut on rotation fed the deer in winter. A boundary fence, called the park pale surrounded the park. This was a cleft oak fence, a bank with a cleft oak fence, or a wall. If there was a bank, it normally had an internal ditch. Park pales often contained structures called deer leaps to entice wild deer into the park. Buildings in parks included manor houses (from Tudor times), keepers' lodges, and banqueting houses. The park was multi-functional and part of the wider economy of the manor. Turf and stone were extracted, mineral coal too if it occurred. Squires and Humphrey (1986) noted arable crops such as cereals grown within the park pale. Deer were a priority but shared the landscape with other domestic stock such as cattle, horses, and even goats. The park at Wharncliffe Chase near Sheffield even acquired North American Buffalo in the early twentieth century (Jones and Jones, 2005). Many parks such as at Wharncliffe near Sheffield had warrens within them or close by and relict 'pillow mounds' and other features may now evidence these. Other parks had productive fishponds that may survive today as ornamental features, but more often are abandoned, frequently obscure complexes of shallow pools and channels for farming fish for the table (mostly carp), or as stock ponds for fish netted elsewhere.

With socio-economic changes, the fashions for parks and the means for their upkeep fluctuated. Most deer parks were created from 1200 to 1350 AD. They then declined following the

Figure 3. Cattle in Hatfield Forest, Essex.

impact of the Black Death (Mileson, 2005). Subsequently, boundaries moved. Small parks were enlarged or replaced by new creations, as parks and their relationships to great houses, changed with time and fashion. Originally an enclosed area at a small distance from the main house, perhaps containing hunting lodges later parks were increasingly the settings for houses and gardens. The house moved to the park, or the park was moved or modified to envelop the house. Expensive and difficult to maintain, many deer parks fell from fashion, abandoned and destroyed. Between the fifteenth and eighteenth centuries, medieval deer parks were deliberately removed (disparkment), to become large, compartmented coppice woods, or farmland. As the rural economy changed so did the values and costs of a park. Many were abandoned during the English Civil War (1642-1649), and few survived intact as the wave of agricultural improvement swept through the landscape from 1600 onwards. Some such as Tinsley Park in Sheffield, and Tankersley Park in Barnsley, were lost to industrial development as landowners discovered coal and ironstone beneath their land. A small number retained their medieval character, and some of their functions to the present day.

It seems that the greater medieval parks may have shared common origins from facets of Vera's primeval savannah. However, it is further suggested that the other areas referred to, upland moors and moorland fringe, and lowland heaths, commons and downs, probably reflect this same lineage. These are the lands unenclosed in medieval times and linked, albeit tenuously, to Vera's open and fluid primeval landscape. For example, some of the species-rich grasslands such as the Derbyshire Dales limestone pastures are in effect, the remains of the open areas of Vera's landscape. Here we have ancient complex and species-rich grasslands but within a landscape of hazel and patches of ancient woodland identified by Pigott in the 1960s. This then presents us with the question of whether there may be ecological evidence to support this contention.

The ecology of parks and other grazed wooded landscapes

The ecologies of working parks and other grazed wooded landscapes reflect the factors described above. What survives today mirrors these events and pressures. Park landscapes had unimproved grassland across much of the grazed area, species and communities varying with grazing intensity, soil type and wetness. Many grassland plants and associated invertebrates cannot cope with short swards and intensive grazing. However, if grazing levels were low or areas seasonally protected from livestock, the vegetation would grow tall, flower and set seed; similar to modern unimproved pasture and hay meadow. Such areas would be rich in wild flowers and in associated invertebrates such as butterflies, bees, and hoverflies. They would be part of a patchwork of shorter grass, bare ground, and in acidic locations, heath. Wet areas such as valley bottoms, or land with impeded drainage, had extensive moist grassland, marsh or bog. The typical plants of ancient woodlands (such as dog's mercury (*Mercurialis perennis*), wood anemone (*Anemone nemorosa*), primrose (*Primula vulgaris*), and bluebell (*Hyacinthoides non-scripta*)) would have been restricted and found only in enclosed woods, copses, lane sides, hedgerows, or streamsides. They survived perhaps in areas of less intensive grazing, and in the protection of prickly bramble and blackthorn.

Keystone species in the park were deer, with other grazing mammals of varying domestication; these animals being the main drivers in the deer park ecosystem. Other important ecological components were fungi in the unimproved grasslands, and associated with extensive animal dunging. There would have been a rich fungal flora of both mycorrhizal associates of both trees (ectomycorrhizas), and of grasses and forbs in the sward (vesicular-arbuscular mycorrhizas). These would present as both individual groups of toadstool fruiting bodies as can be seen today with the dung-associated species such as the shaggy ink caps (*Coprinus* sp.), and as spectacular '*fairy rings*'. Associated with animal dunging would be rich faunas of coprophagous and predatory flies, and dung beetles. It can be assumed that high numbers of animals would lead to carcases and faunas of species such as burying beetles. With the high numbers of mammals were rich faunas of parasites such as mites, ticks, and biting or egg-laying flies, and further associated food chains of complexity.

Imparking sometimes included deliberate or accidental preservation of domesticated, semi-domesticated, or wild grazing mammals within the enclosure. The white park cattle are a case in point, with the Chillingham Park herd in Northumberland perhaps the best example; aside from a small herd established some distance away as a precaution against foot-and-mouth disease, this unique breed of ancient cattle survives at only one location. Whitaker in 1892 described the park as 1,500 acres, well wooded, and with moor and wild grounds (Whitaker, 1892). This ancient and extensive park enclosed and encapsulated an entire ecosystem that has been maintained ever since, though with considerable modifications as described by Stephen Hall (2007). Outside the park, species including the cattle have long since disappeared. Enclosure of large areas of semi-natural landscape was not the exclusive prerogative of the deer parks. Ornamental parks of the seventeenth and eighteenth century often involved similar scales of enclosure, sometimes from common fields but often from the 'waste'. This may have included marshes, grasslands, heaths, and extensive bogs. Hotham and North Cave Park in the East Riding is such an example (Neave and Turnbull, 1992). Management as a park also affected other species both within and beyond the pale. In particular, predators were vigorously controlled and this would have impacts on ecology that were deep and long lasting; the control of both foxes and wolves noted in estate accounts.

The importance of ancient or old wood, living and dead or dying, standing or fallen, has been recognised in recent decades. Key publications (Read, 1999; Speight, 1989; Kirby and Drake, 1993) have highlighted the role of wood for saproxylic invertebrates, especially insects. Others (Rose, 1974, 1976; Harding and Rose, 1986) have noted the habitat value for epiphytic plants, lichens, and fungi. A characteristic of most, but not all, parks were large, often very old, trees. In the best cases, these provide good quality saproxylic habitats and important continuity of resource over many centuries. Other anciently grazed wooded landscapes also have old trees and dead wood but these are generally less obvious.

Park trees may have been a mixture of timber trees enclosed when the park was formed, and others deliberately planted as part of the park management. Many parks such as Chatsworth in Derbyshire include later additions through the conversion of field systems and their hedgerow trees. These trees are now veterans in the contemporary landscape but originated in an agricultural environment. Most of the very old trees, often oak (*Quercus robur*), are specimens that have been actively managed for at least several centuries and then abandoned. Now ranging from youngsters of maybe 400 years, to real veterans of anything from 800 to 1,200 years, these specimen trees represent one of the most precious resources of former medieval parks. Large trees performed many functions in working parks, providing shelter in winter and shade in summer for cattle and deer. Importantly, they could also provide herbage to feed to the livestock; most deer and cattle preferring to browse on leaves and shoots, than graze grass. To ensure a continuous supply of branches and leaves, the trees were cut high, several metres above ground, keeping re-growth out of the reach of the grazing animals, until the parker cut it for fodder. The technique was known as pollarding and is in effect a high coppice. Furthermore, the provision of special hollins and hags ensured that herbage was provided for livestock throughout the winter. For several months of the year, and longer during colder periods, grass does not grow in Britain and livestock depend on stores of hay, a valuable and often scarce commodity, and cut branches of evergreen holly. Pollarding extended the lifespan of trees beyond that normally achieved and in so doing ensured a major supply and continuity of dead wood, a highly important wildlife habitat.

Large oaks were grown for timber, in some cases, the trunks and boughs were carefully nurtured to form particular shapes and sizes for specific functions. Careful planning and management over many decades are key aspects of park historical ecology. The records of great estates often give precise details of the removal of trees, their price, and destination. Around the park, sometimes as individuals or as small groups, trees of a diversity of species, native and exotic, were planted. The form and the species obviously varied with time and fashion. Now neglected, these younger veterans add to the resource of dead and dying wood in the contemporary park landscape.

Parks are the most obvious landscapes that mix trees and grazing animals. However, once one starts to examine the landscape more critically, it is apparent that many other systems have a similar approach. The once vast lowland fens of eastern England (see for example Rotherham, 2010) had extensive woodland and large numbers of grazing animals. Heaths, commons, and unenclosed pastures (such as at Longshaw in North Derbyshire), mix ancient trees and open grazing lawns with long-term continuity of management to match that of the nearby Chatsworth Park. A major difference is that the ancient trees in these landscapes are generally smaller in stature, and may be species such as hawthorns, which are always small and often overlooked. If we examine the ecology and pedology of these wider landscape features, we also see the imprint or 'shadow' of former 'woodland' status. These are indeed, 'ancient wooded landscapes'. As discussed earlier, we see the origins or at least the recognition of the components of these ancient landscapes in medieval legislation. In particular, the Statute of Merton (or the

Figure 4. The Statute of Merton: a Magna Carta of the Landscape 1235 Henry III

Whereas in a Statute made at Merton, it was granted that Lords of Wastes, Woods, and Pastures, might approve the said Wastes, Woods, and Pastures, notwithstanding the contradiction of their Tenants, so that the tenants had sufficient Pasture to their Tenements with free Egress and regress to the same; and Forasmuch as no Mention was made between Neighbours and Neighbours, many Lords of Wastes, Woods, and Pastures, have been hindered heretofore by the Contradiction of Neighbours having sufficient Pasture; and because foreign Tenants have no more right to Common in the Wastes, Woods, and Pastures of any Lord than the Lord's own Tenants; It is Ordained, that the Statute of Merton, provided between the Lord and his tenants, from henceforth shall hold place between Lords of Wastes, Woods, and Pastures, may make Approvement of the residue …………….from henceforth no Man shall be grieved by Assise of Novel Disseisin for Common of Pasture.

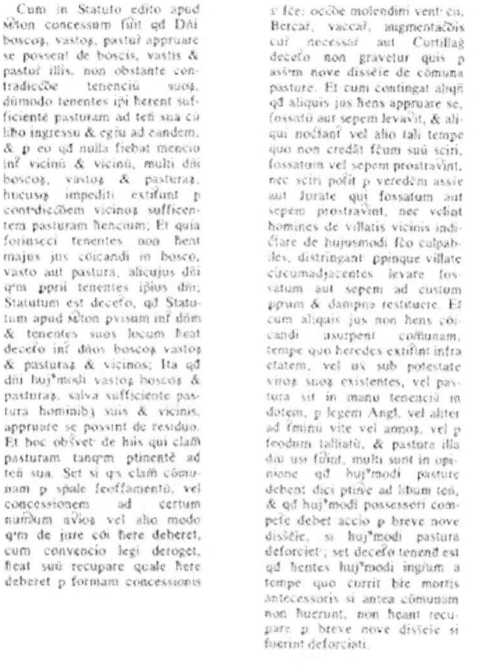
Cum in Statuto edito apud Mton concessum fuit qd Dñi boscoꝝ, vastoꝝ, pastuꝝ appruare se possent de boscis, vastis & pastuꝝ illis, non obstante contradiccōe tenenciū suoꝝ, dūmodo tenentes ipi hērent sufficientē pasturam ad teñ sua cū lībo ingressu & egřu ad eandem, & p eo qd nulla fiebat mencio inř vicinū & vicinū, multi dñi boscoꝝ, vastoꝝ & pasturaꝝ, hucusq impediti extitūnt p contradiccōem vicinoꝝ sufficentem pasturam hencium; Et quia forinseci tenentes non hent majus jus coīcandi in bosco, vasto aut pastura, alicujus dñi qm ppii tenentes ipius dñi; Statutum est decetero, qd Statutum apud Mton pvisum inř dñm & tenentes suos locum heat decetero inř dños boscoꝝ vastoꝝ & pasturaꝝ & vicinos; Ita qd dñi hujusmodi vastoꝝ boscoꝝ & pasturaꝝ, salva sufficiente pastura hominibꝫ suis & vicinis, appruare se possint de residuo. Et hoc obsvet de his qui clam pasturam tanqm ptinentē ad teñ sua. Set si qs clam coīunam p spale feoffamentū, vel concessionem ad certum numerum avioꝝ vel alio modo qm de jure coī hēre deberet, cum convencio legi deroget, heat suū recupare quale hēre deberet p formam concessionis sue: occōe molendini vent' cū Bercar, vaccar, augmentacōis cur necessar aut Curtilag decetero non gravetur quis p assīsam nove disseisīe de coīuna pasture. Et cum contingat aliqñ qd aliquis jus hens appruare se, fossatū aut sepem levavit, & aliqui noctanr vel alio tali tempe quo non credāt factum suū sciri, fossatum vel sepem prostravint, nec sciri posit p veredcm assise aut Jurate qui fossatum aut sepem prostravint, nec velint homines de villatis vicinis indictare de hujusmodi facto culpabiles, distringant ppinque villate circumadjacentes levare fossatum aut sepem ad custum pprium & dampna restituere. Et cum aliquis jus non hens coīcandi usurpent coīunam, tempe quo heredes extitint infra etatem, vel ux sub potestate viroꝝ suoꝝ existentes, vel pastura sit in manu tenenciū in dotem, p legem Angl. vel aliter ad tminū vite vel annoꝝ, vel p feodum talliatū, & pastura illa diu usi fuint, multi sunt in opinione qd hujusmodi pasture debent dici ptine ad libum ten, & qd hujusmodi possessori competē debet accio p breve nove disseīe, si hujusmodi pastura deforciet'; set decetero tenend est qd hentes hujusmodi ingrum a tempe quo currit bre mortis antecessoris si antea coīunam non huerunt, non heant recupare p breve nove disseīe si fuerint deforciati.

Act of Commons) (1235), provides a window into a watershed in the historic development of these landscapes.

It is suggested that this legislation represents a watershed and a landmark moment for the English landscape. It may be that the Act merely reflected what was happening and gave it legal recognition. Nevertheless, this sets down the rights of land use and function at a manorial level. I suggest that what was before very fluid and extensive, became fixed and localised. A 'wood' was now set in its landscape, bounded by fence, wall, hedge or ditch, and given a name. Similarly, the common, the heath, the fen, the field, or the waste, were also marked and recorded. This process has huge implications for the transformation of Vera's landscape to what we see today, and especially for 'wooded' areas left outside the 'woods'. The exciting thing about a great, early medieval deer park is that it enclosed this landscape, as it existed before Merton, including within it woods and other wooded features. It is suggested therefore that these are indeed good places in which to search for the ecological shadows of these once extensive wooded landscapes.

Transformation and fashion

We need to understand the cultural transformations that have occurred in the great parks if we are to understand better their ecologies and those of the associated areas. Rackham (1986) stated that parks were troublesome, precarious enterprises. The boundary in particular was expensive to maintain, especially for large parks. Owners were often absent for much or all of the year, a situation that could lead to mismanagement and neglect. Deer often died of starvation or of other rather vague causes such as 'Garget', 'Wyppes', and 'Rot'. In Henry III's deer park at Havering, Essex, in 1251 the bailiff was instructed '*to remove the bodies of dead beasts and swine which are rotting in the park*' (Rackham, 1978). Even well run parks faced ongoing problems of maintenance. Rackham (1986) noted that many smaller parks were short-lived, and by the thirteenth century, some were already out of use. On occasion, a park was retained but its location changed within the manor, with consequent impacts on their delicate ecologies.

During the sixteenth century, the primary function of the park shifted from game preserve and source of wood and timber, to grand setting of the country house. A disused park might revert to woodland through neglect or deliberate re-planting and many former parks were converted to farmland. Some like Trelowarren in Cornwall retained the park pale, bounding the newly enclosed fields. The late seventeenth and early eighteenth centuries witnessed a fashion to impose formal design and rigid regularity on both existing and new parks. Straight, tree-lined avenues, walks, and straight canals dominated landscapes. At the same time, there came a renewed interest in planting trees, and with wide vistas cut through existing woodlands. New woods were designed in regular patterns within the overall vision. Nature was perceived to be under strict control, and the parks paralleled the great gardens and houses they accompanied (Lasdun, 1992). Changed fashions provided a new lease of life for some old landscapes, but an injection of capital was necessary to maintain them against pressure to 'improve' *per se*. If changes allowed habitat-continuity, then some original ecology such as rare dead wood insects might hang on. As Rackham (1986) pointed out, new parklands were not created from a blank canvas, designers of parks and gardens generally adapted and imposed on earlier landscapes. Indeed, it is this recognition that may provide evidence of the connectivity in time to the ecology of much older landscapes (Rotherham, 2007a, b). The demand for these later parks could mean working with and maintaining elements of an original park. It might also lead to the creation of a new park that incorporated earlier features from a non-park landscape and so features not previously enclosed might come within the park pale. Even when formality was very much in vogue it was still felt that venerable trees added dignity to the feel of a country residence. In a social landscape, where lineage and continuity were highly valued, then a park that was new but looked and felt old, made an important statement. Antiquity, real or perceived, was a commodity with a value. The designer would therefore not only plant anew but would incorporate elements of ancient countryside into their new landscapes. Old pollards and other trees from ancient hedgerows, lanes, or other boundaries, were retained and given heightened significance in their new settings. In effect, these are what we describe elsewhere as 'grubby landscapes' (Wright and Rotherham, 2011). This ensured that ancient pollards and sometimes coppice stools could now be found embedded in a landscape dominated by seventeenth- and eighteenth-century plantings.

In relation to designed parklands, Rackham described these as 'pseudo-medieval' parks. He suggests that this phase of landscape history both preserved some ancient parks, and created these new sites. He notes the New Park at Long Melford Hall, Suffolk incorporating earlier field boundary trees, similar to the situation in the eighteenth-century landscape park at Chatsworth, Derbyshire. At Chatsworth in the eighteenth-century landscape park, are trackways, boundaries, ridge-and-furrow fields, and veteran trees from the old field-system. Oakes Park, formerly in North Derbyshire, shows a similar use of old field-boundary trees to lend an air of elegance and antiquity to a created eighteenth-century park landscape. These sites can be identified not only from archives and records, but also from field archaeology and their ecology. The landscape archaeology may include early non-park features alongside those of the park itself. They lack some of the ancient deer park indicators discussed previously, but can hold species of medieval woodlands, of hedgerows, and perhaps of veteran pollard trees. Again, this gives a site what I describe as 'acquired antiquity'. In other words, the landscape has elements that would normally be associated with a genuinely ancient feature or area, but which it has acquired or 'borrowed' from fragments of an earlier period incorporated into a later design. Sheringham Park in Norfolk is a wonderful example of this, with veteran trees and ancient banks, not of a medieval park, but absorbed from commonland when the owner imparked the area in the 1700s. In many ways, this presumably is what the designers hoped to achieve, though perhaps not at the ecological level. What we see over this period of time is a fluxing of species and communities increasingly influenced by human intervention.

The ebb and flow of woodland and grazing

The question is then what became of the thousands of medieval parks, large and small, that dotted the landscape. The fate of the non-parkland grazed woodlands is even more obscure. For some landscapes, there are tantalising glimpses of their fate, and the approach that we have developed provides a fascinating insight into landscape change. Ecclesall Woods in Sheffield is the region's premier conservation woodland today, but detailed studies of deadwood indicators of ancient woodlands, undertaken in the 1980s, identified it as an anomaly. Ecclesall Woods lacks key species of invertebrates that its assumed antiquity would suggest that it should have. Following in-depth studies of field archaeology and archival research however, the circumstances make eminent sense. Ecclesall Woods was open farmland with small areas of very wet and riverside woodland throughout a long period from Late Neolithic, and through the Bronze Age, Iron Age, and Romano-British periods even until the late Saxon. Following the Norman Conquest, the lands changed hands and by 1317AD, the area has its origins as a medieval hunting park. In 1317, Robert de Ecclesall was granted a licence to impark, and this is reflected in modern place names such as Parkhead, Warren Wood, Park Field, and Old Park (Hart, 1993). An overview of the issues of interpretation of the landscape here are presented by Rotherham and Ardron (2006). As noted by Hart (1993) there is further evidence of the use of the Woods for hunting, with a set of depositions taken on October 2nd 1587. These were from George Sixth Earl of Shrewsbury. He stated that he, his father and his grandfather:

'……..used sett and placed Crosbowes for to Kyll the Deare in Ecclesall Afforesaied and to hunte at all tymes when it so pleased them there.' Thomas Creswick noted that ' ……….ye said Erle George grandfather to ye said now Erle of Shrewsbury hath sett Netts & long bowes to kill deare in Ecclesall and hunted dyvers tymes there and he thinketh that ye said Erle ffrancis father to ye Erle that now is did the lyke.' Richard Roberts confirmed that '…..he hath sene the lord ffrancis hunting in Ecclesall byerlow and that said lords officers sett decoers there at such places as they thought convenyent.' (Hart, 1993).

In the early 1700s, there were also livestock pastured in the woods with horses, mares, foals, cows, heifers, calves, and sterks recorded. Gelly's map of 1725 shows a 'laund' in the centre of the Woods and this was planted up in 1752 (Jones and Walker, 1997). In the 1587 deposition (Hart, 1993), it is also clear that wood and underwood are also being taken, and it was this use that was to dominate the former deer park for the next few centuries. It seems perhaps that the hunting use was falling from fashion by the late 1500s, with references to deer hunts certainly from the late 1400s and early 1500s. Was this the reason for the deposition? Excitingly, in the late 1990s, Paul Ardron, working with the author, located the western boundary bank of the medieval park (Rotherham and Ardron, 2001). Here we have some insight into the evolution of a specific wooded landscape, for which the medieval imparkation was probably the critical moment in it becoming woodland today. However, this 'ancient' woodland is not all it seems, and its ecology and pedology reflect its unique history. From the 1500s onwards, the Woods were individually named and being exploited for intensive manufacture of charcoal and whitecoal. By the mid-1800s, the coppice exploitation ended. Gradually the woodland was converted to high forest with exotic tree species, and then largely abandoned as 'amenity woodland'. This site is now locked within a sea of urbanisation and separated from its past by the process of 'cultural severance' (Rotherham, 2008, 2010). However, the key issue is that for long periods of time this site was mostly un-wooded and included large areas of arable land, and for much of the rest of its history it was grazed parkland. Today, culturally severed from its working past and managed as an urban amenity space, it is rapidly becoming '*parkified*' but aside from occasional deer and rabbits, there is no grazing.

We see similar processes at work across the English landscape as by the late nineteenth and early twentieth centuries many houses, parks, and gardens were subject to neglect or became financial liabilities. In the 1950s, even famous and now highly valued locations like Chatsworth Park in Derbyshire were seriously considered for demolition. Many smaller houses and their parks have long since gone. Other imposed parks on farming landscapes, such as Oakes Park at Norton (formerly North Derbyshire), are now amongst the richest ecological sites in their region. However, despite the well-documented conservation value, they lie uncared for and neglected, social misfits in landscapes of urban sprawl. The losses and severance of the landscape lineage is beyond calculation, and the more so for genuinely medieval parks. The loss of Ongar Great Park, Essex, and a pre-Conquest survival was possibly the worst loss of a visible Anglo-Saxon antiquity in the twentieth century (Rackham, 1986). So what have we left? The nineteenth-century clergyman and diarist, the Revd Francis

Kilvert gives some idea, describing the ancient oaks of Moccas Park, Herefordshire:

'........grey, gnarled, low-browed, knock-kneed, bowed, bent, huge, strange, long-armed, deformed, hunchbacked, misshapen, oakmen with both feet in the grave yet tiring down and seeing out generation after generation.'

Parks and great trees may '*survive*' in new landscapes, housing or agriculture, but most are erased from land and memory. Even if the trees survive, there is no means to replace them as time and nature run their course. Therefore, whilst the remaining sites are conservation icons, they are often isolated in time and space. They possess a unique resource of ecology: lichens, bryophytes, insects, spiders and more, enmeshed with a cultural lineage from the great forests of north-western Europe and are absolutely irreplaceable conservation resources. Beyond the park pale is a further resource but one largely overlooked and unrecognised.

The removal of the evidence

In writing about heathlands and their origins, I have drawn attention to the upland-lowland divide. This is a reflection of landscapes and the resistance to cultivation and 'improvement' of the great mass of northern upland landscapes and vegetation communities. As enclosures and drainage swept through the English lowlands in the 1700s and 1800s, much of the uplands remained relatively intact. They were not unchanged, as drainage and intensive use for sheep and grouse had major impacts, but they stayed stolidly resistant to removal. In the lowlands, the once extensive and expansive moors, fens, bogs, marshes, woods, forests, and commons spiraled into a terminal decline from which there has been no recovery. A consequence of the Parliamentary enclosures was a separation in fates between the upland and lowland situations. With a few examples and exceptions where perhaps forest or parks prevailed, the extensive medieval landscapes and I suggest their 'Vera'esque' connections, were almost entirely removed. In the uplands, though drier and ecologically simplified, the ecological landscape retains more integrity and therefore more connectivity to the past. In the search for the shadows of the primeval or the medieval, and for our wooded landscapes outside the 'woods', it is here that we must look. The evidence in upland heath, moor, bog and sheep walk, and in lowland heath, common and ancient grassland is there to be found.

Looking for the indicators

Part of our current research has been to investigate the uses of ancient woodland indicator species. In Britain, 'ancient' woodland (Rackham, 1986; Peterken, 1981) is that which has existed since at least 1600 AD, and possibly much longer. Prior to this date, planting of woodland in Britain was very uncommon. In this case, if a wood was present in 1600, it is likely to have been there for some considerable time previously. It has even been argued that

Figure 5. Grazing Exmoor ponies at the Valley of the Rocks, Devon.

Figure 6. Goats grazing bracken at the Valley of the Rocks, Devon.

it may be a remnant of the original 'wildwood' that once covered most of Britain, though this idea is generally considered untenable (See Beswick and Rotherham (Eds.), 1993; Pigott, 1993). However, assuming that ancient woods have a significant degree of antiquity, the continuity of woodland cover at a site will have provided refuge for a great variety of plants and animals over the centuries. Whilst this is the case within the wood, there will have been major changes in the surrounding landscapes. Consequently, ancient woods are often very rich in wildlife, and have undisturbed soil profiles and natural water features. Ancient woodland can also provide a living record of past woodland management practices and the organisation of the landscape. This is through the presence of features such as wood-banks, old pollards and coppice stools, remnant charcoal pits, ore furnaces and kilns. There have been two broad types of ancient woodland identified in Britain:

1. That which has been continuously wooded since 1600 AD and is composed of native tree species that have not obviously been planted. This is known as semi-natural ancient woodland.

2. That which has been continuously wooded since 1600 AD but where former tree cover has been replaced with planted trees (often conifers or exotic broadleaved species). This is known as replanted ancient woodland.

In Britain, ancient woodland (and particularly that which remains semi-natural) is considered the most important for wildlife conservation and a vital link to past landscapes and heritage. Identifying ancient woodland is therefore essential to:

1. Promote appropriate management for such woods and their surrounding landscapes;

2. Ensure the importance of ancient woodland is recognised where it is affected by planning proposals or other land-use changes;

3. Encourage new woodland planting to take account of the needs of ancient woodland;

4. Highlight possibilities for restoration (of replanted ancient woodland) to more 'natural' condition.

In this context, it is important to recognise the diversity of woodland types and origins that exists. The main forms of potentially ancient wooded landscape fall into the following categories or variants of these: mediaeval and industrial coppice, park and pasture wood, ancient forest, wooded common, linear remnant, and fragment (Rotherham, 2007a and b). However, the research we have done emphasises very clearly that most evidence for ancient woodlands and the use of botanical indicators in particular, relates to coppice woods of various forms (Glaves *et al.*, 2009a, b, and c). The studies include ongoing research undertaken over a twenty-year period and long-term action research with expert stakeholders (see Rotherham, 2007), together with detailed regional audits in the English midlands and in Cumbria. A two-year project to develop the *Woodland Heritage Manual* (2008) led to a series of expert stakeholder workshops to examine and review issues of woodland indicators, woodland inventories, and related landscape issues. The outcomes of the research included major reviews of literature and of evidence-bases and approaches (Glaves *et al.*, 2009a, b, and c), and a toolkit for practitioners (to be published elsewhere). The latter involves a decision-making tree and an Evidence-based Ancient Woodland Status Grid (Rotherham, 2011a). The approach has resulted in a re-visiting of the use and interpretation of indicator species and of inventory lists, and the advocacy of a more holistic evidence-based evaluation of wooded landscapes and woodland sites.

A result of the issues noted above, and because of long-term studies and interest in wooded landscapes and indicators, there has been a growing need for the evaluation of woodlands in a landscape context. In order to do this, it is necessary to develop new and robust methods for woodland assessment and to grow the academic research that underpins these. On-going work at Sheffield Hallam University and with the Biodiversity and Landscape History Research Institute is doing exactly this with support from the British Ecological Society, the Forestry Commission, the Heritage Lottery Fund, and in partnership with the Woodland Trust. The intention is to develop a robust and evidence-based methodology for assessing and defining ancient woodland. This integrated approach guides the user through a system of logical steps with a decision-making tree around which the process works, that is evidence-based. Importantly, the method is defensible in the case of enquiry disputes or other potential conflicts. The approach evolved from the firm foundations and baseline of the *Heritage Woodland Manual* (2008). The methodology involves the use of carefully considered steps and decisions to address and evaluate information on site documentation, site ecology and pedology, site archaeology, and where available site history. Together these establish a logical framework for the assessment of woods and woodlands. This builds on established definitions of ancient woods but takes into account a broader sweep of information than was formerly available.

Given the conservation interest in ancient woods and old growth forests, we need to consider the range of information sources for antiquity or ancientness in woods and forests. Recognition of the wider resource of ancient wooded landscapes provides a further impetus for this work and a challenge to the models. The information used in evaluation may be ecological, pedological, historical, or archaeological. Glaves *et al.* (2009a, b, and c) and the *Woodland Heritage Manual* (2008), describe in detail the possible approaches to gathering and interrogating information, and the key sources of the data. In undertaking surveys and in listing woods in Ancient Woodland Inventories, botanical indicators of antiquity have played an important role, but this is inadequate for the broader purpose of this research. However, the established use of indicators does provide a platform for the new methodology.

Part of the approach that we are adopting and developing (reported in Rotherham, 2011a), is based around the idea of '*Intelligent Interrogation*' of the lists. There is a danger that the use of indicators becomes too formulaic and users expect a definitive numerical answer of indicator occurrence and worth. Indeed, it may be useful for an overall assessment of woodland status to generate some form of numeric index or gradation. However, the evidence must be considered on a wide front and the lists of botanical indicators require scrutiny and assessment at many levels. They need to be assessed in terms of site history, of map-based evidence of land-use, of archaeological evidence of human activity and plant cover, of other documentation or historical sources, and in terms of the core ecology of the plants themselves. There is much to take in, including soils and other sediments and the evidence they hold; of working and worked trees and the stories they tell; and the variation and patterns of landscape history through time and space. The system that is emerging will help draw together key evidence. The intention is that it will then aid the interpretation and presentation of such evidence to the benefit of woods and woodland and tree practitioners.

A part of the story that emerges from this research, and an answer to some of the quandaries, may lie in exactly what we define firstly as woodland, and then as ancient. Unfortunately, this is not always as simple as might be assumed, and most sites recognised through both indicators and historical sources are in fact medieval coppice woods. This implies that many sites with different time-lines and histories may be omitted when ancient status is assessed. The consequences for conservation and for management may be serious. There are two main issues arising from the work so far. The first is the need for robust indicators and for these to be integrated in to a broader framework for integration and interrogation. Rotherham (2011) suggested five main conclusions from these studies:

1. **The need for robust and appropriate indicators:** the classification of a site as an ancient woodland provides it with extra protection under British planning policy guidance. Species evidence can and has been used to help determine ancient woodland character. However, there are concerns about the robustness of current indicator lists and their misuse. It was concluded from the study that there is a need for robust and locally appropriate indicators to aid reliable identification of ancient woodland sites. Current lists generally do not take into account other factors that may influence the presence or absence of an indicator, for example internal variation within woodland, woodland size, soil

acidity and wetness. Unless these factors are considered and accounted for, there is a tendency to identify base-rich woodlands (with greater diversity), as probable ancient woodlands and to omit more acidic sites of comparable antiquity. Ancient coppice woods subjected at some point to prolonged and intensive grazing (such as for example, in the uplands of northern England), may also be omitted because they are species-poor. Analysis of local and regional trends, and specific sites and datasets is needed to provide a richer context for interpretation.

2. **Use of indicator species to confirm ancientness:** an important conclusion from the study is that indicator species can be used to confirm historic records of woodland continuity and ancientness of a wood. However, if historic records are lacking for the particular location then woodland indicators can also 'indicate' ancient woodland status and a degree of confidence can be placed on such indication. This is based on an integrated interrogation and, in the absence of other information, does not necessarily confirm status. It was also noted that there may be no individual species that can be shown to be confined to ancient woodland, and therefore no single perfect ancient woodland indicator. All species and communities of species must be assessed in the wider context of the location.

3. **Perception and use of the term 'ancient woodland':** ancient woodlands are considered to be more valuable than non-ancient woodland. The 'age' or lineage of a wood is used as a surrogate for nature conservation or historical value. In other words the longer something has been there, the longer features will have accumulated: cultural artefacts, biodiversity etc. However, there is a need for better underpinning science of how strongly particular species are associated with woodland continuity on a site. This includes improved understanding of how the rates at which species can colonise woodland vary, and how quickly key species decline when conditions change. Issues related to this are discussed below. The heritage importance of the woodland archaeology and of worked trees, also present problems of evaluation, of comparison, and of recognition.

4. **Indicators of ancientness or indicators of continuity of environmental conditions and management:** as noted, ancientness implies a long continuity of woodland and its associated environmental characteristics (generally including shade, high humidity *etc*), though these relate mainly to ancient woods such as medieval coppices and there are notable exceptions. It is in part this continuity of environmental conditions, which determines the species present. Are we really talking about 'species associated

with environmental continuity' or an 'index of ecological continuity' rather than indicators of ancient woodland? In addition, most if not all British woodlands, will have been cleared in the past; therefore, woodlands that appeared on early maps and again on later maps could have been clear felled and treated as arable land in the intervening period. It is uncertain how woodland indicators respond to such gaps in continuity. How long can a clearing remain un-wooded and still be regarded as ancient woodland when the canopy returns. Woodland management has changed over history, and many but not all ancient woodland indicators are associated with dense enclosed high forest. However, in the past other types of wooded environments including wood pasture were common. There is a need for indicators of these other types of ancient treed and wooded environments.

5. **Survey and analysis methods:** the type of survey method used (e.g. walk through surveys, transects *etc*) will influence the number of species and indicators recorded (e.g. Kirby *et al.*, 1986). Analysis therefore must take the strengths and weaknesses of survey techniques into account. From a practitioner perspective there is a clear need for a rapid and robust method for identifying ancient woods and so the use of indicators benefits from robust threshold values for ancient wooded sites. However, in undertaking surveys and in analysing any findings, it is important that users understand the issues around the concept of ancient woodland and the problems that may arise.

Imposed on these ideas relating to ancient woodland are the emerging concepts of '*wooded landscapes*' and of '*shadow woods*'. These further complicate an already multi-faceted concept. However, to ignore or overlook these issues potentially devalues the whole system and puts many good sites at risk.

Conclusions

I suggest that grazed wooded landscapes are more widespread than is generally recognised, and many ancient areas are overlooked. Some of these sites may have uniquely long timelines of grazing impacts and influences, and they complement those of the historic parks and forests. Following this approach, it is possible to develop a vision of historical ecology which begins to join the ideas of Frans Vera and his primeval savannah, to the landscape and countryside history of Oliver Rackham. The evidence is there if only we have the eyes to see.

How we find, preserve, and conserve this complex and often-intangible heritage is a huge challenge. There is no single approach or correct answer, and much that remains, is threatened by cultural severance and the ending of traditional management (See for example Rotherham, 2008 and 2010). The research on woodland indicator species is providing good evidence to support these ideas and models to capture and present the landscape vision are being developed (Rotherham, 2011).

To raise awareness, identify sites and to encourage good management, involving local people and engaging with local communities, must be a key. This is the approach that we used to develop the *Woodland Heritage Manual* (Rotherham *et al.*, 2008). Ongoing studies in the Peak District and surrounding areas is proving very productive in terms of placing these ideas and theories into a framework to reflect the specialist research in parallel disciplines such as palaeo-ecology, palynolgy, and archaeology. We will present these findings at the 2012 conference on *Trees Beyond the Wood*.

There is a further issue too. It is now suggested and accepted, at least in part, that remnants of medieval parks are vestiges of very ancient landscapes; albeit transformed and manipulated by human hand over the centuries. These may precede human domination and agriculture, and with Vera's vision of forested savannah indicate a lineage to great primeval origins of the European forest. Harking back evocatively to the past, this view also informs the future. The vision of landscapes is freed from anthropogenic constraints of medieval agricultural and pastoral scenes, setting new challenges for deeply embedded precepts of nature conservation. The best working examples are in the remains of once numerous and great, medieval parks, a powerful lineage. Individual case studies prove hugely rewarding and informative and the recent seminal volume on the Duffield Frith in Derbyshire (Wiltshire *et al.*, 2005) is a wonderful example of what can be achieved.

Acknowledgements

I wish to thank all those who have worked on the projects on the *Woodland Heritage Manual*, *Shadow Woods*, on *Wooded Landscapes*, and on *Ancient Woodland Indicators*. Contributions by Paul Ardron, Christine Handley, Dave Gash, Ondřej Vild, Rikard Andersson, and Melvyn Jones are gratefully acknowledged.

Bibliography

Agnoletti, M., Anderson, S., Johann, E., Kulvik, M., Saratsi, E., Kushlin, A., Mayer, P., Montiel, C., Parrotta, J. and Rotherham, I.D. (2007) *Guidelines for the Implementation of Social and Cultural Values in Sustainable Forest Management: A Scientific Contribution to the Implementation of MCPFE - Vienna Resolution 3*. IUFRO Occasional Paper No. 19, ISSN 1024-414X, IUFRO Headquarters, Vienna, Austria.

Agnoletti, M., Anderson, S., Johann, E., Kulvik, M., Saratsi, E., Kushlin, A., Mayer, P., Montiel, C., Parrotta, J. and Rotherham, I.D. (2008) The Introduction of Historical and Cultural Values in the Sustainable Management of European Forests. *Global Environment*, **2**, 172- 193.

Beswick, P. and Rotherham, I.D. (Eds.) (1993) Ancient Woodlands – their archaeology and ecology - a coincidence of interest. *Landscape Archaeology and Ecology*, **1**.

Bettey, J.H. (1993) *Estates and the English Countryside*. Batsford, London

Blüchel, K.G. (1997) *Game and Hunting*. Könemann Verlagsgesellschaft mbH, Cologne.

Buckland, P.C. (1975) Synanthropy and the death-watch; a discussion. *Naturalist*, **100**, 37-42.

Buckland, P.C. (1979) *Thorne Moors: a palaeoecological study of a Bronze Age site*. Occasional Publication No. 8) Department of Geography, University of Birmingham, Birmingham.

Cantor, L.M. and Hatherly, J. (1979) The Medieval Parks of England. *Geography*, **64**, 71-85.

Cummins, J. (1988) *The Hound and the Hawk*. Weidenfeld & Nicholson, London.

Fagan, B. (2006) *Fish on Friday. Feasting, Fasting and the Discovery of the New World*. Basic Books, New York.

Fowler, J. (2002) *Landscapes and Lives. The Scottish Forest through the ages*. Canongate Books, Edinburgh.

Glaves, P., Rotherham, I.D., Wright, B., Handley, C. and Birbeck, J. (2009) *A Report to the Woodland Trust. Field Surveys for Ancient Woodlands: Issues and Approaches*. Hallam Environmental Consultants Ltd., Biodiversity & Landscape History Research Institute, and Geography, Tourism & Environment Change Research Unit, Sheffield Hallam University, Sheffield.

Glaves, P., Rotherham, I.D., Wright, B., Handley, C. and Birbeck, J. (2009) *A Report to the Woodland Trust A Survey of the Coverage, Use and Application of Ancient Woodland Indicator Lists in the UK*. Hallam Environmental Consultants Ltd., Biodiversity & Landscape History Research Institute, and Geography, Tourism & Environment Change Research Unit, Sheffield Hallam University, Sheffield.

Glaves, P., Rotherham, I.D., Wright, B., Handley, C. and Birbeck, J. (2009) *A Report to the Woodland Trust Field Surveys for Ancient Woodlands: Issues and Approaches*. Hallam Environmental Consultants Ltd., Biodiversity & Landscape History Research Institute, and Geography, Tourism & Environment Change Research Unit, Sheffield Hallam University, Sheffield.

Harding, P. T. and Rose, F. (1986) *Pasture-Woodlands in Lowland Britain – A review of their importance for wildlife conservation*. Institute of Terrestrial Ecology, Monks Wood Experimental Station, Huntingdon.

Harding, P.T. and Wall, T. (Eds.) (2000) *Moccas: an English deer park*. English Nature. Peterborough.

Hart, C.R. (1993) The Ancient Woodland of Ecclesall Woods, Sheffield. Proceedings of the National Conference on Ancient Woodlands: their archaeology and ecology - a coincidence of interest, Sheffield 1992. Beswick, P. and Rotherham, I. D. (Eds.), *Landscape Archaeology and Ecology*, **1**, 49-66.

Hayman, R. (2003) *Trees. Woodlands and Western Civilization*. Hambledon and London, London.

Henderson, A. (1997) From coney to rabbit: the story of a managed coloniser. *The Naturalist*, **122**, 101-121.

James, P.W., Hawksworth, D.L. and Rose, F. (1977) *Lichen communities in the British Isles: a preliminary conspectus*. In: Seaward, M. R. D. (Ed.) *Lichen ecology*. Academic Press, London, 295-413.

Jones, M. (1996) Deer in South Yorkshire an historical perspective in Deer or the New Woodlands? Jones, M., Rotherham, I. D. and McCarthy, A. J. (Eds.).*The Journal of Practical Ecology and Conservation Special Publication*, **No. 1**, 11-26.

Jones, J. and Jones, M. (2005) *Historic Parks and Gardens in and around South Yorkshire*. Wharncliffe Books, Barnsley.

Jones, M., Rotherham, I.D. and McCarthy, A.J. (Eds.) (1996) Deer or the New Woodlands? T*he Journal of Practical Ecology and Conservation, Special Publication*, **No. 1**.

Jones, M. and Walker, P. (1997) From coppice-with-standards to high forest: the management of Ecclesall Woods 1715-1901. In: Rotherham, I. D. and Jones, M. (Eds.) The Natural History of Ecclesall Woods, **Pt 1**. *Peak District Journal of Natural History and Archaeology Special Publication*, **No. 1**, 11-20.

Kirby, K. J. and Drake, C. M. (Eds.) (1993) *Dead wood matters: the ecology and conservation of saproxylic invertebrates in Britain*. English Nature Science, 7, English Nature, Peterborough.

Langton, J. and Jones, G. (Eds.) (2005) *Forests and Chases of England and Wales c.1500-c.1850. Towards a survey & analysis*. St John's College Research Centre, Oxford.

Lasdun, S. (1992) *The English Park: Royal, Private and Public*. The Vendome Press, New York.

Liddiard, R. (2003) The deer parks of Domesday Book. *Landscapes*, **4 (1)**, 4-23.

Mileson, S.A. (2005) The importance of parks in fifteenth-century society. In: Clark, L. (Ed.).*The Fifteenth Century V*. Boydell and Brewer, Woodbridge, 19-37.

Muir, R. (2005) *Ancient Trees Living Landscapes*. Tempus, Stroud.

Neave, D. and Turnbull, D. (1992) *Landscaped Parks and Gardens of East Yorkshire*. Georgian Society for East Yorkshire, Bridlington.

Perlin, J. (1989) *A Forest Journey*. Harvard University Press, Massachusetts

Peterken, G.F. (1981) *Woodland Conservation and Management*. Chapman & Hall, London

Peterken, G.F. (1996) *Natural Woodland: Ecology and Conservation in Northern Temperate Regions*. Cambridge University Press, Cambridge.

Pett, D.E. (1998) *The Parks and Gardens of Cornwall*. Alison Hodge, Penzance, Cornwall.

Pigott, C.D. (1993) The History and Ecology of Ancient Woodlands. *Landscape Archaeology and Ecology*, **1**, 1-11.

Rackham, O. (1976) *Trees and Woodland in the British Landscape*. J. M. Dent & Sons Ltd, London.

Rackham, O. (1978) Archaeology and land-use history' in Epping Forest – the Natural Aspect? Ed. Corke, D. *Essex Nat.*, **N.S. 2**, 16-57.

Rackham, O. (1980) *Ancient Woodland; its history, vegetation and uses in England*. Arnold, London.

Rackham, O. (1986) *The History of the Countryside*. J. M. Dent & Sons Ltd, London.

Rackham, O. (2004) Pre-Existing Trees and Woods in Country-House Parks. *Landscapes*, **5 (2)**, 1-16.

Read, H. (1999) *Veteran Trees: A guide to good management*. English Nature, Peterborough

Rollins, J. (2003) *Land Marks: Impressions of England's National Nature Reserves*. English Nature, Peterborough.

Rose, F. (1974) *The epiphytes of oak*. In: *The British Oak, its history and natural history*. XXXX, M. Morris, G. & Perring, F. H. (Eds.). Classey, Faringdon, 250-273.

Rose, F. (1976) *Lichenological indicators of age and environmental continuity in woodlands*. In: Brown, D. H., Hawksworth, D. L. and Bailey, R. H. (Eds.) *Lichenology: progress and problems*. Academic Press, London.

Rose, F. and James, P.W. (1974) Regional studies on the British lichen flora, 1. The corticolous and lignicolous species of the New Forest, Hampshire. *Lichenologist*, **6**, 1-72

Rotherham, I.D. (Ed.) (2005) Crisis and Continuum in the Shaping of Landscapes. *Landscape Archaeology and Ecology*, **5**, 117 pp

Rotherham, I.D. (2007a) *The Historical Ecology of Medieval Deer Parks and the Implications for Conservation*. In: Liddiard, R. (Ed.) *The Medieval Deer Park: New Perspectives*, Windgather Press, Macclesfield, 79-96.

Rotherham, I.D (2007b) The ecology and economics of medieval deer parks. *Landscape Archaeology and Ecology*, **6**, 86-102.

Rotherham, I.D. (Ed.) (2007c) *The History, Ecology and Archaeology of Medieval Parks and Parklands*. Wildtrack Publishing, Sheffield.

Rotherham, I.D. (2007d) The implications of perceptions and cultural knowledge loss for the management of wooded landscapes: a UK case-study. *Forest Ecology and Management*, **249**, 100-115.

Rotherham, I.D. (2008) *The Importance of Cultural Severance in Landscape Ecology Research*. In: Dupont, A. & Jacobs, H. (Eds.) (2008) *Landscape Ecology Research Trends*. Nova Science Publishers Inc., New York, 71-87.

Rotherham, I.D. (2009) *Hanging by a Thread - a brief overview of the heaths and commons of the north-east midlands of England*. In: Rotherham, I.D. and Bradley, J (Eds.) (2009) *Lowland Heaths: Ecology, History, Restoration and Management*. Wildtrack Publishing, Sheffield.

Rotherham, I.D. (2009) *Habitat Fragmentation and Isolation in Relict Urban Heaths - the ecological consequences and future potential*. In: Rotherham, I.D. & Bradley, J. (Eds.) (2009) *Lowland Heaths: Ecology, History, Restoration and Management*. Wildtrack Publishing, Sheffield.

Rotherham, I.D. (2010) Cultural Severance and the End of Tradition. *Landscape Archaeology and Ecology*, **8**, 178-199.

Rotherham, I.D. (2010) *Yorkshire's Forgotten Fenlands*. Pen & Sword Books Limited, Barnsley. 181pp.

Rotherham, I.D. (2011) *A Landscape History Approach to the Assessment of Ancient Woodlands*. In: Wallace, E.B. (Ed.) *Woodlands: Ecology, Management and Conservation*. Nova Science Publishers Inc., USA, 161-184.

Rotherham, I.D. (2011) The implications of cultural severance in managing vegetation for conservation. *Aspects of Applied Biology*, **108**, 95-104.

Rotherham, I.D. and Ardron, P.A. (2006) The Archaeology of Woodland Landscapes: Issues for Managers based on the Case-study of Sheffield, England and four thousand years of human impact. *Arboricultural Journal*, **29 (4)**, 229-243.

Rotherham, I.D. and Ardron, P.A., (Eds.) (2001) *Ecclesall Woods Millenium Archaeology Project*. Sheffield Hallam University, Sheffield.

Rotherham, I.D. and Bradley, J. (Eds.) (2009) *Lowland Heaths: Ecology, History, Restoration and Management*. Wildtrack Publishing, Sheffield.

Rotherham, I.D. and Bradley, J. (2009) *Preamble and Overview. Lowland Heaths: Ecology, History, Restoration and Management*. Wildtrack Publishing, Sheffield.

Rotherham, I.D. and Egan, D. (2005) *The Economics of Fuel Wood, Charcoal and Coal: An Interpretation of Coppice Management of British Woodlands*. In: Agnoletti, M., Armiero, M., Barca, S., and Corona, G. (Eds.), *History and Sustainability*. European Society for Environmental History. 100-104.

Rotherham, I.D. and Jones, M. (2000) Seeing the Woodman in the Trees – Some preliminary thoughts on Derbyshire's ancient coppice woods. *Peak District Journal of Natural History and Archaeology*, **2**, 7-18.

Rotherham, I.D. and Jones, M. (2000) *The Impact of Economic, Social and Political Factors on the Ecology of Small English Woodlands: a Case Study of the Ancient Woods in South Yorkshire, England*. In: *Forest History: International Studies in Socio-economic and Forest ecosystem change*. Agnoletti, M. and Anderson, S. (Eds.), CAB International, Wallingford, Oxford. 397-410.

Rotherham, I.D., Jones, M., Smith, L. and Handley, C. (Eds.) (2008) T*he Woodland Heritage Manual: A Guide to Investigating Wooded Landscapes*. Wildtrack Publishing, Sheffield.

Rotherham, I.D. and Wright, B. (2008) Searching for the Ghosts: how a forester reads the woodland landscape. *World of Trees*, **16**, 40-41.

Rotherham, I.D. and Wight, B. (2011) Assessing woodland history and management using vascular plant indicators. *Aspects of Applied Biology*, **108**, 105-112.

Speight, M. (1989) Saproxylic invertebrates and their conservation, Council of Europe, Strasbourg. *Nature and Environment Series*, **42**.

Squires, A.E. and Humphrey, W. (1986) *The Medieval Parks of Charnwood Forest*. Sycamore Press, Melton Mowbray.

Taigel, A. and Williamson, T. (1993) *Parks and Gardens*. Batsford, London.

Vera, F. (2000) *Grazing Ecology and Forest History*. CABI Publishing, Oxon, UK.

Warde, P. (2005) *Woodland Fuel, Demand and Supply*. In: Langton, J. and Jones, G. (Eds.) *Forests and Chases of England and Wales c.1500-c.1850. Towards a survey & analysis*. St John's College Research Centre, Oxford.

Whitaker, J. (1892) *A Descriptive List of the Deer-Parks and Paddocks of England*. Ballantyne, Hanson & Co., London.

Whitehead, G.K. (1964) *The Deer of Great Britain and Ireland*. Routledge and Kegan Paul Ltd., London.

Whitehead, G.K. (1980) *Hunting and Stalking Deer in Britain through the Ages*. Batsford, London.

Williamson, T. (2006) *The Archaeology of Rabbit Warrens*. Shire Publications Ltd., Risborough, Buckinghamshire.

Wiltshire, M., Woore, S., Crisp, B. and Rich, B. (2005) *Duffield Frith: History & Evolution of the Landscape of a Medieval Derbyshire Forest*. Landmark Publishing Ltd, Ashbourne.

Encouraging the use of stock to enhance woodland biodiversity: a new web-based toolbox

Helen M. Armstrong[1], Bob Black[2], Kate Holl[3], Nick Mainprize[4], Lucy Sumsion[5], Richard Thompson[6].

Forest Research[1], Argyll Woodlanders[2], Scottish Natural Heritage[3], Forestry Commission Scotland[4,6], National Farmers Union of Scotland[5].

Background

In the 1990s, there was much concern about the condition of ancient and semi-natural woodlands and in particular about the prevention of natural regeneration by deer and livestock browsing. In 1995, through the Woodland Grant Scheme (WGS) administered by the Forestry Commission, a pilot Livestock Exclusion Annual Premium (LEAP) was introduced to compensate farmers for loss of grazing income following the removal of livestock from woodlands. LEAP grants were paid on the presumption that grazing agricultural stock would otherwise prevent the natural regeneration of woodland, or impede the development of the woodland field layer. LEAP grants required stock to have been excluded prior to the first payment, and the grant was then paid for up to 10 years from that point. As time went on, however, we became aware that woodland management delivered through LEAP, which was aimed at improving woodland condition by removing herbivore impacts through fencing, was, for some woods, apparently leading to a loss of biodiversity. Some LEAP woods were experiencing dense tree regeneration leading to low light levels and a consequent decline in field layer biodiversity, lower plant interest, and other associated biodiversity. Other LEAP woods, where the ground layer vegetation closed over before tree regeneration took place, experienced very low, or no, tree regeneration, the field layer became dominated by tall, fast growing species and biodiversity declined. In 2001 the WGS, and with it LEAP, were discontinued but payments for livestock exclusion continued under the Scottish Forestry Grant Scheme (SFGS) for terms of ten years (with a review after five), until August 2006 when both elements were withdrawn for new applicants in anticipation of the introduction of the Scottish Rural Development Programme (SRDP).

Over the last fifteen years or so, since the introduction of LEAP, our understanding of the impact of a complete lack of grazing on a wide range of woodland biodiversity interests has deepened. There has also been a corresponding growth of interest in controlled livestock grazing to encourage natural regeneration and enhance the biodiversity of native woodlands. There has until recently, however, been a lack of support in the grant system to facilitate this. In response to demand, and in recognition that some woods need to have grazing re-introduced to prevent a further decline in biodiversity value, in spring 2005, Forestry Commission Scotland (FCS) launched a pilot '*Stewardship Grant for Controlled Livestock Grazing in Woodlands*', to promote sustainable grazing of woodlands. This scheme was set up under the now defunct SFGS and applicants were invited to participate in a ground-breaking project that aimed to advance our understanding of sustainable woodland grazing. Every entrant had to produce a woodland grazing management plan and carry out regular monitoring of the impact of stock (and deer) on their woodland. Twenty-six sites joined the scheme and information gleaned from this pilot led to the development of a woodland grazing measure in the Scottish Government funded SRDP.

A new type of grant scheme

The SRDP is a programme of economic, environmental and social measures worth around £1.5 billion. It is designed to support rural Scotland from 2007-13, and includes measures to address economic and social, as well as environmental goals. It is outcome-focused and primarily aims to deliver a "*greener, wealthier and fairer*" rural Scotland. The SRDP brings together a wide range of formerly separate support schemes through a single web-based gateway. It embraces grants for farming, forestry and primary processing sectors, as well as support for rural enterprise and business development, diversification and rural tourism. The main agri-environment arm of the scheme is '*Rural Development Contracts - Rural Priorities (RDC - RP): an integrated funding mechanism that aims to deliver targeted environmental, social and economic benefits*'. To ensure that contracts are awarded for the proposals which are best able to deliver the agreed regional priorities the RDC – RP scheme is competitive. Applicants enter the scheme by first selecting one of thirty-two rural priorities. The priorities on offer vary from region to region depending on locally and nationally determined priorities. They cover a wide range of issues including biodiversity, climate change and diversification of rural enterprises.

The new controlled livestock grazing option is available through RDC - RP for the sustainable grazing of forests and woodlands of high environmental value, where controlled livestock grazing could be used to enhance the woodland's biodiversity and ecological condition. This option might be appropriate in woods that are in unfavourable condition and where controlled livestock grazing could be used to help deliver, amongst other things, a diversification of woodland structure, some open space, or the presence of some established regeneration. Controlled livestock grazing of woodland will be supported at a rate of £87/hectare/year for up to 5 years, and a range of relevant capital items are also available through Woodland Improvement Grants.

Before being awarded the grant, applicants must produce a site specific grazing management plan for the wood which will give detail on the wood, the management issue, the desired biodiversity or human heritage outcome and the specific livestock grazing regime proposed. The production of a grazing management plan has not been a pre-requisite for any previous grant scheme and it was anticipated that many applicants would need easily available guidance on how to produce one. To address this issue, we developed, over several years, the web-based '*Woodland Grazing Toolbox*'. The *Woodland Grazing Toolbox* now underpins the controlled livestock grazing option of the RDC - RP.

One of the new and exciting aspects of this grant is that it relies on the use of adaptive management. Under previous agri-environment support for conservation grazing, the land manager was paid to graze with a specified number of livestock units over an agreed period. This type of prescription, however, rarely seemed to match individual site requirements as these vary between sites as well as between years depending on many factors including the nature of the site, the specific objectives, the weather and the type of stock used. In the new scheme land managers are, instead, being paid to deliver specified outcomes. The grazing management plan specifies the desired biodiversity or human heritage outcome(s) for the woodland in terms of woodland structure, and it is then up to the land manager to deliver this structure using the combination of livestock numbers and timing that works best for their individual circumstances. For designated sites the biodiversity objectives would be agreed with Scottish Natural Heritage (SNH). The *Woodland Grazing Toolbox* contains guidance on assessing current, and desirable, woodland structure as well as guidance on determining current grazing levels. Land managers are expected to undertake regular monitoring of the impact of stock (and deer if present) and to adjust the grazing regime accordingly if necessary. This adaptive management allows land managers the flexibility to develop the most appropriate grazing regime for their site so as to maximise benefits both for the natural and /or human heritage as well as for their farming interests.

The Woodland Grazing Toolbox

For this new sort of grant scheme to work, assistance was needed to help land owners /managers and their agents to write suitable woodland grazing management plans. There was a huge fund of relevant information available but it had not been collated with this purpose in mind and finding the information that was relevant for a particular site would be practically impossible for most potential grant applicants. The solution was to find a way of making the information available in an accessible way. Traditionally, it would have been published in the form of a handbook.

We decided, however, that a web-based handbook would have many advantages over the more traditional, static format:

- the structure can be hierarchical with the user only having to delve into the handbook as deep as is necessary for their requirements.

- it can be regularly updated and everyone with access to the internet has access to the most recent version.

- it can contain links to other, relevant documents.

- documents, and other information, can easily be downloaded by the user and adapted for their own use.

- users can search for information on a particular topic either using the site map or by using the search facility.

- large numbers of high quality photographs can be made available.

- users can easily provide feedback on both the structure and content.

- worked examples of Woodland Grazing Management plans can be added as they are produced.

- spreadsheets to help with calculations can be made available to download.

- where hard copies are needed, relevant information can be printed out in the format most suited to its use.

On balance we decided the advantages of a web-based handbook out-weighed the disadvantages and in 2007 we started thinking about what the Toolbox might look like and do. We considered whether the Toolbox itself could produce the grazing management plan, or at least specify appropriate grazing regimes for a site. However, the more we considered the range and quantity of information that would be needed from the user, and the complexity of any program that would be needed to produce the recommendations, the more it became clear that this would not be practical. Instead we decided to design a Toolbox that led users through the process of writing a woodland grazing management plan for their woodland. We designed the structure of the Toolbox to mirror that of the plan itself and we made a template Woodland Grazing Management plan available to download and edit.

Much of the information in the Toolbox applies to all woodland types but, where it does not, we have used a very broad classification of semi-natural woodland using just five types, based on soil moisture and acidity. This was the minimum that we judged necessary to provide reliable information that was tailored to site type. A user with just one woodland type can download many of the documents and edit them to provide only the information relevant to their woodland type. Much of the information can then be copied directly into the template Woodland Grazing Management plan.

The Woodland Grazing Management Plan

The Woodland Grazing Plan is at the heart of the Toolbox. Once it has been decided that livestock grazing could be an appropriate management tool for the woodland, the plan template, which is downloadable from the Toolbox, provides a framework for working out a grazing regime that meets biodiversity and cultural heritage objectives.

The plan is divided into eight sections, corresponding to the eight sections of the Toolbox. These cover the key management issues that need to be considered when drawing up a plan. They can be summarised as:

- background information, covering such things as the overall management objectives for the wood, its physical characteristics, whether it has conservation designations and any surveys or management plans already written.

- defining and mapping very broad habitat types. This includes associated open ground habitats as well as woodland habitats. Woods that lend themselves to conservation grazing often contain a mix of wooded and unwooded habitats. The latter may have high conservation value and are likely to include habitats that need to be taken into account when working out the carrying capacity of the woodland for livestock.

- assessing woodland structure and current impacts of large herbivores on habitats. The toolbox contains a large amount of background information on this subject and to help in the assessment a methodology has been developed for identifying the characteristics of each habitat and for recording these on a survey form.

- defining the biodiversity and/or cultural heritage objectives for the key habitats. Again there is information in the toolbox to help define objectives and from that to determine how much grazing and/or browsing is compatible with meeting those objectives.

- consideration of what have been called 'constraints'. These may include physical barriers such as rivers or cliffs, legal obligations, the resources of the grazier and whether any of the objectives are incompatible. Deer browsing is also covered in this section. This is a big subject and ideally a deer management plan will go along with the grazing plan. The minimum would be a brief assessment of the current impacts of deer on the woodland and an idea of how deer populations are going to be monitored and, if necessary, controlled.

- drawing up a grazing regime. This section covers the characteristics of different livestock breeds, the impacts of year-round or seasonal grazing and the productivity of each of the identified habitats. With the help of a calculation template, all this information is brought together into a proposal for a grazing regime that specifies type of animal, number of animals and the duration of grazing. If any objectives are truly incompatible, the wood may need to be divided into more than one grazing management unit.

- monitoring the progress of the project. The essence of the plan is that it is adaptable. It starts with a grazing regime that is within a range of acceptable alternatives. The impacts are then monitored regularly over the lifetime of the plan so that the regime can be fine-tuned as needed.

All this is potentially a lot of work. The aim of the plan and the Toolbox is to simplify what is a complex and interlocking set of issues without oversimplifying them. Experience of writing grazing plans has shown that the key to keeping the amount of work within acceptable limits is to be very disciplined in the initial identification and mapping of habitats that have to be assessed, ideally restricting the number of habitats or habitat mosaics to no more than seven. In this way, after a bit of practice, it is possible to survey a large wood and produce a plan in about three days.

Producing the plan does not require specialist knowledge. With the help of the Toolbox, it could be produced by an interested land manager, maybe with initial input from a habitat surveyor. Graziers are the people 'on the ground' and they are likely to have invaluable knowledge of their woods. The importance of their involvement and commitment should not be overlooked. If at all possible they should be involved from the beginning in developing grazing plans and afterwards in monitoring progress.

A workable plan, an involved grazier, regular monitoring and an ability to adapt the grazing regime as necessary should result in a scheme that combines livestock farming and sound woodland management.

A subjective method of assessing grazing impact

During the early stages of the development of the Grazing Toolbox, it became clear that the grazier and agent/woodland manager would need a method to assess the impact of domestic livestock and deer on their woodland. This would be needed to allow them to set an initial grazing regime, to assess how effective the selected grazing regime was and to modify the grazing regime if needed to achieve the objectives. The method would have to be reliable yet easy to learn and quick to implement. A quantitative method that required detailed measurement would be too time consuming to learn, implement and analyse, so we decided to develop a method where indicators were used to make subjective assessments of large herbivore impacts. The method that was developed as part of the Grazing Toolbox uses two sets of indicators of grazing level. One set allows the user to assess the impacts of past grazing, and other management, on woodland structure and the other set is used to assess current herbivore impacts. Users are provided with written and photographic descriptions of indicators.

Woodland structure

Woodland structure is a result of past management as well as of past impacts of large herbivores over the medium to long term. The method of assessing herbivore impacts uses eight woodland structure classes, each one representative of a different level of past herbivore impact. For each of five woodland /habitat types based on soil wetness and pH., descriptions are provided of the appearance of each structure class. Figure 1 lists the structure classes and the woodland / habitat types used and shows the format of the description tables.

Current impacts

Woodland structure often takes many years to change from one class to another so woodland managers also need a means of assessing current levels of impact of large herbivores where 'current' is defined as within the last twelve months. We built on existing indicator methods (Armstrong et al., 2003; Thompson et al., 2004; Thompson, 2007) to produce a set of seven indicators along with descriptions of each indicator for each of the woodland /habitat types. Figure 2 lists the indicators and shows the format of the description tables. Within the table differences between different woodland /habitat types are noted.

Field assessment

We recommend that the description tables are downloaded from the Grazing Toolbox and customized for local conditions. For example, a preferentially

Figure 1. Structure classes and woodland /habitat types and format of description tables.

Structure Class	Woodland Type				
	Acidic dry	Neutral dry	Base-rich dry	Acidic wet	Neutral to base-rich wet.
1. Open ground simple					
2. Open ground complex					
3. Dense regeneration					
4. Thicket and stem exclusion					
5. Open canopy complex					
6. Open woodland simple					
7. Canopy tree mortality complex					
8. Canopy tree mortality simple					

In each cell is a description of the appearance of each structure class.

Example description:
Sparse birch, rowan and pine seedlings /saplings (more rarely, oak) may occur within the well-developed field layer.

grazed plant only common in the particular region could be added and any not found at the site could be removed. Similarly, site-specific photographs of different indicator levels can be added. This will help to reduce observer error either between years or between observers. In the field, the structure class and current impact are recorded at ten points within each woodland, or open ground, type and the most common class and current impact are recorded. When subsequent assessments take place, any change to the most common class or impact level is noted. Changes in the most common level of individual indicators of current herbivore impact can also be noted to provide additional information on the nature of any changes. The location of each point, along with its structure class, can also be recorded on a map so that the spatial distribution of different structures can easily be seen. If subsequent assessments use the same points, then the spatial distribution of any changes over time can also be easily seen. Assessments are best carried out in February or March when the cumulative impacts from the last twelve months are most apparent and before new growth from the following growing season obscures evidence of winter browsing.

Benefits of the method

Quantitative trials of observer error have not been carried out but, from experience of using the method, we believe that it will normally be repeatable to within one class either way. Despite the non-quantitative nature of this approach, we feel that its relative simplicity will allow a wide range of people to use it. Whilst many managers and graziers are used to assessing the condition of their woodlands in general terms, we hope that, by using this

Figure 2. Indicators of current impacts and format of description tables.

Indicator	Level of Impact				
	Very High	High	Medium	Low	Absent
Basal shoots					
Epicormic/lower shoots on adult trees		In each cell is a description of the appearance of each indicator.			
Seedlings and saplings					
Bark stripping and stem breakage					
Preferentially browsed species					
Sward					
Ground disturbance					

Example description:
Great woodrush moderately grazed, heavily grazed if cattle are present.

method, they will be encouraged to observe indicators that could easily be overlooked and to record their observations in a more structured way. They will also have a common language with which to discuss current and desirable large herbivore impacts.

A knowledge of both past and current impact levels is quite powerful in describing the processes that a woodland has been through and is currently experiencing, even where very recent changes to a grazing regime have taken place. For example, prolonged heavy grazing would result in an open woodland with canopy gaps caused by death of old trees. A reduction in the browsing and grazing in the recent past, e.g. the last 2-3 years, would then lead to the development of a field layer. The structure type would be 7 (canopy tree mortality complex). However if, within the last twelve months, grazing and browsing levels have increased and current impacts are 'Very High', this indicates that the woodland is now heading towards structure type 8 (canopy tree mortality simple) and its future may be at risk if impact levels are not reduced.

Putting the method into practice

The Grazing Toolbox method has been used at a number of sites since the Toolbox was launched. At Loch Sunart, woodland owners and FCS staff were trained in the use of the method so that they could assess the impact of deer and Highland cattle on native woodland across multiple ownerships on the north side of the loch. The main benefits of the method perceived by participants were that it is straightforward to undertake in the field and quick to analyse the results. Despite all the participants having many years of experience in observing native woodlands, the discipline of working through the different parts of the method alerted them to the usefulness of the indicators in telling a story about past and recent herbivore impacts. For example, the hazel trees had old, dead stems arising from their base. There was evidence of heavy browsing on these old stems. Young stems were also developing from the base of the hazel trees and these were less heavily browsed, probably because sheep had been excluded and deer numbers reduced some years previously. These young shoots had browsed tips, indicating a recent increase in browsing pressure.

Method development

One of the benefits of the method being available on the internet is that it can be regularly updated. Feedback from the Loch Sunart training event led to several improvements to the method. FCS is also using the Toolbox method at Loch Katrine and Aird Trilleachan to assess cattle and deer impacts. Observations made at these sites will be used to refine descriptions of the structure types and impact levels and additional photographs will be taken and added to the documentation. As the Toolbox method is used more widely, we hope to receive more feedback from users to assist us with developing the method further and improving the guidance.

Uptake of the woodland grazing grant scheme

The new controlled livestock grazing option which is available through RDC – RP, was well publicised in Spring 2010 with reports of the formal launch by the Scottish Government's Minister for the Environment appearing in both the national and farming press. Training events were also held for Scottish Government organisations (FCS, SNH and Scottish Government Rural Payments and Inspections Directorate) together with conservation advisors and woodland managers. Uptake of the grant has been very slow to date with only a handful of applications, none of which has yet reached the final contract stage. Possible reasons why it has not been widely taken up so far are:

- The Pilot grant scheme, run by FCS under the Scottish Forestry Grant Scheme (Sustainable Woodland Grazing option) attracted over 60 applications of which 31 were considered suitable and were invited to participate. Twenty-six sites, mainly in the north and west of Scotland, eventually signed up. It is possible that the immediate demand was satisfied through the Pilot and that the applications that were turned down were never going to be suitable candidates for either the pilot, or the mainstream scheme.

- Many native woodlands in the north and west of Scotland are the subject of previously awarded grants that are still running even though the grant scheme under which they were awarded no longer exists. In some cases, the existing grant conditions are not compatible with the requirement of a woodland grazing grant under the new scheme. The main issue is the *Farm Woodland Premium Scheme* which provides an annual income for 15 years to offset income forgone for removal from agriculture (usually the removal of sheep or cattle). One of the conditions of this grant is that the area is excluded from agricultural production for a period of 30 years. Livestock can only be re-introduced if the grant is repaid in full with interest.

- The grant application process is seen as quite complicated by users who are not using it on a regular basis. Although this perception is slowly changing there is anecdotal evidence that this can be a barrier to uptake of grants under the SRDP.

- There is a perceived lack of conservation advisors who have sufficient knowledge of the subject and therefore the confidence to put applications together for woodland owners/managers.

- The delay in introducing the updated grant scheme has meant that many conservation advisors have spent their time drawing up more straight forward agri-environment grant applications for their clients.

- The '*Sustainable Management of Forests*' annual payment for controlled livestock woodland grazing, at £87/ha, is less than that on offer in the Pilot grant scheme (£100/ha). Anecdotal evidence suggests that the rate is too low to attract applicants many of whom were expecting a rate similar to, or higher than that offered in the Pilot. The next opportunity to review the incentives and mechanism will be under the revised SRDP for 2013 – 2020.

- Only 50% of the cost of drawing up a woodland grazing management plan (and undertaking any associated survey work), up to a maximum of £400, is available through SRDP and then only if the plan is prepared by an agent or specialist.

- Many land managers are reluctant to embark on significant changes to the management of their land with the uncertainty of forthcoming reform of the Common Agricultural Policy and with further changes to the SRDP only three years away.

- Recent history has shown that farmers, in the main, are reluctant to get involved with woodland management.

FCS and SNH officers are continuing to promote the new grant scheme where woodland grazing is likely to bring conservation benefits to woodlands that are designated as Sites of Special Scientific Interest or Special Areas for Conservation especially where the sites are in unfavourable condition due to inappropriate grazing. Wider promotion is being left until the future of land management incentives is clearer and land managers are in a better position to make informed decisions.

Conclusions

There are many factors to be considered in developing a sustainable woodland grazing regime for any given woodland and, as this is a new or perhaps re-discovered 'science', many land managers and experts alike lack experience and examples that they can draw on. The *Woodland Grazing Toolbox* is designed to overcome some of this lack of experience however we have probably under-estimated the level of support needed at this stage for new entrants to the grant scheme. We think that currently the Toolbox will be used more by advisers than by land managers. However, by recording the impact of different grazing regimes in different parts of the country, and in different woodland types, we can begin to build up our knowledge and understanding. As woodlands are entered into the new grant scheme, grazing management plans written and monitoring undertaken, we will aim to make an ever-increasing number of case studies available through the *Woodland Grazing Toolbox*. Though uptake of the woodland grazing grant scheme has been slow to date for a variety of reasons, there is an increasing interest in sustainable grazing of woodlands by stock and we expect this to grow in future. There is also increasing demand for subjective, indicator-based, methods of assessing impacts that can be used as part of an adaptive management approach. The assessment and monitoring methodology described here is being used increasingly widely to help with the management of both deer and stock.

References

Armstrong, H.M., Chesterton, C., Currie, F., Kirby, K.J. and Latham, J. (2003) *Developing survey methods to assess over-grazing of upland woods*. Unpublished report to DEFRA, London.

Thompson, R. (2007) *Assessment of overgrazing methodology in lowland semi-natural woodlands*. Report to Natural England, Peterborough.

Thompson, R., Peace, A. and Poulsom, E. (2004) *A judgement-based method to identify overgrazing in English upland native woodland*. English Nature Research Report No. 621, Peterborough.

Man, Swine and Miradal
Hans Baeté
University College, Ghent

Introduction
In 1146, a place on the loess plateau in central Belgium was known to man as *silua de miradal*. From 1406 until the end of the eighteenth century this woodland was endowed with the statute of Free Wood, which, for example, refers to its independent lawcourt. History reminds us of Miradal's long-term relationship with pigs, wild boars, their hybrids, and several kinds of fruit-bearing trees. Man's approach to swine and treescapes in Miradal remains a beguiling issue to this very day.

Celtic pork
In Ancient Rome, the Belgians were not only considered the bravest, as they were also esteemed for producing 'Celtic pork' in or near woodlands. This quality was still appreciated in the sixteenth century by the famous botanist and physician Rembert Dodoens. He described the meat of acorn-eating pigs as *firm and by no means watery* (translation). So the keeping of 'woodland pigs' was lucrative and leased. Numerous documents give evidence of pannage in the Ducal Free Woods of Brabant during the dark and cold months of the sixteenth, seventeenth, eighteenth and early nineteenth century. The pannage in Miradal was obviously well-adjusted to forestry, as this place kept its age-long reputation for high-quality oak timber up to the present day. Pigs were restricted to well-appointed areas and evidently kept out of young stands by swine herders, who also built wooden cages for the animals. The season of pannage traditionally ended on Februay 2, the feast – and Mass - of light.

Juicy fruit-treescape
Miradal was not only a place for pannage, coppice or timber. This Ducal Free Wood also had to keep up a reputation as a chase, housing wild boars and their hybrids with domestic pigs. In this realm we encounter a common feature of man and swine: we only have one stomach and cannot digest grass like ruminants, so we are both happy eating juicy fruits like apple, pear or cherry (indeed, unless there is a matter of food allergy). Accordingly, the fines for gathering fruit and cutting fruit trees were high in the Ducal Free Wood. *Who carries off wood that bears fruit, knowingly apple trees, pear trees (!), cherry trees, hazel trees or the like, forfeits twenty golden reals* (1560, translation). Exactly the same fine was imposed on someone who cut timber illegally... Another explicitly protected 'larger fruit' in Miradal's coppice-with-standards was Medlar (*Mespilus germanica*), which was also prized for its wood, renowned for making cogwheels in water mills. The careful protection of fruit-bearing trees other than Oak (*Quercus robur, Q. petraea*), Hazel (*Corylus avellana*), Chestnut

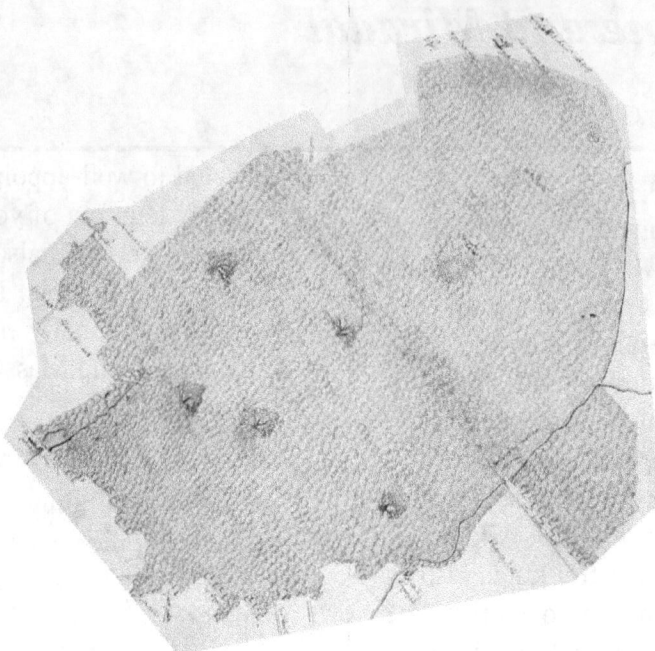

Figure 1. The two main valleys (with ponds) in Miradal according to a late sixteenth century map.

(*Castanea sativa*) and Beech (*Fagus sylvatica*) implied an almost forgotten juicy fruit-treescape. Pear (*Pyrus communis*) sadly disappeared completely, but 'wild' apple trees (*Malus sylvestris*) still survive in the two main, forested valleys of Miradal (Figures 1 and 2).

Black game residency

Pannage in Miradal was abandoned around 1730, but the presence of 'wild' boar was still a beguiling issue in 1781, when the Austrian emperor Joseph II prohibited the roaming of swine in the Southern Netherlands. Clearly, the nutritious roots, truffles, mast and other fruits of Miradal were insufficient to support the duke's favourite game the whole year round and hence the animals regularly feasted on adjacent fields to the dislike of farmers, villagers and businessmen. According to the archives, the duke offered his black game residency in a large, partially forested brick-walled cloister-domain next to Miradal. But apparently these animals didn't survive the revolutionary turmoil during the 1790's.

Twenty-first Century Issues

While all domesticated pigs were confined to pigpens, wild boars reappeared in Belgian forests from the nineteenth century onwards. For the most part as a result of both introduction and migration from France and Germany. The roaming of swine in and out of woodlands has remained a touchy subject ever since. In 2007, the hunting lobby was accused of introducing half-tame swine 'into the

Figure 2. The present distribution of crab apple (*Malus sylvestris*) in Miradal.

wild'. Many conservationists are still in doubt or ignorant concerning the potential role of pigs and wild boars in treescapes. Therefore, amongst many other features, the possible long-term impact of rooting swine on dense structures (e.g. compacted loess soils, thick mats of Bracken), their intriguing relation to fungi (e.g. mycorrhiza, saproxylic fungi as food), and, of course, trees, deserve further attention.

References

Baeté, H., De Bie, M., Hermy, M. and Van Den Bremt, P. (eds.) (2009) *Miradal. Ergoed in Heverleebos en Meerdaal*, Davidsfonds, Leuven.

Dodoens, R. (1644) *Herbarius oft Cruydt-Boeck Remberti Dodonaei: volghens sijne laetste verbeteringhe, Plantijnsche Druckerije van Balthasar Moretus*, Antwerpen, (posthumous edition).

Lindemans, P. (1952) *De geschiedenis van de landbouw in België* (2 parts). De Sikkel, Antwerpen.

State Archives in Belgium (Brussels), *Archief van het Arenbergpaleis te Brussel.*

The Arenberg Archives and Cultural Centre (Edingen/Enghien).

University Library Katholieke Universiteit Leuven, *Archief van het kasteel van Arenberg te Heverlee.*

Continuity and Change: Fluctuations in Woodland Cover, Arable and Pasture in Prehistoric and Modern times: Cycles of intensive land-use and abandonment

Graham Bathe[1], Ben Lennon[2], Jonathan Spencer[3]

Independent Researcher (formerly Natural England)[1], Forestry Commission Scotland[2], Forestry Commission[3]

Introduction

This paper looks at how woodland cover has varied, and sometimes alternated, with agricultural use, over history and pre-history. It draws examples from about 250 square kilometres of land south of Marlborough which once fell within the Royal Forest of Savernake, where extensive documentation has survived from the twelfth until the twenty-first centuries, and where modern aerial reconnaissance by Lidar has revealed the pattern of ground features beneath the canopy. It interprets these findings in terms of our conceptual understanding of the term 'ancient woodland', raising questions about the meaning and application of this category.

Britain's Ancient Woodland Policy

Ancient woodland is a mainstay of conservation policy, heralded as one of its enduring successes, enshrined in legislation, attracts substantial funding from the public purse and forms a central plank of environmental organisations. It is featured in the UK Forestry Standard and the voluntary UK Woodland Assurance Standard.

Development of the concept of ancient woodland

By the mid nineteenth century it was widely considered that some British woodlands represented the modified remains of some aboriginal forest (Watkins, 1988: 238). The term *'ancient and ornamental'*, introduced through the New Forest Act of 1877, is still in common use today. Botanists in early editions of the Victoria County Histories suggested that the relationship between certain plant assemblages and long established woodlands, derived from their primeval origins (Watkins, 1988: 240). Similarly Clement Reid (1899) recognised a connection between molluscan and botanical refugia and what he called *'ancient woodlands'*, although in such early work the term was not often clearly distinguished from primary, indigenous or aboriginal. Building on the theories of successional development towards stable equilibrium, Tansley identified woodland as the climax vegetation in much of Britain. It was in 1910, working within the emerging disciplines of ecology and phytosociology, that Moss, Rankin and Tansley (1910) concluded that the majority of British woodlands could be classed as *lineal descendents of primeval forest*.

To identify sites with long continuity, George Peterken had initially sought to distinguish between primary and secondary woodlands. However, as it was difficult to demonstrate that any particular site had always been woodland, Oliver Rackham suggested it was preferable to select a cut-off date, and concentrate on what was provably old (Peterken, 1996). Ancient woods were defined as those present since at least 1600. This date was chosen because it marks the time when cartographic evidence becomes available, and the time when the planting of trees became widespread (Spencer and Kirby, 1992).

Peterken, adopting the phrase from 70 years earlier, considered that ancient woodlands were *lineal descendents of primeval forest*. The concept was enthusiastically adopted by the conservation bodies. Officers of the Nature Conservancy Council frequently told landowners that their ancient woods had probably been there since the ice-age. The phrase was re-quoted as recently as 2007 by Goldberg *et al.* (2007) who expounded further the principle that once destroyed, they cannot be re-created. The romantic image of ancient woodland still governs national policy. The Government's Environmental White Paper of June 2011 *'The Natural Choice: securing the value of nature'*, states *'Most ancient woods are likely to have been continuously wooded since the Ice Age'* (HM Government, 2011).

Resistance to the protection of ancient woodland

Despite its long incubation, acceptance of the categorisation of woodlands in this way was a slow and painful process. The notion of *'so-called ancient woodland'* was initially rejected by the Director-General of the Forestry Commission (FC), who denied it really existed (Peterken, 1996). The issue became a struggle, with power conferred on those whose classification system prevailed. In relation to Broadleaves policy, Peterken (1983) observed that most of the positive thinking had occurred outside the Forestry Commission.

In 1979-80, the House of Lords Select Committee on Science and Technology had observed that 30-50% of all ancient woodland in Great Britain had been lost since 1947, often by the FC, or using FC grants and subsidies. This was equivalent to losses in the last 400 years combined (HoL SCSC&T 1979-80: 18). The committee endorsed an inventory prepared in Norfolk, and the Nature Conservancy Council commenced work on a national assessment in 1981. As Tsouvalis (2000) observes, *'by 1990 ancient woodland had become thoroughly objectivised and institutionalised'*.

Marketing Ancient Woodland

The success of ancient woodland, as a concept, derives in part from its branding. It conforms to recognised principles evoking a vivid image through its name, conveying the impression of unique characteristics, and appealing to psychological motivations involving beliefs and attitudes. Peterken (1996) reflected that the word 'ancient' had been deliberately chosen because it would mean most to people. Who would dare suggest that ancient woodlands were a bad thing? If it is permissible to draw the analogy with the commercial world further, as a branded object it would be expected to have associated properties, some of which could be actual, some putative and some pretended, and these contribute to both its identity and image.

And yet, for all its success, both parts of the name ancient woodland raise significant issues, especially as our understanding of historic and prehistoric landscapes change, as revealed by definitions in the Oxford English Dictionary (OED).

Ancient: early in the world's history, the period before the fall of the Roman empire.

Woodland: land *covered* with wood or trees.

Wood: a collection of trees growing *more or less thickly together*, a piece of ground *covered* with trees.

There is a danger that a high proportion of sites classified as ancient woodland are neither ancient, nor woodland, at least using the definitions of the OED. The mismatch between historians and natural historians, is exacerbated by the former applying the term Early Modern to the period 1500-1800.

The primacy of ancient woodland within conservation policy to some extent has militated against subsequent rational debate. People who query ancient woodland policy, like those who question climate change, can be treated as if they are denying some universal, self-evident and historically-provable fact.

Methodology employed in preparing the Ancient Woodland Inventory (AWI)

It needs to be remembered that the AWI was prepared in response to a perceived threat, and that the mechanism by which sites were identified relied on a series of proxy decisions.

The argument was broadly as follows:

- Our traditional woodlands are rapidly being converted to plantation.

- We need to retain examples of the most biologically diverse and representative examples of woodland found in Britain.

- There is evidence that sites with long continuity have high biodiversity value.

- Because we cannot trace continuity over protracted historical periods, we will use 1600 as a cut-off date; woods present in 1600 are likely to have been present for centuries or millennia before.

- Estate and manorial records are incomplete and torturous to research, so the first edition Ordnance Survey maps of *c*1810 will serve as the baseline for site identification.

- In certain cases OS maps may not be available until 1830, or are obscure, and need to be supplemented by later 19th century maps.

Where there was any doubt, sites were included on the Inventory (Spencer and Kirby, 1992: 83).

Constructing Reality through Classification

The change in thinking which led to ancient woodland being protected derived from a process to which Foucault applied the ungainly term '*problematization*', but which we could put more simply as '*questioning received wisdom*'. The old models and thought processes no longer seem to apply. Hence the classification of broadleaved woodland as scrubby and unproductive, where its replacement with high yielding conifers was '*a good thing*', was supplanted by an alternative concept of reality. Ancient woodland forms part of our national heritage, where its conservation and enjoyment is also '*a good thing*'. Arguably, if the two are in conflict, conservation could be '*a greater good*'.

As Tsouvalis (2000) observes, reality is *constructed* through conceptualization and classification. The ancient woodland debate enabled a '*long-forgotten reality to be rediscovered and made visible once more*'. Classification was at the very heart of the argument. Taking matters further, as Olwig and Lowenthal (2006) have emphasised '*The heritage of nature, no less than that of culture, is fundamentally cultural in origin*'. In other words we cannot value or protect environmental features, unless we have first classified and conceptualised the landscape, furnishing it with meaning and assigning what is important. Once these categories have been learned, it is difficult to see the world in any other way. *Classification takes possession of us, shaping our perception and thereby our behaviour* (Thomas 1984: 52). Such classifications are human constructs, and provide us with models of reality, but there is a danger that once taken for granted, may be mistaken for reality itself.

Furthermore, in the same way that Victorians perceived Stonehenge as a Druid temple, whereas modern workers focus on its astronomical relevance, we tend to interpret past landscapes in accordance with observations from our own era. Today we distinguish a highly-polarised landscape of ungrazed, dense-canopy woodland, enclosed pasture, and arable, and may be in danger of projecting these modern divisions onto assumed historic land-use patterns, where such dichotomies have no foundation. Habitats which do not conform to modern compartmentalisation, may be perceived as intermediate, and assigned pejorative terms such as "scrub", implying that they are not fulfilling their potential.

The Study Area of Savernake

Problematization, where the former models no longer seem to fit, has been experienced recently by some of us working on the area covered by the Royal Forest of Savernake, which at its maximum, covered 250 square kilometres south of Marlborough, to whose castle it was linked (Figures 1 and 2). The Forest is remarkable, because it has been in the hands of the same family of hereditary wardens from Domesday until today. This has probably contributed to the preservation of a remarkable range of documentation from the twelfth century onwards, nearly all of which are in the public domain. The historical record has been supplemented by extensive aerial photographs, including those taken in the 1940s after wartime felling revealed ground based features, and very importantly by highly detailed Lidar imagery of surviving woodlands undertaken in 2006-7.

Lidar (Light Direction and Ranging) is a non-intrusive, laser-based, aerial reconnaissance system which can be used to construct detailed images of

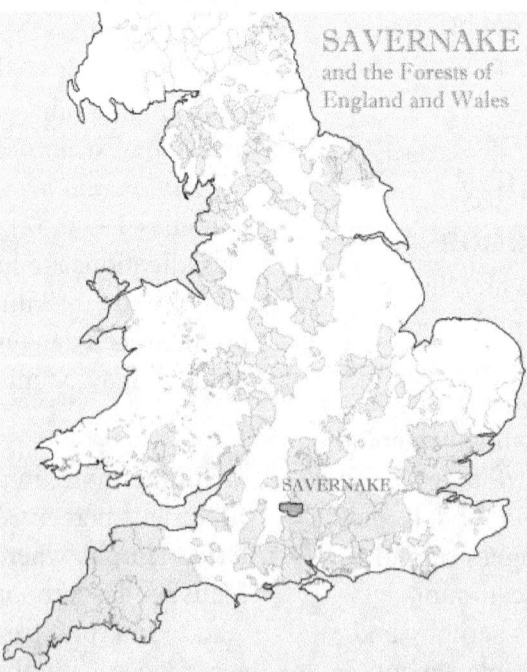

Figure 1. Location of Savernake Forest in the context of the Royal Forests of England and Wales, shown at their maximal extent (not necessarily contemporary). After Langton and Jones, 2005.

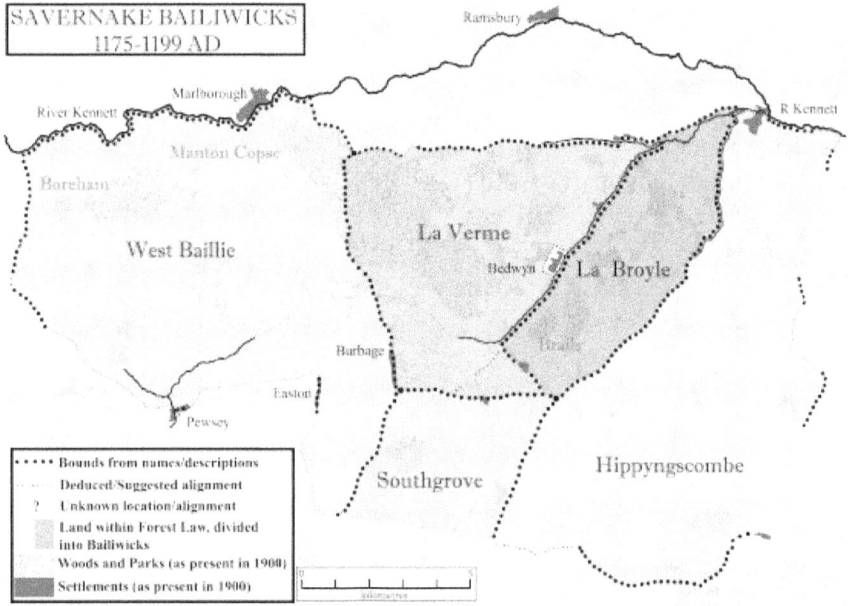

Figure 2. Savernake in the late twelfth century, then covering $c250$ km², as divided into bailiwicks. Also showing the locations of three case-study woods of Boreham, Manton Copse, and The Brails.

ground features. An aircraft flying at constant height emits thousands of laser pulses each second, and records reflections from each pulse (Lennon and Crow, 2009). Delays between transmission and recovery indicate distance travelled, enabling detection of changes in ground level (Figure 3). Over a porous surface such as woodland, a proportion of laser energy is reflected back from the canopy, but a significant proportion will penetrate to the forest floor. Software can be used to eliminate the first return (canopy) data from images, as if stripping woodland cover to reveal ground features (Figure 4). These can be emphasised further by artificially creating shadows from light sources at different compass points, combining as a final product those images with strongest shadows, to construct a three dimensional terrain model (Figure 5).

Woodlands have comparatively few archaeological features listed in Historic Environment Records, leading to claims that they have been less subject to radical land-use alteration through human agency. However recent work suggests that this paucity derives from the difficulty of using aerial photography to record features, or conducting archaeological surveys amidst thick vegetation, poor light and intrusive tree roots. Lidar has demonstrated that, far from having fewer archaeological features, there are more, because the woodland has prevented their loss through ploughing. They are just harder to detect without sophisticated technology.

Figure 3. Lidar Reconnaissance Mechanism. Plane at constant height transmits laser pulses (A) to forest below and detects reflected beams. Time between transmission and return indicate distance travelled, enabling detection of tree canopy (B) and minor changes in ground level (C-D).

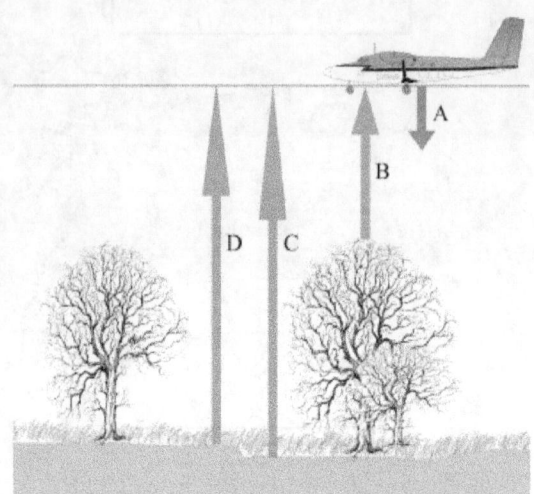

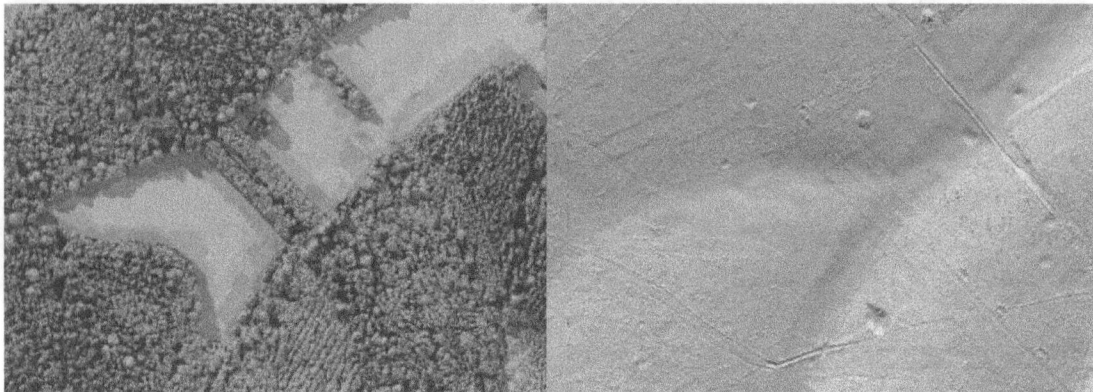

Figure 4. Two Lidar images of the same area, Woolslade, Savernake. The left picture shows the 'first return' from laser beams reflected by the tree canopy. When these are eliminated from the data, the 'final return' shows the forest floor beneath the canopy. In this case it reveals inter alia lynchets, a prehistoric cross valley dyke, a tumulus, Roman road and second world war ammunition stores. © Forestry Commission.

Case Studies of Ancient Woodlands within Savernake

Adopting a multi-disciplined approach to research demonstrates that there are features of former land-use everywhere within the ancient woodland of Savernake. Three case examples will be explored here:

1. Manton Copse.

Manton Copse is the sole surviving relict of an extensive woodland called Hanckeridge situated just south of Marlborough which features in Forest perambulations from the thirteenth century. Before the 1500s this had been enclosed as a series of banked and hedged coppices known as Manton, Hurlmore, Granham and Woodhouse Coppices. These were subject to depredation from people in the adjoining towns. In 1586 alone, there

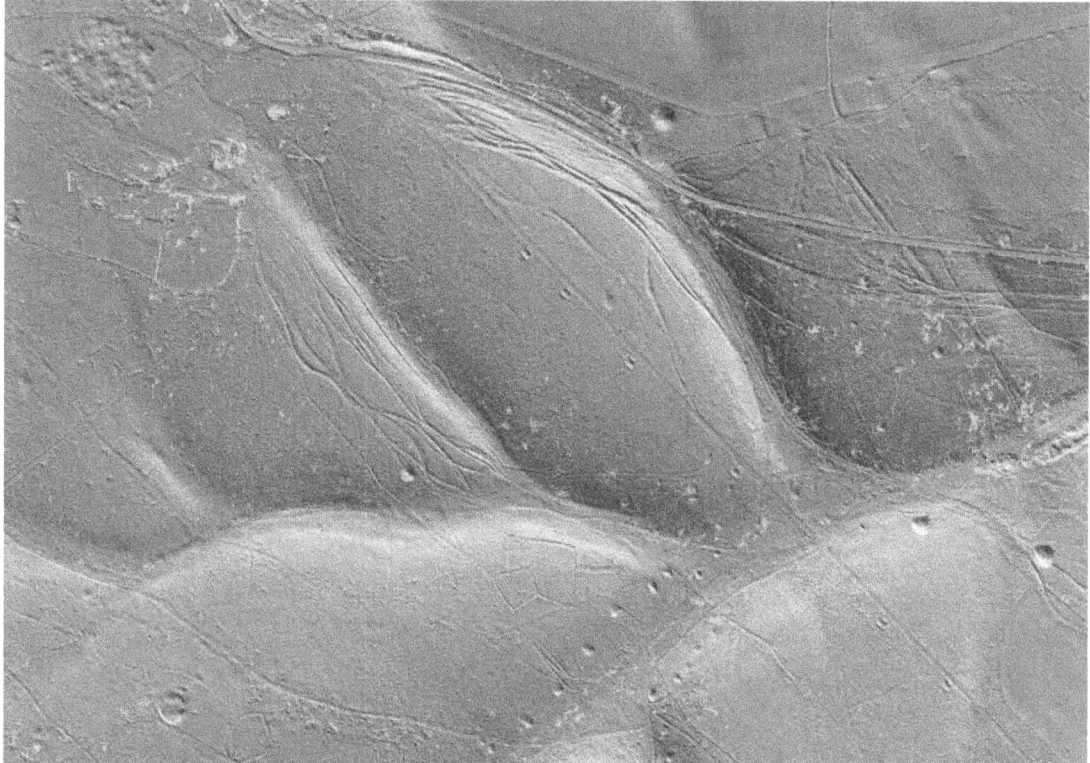

Figure 5. Lidar image of the forest floor at Braydonhook, Savernake. In the centre was formerly a coppice called Bolesoak, and the scars around it show braided tracks. Below centre there is a probable iron-age enclosure, with another bottom left. The image also shows the course of Roman roads, equidistant pits possibly marking a common-land boundary, and wartime relics. © Forestry Commission.

were thirty incidents reported to the Forest Courts, many of them relating to multiple occasions. They were often perpetrated by women, servants or children. For example, Batt's wife, Foches's wife, Mattock's wife, Taylor's maid and Potter's maid cut down Hurlemore Coppice, whilst Potter's boy, Panter's boy, Robert Hiscock's daughter, Thomas Tarrant's son and wife, John Looker's wife and Robert Tarrant's wife were all reported to *"tear up the hedge and coppices continually"*. When challenged, the keeper could be met with defiance. Mattock's wife, Batt's wench and Potter's wife were caught cutting browse from a tree, but said that they would carry on anyway. On the same day the keeper reported that Alexander's and Potter's wives said they would continue *"in spite of my teeth and his that set me there"*. Many of these people *"fetched rods and row continually, yet dwelleth out of the liberty"*. Some came daily and carried home '*hazels and thorns as big as a man's middle*'. The unruly locals took row (deadwood), browse, whole trees, faggots, knitches (smaller bundles, sometimes called kitchen faggots), fleetornes (saplings) and moots (rootstocks) (WSA 1300-87).

When coppices were leased to Francis Lord Seymour in 1652, '*liberty was given to grubb these coppices and convert them to tillage*'. A legal brief of 1754 states that it is '*presumed it was soon afterwards done*' (WSA 9-22-225). Their demise can be mapped subsequently. By 1900 just the southern tip of Manton Copse was the sole relic of Hanckeridge wood. So Manton represents an example of where abuses led to destruction and grubbing. Whilst nearly all the coppices were eliminated, their banks and hedges persisted, imposing their rounded outline onto a landscape otherwise covered in straight-edged fields. Their late grubbing has also revealed the presence of a pre-historic rectilinear field system which predated even Hanckeridge wood, and which extended beyond the bounds of the former coppices (Figure 6). So the known sequence here is:

1. Pre arable landscape.

2. Prehistoric arable 'Celtic' fields.

3. Cessation or Abandonment – development of Hanckeridge Wood.

4. Incorporation into Royal Hunting Forest 1086-1130.

5. Medieval encoppicement.

6. Disafforestation c1550 (= ie removal from Forest Law and transfer to private occupation).

7. Inclusion in Deer Park 1570s.

8. Abuses and depredation late sixteenth century.

Figure 6. Aerial view of Manton Copse, relic of a former extensive woodland. The copse was pear shaped, and its outline is defined by the track to the right, and a right-of-way (shown as dotted line) still existing through the arable field to the left. Clearance of the woodland has revealed the outline of a 'Celtic' field system, with unrelated boundaries.

9. Grubbing 1650-1900 to reveal former arable fields.

10. Relict of Manton Copse mapped as ancient woodland.

2. Boreham Wood

This is a woodland which features in documentary records from the 1200s. In the 1960s most of it was cleared using public subsidies, revealing a prehistoric field system lying beneath, which Lidar shows extend into the remaining section of the wood. The sequence revealed here is:

1. Pre-arable landscape

2. Prehistoric 'Celtic' arable fields.

3. Cessation or abandonment (sufficient to remove significance of field boundaries).

4. Development of scrub and trees.

5. Incorporation of whole landscape into Royal Forest 1100s.

6. Unauthorised 'wasting' of trees at Boreham Wood in 1225-6 by Henri de Lune, and land seized into King's hands (Brentnall 1941).

7. Because it was seized, the wood was retained as a Forest outlier when Forest bounds were contracted to just the King's lands in thirteenth and fourteenth century perambulations.

8. In the early fourteenth century Boreham was described as a wasted wood, a *haya* of the Lord King part of which was lawn, and a pasture for beasts of the chase (PRO E32-217 and E126-2-27; WSA 192-25).

9. Adjoining medieval village of Shaw deserted by about 1388, shortly after Black Death (English and Brown, 2009).

10. Medieval encoppicement established. Pigs were agisted there in the late fourteenth century, and licence issued for gathering cartloads of sticks (WSA 125-25).

11. Transferred from the King into private hands 1550s.

12. Cleared 1960s using public subsidies revealing the field system beneath.

13. New woodland planted on adjoining land using public subsidies.

14. The parcel of Boreham remaining is mapped as ancient woodland.

3. The Brails

The two woodlands known as the Brails are situated on ridges separated by a minor valley. These have a far more complex history, with Lidar and archaeological data supplementing significant historical data from 1199 until the eighteenth century.

The sequence here appears to be:

1. Early unknown landscape.

2. Bronze Age dykes and probable settlement (as suggested by urn field and burnt flint).

3. Probable Iron Age enclosures.

4. 'Celtic' arable fields established (unknown date).

5. Large Roman Villa. Archaeo-environmental remains of oak, hazel, sloe, elder, plus red and roe deer, jay and woodcock, suggest nearby woodland.

6. Unknown post Roman landscape.

7. Brails 'thicket' recorded by twelfth century.

8. Incorporation into Royal Forest between 1086 and 1130.

9. Records of deer, fuel collection, and common land for ox and sheep in medieval times.

10. In the early fourteenth century *The Brails* were described as a wood, a cow pasture, a *haya* of the Lord King, and pasture for beasts of the chase (PRO E32-217 and E126-2-27).

11. 'Disafforestation' – ie removal of Forest Law and transfer into private hands after death of Queen Katherine Parr.

12. 250 men employed in park landscaping for grand mansion (never finished) 1548.

13. Site described as holding two thousand mature timber oaks, felled *c*1553.

14. The Brails is mentioned in 1590s as '*a former wood-ground now converted into pasture*' (WSA 1300-104).

15. Site remains as common pasture for cattle and sheep, with a right of estovers (fuel).

16. Landscaping plans for integrating with Tottenham Park discussed with Lancelot 'Capability' Brown.

17. Inclosure (*ie* common rights extinguished) in 1772 (WSA Inclosure Award 68).

18. Planted with over 200,000 trees and 27 bushels of acorns and hazelnuts in 1770s (WSA 1300-2617).

19. Mapped as ancient woodland.

The pre-historic 'Celtic' fields might derive from any time from the Bronze Age to the Romano-British period. We have no knowledge of their duration, or the landscape present before such 'Celtic' systems were established, including whether it was ever wooded. Recent interdisciplinary work on prehistoric landscape development in the Allen Valley of Cranborne Chase by French *et al.* (2007), has thrown doubt on the received wisdom that such areas had woodland cover. Here integrating archaeological investigation with new palynological, molluscan, soil micro-morphological, and other palaeo-environmental data, suggests that woodland development in the early Holocene was patchy and variable, and there were substantial open areas present in the Mesolithic. If there had been major changes in vegetation and soil, these had already occurred before the Neolithic, and the area has remained relatively stable since.

Models of Physical Stability

All three case examples may be interpretable in accordance with models of physical stability, which can be adapted for biological systems (e.g. Gray and Elliott, 2009). These are depicted in Figure 7. There appear to be no stable landscapes at Savernake, such as might be envisaged if ancient woodlands really are lineal descendents of primeval forest. There are some areas which have undergone perpetual and frequent change, where a number of stable options are available. This equates with meta-stability or what could be called a *'Restless Landscape'*. However some sites, such as The Brails appear to be used and revert to woodland again and again. This is largely governed by the geology. The area replanted in 1770 conforms almost exactly with the Reading Beds and London Clay, areas notoriously difficult to use for other purposes. This conforms with a metastable model of landscape. In this, marginally stable conditions can be maintained by a continuous effort, but the land is predisposed to recover a low-energy state. Metastability would be characteristic of marginal lands, which may be used intensively for short periods following alteration in the balance of demand and opportunity. A fourth model, where the landscape cannot recover once disturbed, could relate to woodland sites where clearance leads to the irreparable loss of soils. No certain examples of this are in the study area.

A: Stable

B: Multiple Stability - discrete or continuous: Restless Landscape

C: Superficial stability: Vulnerable and Irrecoverable

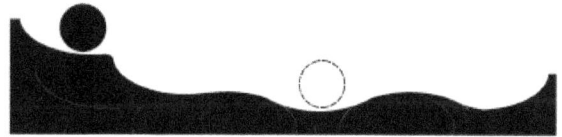

D: Metastability: Marginal Landscape

Figure 7. Landscape Stability models. A: Stable. B: Multiple Stability. Various discrete or continuous stable options are available, equating with a *'Restless Landscape'*. C: Superficial stability: If stability is lost it cannot be recovered (eg because soils/substrates are eroded or irreparably changed). D: Metastability. Temporary stability can be maintained by constant effort, but the landscape has a propensity to return to a lower energy state. Characteristic of marginal lands.

Drivers for Change

The drivers for change in the landscape in the study area, can be demonstrated to include land hunger associated with population pressures, market demands for grain including from occupying Roman forces, social-economic collapse with departure of the same forces, grazing pressures from deer and commoners' stock, disease of stock (perhaps associated with overgrazing), market demands for wool, and Black Death. Such changes may be incremental or instantaneous and catastrophic.

Grazing and browsing in Savernake

Documentation suggests that the whole of the King's lands in the Royal Forest of Savernake was grazed, including all the woodlands and coppices. There were areas referred to as downs, heaths, lawns, hays, thickets, groves and woods. However, it may be more appropriate to think of the landscape as a complex admixture of these habitats rather than a mosaic of demarcated facets, and the extent of the components varied in time as well as space.

The grazing in Savernake stemmed from a number of sources:

1. Common rights established by custom and practice.

These appear in twelfth- and thirteenth- century documentation, but many are probably pre-Norman. Savernake, like many other Forests, had few settlements within its bounds, but neighbouring villagers, called 'borderers', often had rights of grazing. Even within the Royal Forests, where it might be anticipated that the King's prerogative need have little regard to commoners, their rights were given protection in law. The *Carta de Foresta* (Charter of the Forests) of 1217 makes explicit reference to the commoners. The Charter had been drawn up alongside the Magna Carta, and was issued after King John's death, and re-asserted at various times by Henry III, Edward I and Edward II. It states *'All woods which belong to the King, which have been afforested, shall remain forest, saving the common usage of pasture and other matters, to those who were accustomed to the same'*. The barrister John Manwood (d1610), who was a Justice in Eyre of the New Forest, and who produced *A Treatise of the Lawes of the Forest*, observes: *'where the King doth afforest his own woods or lands, he doth not prejudice any man to have common in the same that used to have common therein, but does still reserve the common of herbage'*. The stock which commoners had a right to graze in Savernake included sheep, cattle and horses, with pigs in the mast season when acorns and beechnuts were present. Numbers could fluctuate, and very rarely a common was described as *'so overgrown with trees and bushes as to render it of very little value for sheep'* (WSA 1300-2029). Generally however the number of stock increased dramatically until the sixteenth century. Rights were often not quantified, because commoners were entitled to put out as many animals in summer as their own holding could hold in winter (a principle known as *levancy* and *couchancy*). However, it is certain that thousands of animals were involved. Such practices evolved as populations adjusted, and these in due course became recognised as rights protected by law. In 1580 the *Forest View* (a local commoners' court) heard that 15 smallholders had each established cottages and a few acres of ground on the waste '*and every of them claims to have common pasture in all the Forest of Savernake*' (WSA 1300-87).

2. Common rights specifically granted or gifted in perpetuity.

Such gifts were often made to religious institutions, frequently on condition that they maintained prayers and kept candles burning for the souls of named departed. In 1270 Henry III granted the Priory of St Margaret's the right to depasture sixteen oxen and four cows in the Forest of Savernake, excepting the lawns, without having to pay the usual fine (known as *exchapium*) if the cattle accidentally strayed, but instead driving them back into the Forest pasture, '*for ever*' (IPM 54 Henry III; Cal Close Rolls). Similarly in 1344 Queen Philippa granted to the same priory common pasture for 100 swine, quit of pannage, in the Queen's Forest of Savernake, except in her lawns there, '*for ever*' (Patent Roll, 23 Edward III, 1350).

3. The practice of *agistment*, whereby animals were turned out for payment.

The sums were often modest, and *agistment* also became established as a recognised entitlement to turn out animals in accordance with ancient custom. In Savernake for a penny it was possible to depasture 1 pig, 2 piglets, 1 ox, 1 cow, 1 horse, 2 calves, 2 foals or 10 sheep. Incomplete records from 25 Swainmote Courts held 1371-1380 record payments taken for over 11,000 animals (WSA 125-25).

4. Fallow Deer.

There were some hundreds of deer in Savernake, reserved exclusively for the King's table or hunting, that undoubtedly exerted a major influence on the Forest pasture, browse and regeneration. Evidence of overpopulation is found repeatedly in the local court proceedings known as '*Forest Views*'. Within a twenty year period in the sixteenth century some 506 deer were reported to have died '*from the murrain*' (a term for an unspecified condition or infection, perhaps associated with overpopulation). Death occurred especially in the winter, including 99 reported at one court sitting in December 1542 (WSA 1300-86).

A combination of all these factors led to widespread overgrazing, with a dramatic impact on the landscape. By late Tudor times there was despair over the '*the great decay and spoils of* woods, so that now much wood ground is converted into pasture' (WSA 1300-1484).

The coppices and enclosed woods of Savernake

The earliest perambulations suggest a diffuse landscape across the King's lands, although in the manors adjoining, woodlands could be named after local holdings or Lords. A perambulation from about 1225 mentions '*a wood of Boreham belonging to Shaw*', whilst later in the same century there are references to '*the wood of Nicholas of the Barbefield*' (later: Manton Coppice), and '*the wood of William de Harden*' bordering the Brails (WSA 2667-24-5-1). By the fourteenth century, many woodlands within the King's extra-manorial Forest, were also in discrete blocks, separated from their immediate environment. Nearly all woodlands mentioned are identifiable through their twenty-first century names, or in certain cases where grubbed, through surviving documentation.

Progressively such parcels were banked and generally temporarily hedged to protect them from browsing animals for part of their cutting cycle. All except a few scrubby thickets were called coppices or copses from the sixteenth century, showing that they were managed to provide poles and underwood for fuel and fencing. The word coppice does not feature in English much until Tudor times, when there was a sudden explosion of the term use in documents ranging from Shakespearean plays to legislation.

However, by this time they were clearly widespread, providing one of the mainstay land divisions of rural economies throughout much of England, alongside arable, meadow and pasture.

The Savernake coppices appear to have developed from general woodlands identifiable in early documentation. Evidence from the adjoining Forest of Chute shows increasing attention to efficient coppice management in the late thirteenth century. For example, in 1281 the Abbess of Wherewell was permitted to cut 20 acres of underwood in Harewood on condition that she enclose it with a low hedge for four years (Cal Close Rolls). Similarly in 1297, Oliver de Punchardon was permitted to take 50 acres of coppice in Faccombe, on condition that he enclose it with a dyke and hedge (Cal Patent Rolls). The first certain documentary evidence of the enclosure of coppices at Savernake comes from 1360, when it was ordered that money raised by the sale of underwood should '*be applied to the enclosure of two coppices in Iwode in that Forest* [Savernake] *late made*' (Close Rolls 1360). This evidence conforms with the general impression that there was widespread planned enclosure of woods to form coppices in the late thirteenth and the fourteenth centuries. This does not preclude there possibility of Norman or even Saxon coppices in Savernake. In Domesday the description of '*silva ad causura*' (woodlands for fencing) at both Shalbourne and Bagshot, suggests that these were used solely to provide poles, rather than timber.

The earliest coppices tend to be rounded in outline, enclosing maximum area relative to bank length. This suggests their unconstrained establishment within an uncultivated and undivided landscape. Examples include Boreham, Manton, Hurlemore, and Granham. Later coppices are more angular, having to accommodate to neighbouring features within a tightly enclosed and partitioned countryside. Coppice banks were topped by temporary paling or deadwood hedges to exclude domestic stock.

The Savernake coppices were all forged out of denser wood-pasture, which was common land, where rights of commoners enjoyed legal protection. The *Statute of Merton* of 1235 and the *Statute of Westminster* of 1285 had both confirmed the right of the Lord of the Manor to *approve* land – that is to inclose such land as was surplus to the needs of the commoners. However, this did not apply in Forests which were extra-manorial. The Royal Forests therefore conferred greater protection on common rights, but arguably less on the management of enclosed woodlands, than manorial land. Animals could be excluded for a while, but then coppices were thrown open to animals, and the old deadwood hedge sold for firewood, once the new growth had established. The *Statute for the Preservation of Woods* of 1544 required coppices to be enclosed for at least four years after cutting. In Savernake the coppices were traditionally opened to cattle after seven years (WSA 9-26-515).

When Savernake came into the Earl of Hertford's hands in 1553, the woodlands were in a poor state. He was told by his steward that there were no trees suitable for use as building-timber in the whole of Savernake (Seymour Papers). Despite owning a Forest and vast estate beyond stretching to thousands of hectares, Hertford had to purchase 640 oaks growing on his neighbour's land for building his new mansion (WSA 9-26-512). Hertford resolved to re-establish his woodlands. This required the eviction of commoners from some part of the Forest, and because of uncertainty over his right to do this, legal advice was sought. Instructions were sent to his lawyer concerning *"the lawfulness of his Right to Inclose the Coppices of Savernack"*. The instructions state that *"much wood ground is converted into pasture, the Great Wood in Savernack is very leere* [empty] *and old, and underwood is much decayed"*. The Earl's officers claimed that *"the borderers do not only oppress the said Forest with more cattle than in former times, but many of them connive to bring cattle from foreign townships* [ie those without true rights] *which ought not to be allowed. And they also pasture old oxen and cattle and spoil the first spring of wood as well of coppice, which were formerly preserved"* (WSA 1300-104).

The commoners however mounted opposition, and thwarted workmen building the new dyke and pale. The plan ultimately was abandoned. Hertford's steward bemoaned the *"needless fault finders and repiners"* [complainants]. In a general rant against destruction of the Estate woods overall he bewailed *"these commoners do marvellously murmur and grudge"*, and continued: *"this Realm will, in short time, rue the waste of it"*.

From the eighteenth century, commoners' rights were progressively regulated, enabling coppices to be protected, where they could develop a denser canopy. At a case concerning the straying of commoners' animals heard before Salisbury Assizes in July 1763, thirteen shepherds, cow-wards and other witnesses presented evidence. One, John Bright, 55, born in a house adjoining Furze Coppice, said his father was employed at 40s a year to maintain the boundary, nothing being suffered in the woods but two cows and a horse which he was allowed. John Webb, aged 45, said that when he was a boy he was given 4d or 5d a day for looking after the sheep, and his father beat him if they strayed in the woods (9-2-388). Only upon the eventual extinguishment of all commoners through the inclosure movement was the remainder of the Forest planted to dense tree cover.

In 1716, there were over 1,300 acres of coppice in Savernake. They were cut rotationally, normally at 14-year intervals, and sold for £11 or £12 per acre, during a period when underwood prices were rising year on year. When averaged for the duration of their cycle, coppices raised 17s per acre per year, demonstrating their significant value. Coppices which were not adequately cared for were vulnerable to eventual loss. In 1713, Lord Bruce sought legal advice concerning his entitlement to inclose Cole Coppice. It was claimed that until 25 years previously it had been in good condition, and constantly cut and bounded. However it had been destroyed and lay open to the Forest '*by ye neglect and carelessness of former woodwards who kept not good bounds but let deer and cattle eat and destroy it*' (WSA 1300-1484). In due course it was grubbed, and a team of eight horses ploughed it for conversion to grassland.

Conclusions

After undertaking this study, there are a number of conclusions:

1. The landscape of this area has been more dynamic than hitherto supposed, with periods, often cycles, of intensive use and abandonment.

2. The compartmentalisation of the landscape we observe today with hard boundaries between different land-uses, such as woodland and pasture, is a modern phenomenon, and it is erroneous to project this back to former periods when landscapes were diffuse and variable in space and time.

3. The great majority, and possibly all, mapped ancient woodlands in the 250 square kilometres of the study area have been subjected to other land-uses previously, and many supported arable land at some stage. None are primary or direct lineal descendents of the primeval forest, even in a classic site like Savernake.

4. All woodlands in the study area were grazed, including the coppices, for at least a major part of their cycle. The closed canopy structures of woodlands today are strictly recent phenomena. Until recent plantations were established, the only woodlands which had closed canopies were coppices from which domestic stock were excluded in modern times.

5. Marginal land, ie that which is most difficult to work productively, responds conspicuously to modifications in socio-economic pressures and opportunities. Changes in the landscape have been both incremental (e.g. overgrazing) and instantaneous or catastrophic (eg abandonment following disease or the Roman legion withdrawal).

6. Overgrazing has been responsible for more 'woodland' clearance than the axe.

7. Until modern times abandonment has been responsible for more woodland establishment than planting.

Reflections

We shall not cease from exploration
And the end of all our exploring
Will be to arrive where we started
And know the place for the first time.
          (T. S. Elliott, Little Gidding)

Where does this leave us with respect to the concept of ancient woodland? The answer is 'uncomfortable', and cautious. We recognise that the ancient woodland policy prevented ongoing depredation of the natural heritage of England. We have no challenge to the notion that long continuity leads to high biodiversity, especially where this is complemented by long continuity of consistent management. There is indeed long continuity in the landscape, but as far as we can tell in our study area, there is never unbroken continuity. The countryside is more dynamic, and has developed from a less rigid and divided landscape than we assumed. In the same way that we had to reject the hitherto romantically-held notion that there were primeval woodlands, we need to be very cautious indeed about claims that ancient woodland are primary and the direct lineal descendents of the primeval forest. However, the fact that certain areas seem to have a propensity to be woodland, restoring to this again and again, is particularly interesting. Grazing, and particularly the role of commons, which once covered at least half of England, have been vastly understated. The *Ancient Woodland Inventory* has probably captured medieval encoppicements, with their strictly modern exclusion of animals and recent closed canopies, very well, but been less successful in recognising the majority of the woods and especially the wood-pasture which dominated the scene for much of our history.

We can be optimistic too. Since so many important woodlands are secondary, then surely equally important ones can created anew today, through appropriately tuned policies and forethought. And ultimately, George Peterken's view on classification is fully vindicated: *'Classification all too easily become mechanisms for rigidifying and bureaucratizing thought and action, and provides lifelines to those who lack the confidence to use them with the flexibility of a language'* (Peterken, 1993: 319).

References

Printed Sources:

Brentnall, H.C. (1941) The Metes and Bounds of Savernake Forest, *Wiltshire Archaeological and Natural History Magazine*. **49**, 391-434.

English, J. and Brown, G. (2009) An analytical survey of the earthworks near Old Shaw, Alton Barnes, *Wiltshire Archaeological and Natural History Magazine*. **102**, 222-232.

French, C., Lewis, H., Allen, M.J., Green, M., Scaife, R. and Gardiner, J. (2007) *Prehistoric Landscape Development and Human Impact in the Upper Allen Valley, Cranborne Chase, Dorset*. McDonald Institute for Archaeological Research, Cambridge.

Goldberg, E.A., Kirby, K.J., Hall, J.E., and Latham, J. (2007) The ancient woodland concept as a practical conservation tool in Great Britain. *Journal of Nature Conservation*, **15** 109-119.

Gray, J.S. and Elliott, M. (2009) *Ecology of Marine Sediments*. Oxford University Press, Oxford.

HM Government (2011) *The Natural Choice: securing the value of nature (Environmental White Paper)*. Department of the Environment, Food and Rural Affairs, London.

Langton, J. and Jones, G. (2005) *Forests and Chases of England and Wales, c1500-c1850*. St John's College Research Centre, Oxford, http://info.sjc.ox.ac.uk/forests/Index.html.

Lennon, B. and Crow, P. (2009) Lidar and its role in understanding the historic landscape of Savernake Forest. *Wiltshire Archaeological and Natural History Magazine,* **102** 245-261.

Manwood, J. (1615) *A Treatise of the Lawes of the Forest*. London (Facsimile of 2003, New York).

Moss, C.E., Rankin, W.M. and Tansley, A.G. (1910) The Woodlands of England. *The New Phytologist* **9(3-4)** 113-149.

Olwig, K., and Lowenthal, D. (eds) (2006) *The Nature of Cultural Heritage, and the Culture of Natural Heritage*. Routledge, London.

Peterken, G. (1983) *Woodland Conservation in Britain*. In: Warren, A. and Goldsmith, F.B. (eds.) (1983) *Conservation in Perspective*. John Wiley, Chichester.

Peterken, G. (1985/1993) *Woodland Conservation and Management*. Chapman & Hall, London.

Peterken, G. (1996) *Natural Woodland, Ecology and Conservation in Northern Temperate Regions*. Cambridge University Press, Cambridge.

Reid, C. (1899) *The Origin of the British Flora*. London.

Spencer, J.W. and Kirby, K.J. (1992) An Inventory of Ancient Woodland for England and Wales. *Biological Conservation*, **62**, 77-93.

Straton, C.R. (ed.) (1909) *Survey of Lands of William, First Earl of Pembroke*. Roxburghe Club.

Tsouvalis, J. (2000) *A Critical Geography of State Forests*. Oxford University Press, Oxford.

Thomas, K. (1984) *Man and the Natural World*. Harmondsworth: Penguin, London.

Vera, F.W.M. (2000) *Grazing Ecology and Forest History*. CABI Publishing, Oxford.

Watkins, C. (1988) *The Idea of Ancient Woodland in Britain from 1800*. In Salbitano, F. (ed.) (1988) *Human Influence on Forest Ecosystem Development in Europe*. Bologna.

Primary Sources
Wiltshire and Swindon Archives:

9-2-388, Lawsuit concerning common for sheep and firewood in Savernake Forest, 1762.

9-22-225, Two briefs in a case at Salisbury Assizes, 1754 relating to coppices at Granham, 1754-1777.

9-26-512, Bargain and sale of 210 oak trees in Stock woods, 1575.

9-26-515, Volume of surveys and valuations of the manor of Stock 1690-1738.

125-25, Accounts from Savernake Swanemote Courts Edward III and Richard II.

1300-86, Savernake Forest Views, being a record of Forest Courts, held chiefly at Morleigh, 1542-1564.

1300-87, Savernake Curiae Liber 1577-1609.

1300-104, Letter from Alexander Tutt (steward to Earl of Hertford) to Richard Wheeler, 1597/8.

1300-1484, Volume of Legal Extracts concerning tithes, commons, deer etc in Savernake, collated in 1718 from earlier documentation.

1300-2029, Brief from Charles Bill concerning Tottenham and Puthall Common 1784.

2667-24-5-1 Early 19th cent copies of medieval perambulations of the forests in Wiltshire, compiled by James Everard Lord Arundell.

Wiltshire Inclosure Award 68, Great Bedwyn, 13 April 1792 (enrolled 19 January 1811).

Longleat House:

Seymour Papers, Volume V, Letter from Sir John Thynne to the Earl of Hertford, 1574, fos 56, 57d.

Public Records Office:

E32-217, Savernake Forest Plea Rolls Edward I – Edward III.

E126-2-27, Savernake Pleas of the Vert and Vension, and a Regard.

The Perception of Trees and Forested Environments in Iceland

Adriana Binimelis Sáez
University of Iceland

Abstract

In this paper I refer to the perception of trees and forested environments in Iceland during the period 1950-2000. This is based on the findings of my PhD. anthropology research, done between 2001 and 2004. Framed on phenomenological approaches to anthropology research and using qualitative methodology (ethnography, participant observation, interviews), I researched people's perception of forests, and folk ideas and attitudes towards the development of forestry in the country. In particular, I focused on those involved in the two oldest forestry institutions (the Icelandic Forest Service and the Icelandic Forestry Association).

Forestry in Iceland is in its infancy, that is, of planting and creating new forests. Since 1965, when the first experiments on planting 'on naked land' started, great changes have occurred in people's interest towards trees, and the belief that *'it is possible for trees to grow'* in the country. During the period studied, this activity has moved from enjoying none or very little credibility among the public, even being unpopular among farmers, to being at the core of rural development projects centred on afforestation. Since 1990, these projects have occurred on a scale never seen before. Much of this development is also perceived as a consequence of the decline of sheep farming and the fencing of areas destined for forestry or for soil protection.

However, the impact of forestry on the landscape has become notorious in the last 20 years. It does change the landscape view and composition, and increases local biodiversity. It has affected rural livelihoods, among other things, diversifying the use of the land. Currently, new skills are being learnt by the farmers and new ways of dwelling in the rural areas are emerging.

Introduction

When I visited Iceland for the first time, in August 1997, I was astonished by the lack of vegetation. As time passed, I realised that trees were usually close to the places where people were living, and some patches of greenery could be appreciated when travelling around the country. I became puzzled: How did those trees arrive in these places? In 2000, I visited the office of the Icelandic Forestry Association (IFA) in Reykjavik, and the idea of studying Icelandic forestry started to form. The main questions that guided my research were how - in a treeless land - people involved in forestry perceived trees and forests, and what were the environmental changes they distinguished due to afforestation.

In this study I refer to *perception* as it is defined in phenomenology. According to this, the '*world of perception is the world which is revealed to us by our senses and in everyday life, and seems at first sight to be the one we know best of all*' (Merleau-Ponty, 2004: 39). Therefore, perception is not the achievement of a mind in a body, but of the organism as a whole in its environment, and '*is tantamount to the organism's own exploratory movement through the world*' (Ingold, 2000:3). This implies that '***what*** *we see is inseparable from **how** we see, and how we see is always a function of the practical activity in which we are currently engaged*' (Ingold, 2000:260). Then, perception becomes a matter of searching for constancies in the environment, or what it affords to the perceiver (Gibson, 1979:127); that is, depending on the activity in which we are engaged, we will be attuned to picking up particular kinds of information (Ingold, 2000:166).

Although Gibson suggests that one learns to perceive in the manner appropriate to a culture, this process does not occur by acquiring programmes or conceptual schemata for organising sensory data into higher-order representations, but by hands-on training in everyday tasks. The successful fulfilment requires a practised ability to notice and to respond to salient aspects of the environment. Learning is not a transmission of information but an *education of attention* (Gibson, 1979: 254). Thus knowledge is generated in the course of lived experience:

'*knowledge of the world*' is gained by moving about in it, attending to it, alert to the signs by which it is revealed. Learning to see, then, is a matter of acquiring the skills for direct perceptual engagement with its constituents, human and non-human, animate and inanimate (Ingold, 2000: 55).

In this context, *environment* is understood as what surrounds an individual (Gibson, 1979: 43), therefore, environment and *surroundings* are referred to as synonymous. Environment should not be confused with the physical world, nature or the natural world. The method when presenting the findings has been to avoid the distinction between cultural and natural environment, as from a phenomenological point of view this is a false dichotomy. Environments are continually under construction, and an organism and its environment make an inseparable pair, thus affecting each other. In this context, *change* is simply what we observe if we sample a continuous process at a number of fixed points, separated in time (Ingold and Kurtilla, 2001: 193).

Following Ingold's approach to the perception of the environment, he considers that environment and *landscape* are two concepts that for many purposes may be treated as synonymous. Like the environment, the landscape is '*the world as it is known to those who dwell therein, who inhabit its places and journey along the paths connecting them*' (Ingold, 2000: 193). The landscape is not only land, nature, or space (Ingold, 2000:190); it is modified by human activities, the action of rivers and wind, for example, and the passing of time (Ingold, 2000:203).

In general terms, *forestry* is the science of planting and caring for trees. This includes all the aspects related to trees and forests, from producing seedlings for planting, to management and timber production. This science might be also referred as *silviculture*. In this context, a forester is a person skilled in forestry or in charge of a forest. One definition of forest - known worldwide by foresters- is '*a surface of land of at least 0.5 hectares, covered with trees higher than five metres, and a canopy cover of ten percent*' (FAO, 2010). In spite of this previous definition, I will refer to forests, forested environments, and woodlands as synonymous in this paper. These definitions might vary greatly depending on the context in which they occur. For example, in Iceland areas covered by trees with a minimum height of two metres are classified as forest. This flexibility can be understood in light of that this country is amongst the most deforested places in the world, having only 1.5% of its surface covered by trees.

Bearing in mind forestry technical language, *afforestation* always refers to the setting of new forests or plantations (whether by seeding or planting) on areas where there have not been trees before; and *reforestation* refers to the setting of new forests on areas that have been previously forested. In this paper I follow these definitions.

In terms of the methodology used, I worked with the qualitative approach to social research, as it emphasises description, induction, grounded theory, and the study of people's understanding (Bogdan and Biklen, 1992: 29). Qualitative methodology allows for the investigation of what is not known and is not directly measurable. And because meaning is an essential concern, most of these qualitative methods implicitly assume people's speech or discourse as the object of study. What is said by somebody, in a certain context, is considered the '*critical knot*' where social phenomena is informed, reproduced and transformed. In people's speech both the social order and subjectivity are articulated: in the speech a society or group is subjectivized, and the individual subjectivity is socialised (Canales and Binimelis, 1994:107-108).

The information was gathered by doing fieldwork in Hallormsstadur (north-east of Iceland); through participant observation when attending walks, conferences and social gatherings; and through open-ended interviews. With respect to the research participants, I centred my study on the people involved in forestry, and within this group, in those participating in the organisations which have the longest tradition in the field. Therefore most of the people I came to know were adults between forty and seventy years old, linked to the Icelandic Forest Service (IFS) and the IFA.

The IFS is the state forestry authority in Iceland and influences a large part of the Icelandic forestry. It was created in 1908 (as a department of the Ministry of Agriculture), and in 2004 there were fifty eight people working in the institution. The IFA is a non-governmental organisation (NGO) established in 1930. Today it brings together sixty local forestry societies around the country, with a total of about 7,500 members (which makes it the largest environmental NGO in Iceland). The forestry societies are formed by individuals who are interested in forestry and freely participate as volunteers. Their work is focused mainly around towns and villages, and together with planting on tree-less land, they manage woodlands for recreation purposes, grow and sell Christmas trees, and some societies have small tree nurseries. Throughout the text I refer to my informants as the *forestry people*, that is, the people belonging to either of these two organisations, regardless of whether they had any formal education in forestry. When I refer to *foresters* I am considering only the people who had some formal education in the field.

Historical background: use and abuse of forest resources

After cooler glacial periods, 10,000 years ago the vegetation colonized the land. The only forest forming tree species to survive or return to the present interglacial period in Iceland was downy birch (*Betula pubescens*). Other native tree species found in Icelandic forests today are rowan (*Sorbus aucuparia*), which is uncommon; the extremely rare aspen (*Populus tremula*); and, the Tea-leaved willow (*Salix phylicifolia*), which sometimes reaches tree size but it is usually a shrub (Eysteinsson, 2009:2; Gunnarsson *et al.*, 2005:1).

Up until 600 AD the territory today known as Iceland remained uninhabited. Along the coastline, in valleys, and in large lowland plains, the soil was covered with low, close-growing grass, which in many places was sheltered by birch woods. There were numerous birds, but the only terrestrial mammals were foxes and marine mammals such as seals and whales. The colonisation of the island probably started around this time, but 900 AD is the accepted date for the origin of the Icelandic nation (Karlsson, 2000:1-9).

Most of the settlers came from the West coast of Norway, either directly or via Viking settlements in the British Isles. And although there is evidence that a few settlers were of Irish or other Celtic origin, the prevalence of the Icelandic language shows that the culture was predominantly of Norse origin. These new settlers brought cattle, horses, sheep, goats, pigs, dogs, cats and geese; all sort of implements; grain; and minimal timber for housing as it soon became known that the country had no proper forests (Karlsson, 2000:14).

By the Middle Ages (1100-1311 AD) there were still no towns in Iceland and practically the whole population lived on farms. It has been calculated that there were around 4,000 farmers able to sustain themselves and their families, resulting in a population of approximately 40,000 (Karlsson, 2000: 44). In terms of livelihood, during the colonisation period animal husbandry was always more important than grain-growing in all parts of the country. Wood was the main fuel used, as well as wood-charcoal, dung and peat. The houses were typical Viking Age turf houses, often 15 to 20 metre-long halls, requiring ample use of timber. Thus, by the Middle Ages driftwood had become a valuable commodity provided by the beaches (Karlsson, 2000: 45-48).

Among Icelanders it has therefore become a commonly held belief that before the Settlement period birch woods would have been available. And most of the authors reviewed for this research project support the idea that until the arrival of the Vikings the country was untouched by human activities (e.g. Edwards, 2005; Eysteinsson, 2009; Jónsson, 2009; Ólafsdóttir, 2001).

The livestock brought by the settlers became the main source of their livelihood until the early twentieth century; sheep grazing was the major land-use strategy. These domestic animals were a contributory cause of deforestation, which due to subsequent grazing, prevented nearly all regeneration of the birch and the recovery of the land in many places. In addition, the settlers brought with them agricultural methods that were not created or developed to take into account the environmental conditions of the Icelandic landscape. And, in the birch forests, fire was an effective weapon to convert scrub to grassland to provide fodder for domestic animals (Buckland and Panagiotakopulu, 2005).

Although data on the extent of surface vegetation cover at the time of the Settlement is not available, a rough estimate indicates that cover has diminished from 40,000 to 20,000 square kilometres, and birch cover from 20,000 to 1,000 square kilometres, during the eleven centuries of human habitation in Iceland. Thus, if in the year 1000 AD birch forest and woodland probably covered 25-40% of the land area, by 2000 they covered only 1% of the surface of Iceland. (Eysteinsson, 2009: 2).

Linked to the deforestation of the land has been the problem of soil erosion. Despite the general recognition that there was a soil erosion problem, a comprehensive survey on a national scale was only carried out in the 1990s. The mapping results revealed that 73% of Iceland's 103,000 square kilometres were affected by soil erosion, and that nearly 20% of it was classified as severely eroded (Arnalds, 2001). Looking at the problem of soil erosion, historians such as Ashwell and Jackson (1970) concluded that Icelanders have always regarded themselves as sheep farmers, and it was very likely that the sheep had contributed most to the destruction of the woodlands which led to soil erosion. According to the practices described in the *Egilssaga*, the sheep were allowed to range throughout the winters, so their source of food was the early foliage of the trees. Ashwell and Jackson (1970), contrasted this information with the practices they observed in the 1970s - which actually seemed very similar. They assumed that the sheep in Iceland had survived because they will eat any kind of vegetation; and even where the soil has been disturbed by erosion, it was *'possible to observe sheep laying the eroded hollows on the exposed plant roots'* (Ashwell & Jackson 1970: 164).

The development of forestry in Iceland

By the year 1800, it was acknowledged that a dramatic decrease in woodland cover had occurred from the nineth century. But it was only in 1900 that the first steps towards woodland conservation were achieved, when a law was enacted in order to initiate the enclosing of the remaining forested areas. In 1899, Parliament authorised the enclosure of the woodlands at

Figure 1. Landscape view 'before' and 'after' afforestation, near Rekjavik (2004). The pictures were taken from the same standing point facing in different directions (showing the contrast between the area that was afforested a few years ago, and the other where nothing was done).

Hallormsstadur. The same year, the planting of a '*Pine stand at Thingvellir marked the beginning of organised forestry in the country*' (Gunnarsson *et al.*, 2005: 3). In 1907, the first forestry law was passed which, among other things, promulgated the creation of the IFS. Then, in 1930 the IFA began to operate. Its main objective was the conservation and cultivation of forests (Blöndal and Gunnarsson, 1999: 139).

Between 1930 and 1951, native birch was the most planted species in Iceland, ranging from a few thousand to over 150,000 seedlings per year. Until the late 1940s, birch along with native rowan (*Sorbus aucuparia*) and native tea-leaved willow (*Salix phylicifolia*) were practically the only species available at the four small tree nurseries in the country (Gunnarsson *et al.*, 2005: 3). Other sources indicate that the number of trees planted annually around 1938 were about 20,000 plants (Pétursson, 1999; 1999a). Thus, the afforestation projects started off with predominantly native species.

In spite of these efforts, deforestation continued until the middle of the twentieth century. Although the need for charcoal had decreased by the middle of the nineteenth century due to the importation of steel tools and farming implements, wood was used for fuel until as late as 1940, both for cooking and house-fuel. In addition, the increasing number of sheep and the high levels of summer grazing continued to prevent the extension of woodlands outside the protected areas (Eysteinsson, 2009: 3).

Between 1950 and 1990, the emphasis was on afforestation through planting seedlings. The number of seedlings per year reached 1.5 million during 1960-62, and the main species used were exotic conifers, such as Norway spruce (*Picea abies*), Sitka spruce (*Picea sitchensis*), Scots pine (*Pinus sylvestris*), Lodgepole pine (*Pinus contorta*) and Siberian larch (*Larix sibirica*). The amount of planting declined after 1963 but remained at 500,000 to one million seedlings annually from 1963 to 1989. In contrast, during this period the planting of native birch remained at similar levels or 100,000 seedlings per year, comprising between 5-15% of the total seedlings planted during 1950-1990 (Gunnarsson *et al.*, 2005:3-4; Pétursson, 1999; 1999a).

The year 1990 represents a turning point when a law promoting afforestation on farm land was passed. Although since 1970 the State supported afforestation on farm land, it was only in 1990 that farmers started to receive money for plantation work, whether this was to establish plantations for wood production or for reclaiming eroded land. At least 97% of the plantation costs were covered by the State. These projects could use native birch and other non-timber species, although exotics remained as mainstay in afforestation. Since then afforestation has increased again, reaching about five million seedlings per year, which corresponds to an increase in planted area of 1,000-1,500 hectares per year (Gunnarsson *et al.*, 2005:4; Pétursson, 1999; 1999a).

By 2010, the IFS had developed various research projects that have provided a well-informed view of forest resources. According to this database, the total area of forested land was estimated to be 156,800 hectares, of which birch woodlands were 115,400 hectares and cultivated forests 41,400 hectares. This equates to a covering of 1.5% of the total area of the country (Traustason and Snorrason, 2008).

With respect to forest protected areas, the IFS manages over forty national forests in Iceland, which cover a total of about 7,000 hectares, consisting mainly of birch woodland (Eysteinsson, 2009: 6). An important proportion of this surface is found in Hallormsstadur, the largest and oldest forest of the country. It has an area of 1,850 hectares and contains more species than any other forest in Iceland.

According to the events highlighted by the forestry people regarding the development of forestry in the country, during the 1940s and 1950s there were few farmers who participated in the forestry societies. These farmers were an exception to the rule as in those days there was much controversy between sheep farming and forestry:

'Before there was almost a war due to forestation and agriculture, you had - I would say - almost a war between the sheep and the trees. This had all to do with free grazing. People wanted to plant trees but to do that they had to fence the trees in, and this cost a lot of money. So for quite a while there was a fairly substantive disagreement on whether we should go to forestation in Iceland. That was one of the struggles of the Forestry Association in its early days (..) It was not only the disbelief of Icelanders that you could not plant trees in Iceland, but also there was the farmers' agenda, that planting trees was actually threatening to [the] customary agriculture in Iceland'.

In order to understand this situation, the immediate answer that appeared frequently from informants was that *'there were no forests'*, that is, no man-made forests. Secondly, the land that was around the farms -that had been used for sheep grazing year-round- was usually in a very bad condition. Erosion had started and this was translated by the farmers as *'here* [conditions] *was so difficult to grow, that is why the land is in such a bad state'*.

Eventually, the conflict between pro-forestry people and sheep-farm supporters started to calm down. The idea that nobody believed it was possible to grow trees in Iceland and produce timber - which foresters used to confront - gave way to a new strategy based on the dialogue between the IFS personnel and the farmers, where the former tried to convince the latter about the benefits of becoming involved in forestry. An older informant described this process in the following terms: when presented with the possibility of afforesting some hectares of their farms, most farmers used to say *'I cannot enter in forestry because I need all my land for my animals'*. Then the IFS people would respond: *'Well, if you afforest part of your land, after twenty or thirty years you will be able to produce more meat than now, because you will have a better land after planting trees'*. The farmers were not interested in producing timber, but they understood that more vegetation meant more food for their animals. So in this way they became motivated to set aside part of their land, fence it, and plant it with trees.

Then, other issues occurred during the 1980s which, to some extent, marked the end of the war between sheep and trees. Firstly, in 1980 Vigdís Finnbogadóttir became the president of Iceland. Every time she visited a place in the country she planted three birch trees, as her gift to the local people. By doing this for sixteen years (she was in power until 1996), she became *'the most popular supporter of afforestation'*, making a positive impact on public opinion. Secondly, an awareness of the economic inconvenience of having a huge sheep production subsidised, increased. And thirdly, during this decade a disease appeared among the sheep: when the sheep stock was at its zenith - about 900,000 - the animals in some regions of the country were attacked by a disease (*scrapie*) for which there was no cure other than to slaughter the sheep and keep the area sheep-free for a number of years. It struck in many places, but it was especially hard in Eastern Iceland and parts of Northern Iceland. As the animals had to be killed, in a few years the number of sheep was reduced by half. Some farmers *'lost their courage and quit'*.

These events contributed to the creation of the regional afforestation projects (RAPs) all over the country, starting by the Héradsskógar in the North-East. With the RAPs the *'era of planting in a big scale'* began: '*In 1990 Héradsskógar started and people were ready for it, they saw there was money for forestry. That it was possible to plant big areas of larch, and to take big patches of land for forestry. This latter was a strange idea because until then the sheep had always had the right to use all the land. Forestry seemed not possible on a sheep farm, that was the problem. So it is just few years that this view changed*'.

Environmental changes perceived due to forestry

Icelandic forestry is said to have started about a century ago, but systematic afforestation on bare land did not start until the 1960s, when the first experiments using exotic species were implemented. Only in the 1990s, did afforestation become to be seen as a productive activity that could be developed in Iceland. Therefore, most '*forests*' in the country are very young and mature forests are rare. Almost in their entirety, these environments have been man-made creations, or have gone through some sort of human intervention.

Stepping into this field has meant a '*real conquest*' and realisation for its advocates, in particular, considering that they have had to open the way for forestry in a country historically characterised -and its people '*modelled*'- by the lack of vegetation and the harsh weather conditions (Loftsdóttir, 2010; Sveinsdóttir, 2007). The forestry case in Iceland is a good example of illustrating what can happen to a belief (such as '*trees can grow in Iceland*', or '*when the settlers arrived this country was covered by forests*') when it is invoked, activated, put to work, and realised in the actual world (Jackson, 1996:11).

The forestry people perceived that, within popular public opinion, the interest shown towards trees and afforested environments varied, from being quite indifferent towards them, to manifesting a keen interest in planting trees and creating arboreal surroundings (both, in urban and rural areas). In terms of its scepticism towards the possibility of growing trees, public opinion changed from not believing and/or being sceptical about the possibility of growing trees in the country, to believing that it was possible and desirable to plant trees. These changes could be observed, among other things, in the increase of vegetation in urban areas (both, public and private places), and the financial support and participation in the various activities and funds organised by the IFA and the IFS.

With respect to forestry people and their silvicultural practices, one of the major changes occurred between planting inside birch woodlands and onto bare land. Also, from knowing and using mainly local species - native birch and willows - they incorporated the use of exotic species, which has become the main component of productive forests. Monoculture, the initial way of setting plantations, went out of fashion, currently the option is for multi-species and multi-use forests. For many decades forestry people's concerns and observations of the planted trees revolved around tree height, and if they were growing at all. At present, their main concerns are about how the forests and the exotic species are fitting into the Icelandic landscape. As the concept of environmental impact assessment (EIA) has been incorporated into the local environmental discourse, foresters have needed to emphasise and put more attention into their planning, being particularly careful when choosing the areas suitable for afforestation.

The aims of forestry have also varied. From being centred in the protection of birch remnants and combating soil erosion, since the 1980s there has been a major increase in the planting work. This has focused on five main areas or uses: urban forestry, land reclamation, shelter belts, recreational areas, and productive forestry. In the case of the IFS, when it was created its main task was to enclose and protect the birch forests, as a way of preventing their total disappearance and further soil erosion. As time passed, but always maintaining its original role, the IFS moved into land reclamation and productive forestry. At the end of the period studied, they were doing very little planting as most of this task was '*transferred*' to the RAPs, and their efforts were centred on the management of the areas acquired in previous years, research, and policy making.

By contrast, the IFA have kept a more stable profile and role, always providing a space for ordinary people to become involved in forestry. Since its creation, the IFA had focused on the co-ordination of its many forestry societies around the country; and had informed on forestry issues, in order to educate, generate opinion and awareness among its members and the general public. Those involved in the IFA considered themselves as the advocators of an '*ideology*' - or '*vision*' - which is expressed in the environmental project of '*greening the country*'; that is, improving the surroundings in order to enjoy a '*better*' environment for themselves and future generations. In their view, people can live well only where there is vegetation. In this sense, trees might be considered as a sign of constructive human activity, meaning or providing a symbol of the articulation of time (that is, where past, present and future meet together): trees existed in the past; trees now provide an experience of attachment and belonging; trees will become mature forests that will outlive the current generations, therefore they are the present generations' inheritance to the ones to come.

People involved in forestry were aware of the fact that they were modifying the landscape by afforesting. In their discourse plantations and forests were often used indistinctly, favouring the word forest (*skógur*). The word would apply to afforested areas with native birch that has grown spontaneously, afforested areas with planted birch or other species, areas covered with trees of less than two metres high, or up to fifteen metres. Forestry people did not subscribe to the definition of environmental change as usually understood by environmentalists, that is, of implying a negative or destructive impact. In this sense, they perceived the environment as a very dynamic field, undergoing a permanent transformation. Thus change was a '*natural*' thing to occur. In my view, they have a very practical or utilitarian view towards their surroundings, just as their ancestors did in the past. When the settlers arrived they noticed the mountains, the rivers, the forests, and all the features that would help them to make a living. They were not concerned with the beauty or the magnificence of the landscape (Sveinsdóttir, 2007). In the same way, although the aesthetic value of forests has become an important issue, I would say that most forestry people are concerned, first and foremost, with making their surrounding more liveable. They see the landscape not from a distant point, but as a place to live in and to be used (whether for recreation or production). I do not think that trees are considered among forestry people as '*symbols of conservation*' (although forestry people might be classified as '*tree activists*') (Rival, 1998:3), still they are associated with environmental health, community welfare and prosperity.

The state of a forest was usually assessed in terms of its height (when inside the forest), and the extent of the surface covered (when observing it from far away). In this sense, an afforested environment was in the first place a visual experience, and it would be valued in terms of the '*panoramic view*' it afforded. Thus, although the trees enjoyed a social value, the presence of open spaces and wide horizons remained as a distinctive and a desirable feature of the landscape.

Referring to changes in the local environment, opinions varied greatly depending whether people were living in urban areas and cities, or in rural areas. Among the first group -the city dwellers- the increase in greenery that could be observed in the streets, public areas and private gardens, was higlighted. And when referring to afforestation projects related to parks or on land near the cities and towns, the emphasis was on the total contrast between '*before*' (when there was no vegetation) and '*after*' (of being afforested); people remarked that most of these areas was the result of direct human agency. Amongst the second group -the rural dwellers- the main change pointed out was the growth of trees, giving the experience of being surrounded/sheltered, and resulting in changes in the visibility of the immediate environment. Thus, the growth of the forest was noticed not only by the increase of vegetation in the area, but mainly because of the changes in '*what could be seen*' from those places where people moved daily. The view from their homes, certain points in the area - characterised by the altitude and/or sightseeing possibilities - and the visibility when driving, were often mentioned as points of reference for becoming aware of the changes in the size of the forest. Also, the difference in visibility was also referred to in connection with changes in the vegetation due to seasonal variations. Compared to trees, houses and buildings become a permanent and unchangeable element of the landscape.

The changes observed in vegetation were explained as a consequence of land-use changes. The most noticeable aspect in rural areas was related to the diminishing numbers or the total disappearance of the sheep. Thus, on land were sheep were removed several years ago and planting projects had not been applied, spontaneous re-vegetation was observed.

Relating to afforestation, there had been changes in the '*type of forest*' that had been planted in recent years, basically, evolving from monoculture plantations to mixed forests. For some people this responded to a need for satisfying an aesthetic value, facilitating the '*fitting of the trees*' in the Icelandic landscape, by softening the border lines - and contrasting with the too straight and vertical look of the coniferous species - and creating '*beautiful*' spaces for recreation. Others remarked that this change was done in order to promote the health of the forest, and prevent dramatic losses if a disease or pest should attack them.

An important consequence of the presence of trees was, that from observing the difference between the '*before and after*' of the planting, people became '*convinced of the possibility of having forest farms*'. So the first effect of afforestation was about the presence of trees in the landscape view, that is, the visual effect they had. Changes in the landscape could be noticed after 10 years or less, depending on the species used for afforesting. Exotic species, which could grow ten to twenty times faster than birch, would cause a much more rapid visual impact in the landscape. Tree height was valued as an important indicator of the way trees were growing. Most of the plantations in Iceland were considered to be still quite young, that is, they had not reached yet their adult stage (therefore, their maximum height). The height that trees could reach depended also on which part of the country they grew, and whether they were in the most suitable soil for the species.

Some people mentioned changes in the local weather due to the presence of the forest. Thus, it was often acknowledged that the forest created a type of micro-climate, giving protection from the wind.

In terms of biodiversity, it was considered that by introducing new tree species, the local biodiversity was enhanced. The presence of more birds, even species that had not been seen before, were reported around the forested areas. Also, certain insects had appeared in these areas, which seemed not to be associated with any tree species in particular; and mushrooms linked to certain trees were described.

In the long term, the impact forestry would have in the landscape was not predicted. The development and the future '*behaviour*' of the current plantations will depend on many factors, like weather fluctuations, which cannot be accurately predicted. Despite the increase in the planting work, the total afforested surface of the country will not increase significantly with respect to its current size.

References

Arnalds, O., Gisladottir, F.O. and Sigurjonsson, H. (2001) *Soil Erosion in Iceland*. The Soil Conservation Service and the Agricultural Research Institute, Iceland.

Ashwell, I.Y. and Jackson, E. (1970) The Sagas as evidence of Early Deforestation in Iceland. *Canadian Geographer*, **XIV**, 2, 158-166.

Blöndal, S. and Gunnarsson, S.B. (1999) *Íslandsskógar. Hundrad ára saga*. Mál og Mynd, Reykjavik.

Bogdan, R. and Biklen, S.K. (1992) *Qualitative Research for Education: An Introduction to Theory and Methods*. Ally and Bacon, United States of America.

Buckland, P. and Panagiotakopulu, E. (2005) Insects and Human Impact on Atlantic Islands. *Landscape Archaeology and Ecology*, **5**, 14-15.

Canales, M. and Binimelis, A. (1994) El Grupo de Discusión [The Discussion Group]. *Revista de Sociología. Facultad de Ciencias Sociales Universidad de Chile*, **Nm. 9**, 107-119.

Edwards, K. (2005) Crisis? Recovery? Management? Landscapes of Contrast in Viking Age Iceland and Faroe Islands. *Landscape Archaeology and Ecology*, **5**, 19-20.

Einarsson, Th. (1991) *Jardsaga Íslands*. Mál og menning, Reykjavik.

Eysteinsson, Th. (2009) *Forestry in a Treeless Land*. In www.skograektrikisins.is.

FAO (Food and Agriculture Organisation of the United Nations) (2010). *Global Forest Resources Assessment 2010*. Main Report. Forestry Paper 163. FAO, Italy.

Gibson, J.J. (1979) *The ecological approach to visual perception*. Houghton Mifflin, Boston.

Gunnarsson, K. (1998) *Recent forestry developments and social forestry research in Iceland*. In: Hytönen, M. (ed.) *Social sustainability of forestry in the Baltic Region* (pp. 249-256). Finnish Forest Research Institute, Hakapaino Oy.

Gunnarsson, K., Eysteinsson, Th., Curl, S.L. and Thorfinsson, Th. (2005) *Icelandic Report on Economic integration of urban consumers' demand and rural forestry production COST E30*. Retrieved from http://aslh.nyme.hu/fileadmin/dokumentumok/fmk/acta_silvatica/cikkek/VolE1-2005/iceland.pdf

Gunnarsson, S.B. (ed.) (1995) *Héradsskógar. Náttúruaudlind nyrra tíma - A natural resource for new times*. Héradsprent sf., Iceland.

Ingold, T. (2000) *The Perception of the Environment. Essays in livelihood, dwelling and skill*. Routledge, London.

Ingold, T. and Kurtilla, T. (2001) *Perceiving the Environment in Finnish Lapland*. In: Macnaghten, P. and Urry, J. (eds.), *Bodies of Nature*. (pp.192-198). Sage Publications, London.

Jackson, M. (1996) *Introduction. Phenomenology, Radical Empiricism, and Anthropological Critique*. In: Jackson, M. (ed.), *Things as they are. New Directions in Phenomenological Anthropology* (pp. 1-50). Indiana University Press, Bloomington.

Jónsson, S.A. (2009) *Vegetation History of Fljótsdalshéra_ during the last 2,000 years*. A Palynological study (MSc. Thesis). University of Iceland, Reykjavik.

Karlsson, G. (2000) *Iceland's 1100 Years. History of a Marginal Society*. Mál of menning, Reykjavik.

Loftsdóttir, K. (2010) The loss of innocence. The Icelandic financial crisis and colonial past. *Anthropology Today*, **26**, 9-13.

Merleau-Ponty, M. (2004) *The World of Perception*. Routledge, London.

Ólafsdóttir, R. (2001) *Land Degradation and Climate in Iceland. A spatial and temporal assessment*. Lund University, Sweden.

Pétursson, J.G. (1999) *Skógræktaröldin. Samanteknar tölur úr Ársriti Skógræktarfélag Íslands. Skógræktarritid1999*, **2.tbl.**, 49-53.

Pétursson, J.G. (1999a) *Skógræktarstarfid 1998. Tölulegar upplysingar. Skógræktarritid1999*, **2.tbl.**, 105-107.

Rival, L. (1998) *Trees, from Symbols of Life and Regeneration to Political Artefacts*. In: Rival, L. (ed.) *The Social Life of Trees. Anthropological Perspectives of Tree Symbolism* (pp. 1-36). Berg, UK.

Sveinsdóttir, A. (2007) *The perception and relation between cultural and natural landscapes*. In: Halldorsson, G., Oddsdottir, E.S. and Sigurdsson, B.D. (eds.) *Effects of afforestation on ecosystems, landscapes and rural development. Proceedings of the AFFORNORD conference, Reykholt, Iceland, June 18-22, 2005*, TemaNord 2007:508, (pp. 285-291). Nordic Council of Ministers, Denmark.

Traustason, B. and Snorrason, A. (2008) Spatial distribution of forests and woodlands in Iceland in accordance with the CORINE land cover classification. *Icelandic Agricultural Sciences*, **21**, 39-47.

EU-FIRESMART, Forest and Land Management Options to Prevent Unwanted Forest Fires: SWOT Analyses in Agroforestry Systems

Caroline Boström[1], Maria Julia Yagüe[2], Carmen Hernando[3], Rosa Planelles[4], Armando Buffoni[5], Rosario Alves[6], Marielle Jappiot[7] and Jesús San Miguel[8].

1. Confédération Européenne des Propriétaires Forestiers CEPF; 2. GMV Aerospace and Defence S.A.; 3. Instituto Nacional de Investigación y Tecnología Agraria y Alimentaria (INIA); 4. Entrenamiento e Información Forestal (EIMFOR); 5. AMBIENTEITALIA S.R.L.; 6. Associação Florestal de Portugal - FORESTIS; 7. Centre National du Machinisme Agricole du Génie Rural des Eaux et des Forêts (Cemagref); 8. EC- DG. Joint Research Centre.

Abstract

Fire is one of the environmental risks that is expected to increase in connection to climate change. Fire will be more common in regions where it is today less expected. EU-FireSmart is a project whose objectives are to identify obstacles that hinder the effectiveness of forest fire preventive measures and to derive recommendations to integrate prevention practices into standard forest management plans. The project tackles both the European and local level of addressing forest fire prevention, where the local level has been covered through the implementation of test areas in France, Italy, Spain and Portugal. Documents containing information about different methods and practices of forest fire prevention in Europe have been gathered in a database which now contains more than 1,400 entries. The material available in this database has been analysed according to the strengths, weaknesses, opportunities and threats of different land management practices. This analysis has been performed considering different subjects. The analysis is then used to derive practical recommendations on how to turn current negative fire prevention factors into viable and proactive factors able to strengthen prevention methods. Agroforestry has been found to be a strong preventive method and the strengths and weaknesses of the method as well as the practical recommendations for increasing the preventive values of agroforestry are presented.

Introduction

The EU-Firesmart is a European Framework 7 research project concerned with different land management options that can help to increase forest fire prevention. The project started in February 2010 and has funding for a period of two years. The project is coordinated by GMV in Spain with participants from the individual countries of France, Italy, Spain and

Portugal, as well as from the European Union level. The spread of project participants has made it possible to concentrate the work in several test-areas, one in each participating country. In these areas, the different local and regional aspects have been studied and then the European perspective has been added to give the analyses a broader scope.

The work within the project started by gathering documents with information about fire prevention methods and practices into a database. This database today has more than 1,400 entries related to different topics. The material covers the topics of agroforestry, fire causes, preventive silviculture, awareness raising and training as well as wildland urban interfaces. The database will be made available to the general public through the Firesmart projects website homepage.

Agroforestry is one of the subjects studied within the Firesmart project as a possible land management option to prevent forest fires. Agroforestry systems can be defined as a sustainable land management which integrates both agricultural and forestry practices on the same land area. Agroforestry practices have been defined by different authors as practices that involve the deliberate integration of trees with agricultural crops and/or livestock, either simultaneously or sequentially on the same unit of hand. All types of agroforestry ecosystems integrate people as a part of the system as they are artificial systems to a higher or lower extent. In agroforestry one of the components, either forestry or agriculture, can be promoted over the other, or both simultaneously trying to reach equilibrium (Mosquera et al., 2009).

Agroforestry ecosystems are recognized as beneficial to the prevention of forest fires (Moreira et al., 2009), since these ecosystems often have a lower fuel load due to the fact that the area below the trees is cleared of undergrowth. The lack of a complete canopy cover also reduce the risk for intense crown fires. As fire prevention actions also aim to mitigate the damages caused by fires it should be underlined that agroforestry ecosystems have the capability to reduce fire spread and energy release, thereby allowing fire fighting personnel to carry out for example direct frontal attacks when tackling the fire without exposing themselves to high risks.

Materials and Methods

An analysis of the database material was performed by means of a SWOT analysis. Strengths, Weaknesses, Opportunities and Threats were identified and listed for five different subject areas; agroforestry, awareness raising and training, fire causes and fire risk, preventive silviculture and wildland urban interfaces. The subjects have been analysed first generally and then from the institutional, legislative and socio-economical aspects related to the different topics.

These listed statements were then analysed quantitatively to get a more concrete picture of which statements had a higher importance and which a lower importance. The total importance of the Strengths, Weaknesses, Opportunities and Threats were also made visible through this quantitative SWOT analysis. Through the SWOT analysis it was possible to see which parts of the studied subject areas could be improved and which areas were already quite strong in respect of fire prevention.

In addition to the SWOT analyses, a 96-item questionnaire had previously been designed to obtain information from the respondents about the efficiency and consequences of current management practices. The questions touched subjects such as restrictions, legal issues, social and communication-related activities in terms of wildfire prevention. The questionnaire was addressed to forest managers and scientists and 460 completed questionnaires were gathered, mainly from Spain (62%), followed by Italy (13%) and Portugal (10%). Some results concerning Agroforestry and Grazing as forest fire prevention measures have been taken into account in the present work.

Results

As mentioned, a lower density of undergrowth, in agroforestry ecosystems, lead to a lower fuel level and thus reduce the risk for intense fire events. These ecosystems also have a low level of intense crown-fires, and can through their structure reduce the risks of intense fires through changing the fire's behaviour.

In addition, fires can be detected earlier in agroforestry ecosystems since there are often sheepherders or cattle-herders following their troops through these areas. Human presence is also higher in some regions with a high amount of agroforestry ecosystems because of the long tradition of these practices that can make the landscape and environment attractive to tourists and for touristic activities. Which also contributes to an earlier detection of fires.

Human presence is however double sided since over 95% of the fires in the Mediterranean region are started by human causes, many times these are related to pasture renewal or tourism. Legislation is in place throughout the regions that govern the use of fire when renewing pasture or by tourists. However, these laws are not always followed correctly.

The multifunctional and sustainable use of agroforestry ecosystems can not only contribute by creating employment opportunities but can also contribute to land owners' income through the extraction of, for example, timber, firewood, cork or acorns at the same time in addition to a continuous income from the production of meat or agricultural crops.

Most of the material gathered and connected to agroforestry in the Firesmart database is focused on fire control through grazing in fuel breaks.

One of the crucial **weaknesses** found from the Firesmart SWOT analysis was that a low profitability from agroforestry has led frequently to a decrease in land management. Decreases in the use of agroforestry and the land abandonment which follows this decrease, leaves many areas with an increased fuel load as well as a decreased human presence.

Renewal of pasture lands was also seen as a weakness since this is frequently done without legal permission and when it gets out of control can easily lead to the start of forest fires. The involvement of land managers in forest fire prevention is often low. Increasing the participation of land managers in actions that aim to prevent forest fires could be greatly improved, and could in turn improve the efficiency of the preventive actions. Land managers could be informed about preventive measures within agroforestry in a way that they understood these practices more thoroughly. They could also be involved more in the different schemes that aim to prevent forest fires. Information should be given in particular around the issue that land managers within agroforestry often contribute a lot to societal services just by managing to stay in business. Since it is difficult to make a profit in this type of land management practice it is not easy to get younger people interested in starting up businesses using this type of traditional management.

The use of different branding schemes, for example to indicate the geographical origin of a product could be used in these areas to make a beneficial impact. By increasing the economic benefit of keeping livestock under trees, the abandonment of these lands could decrease and thereby help with the prevention of fires in these areas. Anthropological and ecological values can thus be preserved without extra subsidy input, which gives benefit to all involved parties.

The lack of studies at a national level in the countries studied was also something that was considered to be a weakness in the Firesmart SWOT analysis. These would be needed to adapt grazing practices to the special conditions of each country or region. Another weakness found was the lack of information about agroforestry within the framework of sustainable land management in these areas.

The biggest **opportunity** for agroforestry areas would be their capacity to decrease the speed of forest fires which had already started. A greater use of these areas could therefore, if they were dispersed in a strategic way at the landscape level, be very good for the overall prevention of forest fires in a region. To increase the use of agroforestry as a type of land management it is important that the produce has a higher monetary value so that the practice becomes profitable. Another option would be to develop tourism activities in order to create an extra income for the land manager so widening their income base. Subsidies for biodiversity preservation or special environmental services would also be an option. Some subsidies currently exist for agroforestry such as through the Rural Development program of the European Union. These could be used more and in a more efficient way at member state level.

When it comes to **threats** identified in the Firesmart SWOT analysis, the abandonment of rural areas and agroforestry as a land management practice was the most important statement identified.

When looking at the overall quantitative analysis, the weaknesses of agroforestry and grazing as forest fire prevention measures were dominant with 47% of the importance. Some of the strengths found were also quite weak in their character when analysed quantitatively. Whereas the weaknesses are of a more even character. Strengths and opportunities do however make up almost 40% of the importance. If used properly and improved these could make a difference and give agroforestry even better conditions to succeed as an important forest fire prevention method.

The SWOT analysis on the institutional dimension gives higher importance to the strengths and opportunities than to the weaknesses and threats of agroforestry and grazing as a forest fire prevention method. The general importance of each strength is also higher than for the other statements in the analysis. The strongest strength was the encouragement to increase rural activities that was given by the Spanish government. This encouragement is based on increasing the participation of the sheep-herders in fire prevention and also create agreements between sheep-herders and the land managers. The strongest weakness was also found to be in Spain, which was connected to the lack of communication between different regions within the country on agroforestry practices. Conflicts and disagreements between sheep-herders and land managers in Spain were identified as one of the most important threats. There were only two statements in the SWOT analysis related to opportunities, but there associations were both strong. The strongest opportunity was considered to be the possibility of getting support from the European Union Common Agricultural Policy for different land management practices related to agroforestry.

In the legislative dimension of the SWOT analysis the strengths and opportunities both got about 35% of the weighted importance. The statements were overall strong in both of these categories. The most important strength from the legislative point of view was considered to be the existence of legislation and regulation connected to the practices of using fire for pasture renewal. The conflicts between sheep-herders, farmers and local authorities were considered to be the most important weaknesses. These conflicts are observed on a local level in the Spanish test area and most often they relate to agricultural practices. Integration of grazing in forested areas was the strongest opportunity found in the legislative SWOT analysis since it can reduce the impact of forest fires if used in an efficient way. Overgrazing and other livestock keeping practices that can harm the ecosystems were considered to be the most important threat.

The SWOT analysis looking at socio-economic aspects show that this is an area where the weaknesses dominate. The weighted importance of the weaknesses in this area add up to 68% of the total. However, there are still strengths and opportunities there and these are considered important. The social and economic values generated by agroforestry as a land management practice was the strength considered to be most important. Agroforestry is a sustainable land management and should be economically viable. The fact that agroforestry is not a financially viable and/or socially attractive way of managing land is the strongest weakness found by the project group. Another strong weakness is the low profitability associated with keeping livestock. Income opportunities from tourists were considered to be the most important opportunity and the greatest threat was the conflicts between the different groups with an interest in the land management, e.g. sheep-herders, land managers and local authorities.

In general, most of the strengths were found within the institutional and the legislative SWOT analyses. The weaknesses were clearly dominating in the socio-economic SWOT analyses. To improve the overall picture of agroforestry in regard to forest fire prevention, the weaknesses of the socio-economic SWOT analysis should be targeted to see if they can be improved to reduce their impact. By targeting improvements to the weaknesses of the socio-economic SWOT, the overall general picture would be greatly improved.

In the analysis of the questionnaires, controlled grazing scored higher as an efficient method for the prevention of fires than other techniques for fire prevention. Controlled grazing scored higher in Greece and Spain than in the other countries answering to the questionnaires. Livestock-owner associations were considered to be important, mostly in France and Spain, but overall, respondents found that it was a good way to enforce fire prevention. Conflicting interests were considered to be the factor which made preventive forest management more difficult. This view is also reflected in the results from the SWOT analyses.

Conclusion

The results from the SWOT analyses and the Firesmart questionnaire show that the most efficient way to improve agroforestry in regard to forest fire prevention would be to try to tackle the weaknesses found connected to socio-economic aspects. One could also consider the possibility of using the opportunities identified in the legislative dimension to improve the overall strengths of agroforestry.

It is argued that one of the most important things to tackle is to decrease the abandonment of agroforestry practices. And, one of the most efficient methods for doing this would be to increase the profitability and thereby the attractiveness of using this method. Many different examples on how this can be done exist in the Mediterranean region. Diversification of income is one of the main possibilities to explore which through increasing the possibilities of multifunctional land-use would lessen the impact of different changes. Tourism activities that could provide a local income are one of the possibilities for diversification, but there are other options such as keeping different kinds of animals, or growing trees that can give a continuous income such as cork-oaks or olive trees.

The most important effect of keeping agroforestry as a practice would be that the population in rural areas would get more continuous employment opportunities and as a consequence of more people working the land any fires could be detected earlier and be more easily extinguished. To achieve this more information about agroforestry is needed to both land managers and the general public. Branding schemes for local products could be improved and marketed. The general public should be informed about all the services provided by agroforestry ecosystems. This would greatly help to keep profitability in these systems.

The results from the analysis of the opinions gathered through the Firesmart questionnaire confirmed the results in the SWOT analysis concerning the benefits that could be generated by agroforestry and grazing as forest fire preventive measures. The questionnaire also confirmed that conflicts of interest are an important obstacle in implementing agroforestry and grazing as a forest fire preventive measure.

References

Moreira, F., Vaz, P., Catry, F., Silva, J.S. (2009) Regional variations in wildfire susceptibility of land-cover types in Portugal: implications for landscape management to minimize fire hazard. *International Journal of Wildland Fire,* **18(5)**, 563-574.

Mosquera, M.R., McAdam, J.H., Romero, R., Santiago, J.J., Rigueiro, A. (2009) *Definitions and Components of Agroforestry Practices in Europe*. In: Rigueiro, A., McAdam, J., Mosquera, M.R. (Eds.) *Agroforestry in Europe. Current Status and Future Prospects.* pp.3-20.

Wild Cattle – Wilder Valley
Sharing experiences from introducing extensive cattle grazing to a Lakeland valley

Gareth Browning[1], John Gorst[2],
Forestry Commission[1], United Utilities[2]

Introduction

This report aims to capture some of the stories and emotions that the Wild Ennerdale Partners, visitors and farmers have experienced in the five years since the introduction of extensive grazing to the Ennerdale Valley. It is not written as a scientific report but as a narrative of a valley becoming more self-willed through the introduction of cattle *Bos taurus*. The report tries to capture the interactions between ecological and social benefits that this change in the valley's farming and forestry activities has brought about.

Background

The Ennerdale Valley presents a dramatic picture in a remote position on the western fringe of the Lake District National Park. Extending to fourteen kilometres long and almost five kilometres wide, at its widest it encloses an area of around 5,000 hectares. The

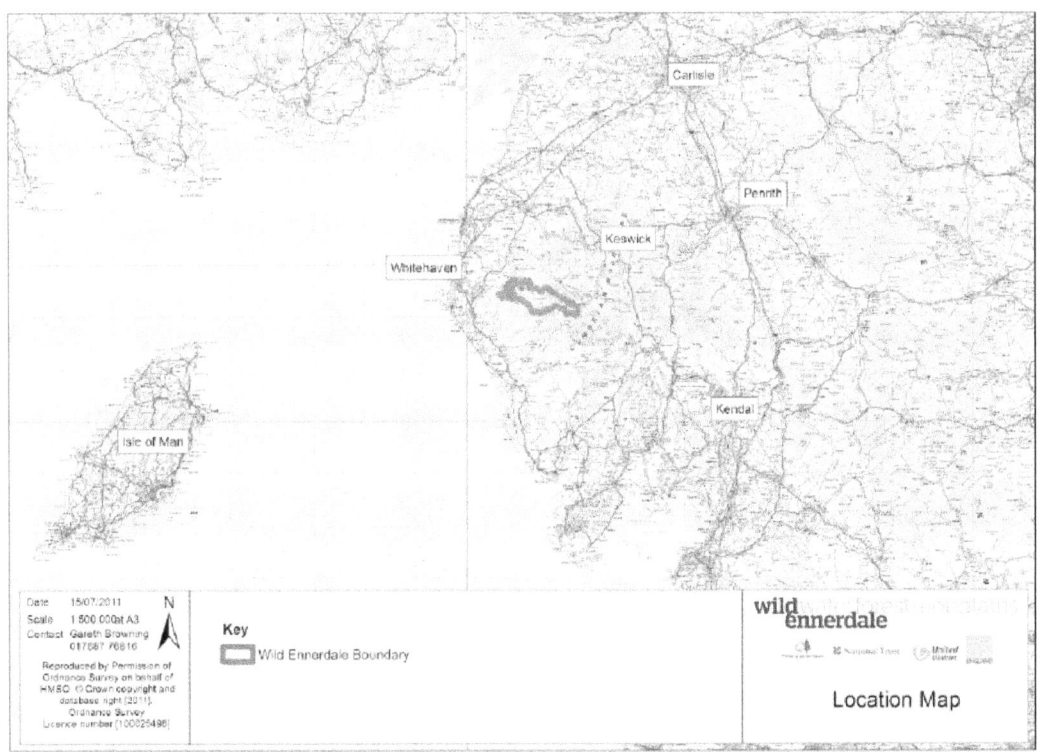

Figure 1. Ennerdale location map

Figure 2. Ennerdale Valley View

valley narrows from west to east and is surrounded by dramatic mountain ridges which include some of Lakeland's highest summits such as Great Gable and Pillar both over 890 metres high.

The large scale and diversity of its landscapes, incorporating farming, mixed forest, rivers, lake, open fell and mountains, combined with the relative lack of roads, traffic, buildings and people all contribute to enhance the sense of Ennerdale as a wild, tranquil and spiritually refreshing place. Over a thousand years of human activity, stretching from the Bronze Age to present day, are etched into the landscape.

The whole valley is highly significant for its rich legacy of archaeological remains and diverse habitats for flora and fauna, all with features which range from regional to international importance. Over 40% of the area is designated as 'Site of Special Scientific Interest' (SSSI) and Special Area of Conservation (SAC) Wild Ennerdale (2006). These designations reflect the outstanding importance of the vegetation and geological features of Ennerdale. The continuous transition of vegetation types, from lakeshore through woodlands and open heath land, to the specialised sub alpine vegetation of its mountain tops, is spectacular.

The River Liza is a major asset, falling wild and unchecked down the valley and is one of few rivers in England to show such uncontrolled dynamism. At the western end of the valley lies Ennerdale Water which supplies over 60,000 customers with drinking water. The network of footpaths, tracks and open access both in the forest and on the open fells provides a wealth of opportunity for people to explore the valley with a sense of freedom, adventure and challenge. The majority of the valley is dedicated Open Access.

Ennerdale is a place, where people can feel humbled by their surroundings, where signs of human influence are less and where nature remains, to varying degrees, the dominating force.

Figure 3. The River Liza, one of England's most natural rivers.

The Wild Ennerdale Partnership

The Wild Ennerdale partnership has been developing since 2000 when the National Trust approached the Forestry Commission about working together. Initial discussion and brainstorming centred on developing ideas about a combined approach to managing the valley and identifying the unique qualities and character of Ennerdale. It was through these discussions that United Utilities were invited to join, recognising the value of Ennerdale Water and water processes across the valley. Following these initial discussions the wild character of Ennerdale was identified as being of primary significance and the three partners agreed on the name '*Wild Ennerdale*'. At the same time a vision statement was developed which sums up the partnerships aspiration for the future of the valley '*To allow the evolution of Ennerdale as a wild valley for the benefit of people relying more on natural processes to shape its landscape and ecology*' Wild Ennerdale (2006).

Over the last five years the partnership has seen its work develop and broaden as individuals such as farm tenants, local businesses, the Youth Hostel Association, local people and volunteers have caught onto the excitement and vision that the original partners have developed. Today Wild Ennerdale is a partnership between people and organisations led by The Forestry Commission (FC), National Trust (NT), and United Utilities (UU) being the primary land owners in The Ennerdale Valley and Natural England, the Government's advisor on the environment.

In 2006, after significant consultation and discussion, the Partnership published its Wild Ennerdale Stewardship Plan which has guided the partners work over the last five years. The Stewardship Plan is currently being reviewed and it is hoped that this paper will add to the review through the time taken to record experiences, from the feedback generated from those contributing and this conference.

The Wild Ennerdale Approach

Wild land is a relatively new concept in the UK and involves giving natural processes greater freedom to develop our future landscapes. Nature conservation in England is generally focused on small-scale interventions where in Ennerdale more weight is given to the landscape scale leaving the detail to natural processes. Wild Ennerdale is one of the UK's largest wild land projects allowing ecosystems throughout the valley to evolve with greater freedom. Its experience in managing land through minimal human intervention is already widely recognised and shared by others.

In the UK, all our landscapes and ecosystems have to some degree been impacted by human influences and in Ennerdale (as elsewhere) any future landscapes and ecosystems will continue to be affected by past management along with influences, such as climate change and airborne pollution, which show no respect for boundaries. As a result using the words 'wild' and 'natural' can be contentious.

The Wild Ennerdale approach involves reducing the scale and altering the nature of human intervention in the valley, so that human processes (whether they be farming, forestry or recreation) do not come to dominate the wide variety of other processes that operate. Put simply, we are trying to place constraints on the way in which people operate in the valley so that they become part of a 'natural system'. This is an attempt to allow a 'wild' place to evolve in which people are and continue to be an important part.

In the context of Wild Ennerdale, the words 'natural' and 'natural system' are not used in an ecologically pure way. We are not attempting to re-create a set of landscapes and ecosystems which might once have existed at a particular point in time. Rather, by acknowledging that natural systems are dynamic and constantly changing, we are using the present as a starting point – a starting point which includes three millennia of human activity and a variety of species which man has both eliminated (or at least seriously constrained) and introduced, of which Sitka Spruce *Picea sitchensis* is perhaps the most obvious. Our concession to the 'un-naturalness' of this starting point is the management approach we have been undertaking over the last five few years and will continue into the near future. This involves introducing some of the more obvious and significant missing processes, such as extensive grazing by large herbivores and broadleaf tree planting, and providing some control on processes we have introduced in the past such as Sitka Spruce regeneration. The intention is to create a more balanced starting point in which a broader array of processes has the opportunity to operate and influence the valley. Wild Ennerdale (2006).

As the valley develops, it is hoped that there will be a series of naturally evolving and interacting ecosystems across the valley that are far more robust in the face of stresses such as climate change and that farming and forestry will maximise ecology and landscape value. It cannot be predicted exactly how biodiversity may develop as natural processes are given greater freedom. However, being able to observe these processes at work, over generations, will be one of the marvels of change in Ennerdale, and ensure that the lessons learnt will have a resonance far beyond the boundaries of the valley.

Why Cattle?

When the Wild Ennerdale partners started to share their new vision with others the feedback from ecologists was unanimous in encouraging the Partnership to introduce a large herbivore into the valley. This was said to be a key missing natural process from many of our modern day forests. The partnership looked around for inspiration and discovered the nature reserve of Oostvaardersplassen in the Netherlands where Heck Cattle *Bos taurus* were introduced in 1983 and graze extensively without tending. The Partnership also visited a grazing scheme in South Cumbria where cattle were rotated across a number of extensive sites.

As we found out more we realised that perhaps cattle could help us achieve our aspiration to see the blurring of the traditional functional management of the valley and the removal of boundaries to natural processes. In the past forestry and farming have been kept separate, often divided by a fence or a wall leading to the development of a stark boundary where landscape texture, colour, look and feel change suddenly. Our vision for the valley challenges us to facilitate the development of more blurred boundaries where the extent of one habitat merging with another is difficult to define and perhaps new habitats

Figure 4. Cattle *Bos taurus* in Ennerdale

develop which challenge our stereotypical understanding of habitat types such as forest and fell.

The introduction of cattle is principally about enabling a number of opportunistic processes where cattle disturb ground creating niches into which the seed from different species can germinate and grow. Whether they make it to full height depends on the availability of nutrients, light and water and grazing by roe deer *Capreolus capreolus*, sheep *Ovis aries* and the very cattle that provide the seedbed in the first place. Unlike other herbivores such as sheep and roe deer, cattle principally by virtue of their weight cause patchy ground disturbance where individuals in the herd engage in activities to determine dominance and rank or where animals create regularly used corridors through vegetation. In addition cattle graze more selectively often ripping vegetation and leave a more clumpy diverse sward than sheep.

Large herbivores in Ennerdale – Historic Context

As the often quoted verse from Ecclesiastes 1:9 says *'there is nothing new under the sun'* so it is with cattle in Ennerdale. Research by Oxford Archaeology North commissioned by the Wild Ennerdale Partners in 2003 found that Winchester (1987, 42-3 and 56n22) identified two vaccaries (cattle farms) in Ennerdale in 1334 and these great walled enclosures can still be explored today. Indeed one of the vaccary, near Woundell Beck, was catalysis for the area known as Silvercove to be identified as the first extensive area for reintroducing cattle. The vaccary however has been given some additional protection with internal fences ensuring the historic walls are not damaged by modern relatives of the original medieval users.

In addition to the tangible remains of medieval cattle farming, the Partnership discovered during one of many discussions with local people that cattle were a part of the valley bottom much more recently. The daughter of the last farmer to live at Low Gillerthwaite (now Low Gillerthwaite Field Centre) recollected how she used to help her father round up Highland cattle from the young planted forest in the 1930s.

Wild Cattle - a brief timeline of introduction

The introduction of cattle to the valley became reality in early 2006 when the first herd of animals was introduced to around 140 hectares of recently clear felled conifer forest, ancient woodland and heather *Calluna vulgaris* fell at Silvercove. Silvercove was chosen as the first area because it had no recent history of grazing and no existing tenancies so was relatively easy to establish.

In 2008, the renewal of a Farm Business Tenancy provided the opportunity to introduce a second herd into the Middle Valley extending to around 250 hectares. This herd was initially excluded from an area of previously intensively sheep grazed inbye fields so that these would become rougher. The concern was that the cattle may decide to spend the whole time in the fields and not explore the valley bottom and forest if the field grazing was too good. This herd's area was to undergo an unplanned expansion in late 2009 when attempts to maintain a fence boundary across the River Liza failed following two successive years of significant flood events. Abandoning this boundary allowed the herd to wander freely in up to 550 hectares of the middle valley.

In 2009, the tenant farmer managing the Silvercove herd suggested reducing his sheep flock at the eastern end of the valley under Great Gable and introducing a third herd into an area of 240 hectares known as Blacksail. This was partly driven by and made possible by the expansion of the Silvercove herd through breeding. The latter herd was now at the capacity for the site and the farmer suggested splitting this herd taking some animals to the eastern end of the valley.

Wild cattle – wilder people

As with the concept of wildness itself the introduction of wild roaming cattle challenged the cultural and traditional values we have of farm animals being regularly tended and managed to a defined end point, the production of meat. Their introduction required a change of philosophy, a standing back and waiting rather than being in control. There are three principal communities that were affected by the introduction of

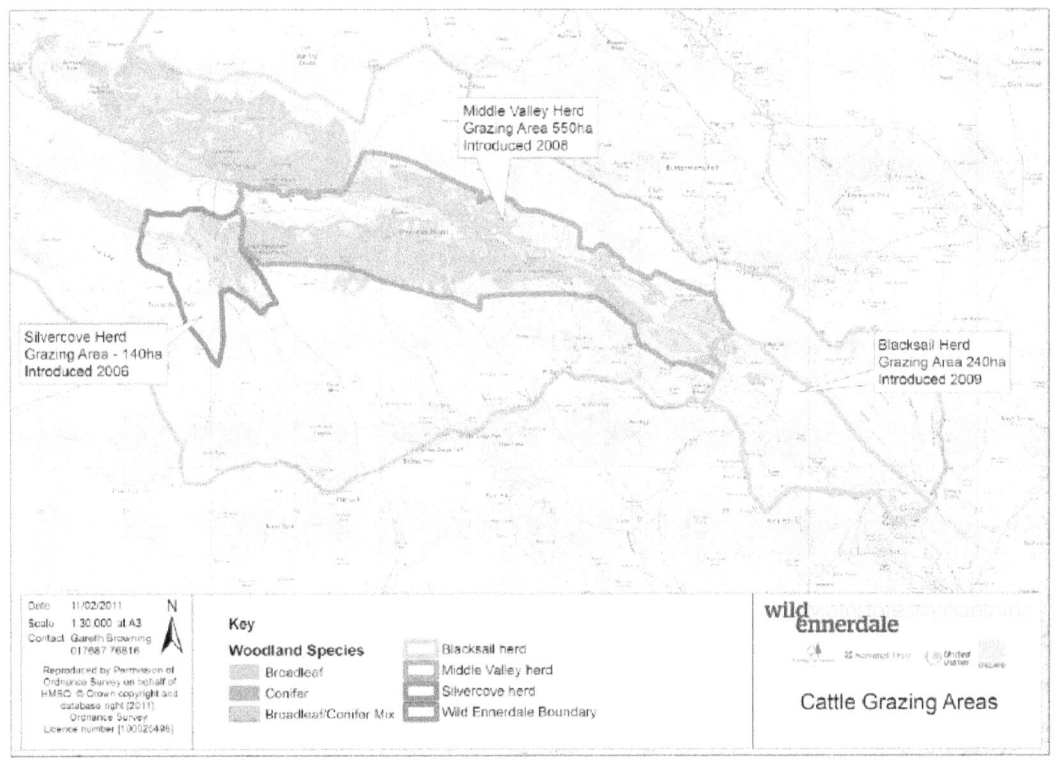

Figure 5. Map of Grazing Areas

cattle, the farming community, visitors to the valley and the Wild Ennerdale Partners as land managers.

To capture the farming communities experience three of the valley's farmers were interviewed. Two of those interviewed now look after herds of extensive grazing cattle and whilst the third does not, they have been involved in sharing cattle grazing with one of the other two.

When the introduction of extensive grazed cattle was first discussed with the farming community there were a number of common responses from existing farmers in the valley. The interviews explored these concerns and also how farmers felt now. These are summarised below.

Welfare and managing

Welfare was the area that solicited the strongest concerns including *'how would they get enough to eat'*, *'would they maintain condition in winter'*, *'would they roam much or just stand at the gate waiting to be fed'* and *'how would they cope'*. Thinking about the situation in 2011 those interviewed expressed pleasure and some surprise with how well the animals coped making comments such as *'they've done everything asked of them'*, *' no bother at all'*, *'they make a lot of decisions'* and *'Galloway cattle know what they are doing next'*.

The size of the area

There was concern that the size of the area that they could roam would make them difficult to manage. This can been seen in comments such as *'How far would they move'* and *'how would you find them'*. The answer to the first

Figure 6. Farmer, cattle and visitors

question has been that they move quite a lot, often some distance in a day. Finding them can occasionally be difficult but they have learnt to recognise the sound of their farmers vehicle and one farmer uses a loud 'yodel' like call which they respond to with their own bellow and rapidly make their way to where the farmer is.

Cultural Change

The valley's farmers clearly saw that this was a change to their previous way of management. Comments such as *'hadn't done anything like this before'*, *'frightened of it failing'* and *'having cattle out all the time was a new concept'* sum up a wider range of comments. By comparison, farmers expressed different feelings now that the cattle were established one saying positively *'The cattle at Silvercove have changed the way we farm cattle at home'*. Other comments included, *'the experiments worked'* and *'Dad was quite surprised it worked but pleased'*.

In terms of members of the public there have been many who have supported and welcomed the new beasts. The choice of Galloways with their thick curly hair has won them regular comparison with bears. There is even a Youtube *drewidofatlips* (2008) video published in 2008 which documents the finding of the *'rarely sighted bears in the Lake District'*. For many visitors the animals do often go unseen as the area they roam is significant. A search of comments left by visitors in the Ennerdale YHA diary revealed no comments about the cattle whilst the presence of the cattle often sheltering around the Blacksail Youth Hostel does draw comment from visitors they, are often only staying a night or two and don't seem to mind too much the animals close presence. The YHA manager has had to live with the regular bringing in of cattle 'pooh' on visitors boots, often just after the hostel has been cleaned. She also recounts a tale of going outside to fix the generator on a dark night only to find a black Galloway cow blocking her way. Even with these inconveniences there seems to be a genuine acceptance of the herds presence in the valley.

When it was first suggested that they be introduced there was concern that dog owners would be chased and people regularly frightened by cows with calves especially given the number of visitors, estimated at around 60,000, and many kilometres of rights of way which criss cross the valley. Five years on from their introduction there have been no formal complaints from members of the public . The worst criticism we have had informally is that the cows *'pooh on the footpaths'*. One of the Wild Ennerdale partners did meet a couple on mountain bikes with a pair of pet wolves on leads who had turned back from riding up the valley because the cattle were encamped on the forest road. However they were not complaining, they accepted that their wolves and the cattle would be wary of each other. Encouraged to follow the Wild Ennerdale partner's vehicle along the road, the bikers and their wolves made it through the herd who moved aside for the vehicle and whilst interested in the wolves *Canis* spp. were not agitated or threatening.

Whilst the introduction of cattle to the valley was instigated by the Wild Ennerdale partners and therefore it is safe to assume that the Partnership had already decided to allow natural processes more self will, the experience of there introduction has at times challenged the Partnership. Initially the partners were keen to see Highland Cattle introduced as they had been farmed in the valley in the 1930's and were the iconic wild cattle breed. For a time we were quite focussed on this iconic species. However, concerns over handling horned cattle and the risk they posed to visitors along with the farmers experience with Galloways suggested they would be a more suitable breed. It was when we returned to our Vision and Guiding Principles that we realised that we were being drawn by the iconic nature of Highland Cattle when in fact introducing Galloways would deliver the same benefits and importantly would reward the enthusiasm of the farmer who was to take on the Silvercove tenancy.

One incident that has reminded us all of our vision and principles was our attempt to maintain a stock fenced boundary across the River Liza. This was aimed at keeping the Middle Valley herd from roaming across the eastern valley where native broadleaves were being planted. Whilst we fully expected to have to maintain this boundary we did not expect to have to completely change our thinking within barely six months of the introduction of the Middle Valley herd. In late October 2008 the River Liza experienced a significant flood event, one that made the National headlines when the Original Mountain Marathon (*The Guardian*, 2008) held to the east of the valley, was cancelled for the first time in its long history. The river smashed its way through the fence across its path burying it under significant amounts of woody debris and gravel. The Wild Ennerdale partners spent much of the following year discussing whether to reinstate the boundary only to be confronted by another headline grabbing flood event in October 2009, this time focussed on Cockermouth and Workington. The River Liza moved 20m or more in places across the valley bottom again, bringing more debris into the river system. It was after this event that we realised that we should celebrate the power of natural forces and accepted that the boundary was not sustainable. The Middle Valley herd's area of roaming increased 100% and has stayed the same since.

Wild cattle – wilder animals

The question often asked is '*Are they wild?*' referring to the cattle themselves. Whilst legally they are still domestic stock a number of episodes have given us an insight into the development of perhaps a more self willed animal.

Our first herd of cattle arrived in the valley in 2006 and we had an inkling that one of them, the oldest matriarch, was already pregnant. She was and gave birth unaided in the late spring. She wasn't unaided out of the desire of the farmer it was clear she didn't want help. Like many a wild animal she took herself away from the herd and gave birth in an area of scrub and bracken. We were all surprised and the farmer was very concerned when one day she went missing from the herd and could not be found. However, this has now become the norm and like it or not we have all had to get used to absent mothers at calving time. Most cows are away for just a few days but the longest absence has been more than a week. Normally the cow rejoins the herd after a few days returning regularly to suckle the calf which is left hidden in scrub as if being sheltered from some predator.

Another story shows how the herd has become a close family unit just like with many wild animals. One of our Middle Valley herd injured its foot to the point where it couldn't walk during its first year on-site. The Wild Ennerdale Partners and the farm tenant discussed what should be done and as the cow seemed in little pain we decided to see if it would recover and see what happened. For a while the cow did not move far at all, preferring to graze a very small area immediately around itself. During this period the rest of the herd exhibited very protective behaviour. They would graze away from the injured animal during the day but would always rejoin and stay with it during the night. As the injured animal improved and started to walk again members of the herd were often seen helping it by pushing it up steeper slopes. Unfortunately something happened after this point and the animal's health deteriorated again so we decided to remove the animal from the herd.

Lastly a more recent story sheds another angle on the strong bonds that develop between animals in the herd. In

Figure 7. Galloway Bull

late Summer 2010 two herds managed by one farmer were both put to the same bull. The bull was allowed to roam with each herd for a couple of weeks. At the time the farmer and Wild Ennerdale partners noticed that when the bull was with the Blacksail herd roaming under Great Gable the bull was never seen interacting with the cows but instead always seemed to be alone. In spring 2011 when the cows were pregnancy tested none of the Blacksail herd was pregnant yet 4 out of 5 of the suitable cows in the other herd were pregnant. Discussing this incident since, the farmer has surmised that the Blacksail herd included two young bull calves which whilst not sexually active may have been blocking the new 'interloper' bull from interacting with the females in the herd. The other herd in which the bull was successful was entirely made up of females.

Whilst the cattle have exhibited what might be described as 'self willed' behaviour they have also exhibited more tame domestic characteristics. Both herds have learnt to recognise the sound of their farmer's vehicle often responding to its arrival with loud calling and sometimes appearing from a long distance away. Recently one of the Wild Ennerdale partners changed vehicles from a small car to a larger four wheel drive type and this now attracts similar attention where before the car did not.

One of the farmers users a very loud call, almost but not quite like a yodel to call the animals when they cannot be seen or found visually. The sound of this call seems to carry long distance as the cattle can be heard only just replying with their own loud call perhaps up to a kilometre away and eventually arrive sometimes five minutes or more after they have been called.

Whilst the animals receive only minimal tending the character of each of the three herds is different yet for the most part tame and far from as wild as a wild animal such as deer are. The Silvercove herd are very sociable and friendly always keen to find out who the latest visiting group are. They are noisy too, bellowing out their recognition for their farmer's arrival. The Middle Valley herd are a more quiet reserved group who are inclined to retreat if you pay them too much attention. The Blacksail herd have yet to establish a different identity. Being only recently made up of cattle from the Silvercove herd they have carried with them the sociable interested character and can often be found standing around walkers staying at the Blacksail YHA.

Wild cattle – wilder treescapes

The process of landscape change across Ennerdale is generally a slow process with tangible, touchable results only becoming visible at the landscape scale after a minimum of ten years. Whilst extensive grazing of the first site at Silvercove is only in its fifth year we are just starting to see the results on the ground. The impact of the Middle Valley and Blacksail herds on the treescapes of the valley are not covered as they have not been active in their areas long enough to show significant results.

Before extensive grazing cattle were introduced into Ennerdale, the Wild Ennerdale Partners decided to establish some baseline monitoring of the Silvercove site so that future managers can see the impact of cattle on the landscape. This focussed on four principal methods, photography, exclosures, vegetation quadrats and satellite tracking. The use of data from a satellite tracking collar fitted to one of the herd provides an estimation for the whole herd's activities as it moves around the landscape. Baseline vegetation quadrat surveys by Miller in 2006 were completed before the cattle were introduced but have yet to be repeated so will not be reported on in this paper. The use of photography for monitoring is well known and will be

Figure 8. Exclosure in 2006 showing post harvesting vegetation dominated by grasses.

Figure 9. Exclosure in 2011 – showing impact of grazing

used to illustrate the main changes discussed as will the satellite tracking data. The use of exclosures is maybe less well known and is described below.

Exclosures are simply small fenced areas which are aimed at keeping grazing animals out rather than in. Typically the exclosures are no more than 0.015 hectare in size, being constructed from one 50 metre long roll of stock net. They take less than a day to erect and can be easily moved if required. They have been extremely valuable in illustrating the impact of grazing on the developing habitat as they are very easy to visit and provide very tangible ongoing and live feedback.

Walking around the site, comparing photographs and looking at the habitats inside and outside the exclosures it is clear that the cattle grazing is having a positive impact in three key areas, diversifying structure and species and opportunities for change.

Inside the enclosures located on the areas where conifers have been clear-felled the habitat is fast developing towards a closed canopy woodland dominated by native broadleaves with a couple of non native pine *Pinus sylvestris*, larch *Larix* spp. and spruce *Picea* spp. Photographs of the exclosures from just before the introduction of cattle compared to today show how quickly woodland regeneration has established and

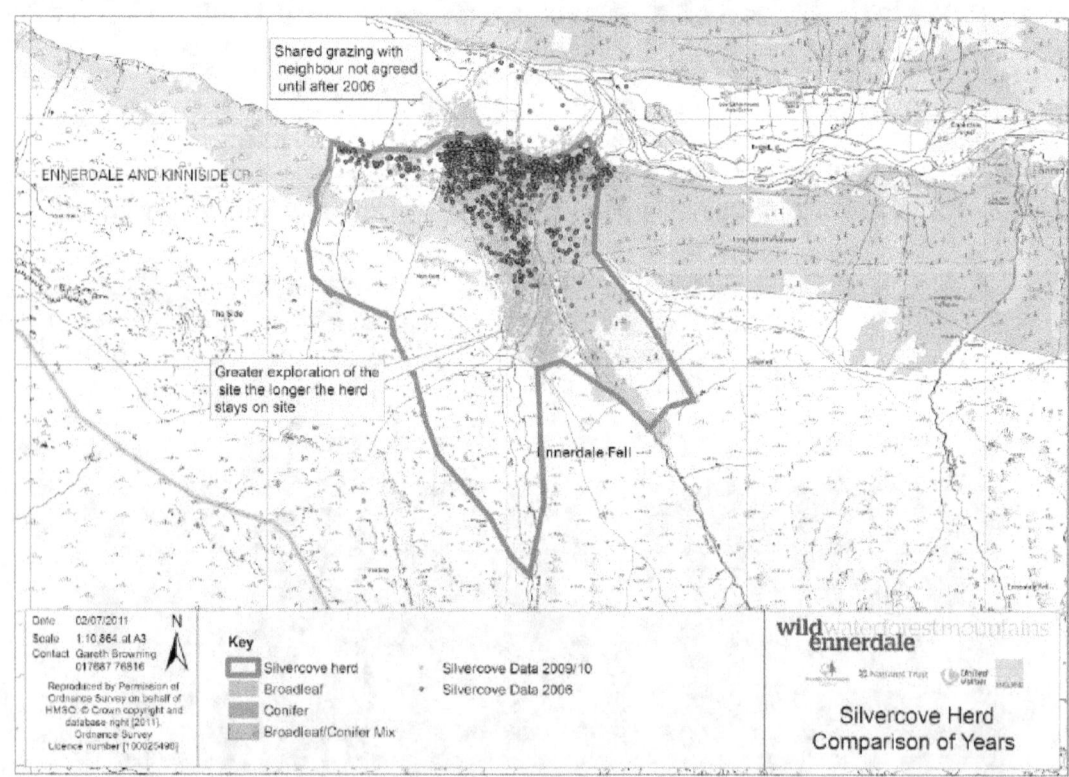

Figure 10. Map of tracking data showing cattle spend more time in the valley bottom.

dominated. During the first two to three years of grazing the habitat inside the exclosures looked the more desirable as there was a mosaic of heathland, scrub and native tree species. However, in the last two to three years this structure has changed significantly as trees have gained succession over shrub and ground vegetation and are shading the latter out.

Outside the exclosures the habitat is much more diverse both in terms of species and structure. The cattle naturally spend more time in the lower valley bottom where forage is better and this has lead to the lower lying areas being significantly grazed. Even so the vegetation is diverse and there are clumps of woodland regeneration and areas of scrub heathland. The upward growth of all species apart from a low stocking of conifer regeneration is being significantly kept in check by grazing.

As you walk towards and onto the sloping ground the distinction between open grasses, heathland, grazed scrub and established woodland is blurred and the future development uncertain. The cattle clearly have preferred and regularly used pathways up and across the slope along which they graze. These areas have regenerated with native woodland species notably birch *Betula* spp. but the cattle are keeping most regeneration under a metre high. The grazed access corridors seem to connect to more defined glades where grazing and perhaps soil type are limiting woodland regeneration significantly. These latter areas currently look destined to stay open whereas the scrub corridors could develop as woodland if the cattle choose a different route across the site and stop grazing along them.

Figure 11. Grazed Corridors in Bracken

When the Silvercove herd were first introduced, data from the tracking collar showed that during the first few months they did not roam far at all (Browning, 2006). This seemed to be a response to ample grazing in the valley bottom brought about by the site not having been grazed before. As time passed the herd have explored further and wider in their search for grazing and perhaps in response to weather and temperature. The tracking collar data shows for example how the herd react to temperature. The set of four maps in Figure 12 shows how during cold periods they tend to stay more in defined areas and don't roam far, presumably to conserve energy. This behaviour will have an impact on the treescape as where the herd spends more time the opportunity for woodland to regenerate is much lower.

Outside of the grazed routes and open glades there are areas of more dense woodland but very few areas that exhibit the same canopy closure as is seen within the exclosures. Leaving alone woodland regeneration the habitats outside the exclosures are developing a much more diverse mix of shrub and heathland species, wetland and wet meadow. In addition to generating a diverse species mix and structure, it is clear that the natural process of opportunistic change is still ongoing. The herd's patchwork ground disturbance caused by social 'pushing and shoving', 'pathway grazing' and

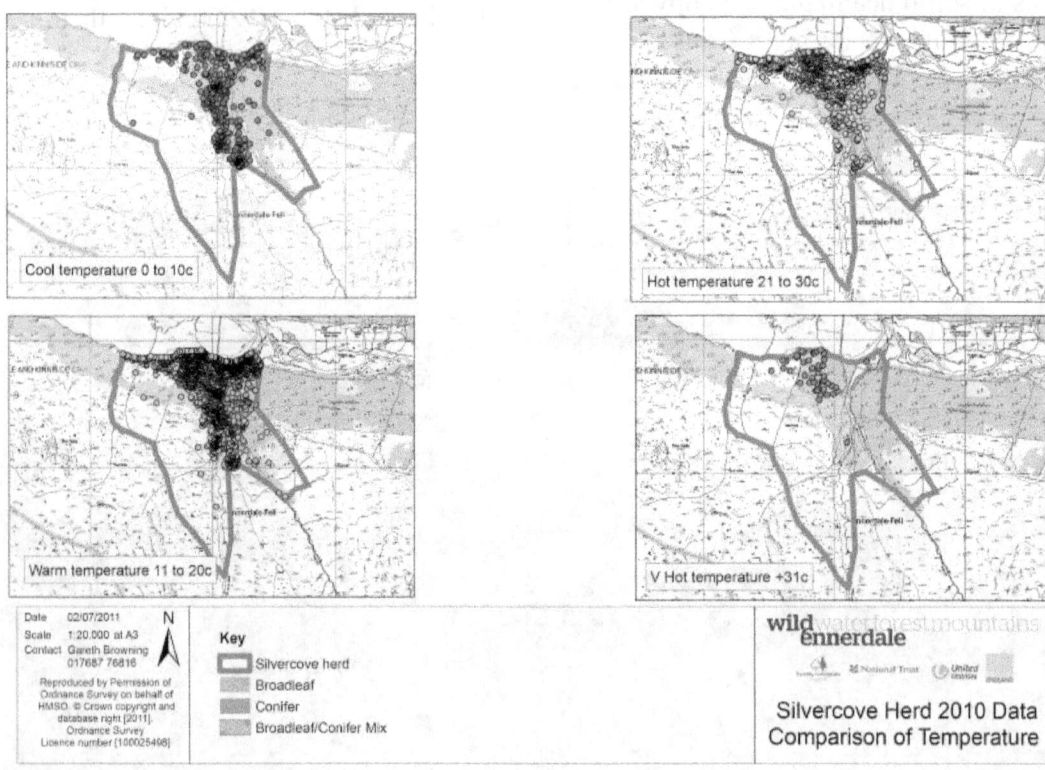

Figure 12. Tracking Data mapped by temperature.

'hill climbing' all create random and newly appearing opportunities for seedling germination and vegetation development. Areas of dense bracken under mature pine trees have been broken up by the cattle creating pathways within which you can find patches of disturbed ground containing young seedlings of birch where under the bracken there is no seedling regeneration just grass.

As this is not a scientific report we do not offer a species list which perhaps would capture the diversity and raw detail but the variety of texture, colour and mosaic of flora intermixed with trees and scrub is a joy to walk through and fascinating to watch develop.

Wild Cattle – future natural landscapes

So we now have three roaming herds of cattle covering around 1,000 hectares of the valley. Whilst they are still considered domestic in the eyes of the law they roam large expanses of landscape, with limited tending, choice in their daily foraging and the freedom to enjoy all that the Cumbrian weather throws at them. We would argue that they are some of the wildest animals in England.

The people involved in the cattle introduction have become wilder as they have let go of past concerns and traditions and now have the confidence to stand back and allow the cattle to decide their own routine or seek them out to gain joy from seeing their calves, their teddy bear faces or learn how they survive the winters.

As a Partnership we continue to aspire to remove boundaries and give our cattle herds as large an area to roam as is possible. The experiment has only just begun, five years of grazing is just showing little glimpses of tangible change and benefit. The treescape of Ennerdale has benefited from these native black animals as they have lived up to the expectations we had for them

Figure 13. Birch seedling in bracken corridor

Figure 14. Middle Valley herd crossing the River Liza.

to blur the boundary between forestry and farming, open and wooded landscape.

We do not know what the valley will look like in the future but one missing natural process is firmly back and helping to make Ennerdale a wilder valley for the benefit of people where nature determines the detail and we, as stewards, can only marvel and be excited by what the future natural landscape may look and feel like.

Bibliography

Browning, G. (2006) *Cattle Tracking Report*. Wild Ennerdale Partnership, Cumbria.

Drewidofatlips, (2008) *Ennerdale Bears*. http://www.youtube.com/watch?v=xqxwlSr25Xo

Miller, H. (2006) *Establishment of Vegetation Monitoring Baseline*. Wild Ennerdale Partnership, Cumbria.

Wild Ennerdale, (2006) *Stewardship Plan*. Wild Ennerdale Partnership, Cumbria.

Winchester, A. (1987) *Historic Landscape Report*, Wild Ennerdale Partnership, Cumbria.

Wearver, M. (2008) Lake District Runners Still Missing. *The Guardian*.

Re-wilding trees for ancients of the future
Jill Butler
The Woodland Trust

Replacement of open grown ancient trees

Ancient and veteran trees are rich reservoirs of biodiversity and cultural icons and in the UK we are lucky that there are so many in our landscape. However, the disappearance of commons, orchards and parkland since the 1850s, and the removal of hedgerows have led to significant losses of open grown trees. There appears to be a growing imbalance between the loss of mature and ancient, open crowned trees and the regeneration of new trees to replace them. The Ancient Tree Forum and the Woodland Trust believe we must encourage tree establishment to ensure we have enough ancient trees in the future.

Some of our oldest trees started life in a very unplanned way – perhaps the least influenced by man in Western Europe – but areas where self-sown trees can regenerate naturally and reach their full potential crown-spread in open wood pasture or parkland are now rare. There are advantages to such natural processes and they should be encouraged where possible to ensure ancient trees for the future. Landowners and professionals who want to establish trees where the landscape is kept open by grazing animals and they can develop full, open crowns have an important role to play. Open tree landscapes are the places which in the past have been celebrated by landscape designers, artists and writers as some of the most beautiful landscapes in the UK and are the most important today for species associated with ancient and veteran trees in old growth[1].

It is however, sometimes necessary to plant trees. While there is plenty of existing guidance on planting to create or restock woods, plantations, orchards and hedgerows, and on planting trees in gardens and streets, there are some important factors to take into account if open crown trees are required in the long term.

Un-tamed regeneration - wild spaces needed for wild trees

Trees have been reproducing themselves naturally for millennia; however the landscape is now subject to so many competing interests that trees and shrubs are usually only allowed to grow exactly where we want them. In some places people value treelessness so much – in calcareous grasslands and heathlands for example - that even scattered trees and shrubs are no longer seen as desirable and considerable resources are invested in clearing 'scrub'.

A planted tree can be placed just where we want it and those that grow 'wild' are often seen as 'neglected' and

Figure 1. The King John Oak at Umborne in Devon has lived all its life in the open and was probably self-sown.

'untidy'. Wood pastures and parkland where wild regeneration of trees and shrubs can take place are now rare and very special and there is still a great deal to learn about the process.

The challenges for self sown - hitting the spot

The seeds of most temperate trees have specialist mechanisms that allow them to disperse naturally either by:

- Wind – the seed cases are light and have wings or other structures to help give them lift so they fly a long way; or

- Birds or other animals – natural selection has enhanced their attractiveness to animals such as by making them a protein-rich source of food. Where seeds escape being eaten they also benefit from having a rich energy source for early development.

Natural selection

When wild regeneration occurs, the tree "selects" its own spot. Those seeds that land in unsuitable places fall by the wayside but any seedling that does take root, starts its life without the stresses of being grown in modern nurseries and the shock of relocation.

Rooted to the spot

Seedling development may proceed under a wide variety of situations provided soil conditions are suitable. The root from the seed needs to be able to explore the soil below where it was deposited and develop in response to the local conditions.

If the soil is in good condition and contains an undisturbed and undamaged microbiology then the root may immediately be colonised by mycorrhizal fungi which help with water and mineral gathering, as well as protecting it from pathogens. Immediate attention from mycorrhizal fungi will increase the chances of the seedling's survival and eventual growth of a healthy tree.

Light and shade

In open habitats such as grasslands both shade-tolerant and light-demanding trees can establish but as shade-tolerant trees may be more vulnerable to drought they may not be able to compete so well in the open where moisture levels may fluctuate more widely.

In woods with continuous canopies only the more shade-tolerant trees such as beech can survive long term and develop under high forest canopies.

Light-demanding seedlings cannot survive under the crown of the parent tree or in shady conditions so the seeds of these trees are dispersed further afield. Oak and hawthorn are light-demanding species needing very open spaces.

Phoenix regeneration

Many trees are able to regenerate vegetatively by suckering or layering. If collapsed trees are allowed to remain *in situ*, intact roots may survive and the tree may continue to grow from a horizontal position. In this way many trees appear to have 'walked' across the landscape. Layering branches will act as flying buttresses propping up aging trunks and making them more stable.

For successful wild regeneration the following is required:

- Places set aside where tree establishment can occur through wild processes;
- Fallen dead wood retained to act as a shelter for wild regeneration;
- Thorny scrub with mature fruit eg bramble, juniper, hawthorn and blackthorn in grazing areas to start scrub regeneration;
- 'Phoenix' regeneration of trees;
- Grazing so that not too much regeneration occurs resulting in closed canopy woodland.

Natural scrub tree shelters

'The thorn is the mother of the oak'
            Humphrey Repton, 1803.

Browsing by livestock affects the establishment, species composition and development of trees and shrubs. However, it is essential to have sufficient browsing by wild animals and domesticated stock to keep landscapes open enough for light-demanding trees and shrubs to thrive - but not too much browsing or from the wrong animals so that seedlings are all eaten or their leading shoots cannot grow on out of reach of animals.

The palatability of leaves to animals influences tree establishment. One reason why most of our deer parks are

Figure 2. Oak sapling protected by bramble – Whiddon Deer Park, Devon.

dominated by oak is that it is much less palatable to deer than ash, for example, and so oak seedlings are more likely to survive. On the other hand many of our cultural landscapes are rich in veteran and ancient trees managed as pollards such as ash pollards in the Cotswolds and the Lake District specifically because their branches were cut for fodder in summer droughts or kept as tree hay for feeding to the animals in winter.

Young trees often survive better if they develop within thorny scrub e.g. blackthorn or bramble, which is less affected by browsing – jays tend to bury their acorn hoards into the edge of thorn clumps. At Hatfield Forest in Essex, there was a tradition of gathering acorns and tossing them into thorn scrub to promote the development of new trees.

Wild regeneration will also occur if other protection is available such as fallen branches or even unpalatable plants – either with chemical (e.g hound's-tongue) or structural (e.g. thistle) defences (Smit et al., 2006).

Grazing by too many browsing animals or by those that can break through thorny defences may mean trees are unable to compete. Goats and sheep from southern and eastern Europe are adapted to browsing leaves through the thorny scrub and are specifically chosen as a 'tool' controlling scrub development in herb rich grasslands and heathland. Exotic muntjac deer from Asia appear to be able to eat plants that are otherwise unpalatable to native wild animals and rare breeds.

Bearing in mind the crown size of mature trees and the need to have a continuous age structure of young trees through to ancient trees, it is preferable to have too little regeneration than too much especially of very long-lived light-demanding trees. It is difficult to remove trees once they are well established and too many of the same age at one time may lead to closed canopy woodland. It may be easier to think in terms of how many trees need to be planted and how frequently and then compare with what is happening in the wild situation.

The key elements are open grown trees, open grass, heath or moorland with wild flowers, scrub, and some groups of trees and occasional establishment of trees to provide succession within the area as a whole. There are no recipes. Some factors to consider:

- Establish grazing practices with the browsing animals that allow sufficient regeneration but not too much.

- Retain 25-75% open ground with the rest a mix of single open crowned trees and a few groups of trees.

- Where there is already too much young tree establishment coppice or pollard trees to reduce canopy cover.

- Cattle, Exmoor or other rare breed horses and deer are probably the best browsers to use.

- Pigs may be an option in the right location or used during the autumn when there is sufficient mast for them.

- Plant scrub to provide a nursery for wild seedling protection.

- Grazing needs to limit regeneration so that some individual trees can grow to maturity and into old age without their crowns touching or being outcompeted by other neighbouring trees.

- Monitor wild regeneration and amend stocking densities to ensure the right level of regeneration.

- Share experiences with other land managers.

- Consider protecting some wild saplings that have regenerated if it is difficult to manage browsing stock and there is no regeneration happening.

Planting for open, full crowned trees that can grow old gracefully

Even when planting, it is important to consider the light-demanding or shade-tolerant characteristics of the trees to be planted. Planting blocks of even aged and closely spaced trees creates structural uniformity that has its limitations in its value to wildlife and will disadvantage light-demanding species of tree. Shade-tolerant trees will outcompete light-demanding saplings and quickly reduce the variety of trees within the first few decades. When planting more formal groups of trees such as roundels or avenues the choice of species and spacing of trees is therefore very important.

Always remember that trees and shrubs grow best when root growth is good and competition for moisture and nutrients from other plants is low. Low nutrient conditions tend to provide the best growing situations for trees and shrubs. Fertilisers negatively affect the growth of mycorrizhal fungi and should not be used.

Although native trees may have advantages, some non-native trees, especially of European origin may be useful in reducing the age-gap in tree populations because they grow more quickly. Sweet chestnut for example has heartwood similar to oak.

Too close for comfort

Scattered, open crowned trees have been shown to be keystone structures in a wide range of landscapes and are objects of great beauty. Trees intended as future replacements must not be planted so close to the older tree that the two trees will be competing with each other for light. The maintenance of a tree free zone around them is important (Manning et al., 2006) or it will lead to the older tree being damaged by shading from the more vigorous younger tree as it matures and the shape of the younger tree being affected as it grows.

The minimum amount of space required by a tree or shrub to grow to its full crown potential – especially lower side branches - depends on the species (and genetics) and also on its situation, eg soil characteristics and landscape. There is not space here to cover the full range however many good tree guides will provide information on the height that trees will achieve. Provide trees with at least an area that has a diameter equalling the height as a minimum.

'Planting' dead trees

Many of the landscape designers of the English romantic garden period in the mid-eighteenth century such as William Kent transported dead trees to incorporate in their landscape design to help create an immediate 'natural' impact and mood.

For open crowned trees to develop to their full potential:

- Allow sufficient space. With oak, for example, lower branch growth can extend as much as 15m from the trunk, maybe more in some situations. For open-grown oak trees with good side branch development that can extend more than 15m from the trunk, the minimum spacing should be 35m between plantings and the same distance away from existing trees; larger spacing is recommended in order to create and maintain open spaces amongst the trees and to leave room for the establishment of new generations of trees in the future.

- Plan planting according to the longevity of trees – more space is needed for trees that may live for many centuries.

- With smaller trees, eg fruit trees, the correct minimum density has evolved from the fruit production industry, enabling optimal flowering and fruiting of trees. In a mature orchard, trees are at about 10m spacing.

- Consider using thorny shrubs such as hawthorn to protect young trees. This was a common practice used by landscape gardeners such as Humphry Repton and 'Capability' Brown.

- For a more rapid crown effect plant a small group of trees close together to form a 'bundle'.

- Consider European non-natives that might provide veteran characteristics more quickly than native trees for wildlife benefits where it is necessary to ensure continuity of the ancient tree habitat.

- Consider planting dead standing trees to enhance wildlife habitat and aesthetic impact.

Resist the temptation to plant too many trees at one time

It is often said that denser plantings allow for the predictable occasional death of a few trees, but such failures are unpredictable and the result generally is an overcrowded stand with a few small gaps. Early thinning to compensate is also often recommended, but rarely actually takes place.

It is better to plant at the desired end density and to replace failures as and when they occur. The biggest problem is with the financial drivers of such projects which normally demand large inputs of activity within a single financial year. This is actually an argument for the final density planting approach as this will produce a closer approximation to the desired outcome than overcrowded plantations and is much less demanding in ongoing maintenance.

Allow for additional planting in decades and centuries to come so that a wide age structure is developed. As oaks can live for 900 years or more there has to be plenty of space in which future generations can be established.

Note

1. Old growth – areas with trees that are over 200 years old where there have been old trees present far into the past.

References

Manning, A.D., Fischer, J. and Lindenmayer, D.B. (2006) Scattered trees are keystone structures – implications for conservation. *Biological Conservation,* **132**, 311-321.

Repton, H. (1803) *Observations on the Theory and Practice of Landscape Gardening.* http://frontpage.woodland-trust.org.uk/ancient-tree-forum/atfgallery/featurespoetryquotes/repton.htm.

Smit, C., Den Ouden, J. and Müller-Schärer, H. (2006) Unpalatable plants facilitate tree sapling survival in wooded pastures. *Journal of Applied Ecology,* **43**, 305-312.

Woodland grazing with cattle – the effects of twenty-five years grazing

Rita Merete Buttenschøn[1], J. Buttenschøn[2]

Forest and Landscape, Copenhagen University[1], Danish Veterinary and Food Administration[2]

Woodland grazing is now considered an important tool in the creation and maintenance of diverse and stable woodlands. In Denmark up to 10% of the forest reserve land is allowed to be used for woodland grazing (*Danish Forest Act*, 2004). Prior to this, from the turn of the nineteenth century, woodland grazing was forbidden in Denmark. For about 200 years this resulted in a division of the landscape into agricultural and forestry land with distinct boundaries between land-use.

In this study we investigate the effect of cattle grazing on structure and vegetation composition in the oak dominated woodland "Skovbjerg" situated in Mols Bjerge National Park. Skovbjerg is one of the very few remnants of ancient woodland in Mols Bjerge. It is surrounded by younger scrub and open grassland. The woodland type is old acidophilus woodland with *Quercus robur* (Type 9192 in the "Habitat Directive") characterised by low diversity of vascular plants but rich in epiphytic lichens.

Over the last 25 years 15 ha of Skovbjerg have been grazed yearly during autumn (October to January) at a moderate grazing pressure (1-1.3 heifer or cow mean weight 500 kg/ha) by crossbred beef cattle. Initially the area was about a third each of woodland, scrub and open grassland. Presently the scrub is developing into woodland proper, while the open grassland is characterised by fragments of scrub and solitary trees. Roe deer are the only wild ungulate present. The roe deer population is estimated to be approximately 20 deer km^{-2} in Mols Bjerge. Pellet group counts indicate an even distribution of roe in and outside the cattle-grazed area.

Autumn grazing was chosen to allow flowering of the field-layer species so enhancing the seed-rain and dispersal by the livestock.

In the present study we compare grazed and un-grazed vegetation over a gradient of gradual cessation of agriculture with subsequent woodland encroachment and ancient oak woodland. The vegetation analyses are made in permanent transects across the vegetation types from ancient woodland to open grassland. The field-layer analysis is made in 1 by 1 metre plots. The tree and bush analysis are made in 10 by 10 m plots. In the woody species analyses we tally the individuals of the different species with reference to four size-groups: (1) = current year's seedlings; (2) = saplings < 0.5m; (3) = saplings 0.5 – 2m. and (4) trees > 2m. Concurrent to the tally we estimate the impact of browse on the individuals using a four step scale: 0 = no browse;

0.5 = slight browse; 1 = medium browse; 2 = heavy browse (Buttenschøn and Buttenschøn, 1985).

Our study demonstrates distinct differences between the cattle grazed and un-grazed woodland.

In the grazed area the browsing horizon on larger trees lies between 1.5 and 2m, whereas there is no distinct browsing horizon in the un-grazed woodland. The grazed area allows more light to penetrate to the woodland floor and thus a denser field-layer to establish as well as providing growth conditions for a wider spectrum of species. Whereas we largely find a persistent or fluctuating bank of woody species saplings in the un-grazed area, there is sufficient light for growth of saplings in the grazed area even if the higher browsing impact slows down growth and individual success. Most woody species are browsed more heavily in the grazed area, oak being an exception (Table 1). Species that are protected by thorns and spikes are generally browsed less than unprotected species.

The germination of many woody species is promoted by grazing through seeds being dispersed by the cattle (Figure 1). In autumn, ripe seeds are available to be eaten and trodden into the ground by the cattle and the autumn grazing leaves the seedlings undisturbed

Table 1. Average browsing pressure on important woody species on Skovbjerg. Browsing pressure > 1.5 is generally critical to long-term survival if no parts of the plant is above the grazing horizon or protected within spikes or thorns. Scale: 0 = no browse, 0.5 = slight browse, 1 = medium browse, 2 = heavy browse.

	Grazed			Un-grazed		
	Saplings < 0.5m	Saplings 0.5 - 2m	Trees > 2m	Saplings < 0.5m	Saplings 0.5 - 2m	Trees > 2m
Cytisus scoparius	1.53	1.52	0.5	0.67	1.17	
Fagus sylvatica	0.61	1.15	1.08	0,29	0.74	
Malus sylvestris	0.41	1.25		0.38		
Populus tremula	1.08	1.10	0.01	0.50	0.92	0.00
Prunus spp.	0.57	1.56	1.11	0.55		
Quercus robur	0.74	1.56	0.15	0.68	1.60	0.05
Rosa spp.	0.41	1.00	0.07	0.50	0.00	
Sorbus aucuparia	1.13	1.50	0.25	0.62		0.25

during the first season of growth. Furthermore, germination on fibre rich cattle dung pats, which may persist and be repulsive for up to a year and a half, enhances seedling survival greatly. While 88% of woody species' seedlings growing on cattle dung survived the first two years, only 26% survived outside the pats (Buttenschøn *et al.*, 2008).

Over the study period the extinction rate of some species is higher than the recruitment rate (Figure 2). This reflects tendencies of actual extinction, thinning of canopy forming individuals as a result of growth or fluctuations in understorey populations of banks of persistent saplings. The latter is seen in the oak and aspen populations. There is no appreciable net recruitment in most species in the un-grazed woodland, *Fagus sylvatica* and *Sorbus aucuparia*. More shadow tolerant species do, however, increase in number. In contrast hereto, some species have an appreciable net recruitment in the grazed woodland, partly due to the preparation of seedbeds and spreading of seeds by the cattle, but also due to the higher influx of light to the woodland understoreys.

The grazed field layer is influenced by the higher influx of light to the surface, the grazing-induced structural unevenness of the sward (grazing *per se* and patchy nutrient reallocation by excreta) and by the cattle's dispersal of seed. Cattle dung pats cover about one percent of the total area, which receive between ten and twenty percent of the nutrients for recycling. The pats contribute between some 5,000 to

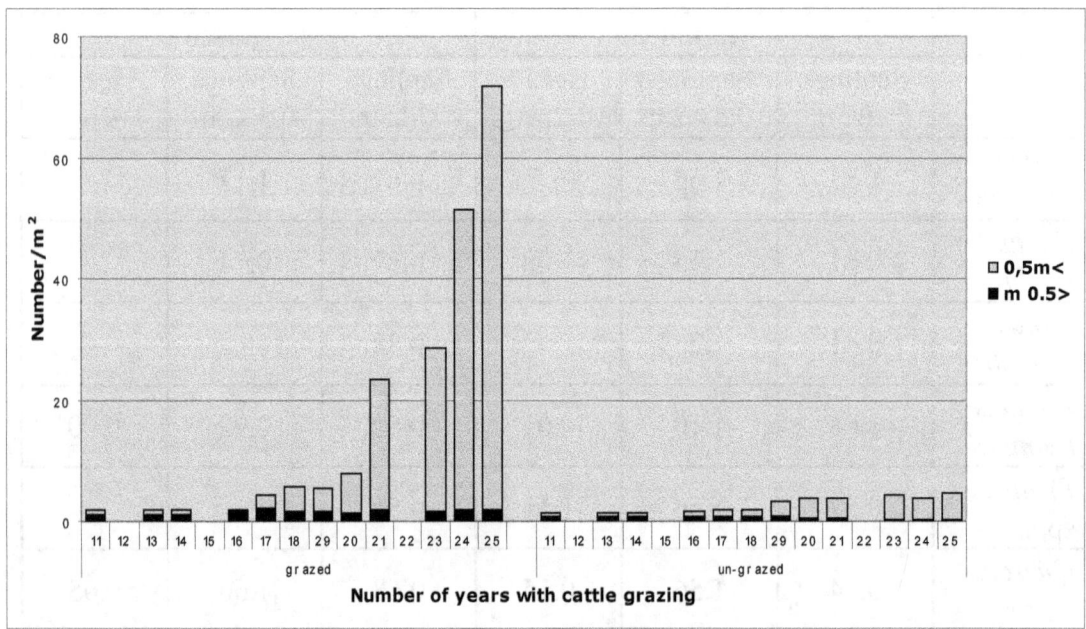

Figure 1. Density of animal spread woody species (*Malus sylvestris*, *Prunus avium*, *P. cerasifera*, *P. spinosa*, *Rosa* spp, *Sorbus aucuparia*) in grazed and un-grazed oak woodland.

10,000 viable seedlings per hectare per year with representation of at least 10% of the Danish higher plant flora (Buttenschøn et al., 2008; R.M. Buttenschøn and J. Buttenschøn, unpublished).

The species number in the grazed woodland is higher than in the un-grazed (Table 2 and Table 3). This applies to woodland character species, semi-shade tolerant species, other herbaceous species and woody species. On the woodland floor in the grazed area cover has become denser during the study with increasing cover in all the above named species groupings, whereas the floor cover is stable in the un-grazed, but shifting towards higher contribution of woodland character species.

While the woodland species proper have a more or less parallel colonisation and expansion under both managements, the assemblage of semi-shadow or woodland boundary species expands largely under the autumn grazing. This is the case with *Melampyrum cristatum* (listed as vulnerable in the *Danish Red Data Book*), which has expanded massively in the present fragmented woodland along the old woodland and now is "present" to "abundant" along the length of the woodland-grassland interface.

The species density increases in young woodland be it grazed or un-grazed (Figure 3). The initial rate of increase and the density, however, is significantly higher in grazed woodland.

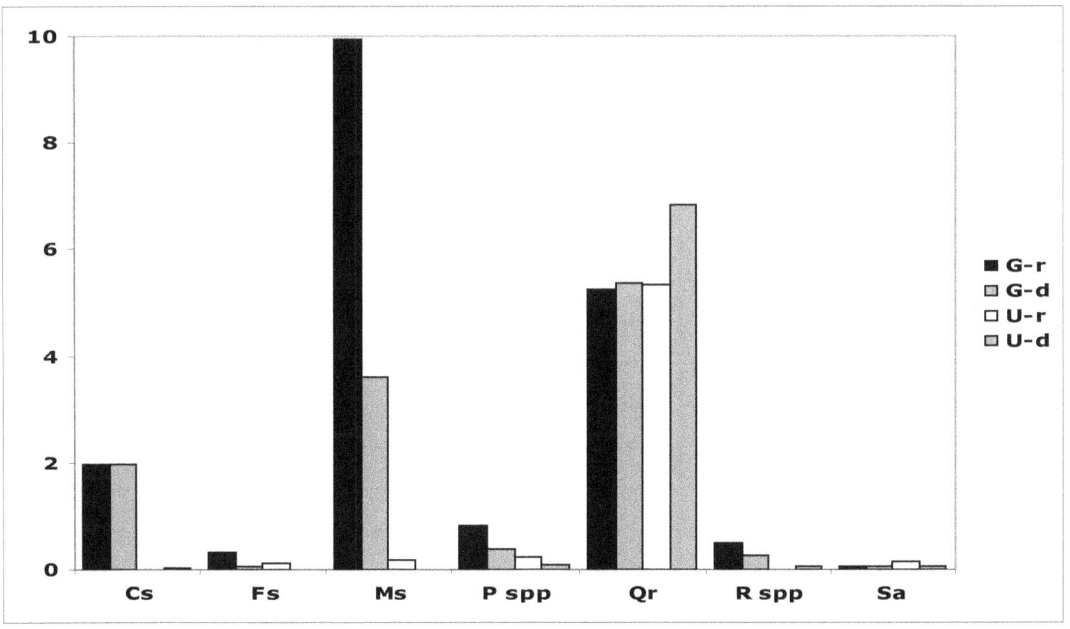

Figure 2. Average recruitment (-r) and death (-d) rate in grazed (G) and un-grazed (U) oak woodland. The species are, left to right *Cytisus scoparius*, *Fagus sylvatica*, *Malus sylvestris*, *Prunus* spp. (*avium, cerasifera, serotina, spinosa*), *Quercus robur*, *Rosa* spp. (*canina, rubiginosa*) and *Sorbus aucuparia*. The rate is individuals per 100 square metres.

Table 2. Numerical presence of species in grazed and un-grazed oak woodland.

Species category	Only grazed	Both	Only un-grazed	sum
Woodland species	2	9	1	12
Semi-shadow species	6	15	2	23
Other species	17	15	5	37
Woody species	4	10	2	16
Sum	29	49	10	

Table 3. Significant increase and decrease (a < 0.001, b < 0.01 and c < 0.5) of the species in young oak woodland based on correlation between time since 1987 and average cover-index. "np" implies not present.

Increase	Grazed	Un-grazed	Decrease	Grazed	Un-grazed
Agrostis tenuis	a	a	*Calluna vulgaris*	a	c
Dactylis glomerata	a		*Galium verum*	a	a
Festuca rubra	a	a	*Hieracium pilosella*	a	
Galium aparine	b	b	*Hypochoeris radicata*	a	np
Stellaria graminea	a		*Luzula campestris*	b	b
Veronica chamaedrys	a		*Pimpinella saxifraga*	b	
Veronica officinalis	b		*Poa pratensis*		c
Carex pilulifera	a		*Rumex acetosella*	b	
Galeopsis bifida	b		*Carex pilulifera*		c
Holcus mollis		b	*Deschampsia flexuosa*	a	a
Poa trivialis	a	np	*Hieracium vulgatum*	b	
Torilis japonica	b	np	*Melampyrum pratense*	c	
Urtica dioeca	a		*Polypodium vulgare*	a	a
Lactuca muralis	np	b	*Cytisus scoparius*	c	
Luzula pilosa	a	b	*Juniperus communis*	a	
Maianthenum bifolia	a	a			
Oxalis acetosella	b	a			
Stellaria holostea	a	a			
Trientalis europaea	b	c			
Viola riviana	a				
Lonicera periclymenum		a			
Malus sylvestris	a				
Populus tremula		c			
Prunus cerasifera	a				
Quercus robur	c				
Rubus idaeus		b			

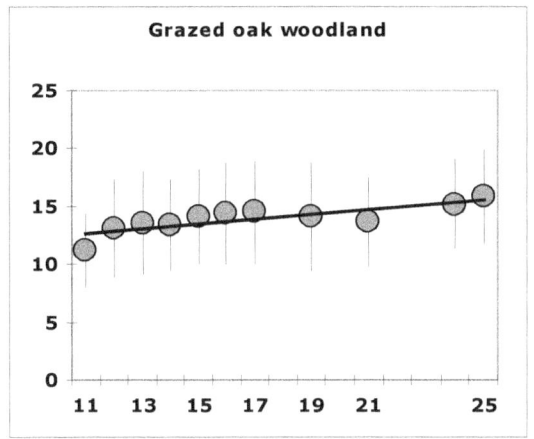 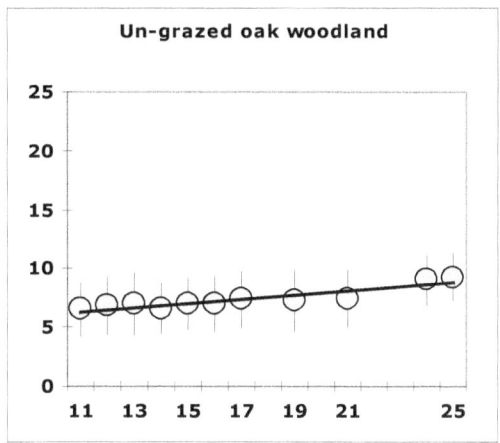

Figure 3. Increase in species density (mean no of species/m^2) in grazed and ungrazed oak woodland 11 to 25 years after grazing was initiated.

From the data from ancient woodland we suggest that density-levels reach a maximum and then decline as the group "other species" decline with falling light levels.

From the up to present 25-year study we conclude that husbandry grazing of woodland with cattle eventually will result in the build-up of a diverse understorey of scrub enriched by animal dispersed species. Without grazing understorey build up is sparse and mostly consists of a persistent bank of minute saplings. The field layer is also more diverse under grazing and the woodland species proper as well as the semi-shade tolerant and less shade tolerant species increase in abundance and cover. The cattle are important for the development as they disperse seeds in their fur or via the alimentary tract, tread seeds into the ground and reallocate nutrients in a patchy pattern, which diversifies growth conditions. Finally, the establishment of the browsing horizon on the larger trees allows more light to the surface.

References

Buttenschøn, J. and Buttenschøn, R.M. (1985) Grazing experiments with cattle and sheep on nutrient poor acidic grassland and heath: IV Establishment of woody species. *Natura Jutlandica*, **(21)**, 117-140.

Buttenschøn, R.M., Odgaard, B, Buttenschøn, J. and Hansen, J.B. (2008) Fra hedeplantage til lysåben græsningsskov. *SKOVEN*, **(03)**, 124-128.

The future potential of wood pastures
Iris Glimmerveen
Woodland Inspirations Limited

Introduction

Wood pastures are intricate usually ancient landscapes as they are an intimate mix of both trees and pasture. Quelch (2010) defines them as: 'Ancient wood pastures in the uplands are areas of grazed pasture, heath or open hill with a scattering of open-grown veteran trees, some of which may have been pollarded in the past', whereas, like Vera (2007) he also described it as: 'a 'Savannah' kind of landscape, being intermediate in character between woodland and (hill) grazing and depending on both' (*pers. comm.* P. Quelch). As wood pastures are so variable, there are probably other ways of describing them and although there might be some difference in emphasis, they still relate to the same habitat.

Having had the opportunity to be closely involved with the discovery and subsequent management of the Geltsdale wood pasture, Cumbria for about eleven years or so (Glimmerveen & Clark, 2008) and latterly with Thornthwaite Hall, Cumbria (Glimmerveen, 2009), whilst also visiting several other upland wood pastures such as Troutbeck, Borrowdale, Langdale in Cumbria, Elan Valley – Wales and Glen Finglas – Scotland and others throughout Europe, I have come to realise that they are very special habitats and on the whole contain four elements, i.e. grazing (Figure 1), trees, archaeology (Figure 2) and wildlife and, depending on the intensity of management, each of those elements and their interactions shape the character of the wood pasture. It generally takes a long time before such interactions become visible or recognisable in the landscape and their clarity further depends on the level of management that has taken place in the past or even currently. However, these interactions not only make for a beautiful landscape, but also create unique opportunities to make use of it.

This paper explores the intricate and multi-functional nature of wood pastures and how people can use it in a sustainable manner.

The potential effects of and use for grazing

Many large grazers, such as cattle, horses, deer and sheep not only eat grass, but also eat leaves and bark to supplement their diet (Figure 3). Young tree leaves are particularly palatable and seedlings and saplings are repeatedly browsed. If there are many mouths to be fed this continues until the trees have either grown tall enough to put their leaves out of the grazer/browser's reach, the trees are protected by fringe and mantle of thorny bushes or by manmade barriers. Without any protection some

Figure 1. Luing cattle grazing in Geltsdale's wood pasture.

Figure 2. Ancient birch in amongst worked stones, Geltsdale.

trees will die, which is why low tree density is a characteristic of wood pastures.

The effect of trees growing up in the presence of continuous grazing can further lead to trees developing a 'basal skirt' (Figure 4), as every year suckers produced by the tree are grazed off by either stock or wild animals. With this process a little bit of timber is laid down causing the tree to produce 'swelling' at the bottom of its trunk. Repeatedly eating leaves from lower branches will further create a browse line, which combined with grass eating will keep the woodland relatively open, at least at low level.

This interest of stock in tree materials could well have been the reason for people to start pollarding their trees, as this enabled them to protect both the tree and to feed the stock its dried leaves or 'leaf hay' at times of low grass production in a controlled manner. The fact that the practice of pollarding has persisted in Cumbria until as recent as the 1970's (pers. comm. C. Brown) shows that both leaves and branch materials (particularly of the more palatable species such as ash) were considered a valuable resource in terms of both minerals and nutrients for stock. Grazing pressure is thus instrumental in shaping wood pasture trees.

Figure 3. Swaledale sheep nibbling ash bark in Langdale, Cumbria.

Figure 4. Basal skirt around alder tree, Thornthwaite Hall, Cumbria.

Table 1. Effects of shelter on livestock

Livestock system	Response to shelter
lamb mortality	10-50% reduction in mortality
milk production	10-20% increase in yield when cows graze in shelter
suckler cows	8% decrease in feed requirements to maintain liveweight with shelter
suckler calves	20% decrease in feed requirements to maintain liveweight with shelter
beef cattle	10-30% decrease to maintain liveweight with shelter
newly shorn ewes	12% mortality in one flock shorn 1-5 days before a storm and turned out in exposed conditions
pasture productivity	10% increase in productivity

Data: Hislop *et al.*, 1999

Large grazers further benefit themselves from the habitat with trees they help to create (Table 1) as it allows them to:

- eat a varied diet, grazing on a wide variety of herbs, grasses and woody materials;
- shelter from wind, rain and sun;
- maintain good condition and therefore increase the chance of producing healthy offspring.

Grazing with livestock not only results in a harvest of a wide range of meat and/or milk products (Table 2), but could potentially also bring a specific type of habitat in favourable/good condition with high biodiversity, and as a spin off also creating ideal deer and game habitat. This so called 'conservation grazing' thus effectively uses grazing animals as a tool to manage or direct the ecological development of certain habitats, but it relies on the herd manager to understand the functioning of the ecosystem he/she is working with and the impact the grazer will have on that habitat. For this kind of management to also be economically viable, the herd manager would further have to be aware of the potential meat and/or milk products his herd can produce. He/she further needs to know how to market them, as the animals generally produce less weight per carcass, but do carry a traditional breed, free range, and/or organic premium from certain buyers (www.thescottishfarmer.co.uk).

Dairy farmers also may have a contract with certain buyers, which could pay them 28-30 p/l for their milk. This is considered a good price for intensive dairy systems in the UK, because they produce milk with a generally low fat content (<5%). More traditional dairy breeds (e.g. Jersey) will demand some premiums, as their milk will have a considerably higher butterfat content (pers. comm. S. Hendry). Further costs for a range of livestock can be found at www.fwi.co.uk, which is regularly updated as these costs fluctuate tremendously.

Table 2. Grazing harvest from livestock

Meat produce	Price at market	Price in shop	Dairy produce	Price in shop
lamb (liveweight)	£1.80-2.20/kg	£15.00/kg	semi-skimmed cows milk	£0.78/l
lamb (deadweight)	£4.50-4.90/kg	£20.00/kg	vanilla ice cream	£0.40/l
venison	£2.50/kg		crème fraiche	£3.30/l
traditional breed beef dead weight	£2.60-2.80/kg	£8.25/kg	yoghurt	£1.50/kg
'ordinary' beef dead weight	£3.00/kg	£4.78/kg	butter	£4.40/kg
ewe	£93 each		halloumi cheese	£8.68/kg
two-year old Scottish Highlander bulls	£2175 average		organic mature cheddar cheese	£8.84/kg
eight-year old oxen sold for logging (Romania)	€1700 each			

Data: www.fwi.co.uk ; www.tesco.com

At first sight Table 2 might suggest that the produce from conservation grazing is valued less than that of the more intensive systems. However, it does not include any of the habitat management benefits the cattle are achieving and is therefore not really a true comparison. To quantify these benefits is difficult, as they include features such as diverse vegetation structure benefiting many ground nesting birds, black grouse in particular, dunging benefiting insects which in turn feed a variety of bird chicks, again including black grouse and cattle tracks for hens to move their chicks through. Other environmental services, such as improving soil health and water quality, are also extremely valuable, and therefore should also be taken into account, but again are difficult to quantify.

To get an approximation however, Knott (pers. comm.) has worked out the income and cost figures for an eighty hectare Forestry Commission site in Scotland, which is grazed with twelve Scottish Highlanders for the specific aim to maintain and enhance the habitat and hence the population of the chequered skipper butterfly (*Carterocephalus palaemon*). He has compared that with figures from other sites, which are mechanically managed, i.e. strimming, for similar purposes (Table 3).

Although the £17.25 per hectare is not a high income, it still compares very favourably with the cost of £112.50 for the mechanical strimming. Moreover, it is likely that private enterprises, as opposed to the Forestry Commission, could benefit from the woodland option

Table 3. Management cost comparison of conservation grazing versus strimming for an 80 ha site.

Income/cost calculations	amount
Beef income from a herd of 12 = £1100 x 12 =	£13,200
Replacement calves = £225 x 12 =	-£2,700
Supplementary concentrates, based on 12.5kg/day for 180 days = 2,250 kg @ £240/tonne =	-£540
Labour to set out concentrates based on 2 hrs/day @ £12/hr x 2 for on costs for 180 days =	-£8,640
Total conservation grazing profit	£1,320
	(£17.25/ha)
Strimming cost based on contract of 2.4 man days/week for 6 months @ £150/day =	£9,000
	(-£112.50/ha)

Data: K. Knott, 2011

within the Scottish Rural Development Programme (RDP) grant, which would generate a further £104 to £111/ha for butterfly habitat improvement, or alternatively £87/ha for basic grazing, which are in addition to for example the beef cattle scheme, which give £100/calf each year if born into the herd; rates for England and Wales RDP may vary. When combined with the rural development grants, conservation grazing can thus be a profitable enterprise.

The potential use of trees and shrubs

Like any tree, wood pasture trees have a wide range of functions, such as production of oxygen, locking up carbon dioxide, reduction of noise and dust, *etc*, but the open grown shape of a wood pasture tree further allows for the creation of substantially sized branches with bends, which are perfect for use in the wooden shipbuilding industry, roofing timbers of churches and other buildings, as well as the bespoke furniture trade (Table 4).

A myriad of other products can be created from wood pasture timbers (Table 5), each of which has a specific end use and therefore takes precise skills and expertise to be produced, e.g. for an oak swill basket the oak needs to be cut to size, steamed in a long tub over a fire for four hours and then split into strips and used to weave the baskets (www.oakswills.co.uk). Although these baskets are created in a traditional manner, they have retained their usefulness through time (Figure 5).

Wood turners particularly favour 'burr' timber, which is created through repeated browsing of epicormic shoots,

Table 4. Estimated timber value of an open grown tree.

1 butt = 33.33 hoppus ft (= 1.2 m³)
(good straight planking quality @ 12' long and 20" quarter girth)
At £10/hoppus feet the butt is worth:
£330 for oak or
£150 for ash at roadside

Data: D. Frost, 2011

as it makes for characterful finished pieces (Figure 6) and can therefore be highly valued (www.jonathanleech.co.uk).

Reinstating traditional practices, or importing them from other places, could well add to the product range of trees. For instance 'leaf hay' was produced from pollarded trees in Scandinavia, where during summer branches with leaves were cut, dried and stored so that additional nutrients could be available when the grass sward is least productive, i.e. at drought or winter times (Quelch, 2009). However, Martin Clark (*pers. comm.*) recently found in south Romania up a wooded valley near Baile Herculanum close to the Danube '*the most stunning wood pasture on a recognised route to a high pasture, so the cattle are taken through and graze on the way. The farmer/cowherd is still pollarding the trees - to get (amongst other things) poles for hayricks & firewood. Most interesting is the use of a hollow beech tree for cooking. He has cut a draft/smoke hole at around 2 metres and the inside is gently smouldering - the fuel being the dead & rotten wood. The bole of the tree was warm to touch, but the forester told me later that day that this was common practice for cooking & smoking food and trees were not killed by it as long as the draft up the hollow trunk was controlled*' (Figure 7).

Pollarded trees further have the advantage that they can produce materials on a relatively short cycle while the main bole keeps growing; it is therefore inherently a very productive system of good straight and similar sized timber. In Cumbria there is still living memory of trees being pollarded

Table 5. Value of some processed tree products.

Product	Price	Unit
Firewood	£50.00	0.5 tonne bag
Charcoal	£3.80	3 kg bag
Large elm burr bowl	£245.00	each
Oak swill basket	£52.00	22" each
Garden bench	±£250.00	4 ft each
Oak beam fireplace	±£200.00	each
Roofing shakes/shingles	£80.00	m²

Data: I. Taylor, 2011; J. Leech, 2011

Figure 5. Owen Jones creating an oak swill basket at Talkin Treemendous, Cumbria.

Figure 6. Burr elm bowl turned and finished by Danny Frost.

in the 1970's (*pers. comm.* C. Brown) and the National Trust now has an active pollarding programme (Figure 8), which is informed by initial tree surveys and leading to prioritized tree management. Objectives for this work include conservation and associated biodiversity, landscape and cultural heritage reasons. Often the cut material is purposefully left in fields for much appreciated stock-browse, before usually being removed for firewood (pers. comm. J. Hooson). Use for leaf hay or other value adding products has not been considered as yet.

Shrubs have traditionally been coppiced (i.e. cut at stump and then allowed to regrow) by people for a wide variety of purposes. Some of these uses have continued to the present day, i.e. paling made from sweet chestnut and hazel spars for thatched roofs, others are seeing a revival, i.e. dead hedging materials to protect tree seedlings from grazing and hazel hurdles, while others still are given a complete new lease of life, i.e. willow rods to weave living arbor seats or large scale sculptures (Figure 9). A wide range of such coppice products can be found on www.coppice-products.co.uk.

Figure 7. Hollow beech used for cooking/smoking food in a wood pasture near Baile Herculanum, south Romania.

Figure 8. Recently re-pollarded ash in Borrowdale.

Figure 9. Willow sculpture, created by Phil Bradley, at Talkin Treemendous, Cumbria.

Figure 10. Hawthorn berries, Geltsdale.

Other shrub produce that has seen a revival in recent years is the use of some for their materials in food or as an active ingredient in herbal remedies. For instance hawthorn berries (Figure 10) are used to make syrups or gels (wildforager.survivalistssite.com), but can also combat heart disease, angina, diarrhea, dysentery and kidney inflammation (www.herbalremediesinfo.com). Both websites give a wealth of other uses for our native shrubs and trees.

The benefits of wood pastures to archaeology

Continuous and relatively light grazing further benefits any archaeology contained in a grazed area, as no ploughing is needed and therefore the features buried within or below the surface of a site are not disturbed, other than perhaps some rubbing from stock on protruding items, which might dislodge some of the smaller pieces. It may therefore not come as a surprise that in the uplands wood pastures with important archaeology have been found on hill slopes and/or tucked away in remote places, such as Geltsdale (Figure 11) as opposed to the more fertile valley bottoms. The archaeology is further more visible with grazing and therefore gives the opportunity for it to be recorded and protected.

Ancient trees contained in a wood pasture site can further contribute to or inform the archaeological study of a site. This is because they are usually the longest living component of the site and therefore their shape, habit, growth form and size, together with tree coring data (should that be available) can reflect its past management. For instance lapsed coppiced or pollarded trees are evidence of those management practices in the past, while repeated pollarding will further show up as a cyclical widening and narrowing of tree ring patterns (Mills, Quelch and Stewart, 2009). Pollard tree location can also be indicative of past land use (Figure 12), as tall well-maintained cropping ash pollards are mostly on the lower slopes, i.e. within easy access to (past) farmers and livestock (Quelch, 2007).

Figure 11. A circular archaeological feature, Geltsdale.

Figure 12. Pollarded ash in Langdale's medieval landscape setting.

This means that a wealth of past information can be contained within wood pasture sites, which with care can be unlocked and combined with historical information, so that today's people can gain insights into the sustainable way past people made use of these places.

The benefits of wood pastures to wildlife

The open grown crown of a wood pasture tree further creates a large volume of three-dimensional space, which can be occupied by a wide variety of wildlife to provide nest and roosting spaces for birds, bats and other animals alike. It further provides the all important shade for (grazing) animals and space for them to shelter from adverse weather conditions (Table 1).

Shrub and bushes also form an integral part of a wood pasture; thorny bushes in particular are instrumental to the regeneration of broadleaved trees in the presence of grazing, as they can form a 'fringe and mantle' to a broadleaved sapling, thereby protecting it from browsing by large grazers (Vera, Buissink and Weidema, 2004). These and other bushes or small trees also provide a good variety of foodstuffs for wildlife, such as berries and nuts (Table 6). They further attract a wide variety of insects, which form food for small songbirds and mammals alike; together they contribute to the wood pasture's biodiversity.

Grazing by large ruminants (Figure 13) further benefits other wildlife in many different ways, as they:

- cut through dense herb layer with their hooves, thereby creating small spaces of bare soil in which seeds can drop and germinate;

- transport seeds in their coats;

- create open space or glades, providing sheltered sunny microhabitats, which is good for most flora and fauna, flowers, fungi and butterflies in particular;

- create diverse edge habitat, providing good habitat for a wide variety of food bearing bush trees;

- allow trees to gain the opportunity to develop their full crown;

Table 6. Foodstuffs from trees and bushes for wildlife.

Animal	Preferred food
insects	nectar, e.g. rose
large tortoiseshell butterfly	aspen, poplar, willow
white admiral butterfly	bramble
vapourer moth	hawthorn, hazel, lime, oak
mistletoe marble moth	mistletoe
song thrush	yew, sloe, elder, guelder rose
waxwing	guelder rose
nuthatch	hazel nut
bullfinch	rowan berry
black grouse	birch buds and berries
fieldfare & redwings	berries (hawthorn, rowan, juniper)
common dormice	bramble
badger	juniper berries
mice & voles	berries

- ensure dappled shade on the tree stem, creating good microhabitat for lichens, mosses, bats and spiders;
- dung and thus provide a good additional food source for invertebrates, who in turn 'fuel' the wood pasture's food web.

For these reasons, large grazers are used as 'tools' in conservation grazing to restore and maintain different types of habitat including wood pastures in favourable condition. Animals used for this type of grazing should be adapted to local conditions and it therefore follows that local, native breeds should be preferred, whether cattle, sheep, deer or horses (Figure 14), as at least in theory they are most suitable. It is further important to graze with a diverse age and sex structure of a herd, as that allows the veteran cattle, for example, to lead the group well and know what to do in adverse weather. Mixed sex herds allow bulls to become more solitary and ranging higher up the hill, while the females stay on the lower land (Quelch & Foster, 2005). These behavioural changes cause significant effects on grazed land, e.g. to set out its territory a bull creates scrapes which, whether wet or dry, add to the diversity of the available micro habitats. A 'Woodland Grazing Toolbox' has been devised by the Forestry Commission to help decide what type of grazing is best for a woodland/wood pasture (www.forestry.gov.uk). In the process they are likely to generate good quality meat and/or milk, which if not completely organic is likely to be produced close to natural conditions.

However, this kind of management relies on the herd manager to fully understand:

- the functioning of the ecosystem his/her herd is to graze;

Figure 13. Highland cattle herd in Anloo, Netherlands.

Figure 14. Konik horses in Oostvaardersplassen, Netherlands.

- the specific type of monitoring required for the desired key species and habitats;

- which type of stock is most suitable to the site/ecosystem;

- type of grazer available;

- health and welfare of the herd(s);

- length of time the herd should be deployed;

- marketability of stock produce (breeding animals, meat, milk);

- immediate positive and adverse impacts on the ecosystem.

These factors combined will determine whether the desired outcome for the habitat can be achieved and whether such management is sustainable in the long term (pers. comm. S. Hendry).

The benefits of wood pastures to people

Wood pastures are thus valued by people for their trees, grazing, wildlife and archaeology and it is particularly the old wood pasture remnants we see today that are extremely important, as persisting over a long time, they have been allowed to grow old and therefore give us an opportunity to study the ecological processes that have taken place over time and to re-learn how people managed such sites in the past. They further give a sense of history, continuity of traditional ownership and a sense of place. Just for these reasons alone they are well worth conserving, let alone the wealth of ancient trees, biodiversity and archaeology they may contain.

However, if we are to sustain the benefits of wood pastures in the future, then we should not only protect and rediscover what still persists today, but also enhance them so that they can develop to their full potential, both in terms of ecology and benefits to people.

Should our existing wood pastures turn out to be too precious because of their bio-cultural historic landscape values to be turned over to productive use, however extensively, then maybe now is the time to create new ones. Already in 2003 the then Royal Society for the Protection of Birds manager at the Geltsdale reserve and myself made use of two consequential Forestry Commission grants (Joining and Increasing Grant Scheme for Ancient Woodlands or JIGSAW and the Woodland Creation Grant), to plant Bruthwaite, a 160-hectare new native woodland (Figure 15). As Geltsdale contains a black grouse population, the Forestry Commission allowed us to plant at relative low densities, which will enable the site to be turned over to wood pasture once the trees are well established. A wide range of locally native tree species mixes were used to maximise the benefits to wildlife, in addition to which a relatively small section (two hectares) was added with a view to produce hazel coppice. The trees are growing well and it won't be long before a cattle herd can be allowed in.

Following some special training events (Figure 16), the Woodland Trust's woodland creation team in Wales have also recognised that wood pastures are beneficial to many situations and are therefore piloting information days to encourage farmers to create new wood pastures or to enhance some existing ones. This pilot will take place over a year to gauge the response and outcome (K. Owen, pers. comm.).

With skill this will enable us to produce many of the food and timber items we need close to home, thereby significantly reducing both food and timber miles, while also making the most productive use of the land. It is recognised that such land use will need to be economically viable too, which should be possible to achieve with even a single, albeit a niche market product, but is much more likely if an income was derived from any combination of produce available. Should we be able to do this in a sustainable and stable manner, than we may even enjoy the wood pastures and their produce for all time.

In addition to all the benefits mentioned above, people in general like to be in wood pastures. Their open spaces makes it safe for them to be in, while the high biodiversity gives them a good chance to see wildlife at a safe distance. The varied components,

Figure 15. 160 ha of new wood pasture at Bruthwaite, Geltsdale.

Figure 16. Wood pasture training event at Elan Valley, Wales.

woodlands, bushes, single trees and open spaces make for a beautiful landscape which are easy to enjoy by both visitors and locals alike.

Wood pastures are thus ideal places for people to be in. This could be because within wood pastures, people can fully experience for themselves what it is like to be an integral part of the idyllic pastoral scene where an animal is peacefully grazing in an open space surrounded by bush fringed woodland and the odd majestic tree (Figure 17). A little stream bubbles through the glade and you yourself can pick at will from the plants or trees to quench either hunger or thirst. Add to this the notion that at any moment you can come face to face with an amazing wild animal, then it is perhaps no surprise that, subconsciously at least, people are reminded of arcadia. Where you can live in harmony within the ideal landscape, where everything you require is within easy reach and where you can be drawn with peace of mind to either tree enclosed spaces for inward looking contemplation, or open spaces for blue sky thinking, or to simply rest safely underneath a tree. No wonder then that many artists have been inspired to use wood pasture landscapes to portray their paradise and that a small wood pasture, the Borkener Paradies in north west Germany (Figure 18), is actually named after it.

Acknowledgements

Brown, C. (pers. comm., 19-2-2011). Retired from National Trust. cliffwalter.brown@gmail.co.uk

Clark, M. (pers. comm., 15-6-2011). Director, Grampus Heritage & Training Limited, Cumbria.

Corbett, V. Photographer, www.valcorbettphotography.com

Frost, D. (pers. comm., 8-6-2011). Furniture designer & maker, www.dannyfrost.co.uk.

Hendry, S. (pers. comm. 2011) Grazing and Livestock Manager, Cowal and Trossachs Forest District, Forestry Commission Scotland, stewart.hendry@forestry.gsi.gov.uk.

Figure 17. Dream of Arcadia, Thomas Cole, 1834.

Figure 18. Borkener Paradies, North East Germany.

Hooson, J. (pers. comm. 18-5-2011). Wildlife & Countryside Adviser, The National Trust, (North West Region), The Hollens, Grasmere, Ambleside, Cumbria, LA22 9QZ.

Knott, K. (pers. comm. 28-6-2011). Environment and Conservation Manager, Lochaber, Forestry Commission Scotland, kenneth.knott@forestry.gsi.gov.uk.

Owen, K. (pers. comm. 30-6-2011). Senior Verifier, Ancient Tree Hunt, Woodland Trust, katherineowen@woodlandtrust.org.uk.

Quelch, P. (pers. comm., 2002). Peter Quelch Woodland Services, Independent Woodland Adviser, peter.quelch@btinternet.com.

Taylor, I. (pers. comm. 10-6-2011). www.lakelandcoppiceproducts.co.uk

References

Glimmerveen, I. (2009) *Thornthwaite Hall's wood pasture*. Unpublished report for Natural England, Cumbria.

Glimmerveen, I. and Clark, M. (2008) *Geltsdale's wood pasture*. East Cumbria Countryside Project (now available from the authors).

Hislop, M., Gardiner, B, Palmer, H. and Bailey, R. (1999) *The value of shelter woods on farms in Cumbria*. Forest Research, Edinburgh.

Mills, C., Quelch, P. and Stewart, M. (2009) *The evidence of tree forms, tree-rings and documented history around Bealach nam Bo, Loch Katrine*. Available from the authors.

Owen, K. *Seeds of inspiration*. Photographer http://www.flickr.com/photos/katherineowen/sets/72157626807701813/

Quelch, P and Foster, S. (2005) Glen Garry woodland grazing project site visit. *Livestock in woods*. Newsletter Spring 2005, **7**.

Quelch, P. (2007) *Seathwaite wood pasture. Bassenthwaite wood pasture project (4)*, Unpublished report, Grampus Heritage & Training Limited.

Quelch, P. (2009) *Woodland Archaeology in Cumbria – Stone Gate Stoups & Drying leaf hay in Norway*. Poster presentation at Time Honoured Trees, Cumbria Wood & Forestry Festival.

Quelch, P. (2010) Upland Wood Pastures. In: *Landscape Archaeology and Ecology – End of Tradition*, **8(2)**, 172-177.

Vera, F., Buissink, F. and Weidema, J. (2004) *Wildernis in Nederland*. Het verhaal van bossen en beesten, page 85. Tirion Uitgevers BV, Baarn.

Vera, F. (2007) The wood-pasture theory and the deer park: the grove – the origin of the deer park. *Landscape Archaeology and Ecology*, **6**, 107-112.

http://en.wikipedia.org/wiki/File:Cole_Thomas_The_Course_of_Empire_The_Arcadian_or_Pastoral_State_1836.jpg

www.coppice-products.co.uk/Glossary.htm, accessed 15-6-2011.

www.forestry.gov.uk/woodlandgrazingtoolbox

www.fwi.co.uk/gr/markets%20AAG.pdf, accessed 17-6-2011.

www.herbalremediesinfo.com/Hawthorn.html, accessed 16-6-2011.

www.jonathanleech.co.uk/my-work.aspx, accessed 15-6-2011.

www.oakswills.co.uk/buy.html, accessed 15-6-2011

www.tesco.com/groceries, accessed 16-6-2011.

www.thescottishfarmer.co.uk/news/this-weeks-news/morrisons-go-native-1.1103670, accessed 17-6-2011.

www.wildforager.survivalistssite.com/edible.html, accessed 16-6-2011.

All images by the author unless otherwise stated.

Impact of the reintroduction of wild boar into the Forest of Dean, UK

Martin Goulding
British Wild Boar Organisation

Introduction

Wild boar became extinct in the United Kingdom (UK) towards the end of the thirteenth century. Since the early 1990s, escaped or deliberately released farmed wild boar, from stock originally imported from continental Europe, have re-established free-living populations in several UK counties. For example, wild boar were reintroduced into the Forest of Dean, in the county of Gloucestershire, in 2004 when 25-30 animals suddenly appeared. The tame demeanour and diurnal behaviour of these animals implied they were captive-bred and had been deliberately released. No person or organisation accepted responsibility for the release nor any owner traced. Since 2004, the population has increased and in the absence of any natural predation (lynx and wolf are extinct from the UK), the Forestry Commission have implemented a year round culling policy to reduce, but not eradicate, wild boar numbers.

Figure 1. Map showing the location of the Forest of Dean, Gloucestershire, UK.

Implications

The implications of the wild boars' return are many. They have overturned areas of amenity grasslands, roadside verges, and sports fields. The Forestry Commission also report wild boar damaging garden fences and entering the private gardens of residential properties. Wild boar can on occasion be aggressive and as such are a potential threat to public safety. Recreational activities such as dog walking, rambling, and cycling are popular throughout the Forest and wild boar have come into contact with the public on numerous occasions. To-date, no-one has been killed or seriously injured by a wild boar, although reports sporadically emerge of people needing to take evasive action after being chased by a wild boar. Only one incident of injury to a human has been reported to the Forestry Commission, whereby an individual hand feeding an adult boar that had become urbanised was slightly injured as the boar reacted to the actions of a second bystander. Domestic dogs off the lead have been attacked and wounded by wild boar, and resulting injuries have led to at least one dog being put to sleep, an incident that was widely reported in the local media. However, the Forestry Commission suggest a greater number of deaths, 'around 5 or 6'. Road traffic accidents have also occurred; 22 wild boar were recorded as being killed in road accidents in the Forest of Dean in the period 1st April 2010 to 31st March 2011. Minor injuries to drivers have been reported. Wild boar have damaged growing crops and rooted up pasture in agricultural fields in close proximity to the Forest of Dean, but to-date no assessment of the scale of damage has been reported. Livestock disease has not

Figure 2. The Forest of Dean

Photograph: Martin Goulding www.britishwildboar.org.uk

to-date become an issue, but one wild boar in woodland close to the Forest of Dean has been confirmed to be infected with *Mycobacterium bovis*, the causative agent of tuberculosis in cattle.

Impacts

The wild boar have not had a significant impact upon the growing of timber trees within the forest as they do not graze on the trees (as do deer species) nor do they damage tree bark. Furthermore, the wild boar are likely to increase species' richness through their rooting behaviour breaking up monocultures of grass and bracken on the forest floor, creating seed beds and allowing dormant seeds or annual plants to germinate. However, the exact effect of the wild boar on woodland flora and fauna within the Forest of Dean is currently unknown. The wild boar have considerable appeal to field sports enthusiasts and entrepreneurial individuals advertise wild boar shooting opportunities on private land adjacent to the forested areas. A survey investigating public perception to the wild boar in the Forest of Dean showed 67% of 950 responses from the resident community were unconcerned by their presence. Visitors to the forest responded with over 80% indicating they were unconcerned.

The wild boar in the Forest of Dean will continue to be managed by the Forestry Commission, whose primary management objective is to maintain a level of population control to reduce the risk of conflict between the general public living in or visiting the Forest of Dean.

References

Stannard, K.G. (2010) *Feral Wild Boar Management Plan, Forest of Dean, 2011 to 2016*. Forestry Commission, England. http://www.britishwildboar.org.uk/Feral Wild Boar Management Plan Forest of Dean.pdf Accessed 23 August 2011

Knepp Castle Estate Wildland Project
Charles Burrell, Bt.[1], Theresa Greenaway[2]
Knepp Castle Estate[1,2]

The Knepp Castle Estate

The Knepp Castle Estate lies to the south of Horsham, West Sussex. Its long history has resulted in a number of features of archaeological, cultural and geological interest, including the remains of the original eleventh century castle. Knepp Castle Estate originated in the Middle Ages, when it was one of King John's hunting parks. It now extends to a total of 1,416ha. The original Estate seems to have been a hunting park throughout the mediaeval period, following which the land was used for iron working in the sixteenth century. Since this industry fell into decay, the Estate has been an area of farmland and woods. Following World War II, it was increasingly under intensive farming. An unusual feature of the Estate is that its historic field system has largely been retained. Many fields are 4ha or less, and are still bordered by hedgerows.

The Estate lies within the Low Weald Natural Area and has a heavy clay soil. It is traversed by the River Adur and some of its tributaries. Kneppmill Pond is a hammer pond constructed for nearby iron workings prior to 1568. There are two Sites of Nature Conservation Interest (SNCI) on the Estate.

Vision for Knepp Castle Estate

Development of the vision

Charlie Burrell, the present owner, has had a life-long ambition to recreate the landscape probably designed by Humphry Repton. This was laid out when the modern Knepp Castle was built by the architect John Nash in about1806 for the Burrell family. As steps were taken to achieve this restoration, the project grew and developed into a far more ambitious scheme to create a landscape-scale wildland in which a variety of large herbivores would roam freely. As far as possible, these animals would be 'de-domesticated'. Near-natural grazing would be replicated with the animals utilising the land with as little human intervention as possible. The intention was that this near-natural grazing system would ultimately include a large part of the Estate.

The Knepp Estate, in conjunction with the Environment Agency and Natural England, also proposes to 're-wild' the part of the River Adur crossing the Estate. This involves restoring the Adur floodplain to its natural function and the river itself as far as possible to its original course before canalisation.

Figure 1. Map showing the extent of the Wildland Project Area.

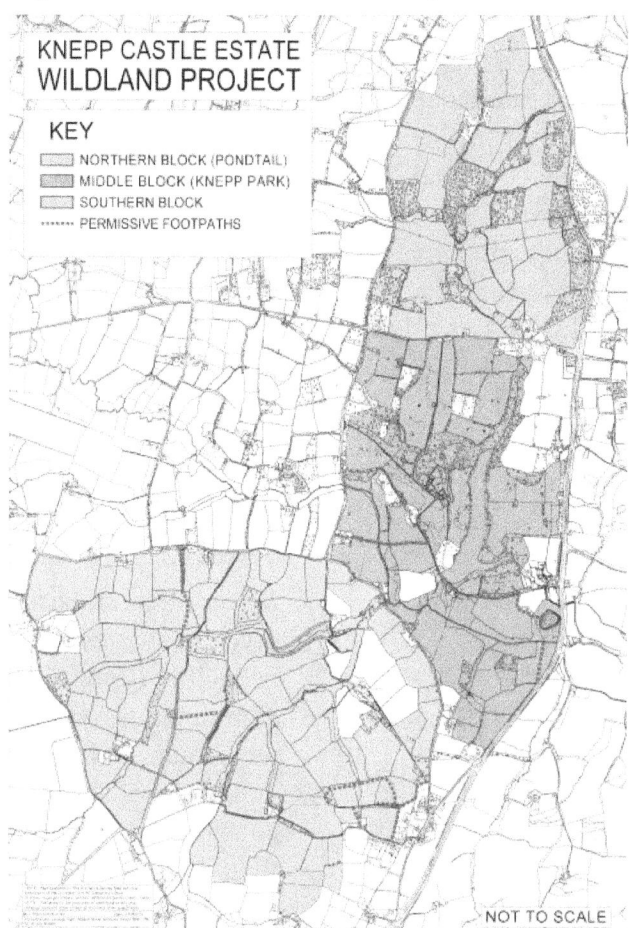

The aim of the Wildland Project

The 'Vision' soon evolved into the Knepp Wildland Project. Unlike the management strategies of nature reserves and designated protected areas, the management of the Wildland project had no ecological targets. Instead, the overall aim was to record and evaluate changes in the biodiversity and vegetation structure following the reversion of land under intensive arable management to a more natural grazing regime. The research emphasis was, and continues to be, on the processes driving such changes and their effects at a landscape scale. It is very rare, especially in southeast England, to have the opportunity to evaluate ecological changes and issues on a site as large as Knepp. This opportunity is immeasurably enhanced by the vision and active participation of its owner Charlie Burrell.

The first stages

Knepp Castle Park has 'historic parkland' status, so it was possible to revert large areas from arable to parkland under Natural England's Countryside Stewardship Scheme (CSS), a reversion of historical relevance. The restoration of the deer park began in 2001, when some 202ha of this former park were taken out of arable and commercial grassland. This land was deer fenced and internal boundary fences were removed. The ground was 'sterilised' by continual cultivation and spraying with herbicide, and subsequently planted with native grasses. About 28ha also included a wild flower seed mix. In 2004, the deer park was extended by a further 106ha, of which approximately 35ha were already in CSS, and the remainder was entered into CSS at this time. This brought the size of the deer park to over 283ha. The additional area of land entered into CSS in 2004 was treated differently. Following the removal of wheat and rape, the seedbeds were cultivated, sprayed with herbicide and drilled with stewardship grasses. In 2005 a second park was created as a further area north of the A272 was entered into CSS, bringing the project area to approximately 322ha.

Fallow deer were introduced from Petworth and Gunton Parks in February 2002, longhorn cattle in June 2003, followed by six Exmoor fillies in November 2003 and a stallion in 2005. In early January 2005, two Tamworth sows and their eight piglets were introduced. This brought the stocking levels up to an estimate of around 550 animals for summer 2005 – about 500 deer, 6-10 ponies, 16 cattle with 13 calves and 10 sows. Roe deer were already present on the Estate and in the wider countryside, and special gates allow them freedom to roam.

In 2009, the project area was extended by a further 445ha to encompass the southwest corner of Knepp Castle Estate. Following the completion of fencing around this third area, 53 head of cattle were put on at the end of May, 10 Exmoor ponies at the end of August and some 20 Tamworth pigs in September. The fencing was mostly funded by Natural England and brought the Wildland Project area to some 1,000ha.

Rationale and background

Landscape-scale ecology

Much attention has traditionally been given to studies on the ecology and behaviour of individual species or small communities, typically on timescales of three years or less and spatial scales of 10m or less. This may accord well with constraints integral to the timescale and funding of academic research but the pressing concerns of conservation biology are on longer time scales and vastly greater spatial scales (May, 1994).

The 'Single Large or Several Small' debate has been going on since the 1970s and the limitations of both options were summarised by Rosenweig (1995). The concept of 'stewardship' (Whitbread and Jenman, 1995) is compatible with the management of small reserves. However, doubts about the effectiveness of this strategy to conserve biodiversity, and the high economic cost of maintaining small areas of habitats and populations of species of high conservation concern, are resulting in increasing support for large-scale areas in which natural or near-natural processes drive biodiversity conservation. Linking nature and planning on a landscape scale has numerous advantages over conservation in small fragmented reserves, and is now considered to be an essential approach in the conservation of biodiversity in Europe (Hodder *et al.*, 2005).

One of the drivers progressing landscape-scale conservation in Europe has been *Natura 2000* which in turn derived from the *Habitats Directive* (Council Directive on the Conservation of Natural Habitats and Wild Fauna and Flora 92/43/EEC) and the *Birds Directive* (79/409/EEC). This initiated a European network of protected nature areas. In the Netherlands, the National Ecological Network comprises a spatially coherent network of existing and new nature areas that should be ready by 2018 (Anon., 2004). In Britain, the concept of restoring near-natural ecosystems by near-natural processes was expounded by Whitbread and Jenman in 1995.

Grazing as a driver for landscape scale ecological processes

Frans Vera's study of the effects of grazing on forest history (Vera, 2000) has excited much interest, invoked much support, raised a number of issues and provoked considerable discussion if not dissent - all of which have served to enliven and enrich ecological theory and, it is to be hoped, practice. This report is not the place to engage upon an evaluation of Vera's lengthy dissertation, but quoting the null and alternative hypotheses may be useful:

- **Null hypothesis**: *"That pedunculate and sessile oak and hazel survive in a closed forest and regenerate in gaps in the canopy in accordance with Watt's gap phase model (1947) and Leibundgut's cyclical model (1959, 1978). Large herbivores present in the natural state are dependent on the developments of the vegetation. According to this hypothesis, they do not have an influence on the course of the succession and regeneration of forests."*

- **Alternative hypothesis**: *"That the natural vegetation consists of a mosaic of large and small grasslands, scrub, solitary trees and trees growing in groups (groves), in which the indigenous fauna of large herbivores is essential for the regeneration of species of trees and shrubs which are characteristic in Europe. According to this hypothesis, wood-pasture should be seen as the closest modern analogy of this landscape."*

Vera's thesis itself was based largely on a literature search. English Nature's interest in Vera's theories resulted in an initial evaluation of his seminal work (Kirby, 2003) followed by a further report by Hodder *et al.* (2005), which concluded that the case for Vera's alternative hypothesis was not proven. Apart from the historical validity (or not) of this hypothesis, there is considerable interest in the use of grazing as a way of generating diverse modern landscapes, inspired to some extent by the Dutch Oostvaardersplassen reserve.

Oostvaardersplassen is one component of the Dutch ecological network. Derived from reclaimed polderland in 1968, it is now a 5,600ha nature reserve (Whitbread and Jenman, 1995) that has become one of the most influential examples of management by the implementation of near-natural processes. The role of free-ranging herbivores in this system has inspired a huge amount of interest, influencing theoretical ecology as well as practical conservation. However, Oostvaardersplassen is unlikely to have any direct analogue in the UK. It started from a low-biodiversity baseline of reclaimed land, inheriting no protected species or priority habitats. The grazing can truly be said to be 'near-natural' grazing rather than 'conservation grazing'. By contrast, in the UK, conservation grazing has tended to be implemented to maintain specific open landscapes or historical pasture woodlands.

It might be useful at this point to clarify what is meant by 'naturalistic' or 'near-natural' grazing and 'extensive' or 'conservation' grazing. These terms do not have formal definitions but depend on compliance or otherwise with the adherence to natural processes, and the following summary is based on Hodder and Bullock (2005): - In *naturalistic grazing*, there would be no specified grazing density, the grazing animals would be the key ecosystem drivers and natural processes would be allowed to proceed. Herbivore populations would be limited by resources, fluctuating according to the amount of food available, the vicissitudes of climate and the impacts of parasites and pathogens. The natural process would be seen as an aim in itself. By contrast, the practice of *extensive* or *conservation grazing* systems acts as intervention that is aimed at achieving targets for habitat and species composition.

In practice, grazing regimes such as that currently in place at Knepp lie somewhere between these two ends of the scale. The main reason for this is that although large in the context of lowland England reserves, the Knepp Estate is still too small to allow natural population fluctuation, especially in the absence of large predators. The term 'more natural', despite its lack of definition, is therefore used here, indicating the intention to allow grazing that is as naturalistic as possible within certain constraints.

The need for more research

Although giving a stimulating incentive to ecological theory, relating Vera's theory to biodiversity conservation is fraught with complexity. Kirby (2003) cites Olff *et al.* (1999), who question whether releasing free-ranging large grazers in former agricultural areas will really counteract the ongoing loss of biodiversity, as it is intensive agricultural practices themselves that have contributed to this loss. Putting a number of large grazers onto arable reversion land thus feeds into the Vera cycle on a far more impoverished level than would have been the case in pre-industrialised Europe. Rewilding including the restoration of 'naturalistic' grazing may be the optimal conservation strategy for the maintenance and restoration of biodiversity in Europe (Vera, 2000), but in the short term, it may be unrealistic to expect much increase in biodiversity, certainly as far as the less mobile species are concerned.

The impacts of a given cattle grazing regime on a particular woodland cannot yet be predicted, and Armstrong *et al* (2003) collated information from cattle-grazed woodlands across the UK. Although focussing on conservation grazing by one kind of herbivore (cattle), this study nevertheless gives a large amount of information gleaned from visited and unvisited grazed woodland sites. Much of this information is subjective and the authors observe that at many sites some form of quantitative monitoring was undertaken but results seldom analysed or published.

The primary objectives for grazing sites may be very different – for example, wilderness creation, biodiversity conservation or enhancement, or to maintain an open habitat such as heathland or wood pasture. In Holland as well as in the UK, grazing has been used as a conservation tool, particularly on open biotopes such as grasslands and heath (Ausden and Treweek, 1995; Kuiters, 2002; Symes and Day 2003), and increasingly, grazing in woodlands is being considered (Armstrong *et al*, 2003). Extracting rigorous scientific information from these, or monitoring the effects of grazing is hampered both because there has been no inventory of the site prior to the introduction of grazing and also because other management measures are implemented at the same time (Kuiters, 2002; Sutherland, 1995). Kuiters also comments that there has been little research on the effects of grazing on the underlying processes of soil microclimate, and the resultant knock-on effects on seed germination, seedling recruitment, invertebrates and reptiles. Studies are often limited spatially and temporally, and their results may appear contradictory. Further knowledge is needed on the underlying mechanisms driving habitat dynamics and diversity both with and in the absence of grazing, and this is relevant to all sites at all scales. Grazing-related issues identified by Kuiters (2002) as needing further research can be summarised as follows:

- Research into underlying processes influenced or affected by grazing.

- Evaluation of effects of grazing on flora, in relation to soil type, topography and other factors.

- Research on effects of grazing on fauna.

- Further exploration of Vera's work.

- Role of thorny scrub in woodland regeneration in relation to soil type.

- Grazing density and timing.

Other Issues

Apart from the issues raised above, near-natural grazing brings with it a number of other issues that need to be addressed. Many of these have been identified, and continue to be appraised, in the Oostvaardersplassen project (Van Leewen *et al.*, 2003):-

- Animal health – risk to farm livestock from spread of diseases such as foot-and-mouth disease.

- Human health – transference of diseases such as anthrax to humans.

- Animal welfare – issues include loss of condition in winter, supplementary feeding that reduces the 'near-natural' ethic; dealing with ill, injured or very old animals; use of preventative treatments such as antihelminthetics.

- Control of animal numbers - lack of predators means less fit animals are not weeded out of the system naturally. Stock may suffer progressive loss of condition and health unless they are 'artificially' culled.

- Herbivore corpses - by law these have to be removed.

- Public acceptance – people often reluctant to embrace changes in what they perceive as their 'natural' surroundings.

- Potential danger to humans – some breeds are more aggressive, or more aggressive at particular times of year, than others.

Reconciling the needs of a near-natural grazing regime with these issues is likely to be difficult. Should the aim be for a consistent number year after year, or should an attempt be made to replicate 'boom and bust' cycles that may have existed naturally? Hard winters, parasite load, predators and summer drought would all have taken their toll in a natural situation, though seasonal migration would have helped to mitigate the adverse impacts of these. Overmars *et al.* (2002) discuss social

Figure 2. Park sign to alert visitors to the different animals in the area.

Comparisons between the different landscapes on the Estate.

Figure 3. The Southern block. A few small woods and narrow river meadows are dispersed amongst hedge bound fields with an average size of just ten acres. Hedgerow oaks are prevalent also giving the landscape the appearance of being quite densely wooded. The area was arable farmed intensively from the 1980s to 2004 and ring fenced in 2009.

Figure 4. The Middle block is believed to have been laid out by Humphrey Repton in the early 1800s, much of this land is Registered Parkland and in 2002 was reclaimed from intensive agriculture with the help of DEFRA's Countryside Stewardship. The centrepiece is the Knepp Lake - a medieval mill pond and SNCI. The parkland character is enhanced by vistas "borrowing" land from beyond the perimeter.

Figure 5. The Northern block This was a mixed farm with dairy as its main enterprise. In the 50's the hedges and rues were removed the ditches were filled in and piped giving it a feeling of open parkland. The oaks still mark where the hedges were. It's the most wooded area on the estate with plantations of firs and pine and mixed deciduous woodland. One of these oak woods, Horsham Common, is designated SNCI. Some of the head water for the Knepp lake is on this land.

structure and heredity in natural grazing. However the more intervention there is with regard to animal numbers and so on, the less the system can be regarded as near-natural.

Koene (2002) explores what is meant by 'de-domestication'. This is an important issue. Humans like the idea of 'natural' herds of large herbivores but we do not want them to kill us. In the original plans for park restoration, Charlie Burrell rejected red deer introduction because of the danger they might pose to his children. So it is essential in order to gain and maintain public support to differentiate 'wild' in the sense of 'untamed' but not 'wild' in the sense of 'savage'. Koene asks whether we want the animals to adapt to their natural surroundings or do we want to adapt the surroundings to the animals?

Charlie Burrell also has other factors to take into consideration as the estate is his only form of income and must generate sufficient surpluses to fund the non business assets such as the castle itself. The former farmland must continue to be used for trading purposes to qualify for certain tax treatments which means that the animals are sold into the food chain. Enjoyment of the land is also an important aspect of private ownership for the Burrells and some traditional country pursuits such as polo and game shooting exist on a very low-key basis. New business ventures are continually considered and it is hoped that some form of ecotourism may develop alongside the project if it proves financially sustainable.

Near-natural grazing at Knepp

The area at Knepp currently under restoration stands at about 1,000ha, which is about three quarters of the entire Estate. Although the area in the Knepp wildland project is far larger than each of the largest three Sussex Wildlife Trust reserves (Malling Downs 215.5ha, The Mens 159.4ha and Ebernoe / Butcherlands 158ha), it is still comparatively small. Even if the entire Estate were put under a more natural grazing regime, the area involved would only be a quarter of the size of Oostvaardersplassen. Nevertheless, this site provides an opportunity for exploring more naturalistic grazing in the short, medium and long-term.

Despite its small size relative to reserves in mainland Europe, Knepp has attracted keen interest from a number of experts, many of whom have visited Knepp since the first moves to reinstate the Repton park. The opinions and advice of those such as Hans Kampf (Senior Policy Adviser, Ecosystem and the Environment), Frans Vera (Staatsbosbeheer), Keith Kirby (Natural England), Tony Whitbread (Chief Executive, Sussex Wildlife Trust), Professor Mick Crawley (Imperial College London University) Matt Heard (Centre for Ecology and Hydrology), Rob Fuller (British Trust for Ornithology), Ted Green and Jill Butler (Veteran Tree Initiative and the Woodland Trust) and others have all helped to shape the direction in which the project has developed.

The rationale outlined by Whitbread and Jenman (1995) has guided the development of much of Sussex Wildlife Trust's recent conservation thinking and has resulted in a number of initiatives that are particularly complementary to the Knepp project. One of the major projects that the Trust is leading is the West Weald Landscape Project. This is focused on a 23,820 ha area at the western end of the Low Weald in the Surrey and West Sussex border area. It encompasses Ebernoe Common/Butcherlands and The Mens, two SACs that are owned by Sussex Wildlife Trust. Chiddingfold Forest SSSI, in the north of the area, straddles the county boundaries and is owned and managed by Forest Enterprise.

The West Weald project is focused on promoting the integrated management of the landscape for the benefit of the people and wildlife that live there. It is also working towards using more naturalistic grazing systems in some areas with the ultimate aim of reconnecting isolated landscape features to create an interconnected mosaic of dynamic habitats across core parts of the project area. A comparison of the long-term surveillance on Ebernoe/ Butcherlands and Knepp, evaluating the effects that more natural grazing has on vegetation process and biodiversity in these two sites will be of considerable scientific interest. The sum total of all this work should contribute significantly to our understanding of the role that less rigidly structured grazing systems may play in twenty-first century landscape management and conservation.

The advantages of the Knepp Estate as a site to explore more extensive grazing may be summarised as follows:-

- with the exception of 2 SNCIs and a few COGS (County Geological Sites) and English Heritage features, no part of Knepp Estate is designated SSSI, SAC or has other protected landscape status.

- there are no rare or protected species for which conservation management measures have already been introduced on site.

- it benefits from an owner who is extremely enthusiastic about and supportive of naturalistic grazing and re-wilding schemes.

- the intention to introduce a more natural grazing regime is highly complementary to SWT's West Weald Landscape Project and the restoration of the Butcherlands acquisition by natural processes.

- the grazing project will run in tandem with the River Restoration Centre's and the Environment Agency's plans to restore and 're-wild' the stretch of the River Adur that crosses the Estate.

- Knepp Castle Estate presents an opportunity for exploring some of the issues raised in both landscape scale conservation and the issues of 're-wilding' and 'naturalistic grazing'.

The Estate has also qualified for grants under Defra's Higher Level Stewardship (HLS) scheme. Biodiversity and habitat information obtained during this project contributed to the production of the Farm Environment Plan that was a requirement of the HLS application.

Is this aim being realised?

With so much potential for research and survey, keeping the Wildland Project to its original brief has presented challenges. As the project has developed, it has been necessary to modify, adjust or extend the original objectives. Constraints imposed by animal welfare compliance and the absence of large predators have had considerable impact on the concept of 'near natural' grazing. With the exception of deer, livestock has to be registered, maintained and slaughtered in accordance with UK legislation. The two very cold episodes of winter weather in January 2010 and again in December 2010 meant that stock had to be given supplementary feed, contrary to the original intention. The lack of large natural predators means that there is no natural herbivore control. In the case of cattle and pigs, this can be mimicked by culling for the market. Ponies are controlled by limiting stallion activity, and deer are controlled by stalking. All sales of meat are for human consumption and whilst the estate hopes that one day each animal based enterprise will be financially sustainable, their primary *raison d'être* is their role in the project, not profit.

Now some ten years on, it is clear that deer numbers in the Repton Park were too high and have caused the woodland under storey to become depleted. The project originally intended that deer would be used to 'thin' the woods as the project moved away from traditional woodland management towards wood pasture, in line with the parkland landscape objectives of the original Countryside Stewardship Scheme. However, as the estate has shifted emphasis away from pure landscape towards biodiversity, deer numbers have been reduced from 280 in March 2010 to 170 in 2011. Aside from the usual annual cull, some animals were caught and relocated to the southern block where about 80 fallow deer have joined the longhorns. Arriving at a balance between deer numbers and an appropriate level of grazing is likely to be an ongoing issue.

Other unforeseen issues include the proliferation of ragwort and thistles, scrub development, and the attitude of a minority of adjacent landowners. The high visibility of toxic ragwort caused much concern among horse or livestock owning neighbours. As an *Injurious Weed* under the *Weeds Act 1959*, Knepp has to comply with the law, and ragwort is now monitored annually. Scrub is an essential and valuable component of the changing vegetation away from arable but its increase in some parts of the Estate is in conflict with meeting the requirements of the Single Farm Payment. Changes in the appearance of the land after the cessation of intensive farming have also not pleased some people.

But there are signs that there are gradual improvements in vegetation structure and wildlife diversity. To date, the greatest changes in vegetation structure are seen in the southern block of land, which was taken out of arable production some years before it was grazed. This has given time for scrub to develop prior to any grazing pressure. The diversity of breeding birds appears to be increasing, including a number of birds on the Red List of conservation concern such as lapwings and turtle doves. Another sign of improving habitat was indicated by the results of a breeding bat survey in 2009 (Greenaway F., 2009). All bat species have different ecological requirements, but in general, male bats occupy less favourable habitats than females, leaving the most productive foraging areas to the breeding and lactating female bats. One of the species recorded, Natterer's bat, forages extensively on insects associated with grazing animals and their dung. The presence of almost equal numbers of male and female Natterer's bats recorded in 2009 suggests that the status of the foraging habitat is changing – perhaps indicating that the more natural grazing regime is having a positive effect on the breeding success. A repeat survey after five years have elapsed will allow a firmer assessment of bat population changes.

The first major evaluation of the Wildland project is due to be carried out in 2015, ten years after the initial baseline ecological survey. This will bring together and evaluate ten years of ecological surveillance, and could also include the wider issues associated with more natural grazing strategies such as economic viability, community support and animal welfare.

Acknowledgements

This article is adapted and updated from the Knepp Castle Estate Baseline Ecological Survey (Greenaway, T.E. (2006) English Nature Research Report No.693.

References

Anon. (2004) *Ecological Networks: Experiences in the Netherlands*. Working Paper, Ministry of Agriculture, Nature and Food Quality, The Netherlands.

Armstrong, H.M., Poulsom, L., Conolly, T. and Peace, A. (2003) *A Survey of Cattle-grazed woodlands in Britain*. Woodland Ecology Branch & Statistics and Computing Branch, Forest Research, Northern Research Station.

Ausden, M. and Treweek, J. (1995) *Grasslands*. In: Sutherland, W.J. and Hill, D.A. (eds.) *Managing Habitats for Conservation*. Cambridge University Press, Cambridge.

Greenaway, F. (2009) *Knepp Bat Survey 2009: A survey of the land within the proposed River Adur restoration site and associated watercourses*. Unpublished report for Knepp Castle Estate.

Greenaway, T.E. (2006) *Knepp Castle Estate Baseline Ecological Survey*. English Nature Research Report 693, English Nature, Peterborough.

Hodder, K.H., Bullock, J.M., Buckland, P.C. and Kirby, K.J. (2005) *Large herbivores in the wildwood and modern naturalistic grazing systems*. English Nature Research Report No. 648, English Nature, Peterborough.

Kirby, K.J. (2003) *What might a British forest-landscape driven by large herbivores look like?* English Nature Research Report 530, English Nature, Peterborough.

Koene, P. (2002) *Ethology and large herbivores: what do we want?* Vakblad Natuurbeheer.

Kuiters, A.T. (2002) *Hoofed animals in nature areas: theory and practice versus research*. Vakblad Natuurbeheer.

Leeuwen, J.M.Van and Essen, G.J.Van (2002) *Health risks between large herbivores, farm animals and man*. Vakblad Natuurbeheer.

Liebundgut, H. (1959) Über Zweck und Methodik der Struktur und Zuwachanalyse von Urwäldern. *Schweizerische Zeitschrift für Forstwesen*, **110**, 111-124.

May, R.M. (1994) *The effects of spatial scale on ecological questions and answers*. In: Edwards, P.J., May, R.M. and Webb, N.R. (eds.) *Large-scale*

Ecology and Conservation Biology. British Ecological Society, Blackwell Science, London.

Olff, H., Vera, F.W.M., Bokdam, J., Bakker, E.S., Gleichman, J.M., Maewyer, K. de and Smit, R. (1999) Shifting mosaics in grazed woodlands driven by the alternation of plant facilitation and composition. *Plant Biology,* **1,** 127-137.

Overmars, W., Helmer, W., Meissner, R. and Kurstjens, G. (2002) *Natural grazing, social structure and heredity*. Vakblad Natuurbeheer.

Rosenweig, M.L. (1995) *Species diversity in space and time*. Cambridge University Press, Cambridge.

Sutherland, W.J. (1995) *Introduction and principles of ecological management*. In: Sutherland, W.J. and Hills, D.A. (eds.) *Managing habitats for conservation*. Cambridge University Press, Cambridge.

Symes, N. and Day, J. (2003) *A practical guide to the restoration and management of Lowland Heathland*. RSPB, Sandy.

Vera, F.W.M. (2000) *Grazing Ecology and Forest History*. CABI Publishing, Oxon.

Whitbread, A. and Jenman, W. (1995) A natural method of conserving biodiversity in Britain. *British Wildlife,* **6 (2)**, 84-93.

Watt, A.S. (1947) Pattern and process in the plant community. *Journal of Ecology*, **35**, 1-22.

Observations on the Knepp Castle Wildland Project
Ted Green
Ancient Tree Forum

Introduction
The philosophy behind the Wildland Project at Knepp Castle can be summed up with the following quote *"where natural processes predominate and long term financial stability is achieved outside of a conventional agricultural framework"* (Knepp Castle Estate, 2011).

Here, much of the land has been 'abandoned' from arable, fences have been put up and animals introduced to develop an extensive pasture system. This is really not land abandonment but agricultural reversion, putting animals back into the landscape for biodiversity benefits and to generate a sustainable income. There have been many examples of this throughout history with land being abandoned and man moving on. The Knepp Castle Wildland Project is a deliberate attempt to re-create a different landscape by taking arable fields out of cultivation and replacing with pasture. The estate is located south of London where the weald and clays are reckoned to be some of the worst soils for farming in Britain. Whenever there was a depression in the past, the first farmers to go out of business were the people on the Weald.

The Estate
The estate covers 1,400 hectares in total and is split into three managment blocks, northern, middle and southern.

The Northern and Middle Blocks
The northern block covers 215 hectares which has been changed from arable to grassland. The trees have been retained but the hedges removed. The middle block is the Humphry Repton designed landscape created in the early nineteenth century, covering 283 hectares, which has benefited from some restoration. Both the northern and the middle blocks retain a number of the old oaks from a former parkland.

In the middle block (Repton landscape) there is a fungus, which we only know from ancient woodland pasture, and can be called a woodland pasture indicator. This is found associated with oak in places like the New Forest, Windsor Park and here. It indicates that we have already got the seeds of biological continuity which I think is going to be a fundamental part of this giant experiment. There are other rare fungi which have been found within the Repton parkland where there are mature and ancient oaks; one of the fungi occurs on sixteen sites in the UK. The key to these fungi is going to be the soil content.

Figure 1. The Knepp Estate.

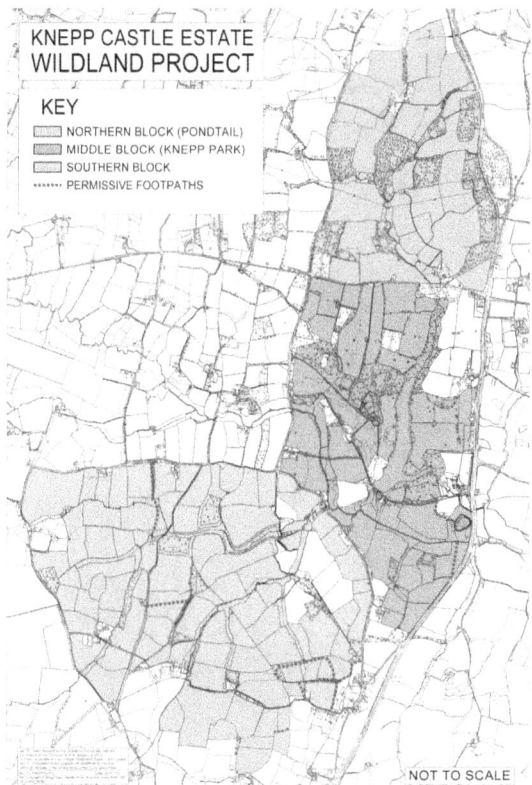

Figure 2. The three blocks of the estate.

The Southern Block

The southern block, which is the focus of the paper is the area which I find the most exciting because of the studies around arable reversion which can be conducted here. Figure 3. shows the year each of the fields in the southern block came out of arable and the crops which were grown in them at the time. An example of how the landscape has changed in a few years is of a wheat field taken out of production in 2004. In 2010, when animals were introduced it had gone from a ploughed field enclosed by hedges to a scrubby grassland with outgrowing hedges. Based on these and similar observations, Figure 4. shows a projection to 2050 of what the landscape might look like using the current vegetation as a starting point. The tree cover and the smaller coppices which will appear over time are shown in dark green.

As fields were taken out of cultivation and animals introduced into areas at different times the rate that fields are reverting to scrubby grassland varies. This can be seen in some areas where on one side of the hedgerow there is taller vegetation and on the other side shorter vegetation presumably mainly grass.

The Drivers

Prior to the Wildland Project, because of the public footpaths across the land, the estate could not contain herds of wild animals. At the start of the project

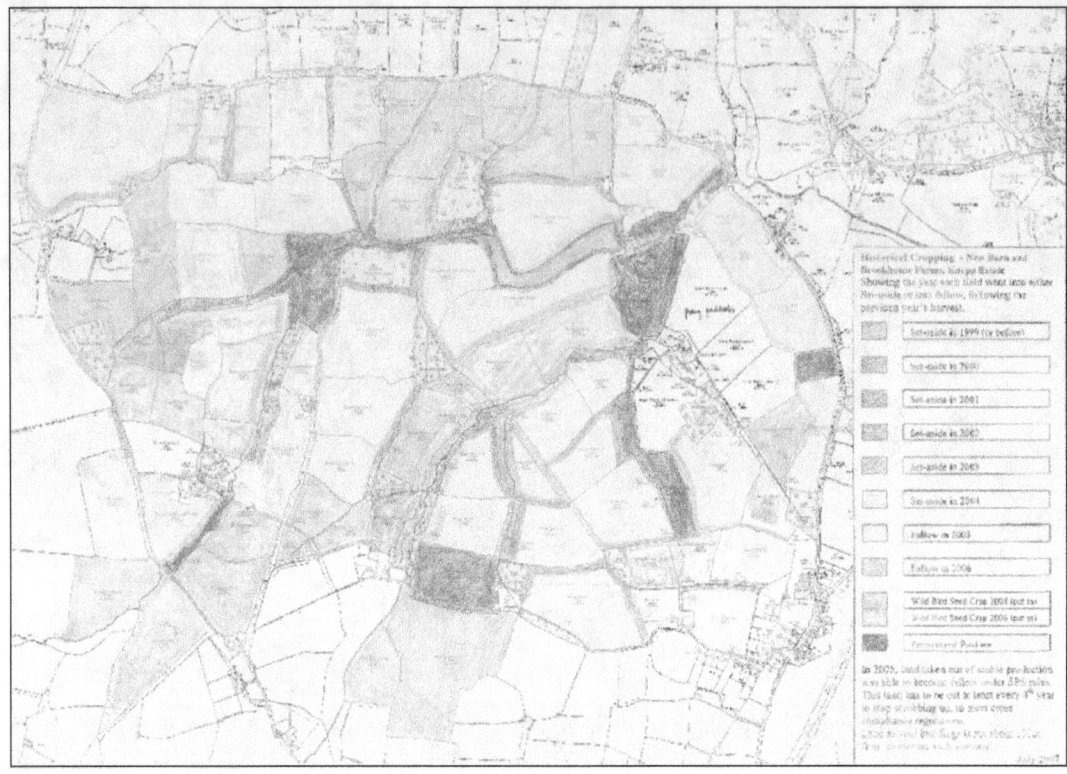

Figure 3. The southern block showing the historical cropping.

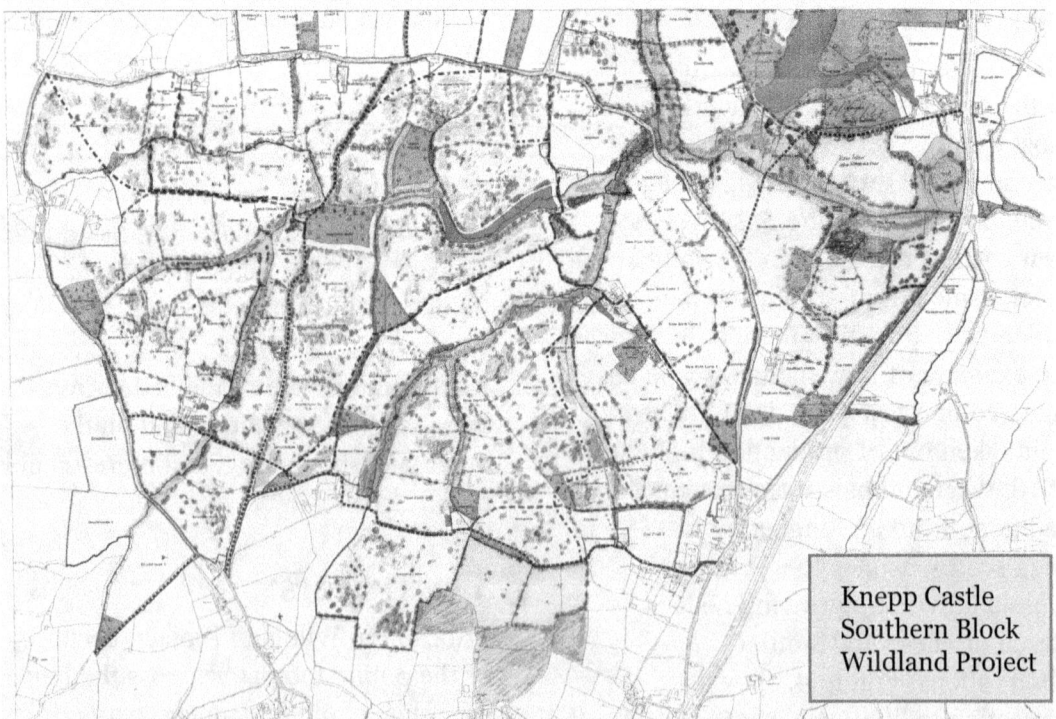

Figure 4. Projections based on managing animal numbers for tree and scrub cover 2050.

Figures 5 and 6. An example of the effect of reversion.

when boundaries were redrawn, the estate looked for analogues of these wild animals which led them to identify the Exmoor pony, oryx and deer as potentially suitable. Since 2009, Exmoor ponies, longhorn cattle, Tamworth pigs, fallow and roe deer have all been introduced into the project area. In addition to these introductions, rabbits are present and their foraging behaviour also has an effect. The impact from rabbits can be large depending on the time of year. There isn't any holly at Knepp but if there was and particularly during the last winter when we had heavy snow cover I think rabbits would have had a heavy impact on it.

Exmoor ponies

Exmoor ponies were first introduced into the park in 2003 and a further fifteen in 2009. The ponies are wonderful animals which should be studied more and more in the context of managing areas under reversion to pasture woodland. We know that they move around in rotation across their territory, constantly on the move but in a pattern which changes throughout the year depending on the availability of their favoured food. As with other grazing animals they also browse leaves from trees and shrubs. We assume that the females lead the way and show their foals how to find the preferred food thus they become very significant movers of seed in their dung. These

Figures 7 and 8. Exmoor ponies' behaviour.

areas are where you see that the wild boar have been digging as well. The ponies' condition is fantastic and in the winter they became curious around a dead fallow deer, they did not eat the animal but could have been eating the antlers as they are a great source of calcium. There has also been some exciting DNA work which says that the Exmoor is probably one of the lines called the mountain horse.

Longhorn Cattle

Longhorn cattle are one of the great old breeds of the UK. My theory on their docility centres on the fact that they used to live with man, in his house and they slept with him and if you got a stroppy one you just hit it with an axe and eventually this led to genetic selection of the traits for docility. After the first year (2003) of their introduction into this area I believe the impact they are having is huge. They are being allowed to go back into a wild situation, but at the same time are being looked after so that they are providing an income for the estate. This is a good marketing strategy – who couldn't resist a steak from an animal that has lived such a happy and contented life and organic of course!

One of the things that happened when the cows arrived was that they made inroads into some of the shrub seedlings within the grassland. Here you will see them in very dense areas finding the areas of vegetation that they want to eat. They browse all through the lean time towards the end of February and March when there is very little grass about, they find small areas of vegetation. They also make very significant tracks through the vegetation but it appears that they only damage small areas of vegetation and keep good vegetation on both sides. The cows do like rubbing against tree bark which we have to expect but the large oaks were well established when the cows arrived so we hope they will survive but there are signs of damage where they rub. Damage may be more severe on smaller or younger trees so if the oak carries on growing, are we going to have a coppice oak or a pollard oak created?

Figures 9, 10 and 11. Longhorn cattle behaviour.

Tamworth Pigs

Following the Exmoor ponies and Longhorn cattle, twelve Tamworth pigs were introduced to the project area in 2005. They have also had a huge impact on the wildlife. One of the reasons for the Tamworths probably being so successful is that the female can raise three litters per year whereas a female wild boar can only raise one.

The animals can roam freely. They appear to enjoy being around the house rootling up the ground next to the road but it might be significant that the area might be more nutritious here – I am unsure. When the animals moved over into the woodlands it was interesting to note that whilst they rootled in the ground they did not touch the daffodils. And one could argue that the daffodils are now on the increase because of the availability of more bare ground so the animals are having some positive impact on the woodland floor at the moment. In the woodland situation, the pigs are not constrained by fences and other barriers but there is very little effect on bracken. Here they are perhaps looking for truffles!

The visual impact on the parkland after it had been dug up by the pigs the first time, looks quite dramatic but it still recovers – amazing! Of course the ground is now very hummocky which means that the actual soil surface has a greater area and probably potential for being far more diverse.

Comparing sites of old sward and former arable dug up by the pigs shows that the older grassland has been dug more significantly than the former arable. This may have implications for future management. Figure 12. shows an ancient footpath which has never been ploughed, herbicided or fungicided but the two fields either side were arable up to two years before the picture was taken. When the pigs arrived they only dug up the footpath so I would coin the phrase "*if only pigs could speak and tell us about it*". I think that this is deeply significant and telling us

Figure 12. Ancient footpath.

Figure 13. Pigs at water's edge.

something about soil biodiversity and how this will probably be so very important to us in the future.

Pigs are highly intelligent and opportunistic. Figure 13 shows two of them actually about to enter the water. They completely submerged and then every 20 seconds they came up, put their snouts up and took a breath and went back down again – we have no idea what they were eating but it does show you how opportunistic they are.

Deer

Both fallow and roe deer occur in the wildland project area. Fallow deer were introduced into Knepp from Petworth Park in 2002. They are said to have been introduced into the UK by the Normans but one could argue now that they really are part of the British countryside and certainly part of the rest of the continent. The fallow deer move around in groups and do have an effect on the woodlands. The male deer also move around in large groups and have a significant impact on the vegetation. Presumably at times when the seed dispersal is in progress, if they eat the heads of the flowering plants then the chances are that they can actually eradicate the plant from the sward. Figure 14. shows the effect they can have on an ancient hedge. In the woodland where they have entered, in this particular instance they have probably browsed out the bramble allowing the grass to come back in but they are also having a serious detrimental effect on the trees. Many of the young trees have been severely damage by the fallow deer. It can be argued that we were going to lose a lot of those trees anyway but the more we lose the worse the effect on the trees that remain. Therefore this damage could in actual fact affect the next generation of trees. However what we are actually looking at is a Repton landscape with fewer trees rather than dense woodland.

Roe are the other species of deer which occur in the project area. They were present in the park and surrounding area before the project started. They are very effective browsers. The population has expanded presumably because they are territorial but it may start to limit itself as capacity is reached.

Figure 14. Deer browse line on hedge.

Figure 15. Outgrown hedges at the side of a field.

Observations

Each of the grazing livestock species has different grazing patterns and strategies. For example, the roe deer are incredibly effective browsers and we have come to the conclusion that ponies nip and cattle chomp by using their tongue. They seem to be able to find tiny little blades that I think they are probably finding in the inner vegetation.

The regeneration of the hedgerows in the southern block has been significant as they were originally cut to within 'an inch of their life' every year after harvest. However, now they have been left to grow and actually expand out, they have become a great source of seed and in these first few years they have contributed a great deal of the seed source for the scrub regenerating in the fields. In this case birds probably moved a large number of the seeds but we know small mammals play a great part as well. It has been found that jays may move acorns up to 25m from their source whereas small mammals may move them up to 75m and then go back for another acorn. We of course cannot rule out rooks and jackdaws but they are more likely to be carrying them away from the tree and just randomly dropping them because they slip out of their beaks. Blackberries, sloes, hawthorn and other berries may all be moved by birds or small mammals who may eat the fruit and then the seeds are deposited as they move around. Figure 15. shows what one field looks like with the hedges along the back consisting of hawthorn, oak and a whole range of species in there. It is very interesting to think about the establishment of the vegetation as new species move in.

Figure 16 a. tree seedlings protected by blackthorn and b. growing outside protection.

Amongst the grassland itself you can see thousands of oaks appearing in an acorn year. Of course they get browsed off if there are grazing animals and they will carry on getting browsed off until at some stage one or two of them get a thorn bush or a patch of thistles growing around them. This protection then allows the oak to develop. Figure 16 shows a tree out of the thorn which has been damaged and the one in it which has not. There is a lovely saying from Windsor in the sixteenth century that *"the thorn was the mother of oak"*.

On other fields grassland species such as ragwort, fleabane and creeping thistle have appeared. It has been noted that there appears to be some sort of competition between ragwort and fleabane which focuses on wet years and dry years. Fleabane appears to be far more successful in wet years whereas in a dry year it is not and this is what has happened in 2011. As ragwort and creeping thistle are agricultural weeds this has been a bone of contention with people who arrived at Knepp in 2009 seeing huge patches of creeping thistle wanting to know what was going to be done about it. But by 2011 they were all gone and we have no idea why (Figure 17.).

Conclusion

I hope this has provided some idea or an insight into where we are today because for us Knepp is an adventure and an open university. We will probably never have mammoths and we may not even be able to get wolves, but the scrub down by the meandering river which is going to be rewilded will include a lot of the other animals. So we finish up by thinking to ourselves that Knepp could be a place of learning in science which has not stood still.

References

Burrell, C. and Greenaway, T. (2011) Knepp Castle Wildland Project. *Landscape Archaeology and Ecology*, **9**, this volume.

Figure 17. The top picture was taken in September 2008, the one on the right in June 2011. In 2010 about 60 acres of creeping thistle disappeared. We have no idea why. A virus, sap-suckers, mildew or browsing - or a combination of them all?

Observations on trees and grazing refuges in the west of Scotland

Richard Gulliver

Honorary Research Fellow, School of Geographical and Earth Sciences, University of Glasgow

Summary

Several types of landform totally or partially prevent the grazing of woody plants by domestic stock. Such features are described in the account as Grazing Refuge Habitats. The relationship between type of refuge and type of native or feral grazer is tabulated; as is the relationship between type of refuge and environmental factors which positively or negatively impact on woody plants. Ellenberg Values are used to elucidate the ecological relations of the main species.

Portraits of seven native species and typical Grazing Refuge Habitats are provided; together with two non-native species, plus horizontal-growing Cotoneasters; and ecological conclusions are drawn/given. Circumspection is needed in the allocation of native status for species native in part of a region and introduced elsewhere in the region. Grazing Refuge Habitats have the potential for being seed sources for currently unoccupied refuges, species-poor woodland and moorland; though seed output may be limited in some species.

One of the species considered, Juniper, is a United Kingdom (UK) Biodiversity Action Plan Species; and two, Rock Whitebeam and Downy Currant, bear the rarity designation - scarce (Stace, 2010). Juniper is normally found in Grazing Refuge Habitats in the prostrate form, often described as *Juniperus communis* subspecies *nana*. Holly can assume a variety of shapes depending on exposure and grazing history. This variety of form may be one means of generating a greater level of community interest in these environmentally important Grazing Refuge Habitats. The potential for community action in planting native species into grazing refuges is discussed.

Introduction

General

Fieldwork has been undertaken over a number of years in the west of Scotland to gain a greater understanding of the importance and ecological complexity of Grazing Refuge Habitats. These are areas where the nature of the landform totally or partially prevents the grazing of woody plants by domestic stock. The United Kingdom Biodiversity Action Plan Species - *Juniperus communis* occurs in such habitats in the region. Rarity criteria follow Stace (2010) and therefore relate to the whole of the British Isles, e.g. including Ireland and the Channel Islands. An earlier scheme related to Britain, e.g. see Rose (2006). Species classed as rare occur in 1-15

10x10km squares; those classed as scarce in 16-100 10x10km squares; and those classed as uncommon occur in 101-250 10x10km squares. Rock Whitebeam (*Sorbus rupicola*) and Downy Currant (*Ribes spicatum*) are both rare and both occur in Grazing Refuge Habitats. The dwarf subspecies of Juniper (subspecies *nana*) has the rarity designation - uncommon. The distribution of the species discussed, plus brief biological accounts, appears in Preston, Pearman and Dines (2002). Grazing Refuge Habitats can contain non-native as well as native species. In this account Grazing Refuge Habitats have the first letter of each word capitalised in references to habitats. For more general references to grazing refuges capitalisation is not used. Scientific names and English names (including capitalisation) follow Stace (2010).

In this observationally-based study, preference is given in the references to literature produced by local plant scientists who knew their study area well, over general review articles where the special characteristics of local individual populations, forms, subspecies and species are not emphasised, as the aim of such reviews is to present a general overview, a process which can 'iron-out' important attributes.

Types of Grazing Refuge Habitat and types of grazer

Table 1 presents information on the types of landforms and landscape feature that act as refuges from grazing by stock in relation to type of potential grazer (domestic, feral and wild). The presentation is a simplification for the purposes of providing an overview, and should be treated as such. It is based on the general assumption that although some of the listed habitats will be accessible to either wild or feral grazers, all are 'unavailable' to sheep (*Ovis aries*) and cattle (*Bos taurus*).

However, in each category there will be some examples on the ground where grazing by domestic stock never occurs, some examples where it occurs extremely rarely and some where it occurs at infrequent intervals. For example small changes in verticality in cliffs and crags may affect animal accessibility greatly. Very hungry animals may graze in areas that would normally be avoided.

For most of the landforms listed in Table 1 the core substrate is rock with woody plants rooted in cracks, crevices and mini-ledges. In the case of boulder scree there may be a rudimentary soil under the large boulders or built up in the spaces between boulders. In the case of river banks there will usually be a mineral soil with little or no humus present.

In this account the word 'gorge' means a very steep sided valley (often with vertical sides) with a watercourse in the bottom, 'ravine' indicates a very steep sided valley with no watercourse in the bottom. Where text is quoted from other authors, they may be using the words in a somewhat different sense.

Table 1. Overview of broad trends of susceptibility of Grazing Refuge Habitats to grazing.

Each element is subject to considerable variation. For example small changes in verticality may affect animal accessibility greatly. Very hungry animals may graze in areas that would normally be avoided.

Boulder scree in this account consists of large blocks of stone and is unwooded (i.e. occurs at very high levels of exposure).

ABT = Above Boulder Tops, GP = Grazing Possible, ITBM = If Transported By Man, SAT = See Also Text (Downy Currant section).

Bracketed entries - may occur very occasionally.

	Cattle	Sheep	Goats	Deer	Lagomorphs	Small mammals
River bank - mineral soil	SAT				GP	GP
Gorge with watercourse					GP	GP
Ravine, no watercourse			(GP)	(GP)	GP	GP
Isolated large boulders					GP	GP
Boulder scree a) inland b) near shore	ABT	ABT	ABT	ABT	GP	GP
Crags & inland cliffs moderate slope			GP	GP	GP	GP
Crags & inland cliffs near vertical					GP	GP
Sea cliffs moderate slope			GP	GP	GP	GP
Sea cliffs near vertical					GP	GP
Islands in lochs	ITBM	ITBM	(GP)	(GP)	(GP)	(GP)

Susceptibility of Grazing Refuge Habitats to environmental factors

Table 2 provides a subjective assessment of the susceptibility of Grazing Refuge Habitats to key environmental factors. Strong winds can cause tissue damage; loss of plant parts e.g. branches; uprooting with some roots retaining a connection with the substrate; and 100% uprooting. Similarly drought can cause tissue damage, part-plant damage or total death. The two factors can act together during dry, windy periods. The nature of the Grazing Refuge Habitat depends greatly on the presence of an established tree canopy. For example a narrow gorge may be subject to intense shade which is a negative factor for tree and shrub growth on the sides of the gorge. However, the overall canopy may provide shrubs and small trees with protection from the desiccating and potentially uprooting effect of strong winds. An equivalent section in the open (i.e. without tree cover) will have high light levels, permitting vigorous growth, and there may be more likelihood of wind blown or animal dispersed propagules arriving; but the negative impact of wind movement may be considerable. The shade column in Table 2 emphasises the fact that grazing refuges can occur in either the shaded or unshaded state, though sometimes shaded examples are rare. Boulder scree discussed in this account and as shown in Table 2 occurs at such high exposure levels as to preclude or greatly inhibit tree growth. Boulder scree does sometimes occur in woodland. Heavy snow fall may result in the breaking of branches or the toppling of snow-laden trees.

There may be considerable variation in Grazing Refuge Habitats in susceptibility to fire, depending, for example, on the presence of a dense tree or shrub canopy, the presence of herbaceous or ericaceous vegetation between the woody plants and the height of the vegetation surrounding the grazing refuge.

Ellenberg Indicator Values

Ellenberg Values indicate the ecological condition at which a plant species performs well. They were originally derived for Central Europe by Professor

Table 2. Overview of broad trends of susceptibility of grazing refuge habitats to environmental factors.

In general the larger the tree or shrub, the greater the degree of susceptibility.
BE = Bank Erosion, BS = Boulder Shower, P = Possible, P-ABT = Possible Above Boulder Tops, P-OS = Possible Open Sites, RF = Rock Fracture, STBS See Text on Boulder Scree, i.e. Boulder scree in this account consists of large blocks of stone and is unwooded (very high levels of exposure).
Bracketed entries - may occur very occasionally.

	Wind	Drought	Shade from established canopy	Heavy snow fall	Catastrophic event
River bank - mineral soil	P-OS		P		BE
Gorge with watercourse	P-OS	(P-OS)	P		(BE), RF
Ravine, no watercourse	P-OS	P-OS	P		BS, RF
Isolated large boulders	P-OS	P-OS	P	P	RF
Boulder scree a) inland b) near shore	P-ABT	P-OS	STBS	P	BS
Crags & inland cliffs moderate slope	P-OS	P-OS	P	P	RF
Crags & inland cliffs near vertical	P-OS	P-OS	(P)	P	RF
Sea cliffs moderate slope	P-OS	P-OS	P		RF
Sea cliffs near vertical	P-OS	P-OS	(P)		RF
Islands in lochs	P-OS	(P-OS)	P	P	

Heinz Ellenberg. They have been modified for Britain by Professor Mark Hill and colleagues (Hill *et al.*, 1999).

The Ellenberg Values for a set of woody species which occur in Grazing Refuge Habitats in the West of Scotland are shown in Diagram 1. Values for moisture - F values - in this diagram range from 3 to 8. The complete range of values runs from 1 to 12. Some species occupy five key positions 1, 3, 5, 7 and 9; some are intermediate in their attributes; value 10 relates to shallow water plants, with plants of wetter sites having values 11 and 12. Values exist for soil reaction - R values - (acidity/alkalinity) on a nine point scale; and for soil Nitrogen - N values - on a nine point scale. Pyatt, Ray and Fletcher (2001) derived a system to gain a measure of soil fertility preferences for each species by adding the R and N values. This system has been adopted in Diagram 1. Any given combined value may be made up of two equal (or more-or-less equal) R and N values; or the combined value may have a relatively low R value and a relatively high N value, or a relatively high R value and a relatively low N value. Pragmatically however, the system works well to give a general picture of a plant's relationship to the environment.

Single underlining in Diagram 1 indicates an Ellenberg light value of 8, i.e. one frequently associated with open habitats. Names in capitals indicate a species with an Ellenberg light - L value - of 4, i.e. one frequently associated with shaded habitats. Non-annotated species have intermediate values.

The diagram reveals a major feature of many Grazing Refuge Habitats. Woody plant size is often limited by wind exposure. Periodic severe drought may result in death of some parts e.g. branches of the plant. Low levels of availability of water may result in slow growth rates even before drought conditions set in. Plant nutrient levels will often be low. Hence at many sites woody plants seldom attain sufficient height and width to allow intra- or inter-specific competition for the major resources to become an important issue. As a consequence some species typically associated with high light levels and some with lower light levels may both occur in grazing refuges e.g. crags. A similar situation pertains to soil moisture and to soil fertility (as Ellenberg R + N). This principle is demonstrated by the use of boxes in Diagram 1 which shows a set of species co-existing on a former low sea cliff now *c.*100 metres from the shore on Islay. Had growth conditions been more favourable, and each plant had attained a larger size, competition would reduce the species complement to a set of species appropriate to the substrate and exposure characteristics of the site. Positive identification of the oak to Pedunculate Oak (*Quercus robur*) was possible at this steep, but not vertical, cliff.

Diagram 1. Array of British Ellenberg indicator values with moisture - F value; presented against acidity/alkalinity - R value and soil Nitrogen - N value combined for woody plants of western Scotland in Grazing Refuge Habitats.

Single underlined - Ellenberg indicator value of 8 for light. Capital letters - Ellenberg indicator value of 4 for light. Native and non-native plants are included. Heavy boxes shows a set of species co-existing on a former low sea cliff now c. 100 metres from the shore on Islay.

		R+N Value											
F Value		3	4	5	6	7	8	9	10	11	12	13	n
3													
4								*Rosa spinosis-sima*	*Sorbus rupicola*	*Cotoneaster integrifolius*			2
5					*Rhododen-dron ponticum*		*Juniperus communis*	*Quercus robur*	*Ilex aqui-folium*	*Populus tremula*	CORYLUS AVELLANA	HEDERA HELIX	1
6						*Sorbus aucuparia* / *Quercus petraea*						*Fraxinus excelsior* / *Prunus padus* / RIBES SPICATUM	7
7			*Picea sitchensis*				*Betula pubescens*				*Viburnum opulus*		5
8						*Salix aurita*							3
9													1
10													
n			1		1	3	2	2	2	2	2	4	

NB: F,N and R values are not given for *Cotoneaster thymifolius* or *C. microphyllus* in Hill *et al.* (1999).

Woody plant shape and exposure - general relationships

As one ascends in altitude, exposure levels increase. Tree cover gives way to scrub cover; then to a zone of stunted shrubs and very stunted trees (Table 2, boulder scree (a)); and finally to open land.

The same phenomenon occurs in reverse as one approaches the shore. Increasing exposure to salt-laden winds results in the sequence of cover types; tree cover; scrub cover; zone of stunted shrubs and very stunted trees (Table 2, boulder scree (b)); then to herbaceous vegetation, rock or shore.

The distribution of scrub communities in Scotland at high altitudes, at high exposure levels near the sea but not on the shore, and by the shoreline is reviewed in MacKenzie (2000).

Native Woody Plant Species

Aspen - *Populus tremula*

Aspen is often considered to be a woodland tree. In the National Vegetation Classification (NVC) five of the six woodland communities containing Aspen are lowland, one is upland (Rodwell, 1991). As well as woodland, the species does commonly occur in Grazing Refuge Habitats, these are frequently in areas devoid of woodland at present. In some cases the Aspen in the grazing refuges may have originally been surrounded by woodland containing Aspen, the woodland having been subsequently lost. However, at a large number of sites Aspen appears to have colonised when the surrounding land was moorland. The habitats in Main Argyll (vice-county [biological recording district] 98) are given by Rothero and Thompson (1994) as '*coastal cliffs, crags and ravines*'.

Evans, Evans and Rothero (2002) describing the situation in Assynt, Sutherland, state: '*although it does not flower or fruit freely, it must sometimes set seed successfully as the majority of its more isolated sites could not have been colonised in any other way*'. Once established, the number of individuals is often increased by means of suckering which produces a line or small group of trees.

As Aspen seed is wind dispersed, the propagule number for an individual of any given size is greater than that for trees and shrubs with berries; but the output will be dispersed generally, i.e. there is no targeted seed deposition as can occur with species whose seed is defecated by perching birds.

Figure 1 shows four Aspens which have developed into upright-growing small trees on a linear crag on Colonsay. The larger any individual tree grows, the more susceptible it is to gale damage. Trees may sometimes be blown over by gales but not uprooted. In the case of a tree originally rooted in a small crag on Colonsay (Figure 2), the trunk was blown over and was supported a little above ground level by the major branches, whilst the ends of the roots retained their purchase in the fissure in the crag. Subsequently the tree then began upward growth, ultimately resulting in a U-shaped trunk.

Two groups of shoots growing from an exposed major root were examined on 12 April 2010. These had been produced over many previous years and were subject to grazing by sheep and cattle. All that remained of the shoots produced pre 2010 were woody protuberance i.e. the shoot bases (Table 3). Every example of new, 2010 growth, was truncated by grazing at its end. As the exposed major root is close to the ground, death of the pre 2010 shoots has been attributed to grazing by sheep and cattle and not to wind exposure. The latter possibility, cannot, however, be entirely ruled out.

Major gales may kill most of the individuals in a line or group of small trees produced by suckering, though one or more may survive. Sometimes strong winds present over a long period of time leads to a development of a low canopy which hugs the rock face. Aspen foliage is especially attractive in spring

Figure 1. Four small Aspen trees (*Populus tremula*), with mid green canopies, on a linear crag on Colonsay (GR NR 40737 95429) on 10 June 2009. The oblique angle of the seaward tree may have been caused by strong winds from the west. The more prostrate tree nearer the east coast, with a thinner canopy, is a Rowan (*Sorbus aucuparia*). No other trees or shrubs grew on the crag.

Figure 2. An Aspen tree (*Populus tremula*) on Colonsay (GR NR 40739 98316) on 12 April 2010. It was once rooted in a small crag, having been partly dislodged, presumably during a gale. The view involves looking along the fallen trunk. Some of the branches support the trunk. Other branches have now started to grow vertically. The two groups of shoots (Table 3) were on a section of root near the trunk base that had been torn away from the rock face when the tree was dislodged.

Table 3. Number and type of shoots in two adjacent groups on an exposed section of root of Aspen (*Populus tremula*), Figure 2, on Colonsay (GR NR 40739 98316) on 12 April 2010.

	Alive, ungrazed.	Alive shoots 4-9cm long, grazed at the ends.	Woody bases of former shots, presumably subject to excessive grazing
Group 1	0	6	67
Group2	0	6	81

and autumn and it makes a pleasing sound when disturbed by the breeze. It is a species which may appeal strongly to community groups interested in planting in Grazing Refuge Habitats; although all the native species discussed in this account have their own particular merits. Aspen has a further advantage in that at some sites individuals of the Poplar Hawk Moth (*Laothoe populi*) may be present; this association has been personally observed on Coll and Islay. Aspen has an Ellenberg value for light of 6. The biology of the species is reviewed in MacKenzie (2010).

Rock Whitebeam - *Sorbus rupicola*

Rock Whitebeam occurs on outcrops of basic rocks in scattered locations in the west of Scotland; it also sometimes occurs on other substrates. The habitats in Main Argyll are given by Rothero and Thompson (1994) as *'crags and coastal cliffs'*.

Rock Whitebeam is a scarce species *sensu* Stace (2010), i.e. occurring in 16-100 hectads in the British Isles. It is normally found as individual plants or in small groups. It has an Ellenberg light value of 8 indicating it performs well in open situations. It is not listed as a component of any NVC woodland community (Rodwell, 1991).

Inland cliffs that were once sea cliffs are an important habitat. One flowering and one fruiting individual occurred in a group of three small plants and one medium plant on an inland cliff near the shore on Lismore (Grid Reference - GR - NM 802 387) on 4 September 1994. The late flowering individual almost certainly had flowers badly damaged earlier in the year; re-flowering in September is a known response to such a phenomenon in some woody species. There is no means of vegetative reproduction. The upright growth form renders the plant particularly sensitive to wind damage. Total death following strong winds and drought are threats to individuals and populations.

Rock Whitebeam is not listed in the classic work *'Planting Native Trees and Shrubs'* by Beckett and Beckett (1979). Common Whitebeam - *Sorbus aria* - is a diploid sexual species (2n=34). Rock Whitebeam (2n=68) is one of twenty polyploid, apomictic species in the *Sorbus aria* aggregate (Common Whitebeam group), (Stace, 2010). Any projected raising of individuals for planting back into Grazing Refuge

Habitats should involve local seed. The foliage is particularly attractive when first produced, being white-felted on the underside; the inflorescences are quite large; and the green-and-red (12-15mm) fruits fairly conspicuous. (The inflorescence is shown 6cm across in Butcher, 1961).

Holly - *Ilex aquifolium*

The habitats in Main Argyll are given by Rothero and Thompson (1994) as '*rocky burn sides and crags*'. Holly has an Ellenberg light value of 4, it often occurs in woods and has a frequency class of I (1-20%) in NVC woodland community W17 (Rodwell 1991).

The prickly leaves provide only minor protection from grazing, the green young stems and new leaves are attractive to grazers. For the historic relationship with man and the possible inference for genetic diversity see Appendix 1.

Describing the situation on Colonsay, McNeill (1910) stated '*trees in exposed situations rarely produce berries*'. Furthermore in shaded situations growth may be reduced, especially shaded gorges; and reproductive output may also be affected. The species does not reproduce vegetatively. The biology of the species is reviewed in Peterken and Lloyd (1967).

Whereas the upright growth form of holly renders the species susceptible to wind damage, it also provides perching positions. Birds, having fed on the berries of other individual plants, may defecate, ultimately resulting in new young trees. Assuming some local regeneration from the established tree, a genetically mixed small stand may result. Holly trees can be male or female; or sometimes hermaphrodite (Beckett and Beckett, 1979). The dense evergreen foliage of holly may generate suitable conditions for roosting in the winter months, the leaves providing some protection from the weather and from predation.

At a moorland site with a peaty soil three kilometres from the sea on Islay (GR NR 43759 54332), twelve young hollies (all less than one metre tall) grew near the base of one small tree and two large saplings on a side arm of the Claggain River. As one proceeded downstream along the Claggain River from this point the incidence of seedlings and of very small trees decreased. The soils became progressively less infertile as a) the altitude got less and b) the areas of mineral soil that were exposed became larger. It is suggested that this change in soil fertility resulted in an increase in grazing pressure by stock as herbage quality increased. Also as one proceeded downstream there was a decrease in the incidence of Holly trees that did not occur in refuge habitats.

Any planned community production of young plants for planting in Grazing Refuge Habitats should involve local seed.

Variation in the shape of Holly trees is considered in the discussion.

Bird Cherry - *Prunus padus*

Bird Cherry produces conspicuous inflorescences (shown 7cm long in Butcher, 1961: given as 10-20cm in Leather, 1996) and small black fruits which are bird dispersed. Seedlings are not often found (Leather, 1996). The plant produces root suckers which can develop into dense thickets (Leather, 1996). It occurs as a native on Mull and Skye and is present on the mainland of western Scotland. It seems possible that its range may be expanding over long periods of time both westward and outward to include some of the medium sized Hebridean Islands e.g. Islay and smaller ones e.g. Colonsay. Conversely it may once have been more widespread and been subject to a range reduction due to habitat destruction. The habitats in Main Argyll are given by Rothero and Thompson (1994) as '*wooded ravines*'. Larger Hebridean Islands tend to have larger watercourses and hence deeper gorges, and this may be important both for the provision of potential colonisation sites and for refuges. On Islay it is an introduction (Ogilvie, 1995). One line of planted path-side trees on the island occurs above a wooded gorge. Assuming some members of this group die and others survive, such situations may provide environmental interpretation puzzles in the future.

Bird Cherry has an Ellenberg light value of 5. It is listed in two lowland NVC woodland communities in Rodwell (1991), plus upland ash woods - NVC woodland community W9. The biology of Bird Cherry is reviewed in Leather (1996).

Pedunculate Oak - *Quercus robur*

Pedunculate Oak appears to be the predominant species of oak in parts of the western fringe of the area. Examples are taken from Kintyre and Mull, both areas having detailed floras. Thus on Kintyre, Cunningham and Kenneth (1979) report that Pedunculate Oak is '*apparently the common oak of the vice-county* [biological recording district - 101] - *general, abundant. The certainly native scrub oak populations of extreme exposure appear to belong here. These - as near Ormsary - grade from* c. *3 ft. on the seaward to* c. *15 ft on the landward side.*' For Sessile Oak they state '*In Knapdale at least undoubted* Q. petraea *has not been seen other than a planted tree, but it appears to grow in upland ravines near Carradale, Kintyre*'. On Mull, Jermy and Crabbe (1978) state '*we believe that* Q. robur *is more frequent in our area than* Q. petraea. *Intermediates have been reported both by ourselves and by others, but there seems to be no agreement among the specialists as to the likely status of apparently hybrid populations. Thus Cousens (1965) states "Introgression in the Pedunculate Oak (*Q. robur*) and Sessile Oak (*Q. petraea*) in Scotland was known to be so extensive that neither could be defined satisfactorily"*'. Clarke and Clarke (1991) suggest that both species were under-recorded in their listing of the Colonsay flora. In Main Argyll both taxa and the hybrid appear to be widespread (Rothero and Thompson, 1994). It is probably best to consider each site separately and not, as yet, develop a regional model for the relative abundance of the two species and the hybrid, for their relationship with human history, for their links to environmental conditions, or for the allocation of one taxon as the locally or regionally indigenous form. The occurrence of hybrids at some locations suggests a greater degree of genetic variation in oaks than in the other species considered in the article. This may assist the evolution of forms that are adapted to exposed Grazing Refuge Habitats.

Oaks occur frequently on crags where they may be present as small trees or as wind shaved carpet-like stands. Where inaccessible to both larger mammalian grazers and humans, taxonomic identification is often impossible. Based on experience at accessible sites, the author's records at inaccessible sites on Colonsay (e.g. Figure 3) have been provisionally allocated to Pedunculate Oak. On Mull, Jermy and Crabbe (1978) state that Sessile Oak occurs '*in scrubby woodland on slopes with birch, in gorges* [a Grazing Refuge Habitat] *and at roadsides*'. On Lismore, Sessile Oak occurs on '*Raised beach cliffs and possibly elsewhere. North of Castle Coeffin and single tree south of Achnacroish (leaves were found below the Druim Mor cliffs but the tree could not be located)*', (Thompson, 1996). There is an 1899 record for Pedunculate Oak on Lismore, but no modern records. The hybrid occurs at a '*Raised beach cliff near Point and south of Kilcheran*', (Thompson, 1996). The biology of both oak species is reviewed in Jones (1959), and Morris and Perring (1974).

Woody plants with berried seeds may be distributed from one grazing refuge to another by birds; wind born seed may be dispersed by air currents. Three classic distribution agents for acorns are jays (*Garrulus glandarius*), red squirrels (*Sciurus vulgaris*) and grey squirrels (*Sciurus carolinensis*). Red squirrels do

Figure 3. In the centre of the view is an inaccessible wind-shaved oak, provisionally allocated to Pedunculate Oak (*Quercus robur*), on 7 May 2011 on Colonsay (GR NR 40364 97147). Also growing on this large crag were Aspen (*Populus tremula*), Hazel (*Corylus avellana*) and Ash (*Fraxinus excelsior*). Note the ungrazed nature of the grassy vegetation.

occur on Arran and Bute. Apart from this, all three are absent from the Hebrides. Nevertheless Pedunculate Oak is not infrequent in Grazing Refuge Habitats on Colonsay. The moderately small size of the plant at several locations suggests a fairly recent occupancy of the individual sites. Red and grey squirrels occur in the southern part of the west of the Scottish mainland (Harris and Yalden, 2008). The mainland occurrence of jays is broadly similar, they also occur in the southern part of the Great Glen (Gibbons, Reid and Chapman, 1993).

Downy Currant - *Ribes spicatum*

The shrub Downy Currant is considered to be native in boulder scree on Skye (Murray and Birks, 2005). It is interpreted by this author as being native on Islay in the equivalent habitat of boulder scree made up of large blocks at the base of cliffs just above the present high tide line on the east coast of Islay, Figure 4. Rain falling on the cliffs which are now located *c.* 20-40 metres inland may ensure a good supply of water for the substrate under the boulders in the scree. Downy Currant therefore occurs in two types of this habitat (inland and by the shore) where high exposure levels prevent or severely inhibit tree growth. Some plants in this area on Islay grow in crevices between boulders. Some grow hard up against boulders and hence obtain a degree of protection from the boulder face behind them.

The passage of rivers through areas of mineral substrate generates a low vertical face i.e. a river bank, of *c.* 0.5 to 1.5 metres tall, and this forms one category of Grazing Refuge Habitat. Such positions are potentially accessible to large grazers especially cattle wading in the river, but are usually ungrazed. At two sites on Islay on the Ardilistry River, parts of plants which are rooted in the river bank are grazed when growth reaches the top of the bank. Red deer (*Cervus elephas*), fallow deer (*Dama dama*), roe deer (*Capreolus capreolus*) and sheep occur in the area. At one site three prostrate stems had penetrated the earth of the bank and had clearly rooted. Downy Currant produces clonal stands (Richards, 2011). Woody

Figure 4. The shrub Downy Currant (*Ribes spicatum*) is centre-right of the view. It is growing behind a boulder at the base of a former sea cliff now 20-40m inland on 29 November 2004 on the east coast of Islay. The wider spaces between the boulders are accessible to large mammalian grazers. The mature twigs of Downy Currant are blackish. An occasional small tree occurs near the base of the cliff.

species growing on river banks may be damaged or eliminated at times of flood. Some parts of the stand may survive such catastrophes while others are washed away, especially if the original connection to the mother plant has died and rotted. Fragments carried in floods may establish elsewhere.

Downy Currant can occur as an escape from cultivation. For example, the species on Mull is described as a denizen i.e. a plant *'growing wild but known or suspected to have been introduced for cultivation as crops or herbs'* (Jermy and Crabbe, 1978). The Mull records are firstly Glen Forsa House *'in damp woodland and waste ground near houses'* and secondly in the Kintra Botanical Recording Area (no further habitat details provided). At locations within a few kilometres of gardens or woods established by estate owners in the west of Scotland it may either be locally native or locally introduced. For Britain as a whole it is shown in sixty 10x10km squares as a native and eight as a neophyte (introduction) for the period 1987-1999 in Preston, Pearman and Dines (2002). In a review of the biology of the species Richards (2011) describes characteristic locations in Britain and states *'Typically, plants of R. rubrum* [Red Currant] *and R. nigrum* [Black Currant] *are found close to the nearest habitation, and as the natural riverside woodland is penetrated further R. spicatum finally appears.'* Downy Currant mostly occurs within 50m of shallow, rocky rivers and streams in north east England (Richards, 2011). It occurs in woods on limestone in Lancashire and Yorkshire, often by streamsides. The fruit is very acid. It is conceivable that plants growing in gardens in the past were little modified genetically from wild plants, though specimens may have been brought in from other areas; its native range extends from Britain through Scandinavia and northern Europe to Manchuria. It may be significant that Islay, Mull and Skye are all islands with several estates.

Downy Currant is a scarce species *sensu* Stace (2010). The restricted extent of suitable habitats and narrow specificity within those habitats appear to be major factors leading to its limited distribution in Britain. At two Islay riverside sites the bank vegetation corresponds to the NVC National Vegetation Classification woodland community W7b (Rodwell, 1991).

On the coastal boulder scree on Islay ten plants occur within 20 metres of each other with an eleventh *c.* 50 metres away. The group was examined on 25 November 2002. The woody tissue produced during the 2002 growing season occurring above the upper surface of the boulders was leafless but alive. However, all older woody tissue protruding above the surface of the boulders was broken at its tips and dead, (it was not truncated by a mammalian grazer). It is therefore provisionally concluded that for this group of plants, the gaps between the boulders provide a refuge from wind. Plants growing in the narrow cracks between boulders have a measure of protection from large mammalian grazers. However, grazers can exploit the grassy vegetation in the wider spaces between some boulders, Figure 4. Deer and feral goat (*Capra hircus*) droppings occurred nearby.

Both river banks and boulder scree areas subject to high levels of exposure are not heavily grazed by large mammals, but neither are totally inaccessible. At its maximum height in these habitats in the study area Downy Currant is within reach of grazing by large herbivores, hence any berries produced could be consumed some, most or all years. In this regard the species differs from the trees discussed previously. For these trees growing in favourable conditions the height of mature plant specimens is sufficient to put the branches bearing fruits and seeds above the reach of large mammalian herbivores. (Grazing would not occur as a normal event in landforms with the broad designation "*grazing refuges*"). Richards (2011) reports that for Downy Currant '*fruit-set is usually very poor*'. Opportunities for bird dispersal may therefore be very limited. Developing fruits were observed at one of the riverside sites on Islay on 25 June 2004.

Downy Currant is not included in Beckett and Beckett (1979). The flowers are green and the fruits, when produced, are red. However the main stems are a blackish shade, which is especially noticeable in winter.

Juniper - *Juniperus communis* subspecies *nana* and *communis*

Juniper today frequently occurs in open habitats and this is reflected in the high Ellenberg Value of 8 for light. However, it can occur as a small tree in woodland (Broome, 2003), and has a frequency class of I (1-20%) in the NVC woodland communities W11, W17 and W18 (Rodwell, 1991). It has a frequency class of V (81-100%) in the W19 - *Juniperus communis* ssp. *communis-Oxalis acetosella* woodland - where it varies in height from 1-5m (Rodwell, 1991).

Particularly in England, there has been a major decline in recent years and this has led to its designation as a UK Biodiversity Action Plan Species (Anon., 2010). The decline is due to one or more of the following factors, change of land use, heavy grazing, minimal or zero grazing leading to unsuitable conditions for regeneration, and losses due to fire. The biology of the species is reviewed in Ward (2007), Thomas, El-Barghathi and Polwart (2007) and Lockton (2011).

The species is extremely drought resistant but dead major branches, Figure 5, and occasional dead entire plants bear testimony to the fact that prolonged droughts can be fatal. In some areas it is an open question whether sufficient female plants of sufficient reproductive output currently exist to allow colonisation of a) the widely scattered Grazing Refuge Habitats to compensate for periodic losses by drought, and b) moorland - where there may be a considerable loss of young plants to grazing.

Dwarf forms, which perform well in environments with high wind exposure, have been allocated to subspecies *nana*. In Scotland they predominately occur in the north west, including near the sea where high levels of exposure can occur at all altitudes. Upright forms, which can perform well in woodland situations, have been allocated subspecies *communis*. At some locations a complete spectrum of forms occurs. Accordingly some plant scientists identify Juniper to the species level only (Pearman, Preston and Dines, 2002). Upright forms are often to be found in open (unwooded) land. They are absent in most of north west Scotland (Pearman, Preston and Dines, 2002).

In dwarf forms the slow growth produces twigs with much woody tissue in relation to the needles. Stace (2010) states that the leaves of subspecies *nana* are '*abruptly tapered to a short almost blunt point*[s] *so that branchlets are scarcely prickly to touch*'. All the dwarf forms felt by the author had very sharp needles and the branchlets also felt sharp. Some were very dwarf mats of plants e.g. 10cm tall, in grazed areas. It would seem logical that the greater the level of susceptibility to grazing due to dwarf-ness, the greater the selection pressure over long periods of time to develop foliage which is strongly unattractive to grazers, e.g. sharply pointed. The topic would bear further investigation.

Replanting of upland areas with Juniper has been successfully undertaken by the Forestry Commission using cuttings in Lochaber, Moray and the Pentland Hills (Broome, 2003). In the North York Moors individuals grown from seed have been planted by children, particularly at locations close to their schools in the Esk Valley (Woods, 2003). Plants are being raised from cuttings for replanting into Grazing Refuge Habitats on Islay by the author and his wife. So far plants raised from cuttings have retained the prostrate growth habit of the mother plant. This attribute would not be disadvantageous when individuals are planted in crags. In moorland with tall vegetation it may lead to poor competitive performance. Small prostrate plants, presumably developed from seed, have been observed in short, heavily-grazed vegetation at the base of crags containing mature plants. Hence the prostrate habit may confer some benefit in certain heavily grazed locations where exposure is not a factor. Plants grow extremely slowly, whether from seeds or cuttings, and this should be born in mind if a community planting exercise is planned. Ideally pre-visits should be made to existing plants in May and the sex determined. Plants of the opposite sex can then be planted nearby, e.g. in the winter months. The scale of many Grazing Refuge Habitats, e.g. Figure 5 provides niches for only small numbers of Junipers to be planted.

Juniper on small, dome-shaped crags will sometimes be rooted near the centre of the crag and grow outwards until the branches reach the adjacent moorland. Similarly Junipers rooted part way up vertical crags will grow downwards to meet grassy and heathery vegetation. In one area on Colonsay, well-grazed by sheep and some cattle, the Juniper which occupied the crag had a browse-line at 1.5 metres above ground level, Figure 6. In another area with a low stock density the plants (usually one per crag) were ungrazed. Hence Juniper may provide a barometer of grazing intensity. New intact growth from a former browse-line will indicate a change from a heavy intensity of grazing to light or zero grazing. It is also possible that increases in stock density will be revealed by newly damaged branchlets at or near ground level.

Figure 5. Juniper (*Juniperus communis*) on a crag near Rubha nan Ron on the west side of 'The Strand' on Colonsay on 16 September 2009. Winds from the west have killed the western (left hand) upper part of the plant, together with other sections of the wind shaved upper mat. The sea is less than one kilometre from the plant to north west, west, south west, south and south east.

Figure 6. A single plant of Juniper (*Juniperus communis*), the sole woody occupant of a small crag to the south east of Kiloran Bay, Colonsay. 19 May 2011; GR NR 40342 96663. Green branchlets can be seen above the ragged browse line circa 1.5m above the ground, a few dead stems protrude below the browse line. Sheep and cattle graze the area.

Juniper can occur in Grazing Refuge Habitats on a wide range of rock types. This is in marked contrast to Rock Whitebeam which typically occurs on basic rocks and Downy Currant which has several narrowly defined habitats.

Non-native Woody Plant Species

Rhododendron - *Rhododendron ponticum*

Seed of *Rhododendron ponticum* from large gardens, woodland gardens and the policy woods of estates colonises many habitats including broad-leaved woodlands, rough pasture, moorland, crags and cliffs. Plants can bloom a few

years after habitat invasion, hence providing further propagules for subsequent colonisation e.g. of a crag or cliff.

Observations suggest that plants on crags and cliffs are less likely to be successfully sprayed during a *Rhododendron ponticum* clearance programme than those on moorland nearby. Hence the habitat may well provide a refuge from this particular form of management.

Sitka Spruce - *Picea sitchensis*

Sitka Spruce colonises Grazing Refuge Habitats from nearby forestry. The upright growth habit will probably result in Sitka Spruce plants in many open Grazing Refuge Habitats ultimately being blown over during gales. While they survive they give an unnatural appearance to crags. However, within the European context, the presence of Spruce species on crags is to be expected.

Horizontal-growing Cotoneasters

Horizontal-growing Cotoneasters, originating from gardens, colonise rock faces close to settlements. They develop into dense, low woody carpets. The colour of the foliage is different from any native woody species thereby generating an unnatural appearance in the landscape. They produce an abundant berry crop. The author has provisionally identified the following taxa on Islay and/or Main Argyll. Thyme-leaved Cotoneaster - *Cotoneaster thymifolius* - naturalised; Small-leaved Cotoneaster - *Cotoneaster microphyllus* - naturalised; Entire-leaved Cotoneaster - *Cotoneaster integrifolius* - on the outside of a garden wall.

In North Wales Wild Cotoneaster - *Cotoneaster cambricus* - grows on limestone at the Great Orme, Llandudno. Stace (2010) classes it as rare, native and endemic. However, in the '*New Atlas of the British and Irish Flora*' (Preston, Pearman and Dines, 2002), it is classed as a neophyte - i.e. a plant introduced after 1500 - and considered to be of garden origin.

Conclusion

Summary of the importance of Grazing Refuge Habitats

Grazing Refuge Habitats can therefore be shown to have great importance in the following areas:

1. the continued maintenance of locally, regionally, or nationally uncommon species in a zone with minimal or zero grazing by domestic stock;

2. as potential sources of seed for the establishment of woody species into currently unoccupied Grazing Refuge Habitats, moorland and species-poor woodlands;

3. as a means of monitoring intensity of grazing as plants grow towards the edge of the refuge; and

4. as habitat types into which planting is possible to compensate for losses in the landscape at large.

In some cases they may act as refuges from upland fires. The advantages of freedom from grazing must be set against disadvantages from increased exposure to wind, proneness to drought, and limited resources e.g. soil water and nutrients. Critical issues for woody species growing in refuge habitats include the level of production of propagules, the genetic diversity of the seed, the effectiveness of the distribution system and the nature and availability of suitable receptor habitats. Research is desirable to confirm the native status of Downy Currant at its presumed native sites; and the native/introduced status of Pedunculate and Sessile Oak on a per-site basis. However, it is potentially time consuming and may conceivably be inconclusive.

Habitats which are refuges from grazing sheep and cattle may still be utilised by several wild or feral grazers.

Overview of four key features of seven woody species

In order to provide an overview, four features of the seven woody species of refuge habitats have been subjectively ranked in Table 4. Based on personal observation, Rock Whitebeam and Downy Currant were most confined to Grazing Refuge Habitats (Column 1); and Pedunculate Oak was least strongly associated with grazing refuges, e.g. also occurred in some quantity in woodlands, both enclosed and unenclosed. The canopy of Juniper was potentially the most prostrate of the seven species, low growth of any one individual plant almost certainly resulting from a mixture of genetic constitution and environmental factors (Column 2). Cuttings of prostrate plants grown by the author in sheltered conditions remained prostrate. The canopies of Rock Whitebeam, Holly and Bird Cherry, plus the upper layer of Downy Currant, resembled stunted and wind damaged versions of canopies that would develop in unexposed locations. The prickles of Juniper and Holly would provide a little protection against casual grazing (Column 3), but in both cases heavy grazing pressure leads to leaf and stem consumption. Oak leaves contain distasteful tannins. In relation to Column 4, growth of Juniper from seed or from cuttings is slow. This, however, has the benefit that nursery stocks can be maintained at a size for replanting periodically over the years by community groups. The low ultimate height plus the ability of Downy Currant to grow new shoots from the base has resulted in its second place in the ranking of the predicted effectiveness of planting native stock in refuge locations. Source material for cuttings may be easier to obtain from coastal sites than inland ones. Re-established plants of Aspen may produce suckers - an insurance against the mother plant being killed by exposure - and hence the third position in the ranking has been allocated to Aspen. The remaining four species can be reintroduced as young plants, supplemented by sowing seeds in an adjacent part of the Grazing Refuge Habitat. (This technique could also be used with Juniper and Downy Currant).

Table 4. Subjective ranking of features of seven woody species of Grazing Refuge Habitats.

Scientific name	Affinity to refuge habitats	Ability to modify height and density to exposure	Minor defences of leaves against mammalian grazing	Predicted effectiveness of planting native stock in refuge locations	English name
Populus tremula	3	3	4	3	Aspen
Sorbus rupicola	1	4	4	4	Rock Whitebeam
Ilex aquifolium	6	4	2	4	Holly
Quercus robur	7	2	3	4	Pedunculate Oak
Prunus padus	3	4	4	4	Bird Cherry
Juniperus communis	5	1	1	1	Juniper
Ribes spicatum	1	4	4	2	Downy Currant

Community groups may also like to prioritise their activities based on the local, regional or national rarity of the species.

Visual and general aspects

Holly develops a unique canopy shape at each site it occupies depending on the level of exposure encountered and, in some cases, the interaction with periodic grazing events. This variety of canopy shape seen as a dark outline against the crag or cliff face in both summer and winter could act as an initial source of fascination to walkers and countryside users. Once an interest in the special nature of the Grazing Refuge Habitat has been kindled, further investigations and activities, e.g. community planting exercises, may result. The variety of forms of Holly has the potential to inspire poets, artists and writers of prose. Hopefully it will also have a strong motivating influence on landscape scientists and geographers as our understanding of the plant/animal/environment/landscape interactions of Grazing Refuge Habitats develops. The many shapes adopted by prostrate stands of Juniper are also potentially inspirational; indicating, in anthropomorphic terms, perseverance in adversity.

Acknowledgements

I would like to thank my wife, Mavis Gulliver, for help and support throughout this study.

The administrators of The Paddy Coker Research Fund are thanked for a grant which helped to fund part of this article.

References

Anon. (2010) *UK priority species pages – Version 2* Juniperus communis. Joint Nature Conservation Committee, Peterborough http://jncc.defra.gov.uk/_speciespages/394.pdf. Accessed 4 July 2011. NB the useful 1999 Species Action Plan, author D. Price, is not at its original web location and appears to have been withdrawn.

Beckett, K. and Beckett, G. (1979) *Planting Native Trees and Shrubs*. Jarold Colour Publications, Norwich.

Broome, A.C. (2003) *Growing juniper; propagation and establishment practices.* Information Note No. 50. Forest Commission, Edinburgh.

Butcher, R.W. (1961) *A New Illustrated British Flora. Part I. Lycopodiaceae to Salicaceae*. Leonard Hill, London.

Clarke, P.M. and Clarke J. (1991) *The Flowering Plants of Colonsay and Oransay*. Published by P. M. Clarke and J. Clarke, Colonsay, Argyll, Scotland.

Cousens, J.E. (1965) The Status of Pedunculate and Sessile Oaks in Britain. *Watsonia*, **6**, 161-176.

Cunningham, M.H. and Kenneth, A.G. (1979) *The Flora of Kintyre*. EP Publishing, East Ardsley, Wakefield.

Evans, P.A., Evans, I.M. and Rothero, G.P. (2002) *Flora of Assynt*. Published by P.A. Evans and I.M. Evans, Assynt, Scotland.

Gibbons, D.W., Reid J.B. and Chapman, R.A. (1993) *The New Atlas of Breeding Birds in Britain and Ireland: 1988-1991*. T. and A. Poyser, London.

Harris, S. and Yalden, D.W. (2008) *Mammals of the British Isles: Handbook, 4th Edition*. The Mammal Society, Southampton.

Hill, M.O., Mountford, J.O., Roy, D.B. and Bunce, R.G.H. (1999) *Ellenberg's Indicator Values for British Plants*. Ecofact Volume 2. Technical Annex. Institute of Terrestrial Ecology, Abbots Ripton, Huntingdon.

Jermy, A.C. and Crabbe, J.A. (1978) *The Island of Mull: a Survey of its Flora and Environment*. British Natural History Museum, London.

Jones, E.W. (1959) *Quercus* L. Biological Flora of the British Isles. *Journal of Ecology*, **47(1)**, 169-222.

Leather, S.R. (1996) *Prunus padus* L. Biological Flora of the British Isles No.189. *Journal of Ecology*, **84(1)**, 125-132.

Lockton, A.J. (2011) *Species account: Juniperus communis*. Botanical Society of the British Isles, www.bsbi.org.uk.

MacKenzie, N.A. (2000) *Low Alpine, Subalpine & Coastal Scrub Communities in Scotland*. Highland Birchwoods, Munlochy, Scotland.

MacKenzie, N.A. (2010) *Ecology, conservation and management of Aspen - A Literature Review*. Scottish Native Woods, Aberfeldy, Scotland.

McNeill, M. (1910) *Colonsay: One of the Hebrides*. David Douglas, Edinburgh.

Morris, M.G. and Perring, F.H. (1974) *The British Oak - Its History and Natural History*. Published for the Botanical Society of the British Isles by E. W. Classey, Farringdon, Berkshire.

Murray, C.W. and Birks, H.J.B. (2005) *The Botanist in Skye and Adjacent Islands*. Published by C.W. Murray and H.J.B. Birks, Prabost, Scotland and Bergen, Norway.

Ogilvie, M. (1995) *The Wild Flowers of Islay: a Checklist*. Lochindaal Press, Bruichladdich, Islay, Scotland.

Pearman, D.A., and Preston, C.D. (2001) *A flora of Tiree, Gunna and Coll*. Published by D. A. Pearman, and C. D. Preston, Dorchester.

Preston, C.D., Pearman, D.A. and Dines, T.D. (2002) *New Atlas of the British and Irish Flora*. Oxford University Press, Oxford, UK.

Peterken, G.F. and Lloyd, P.S. (1967) *Ilex aquifolium* L. Biological Flora of the British Isles. *Journal of Ecology*, **55 (3)**, 841-858.

Pyatt, G., Ray, D. and Fletcher, J. (2001) *An Ecological Site Classification for Forestry in Great Britain*. Forestry Commission Bulletin 124. Forestry Commission, Edinburgh.

Richards, A.J. (2011) *Species account: Ribes spicatum*. Botanical Society of the British Isles, www.bsbi.org.uk.

Rodwell, J.S. *et al*. (1991) *British Plant Communities, Volume 1, Woodlands and Scrub*. Cambridge University Press, Cambridge.

Rose, F. (2006) *The Wild Flower Key*. Warne, London.

Rothero, G. and Thompson, B. (1994) *An Annotated Checklist of the Flowering Plants and Ferns of Main Argyll*. Published by the Argyll Flora Project, Argyll, Scotland.

Stace, C.A. (2010) *New Flora of the British Isles: Third Edition*. Cambridge University Press, Cambridge.

Thomas, P.A., El-Barghathi, M. and Polwart, A. (2007) *Juniperus communis* L. Biological Flora of the British Isles No. 248. *Journal of Ecology*, **95(6)**, 1404-1440.

Thompson, B. (1996) Lismore Flora: Flowering Plants and Ferns. *The Glasgow Naturalist,* **23(1)**, 14-40.

Ward, L.K. (2007) *Juniperus communis* L. Plantlife Species Dossier. Vol. 1, pp. 1–21. www.plantlife.org.uk/uploads/documents/Juniperus_communis_Dossier__part1.pdf. Vol. 2 pp. 22–46. www.plantlife.org.uk/uploads/

documents/Juniperus_communis_dossier__part2.pdf. (last accessed 4 July 2011).

Woods, P. (2003) *Juniperus communis* in Yorkshire's Esk Valley, a Model for Woodland Education in Primary Schools. *Quarterly Journal of Forestry*, **97(1)**, 55-58.

Appendix 1

Historic relationship with man and the possible inference for genetic diversity

In the past, both Holly and Gorse have been crushed for winter feed for stock in various parts of Britain and Ireland. Gorse has been planted in fields in Ireland. Gorse on Coll and Tiree (Inner Hebrides) and all the Outer Hebrides is considered to be non-native (Preston, Pearman and Dines, 2002), having been brought in for agricultural purposes. Holly has been planted on farms in northern England. It is therefore conceivable that there has been some movement of the species by man in the west of Scotland. Any such planted trees are likely to be close to habitation, but berries could be carried by birds to nearby Grazing Refuge Habitats.

Juniper Re-establishment Project - Isle of Islay, Argyll, Scotland

Richard and Mavis Gulliver

Carraig Mhor, Imeravale, Port Ellen, Isle of Islay, Argyll, UK, PA42 7AL

Background

Juniper (*Juniperus communis*) has declined in the UK due to a) very heavy levels of sheep grazing, b) death following burning of upland vegetation and c) change of land use. In some areas minimal or zero grazing has resulted in conditions which are unsuitable for seedling establishment. In the Hebridean Islands, it tends to exist only in places inaccessible to grazing domesticated animals. Such locations may also offer some protection from fire. These are often fringe microhabitats where growth rates are slow, e.g. cliffs and rock crags. Some plants do not produce any cones, and this indicates the suboptimal nature of the habitat. Female cones take two years to mature. Grazing by slugs, sheep, feral goats, deer, rabbits and birds may mean that some cones are initially produced, but do not reach maturity. The low growth rate of Juniper has the consequence that young foliage is susceptible to grazing for a long period of time, and the recovery from one grazing incident is slow. Seeds are contained in the mature female cones. Plants known to be male may only produce cones in some years. A considerable number of plants visited in May in any one year show no signs of either male or female cones. Juniper is reasonably widespread in Argyll but there are serious concerns about regeneration throughout the area, particularly in grazed habitats. In a survey carried out by Scottish Natural Heritage in Argyll West and the Islands, (Sullivan, 2003), only one population where seed production was occurring was located. Young plants are occasionally found on Islay, but are rare; many old and middle-aged plants exist.

Dwarf forms, which perform well in environments with high levels of wind exposure, have been allocated to subspecies *nana*. Upright forms, which are more susceptible to wind damage, have been allocated to subspecies *communis*. At some locations a complete spectrum of forms occurs. Accordingly some plant scientists identify Juniper to the species level only (Pearman, Preston and Dines, 2002). All the Junipers examined up to now which were growing in exposed locations in the Hebrides were prostrate in growth form, and by convention would be considered to be subspecies *nana*. However, due to the widespread occurrence of intermediates at less exposed locations in Britian, Juniper is not divided into subspecies in this account. All cuttings taken from low, prostrate plants have so far retained a prostrate growth form in cultivation.

The pots were placed in fish boxes in the nursery and thereby received protection from strong winds.

The biology of the species is reviewed in Ward (2007), Thomas, El-Barghathi and Polwart (2007), and Lockton (2011); the distribution is shown in Pearman, Preston and Dines (2002). Together with Scots Pine and Yew, Juniper is one of only three native conifers in Britain. The genetic constitution of Juniper is unlikely to have been affected by crossing with material of non British origin.

Project Overview

On Islay in the Inner Hebrides a large number of Juniper plants do not bear female cones (berries), and where berries do occur they are often few in number. Cuttings are being taken from male and female plants. After a period in the nursery they will be planted in locations where grazing by stock is absent - Grazing Refuge Habitats (Gulliver, 2011). At such sites risk from fire is likely to be very low. These activities will ensure a healthy population for the future. Plants will also be offered to Botanical Gardens and other public organisations who wish to build up a collection of native plants of special interest. Juniper has declined greatly in many parts of Britain and has United Kingdom Biodiversity Action Plan Species status (Anon., 2010). The project will demonstrate the importance of horticultural procedures in assisting in plant conservation. The techniques to be used could be operated by community groups and dedicated individuals as well as tree and shrub nurseries. Some of the planting will be undertaken by community groups. Work in the North York Moors (Woods, 2003) has shown the great benefits of community action in assisting with care of Juniper plants post planting e.g. when growth of the surrounding plants becomes an important factor.

Project Procedure

1) Cuttings are being taken from male and female plants on Islay and propagated in pots; labelled to show the sex of the source plant. The growth medium is 50% rain-washed coarse sand from behind the shore and commercial Irish 50% Sphagnum Moss Peat.

2) Cuttings stand outside, protected from winds in fish boxes. Plants are watered if a dry period occurs immediately after initial potting-up. A trial run has indicated that under normal circumstances natural precipitation on Islay is sufficient to keep plants alive over many months. Watering is, however, being undertaken during very dry periods in the summer months.

3) Cuttings are re-potted as they grow in size. The growth rate of Juniper is low.

4) Junipers will be planted out as soon as they reach a sufficient size. Further details are provided in the subsequent section - 'Establishment sites'. On Islay, Junipers from cuttings take three years to reach a size which is ideal for planting. Experiments will be undertaken with planting some

individuals after one or two year's growth. An early trial of planting a small, rooted plant into a crag produced a positive result.

5) Botanical Gardens will be contacted and plants will be offered.

Information on establishment

The techniques utilised incorporate information from the Forestry Commission Information Note 50 (Broome, 2003); and from a community project in North Yorkshire with schoolchildren, (Woods, 2003), though in this case plants were initially raised from seed in a commercial nursery.

Establishment sites

The main establishment sites will be in locations where soil (which is usually largely organic) fills crevices in the rock or occurs on ledges. Situations with some water flow down the crag, e.g. after rain, which keeps the soil moist, will be used by preference. Planting sites will be free from salt laden winds, and will have light or zero grazing from deer and feral goats plus no grazing from domestic stock. They will be located where growth of the vegetation on the crevices and ledges is not too vigorous, i.e. soil conditions suitable for Juniper and suboptimal for some other moorland plant species. As well as crags themselves, somewhat suitable conditions often exist near the base of crags. Such areas are frequently damp as a result of water running down the rock face during rainstorms, but are also subject to grazing by sheep and cattle. Small scale planting will be undertaken at some of these sites.

Stanley Smith Horticultural Trust

This project has been supported by the Stanley Smith Horticultural Trust. Grateful thanks are extended to the Trustees for their assistance.

References

Anon. (2010) UK priority species pages – Version 2 *Juniperus communis*. Joint Nature Conservation Committee, Peterborough http://jncc.defra.gov.uk/_speciespages/394.pdf. Accessed 4 July 2011. NB the useful 1999 Species Action Plan, author D. Price, is not at its original web location and appears to have been withdrawn.

Broome, A.C. (2003) *Growing juniper; propagation and establishment practices*. Information Note No. 50. Forest Commission, Edinburgh.

Gulliver, R.L. (2011) Observations on trees and grazing refuges in the west of Scotland. *Landscape Archaeology and Ecology*, **9**, this volume.

Lockton, A.J. (2011) *Species account: Juniperus communis*. Botanical Society of the British Isles, www.bsbi.org.uk.

Preston, C.D., Pearman, D.A. and Dines, T.D. (2002) *New Atlas of the British and Irish Flora*. Oxford University Press, Oxford, UK.

Sullivan, G. (2003) *Extent and Condition of Juniper Scrub in Scotland.* Unpublished Report to Scottish Natural Heritage, Contract No. BAT/AC205/01/02/96.

Thomas, P.A. El-Barghathi, M. and Polwart, A. (2007) *Juniperus communis* L. Biological Flora of the British Isles No. 248. *Journal of Ecology*, **95 (6)**, 1404-1440.

Ward, L.K. (2007). *Juniperus communis* L. Plantlife Species Dossier. Vol. 1, pp. 1–21. www.plantlife.org.uk/uploads/documents/Juniperus_communis__Dossier__part1.pdf. Vol. 2 pp. 22–46. www.plantlife.org.uk/uploads/documents/Juniperus_communis_dossier__part2.pdf.(last accessed 4 July 2011).

Woods, P. (2003). *Juniperus communis* in Yorkshire's Esk Valley, a Model for Woodland Education in Primary Schools. *Quarterly Journal of Forestry*, **97 (1)**, 55-58.

Re-wilding the Landscape: Some Observations on Landscape History
Della Hooke

The concept of re-wilding

A good many years ago (probably in the 1960s or 1970s) the concept of turning parts of Snowdonia into a 'wilderness' by permitting relatively unrestrained tree growth was broached. I was led to respond on that occasion that there was a very real danger of thus masking or even wiping out the evidence of many centuries of settlement and land use change. Almost every upland valley in Snowdonia still has such remains: even if prehistoric remains are visually few, the footprints of the medieval *hafodydd* can still be detected on the *ffridd* pastures that were often enclosed around the sixteenth century, the encroachments around the lowland and upland commons, upland farm units that were abandoned later with the break-up of some large estates, short-lived mining communities exploring the mineral potential, and all their associated field systems and boundaries – such examples are manifold (Hooke, 1997, 2003). It was even possible to suggest the different periods of stone walling that accompanied this ebb and flow of settlement, clearly distinguishing between the sinuous and apparently precarious walls that pre-dated the formal enclosure movements, built from whatever stone was readily at hand, through to a less random style, often employing large through-stones, that reflect the improved techniques carried out on well-managed estates after the seventeenth century, to the walls of nineteenth-century enclosure that often enclose large intakes on the hills and built by experienced gangs employed at the time. Even locally idiosyncratic styles can be detected. Blanket uncontrolled tree growth would inevitably destroy this kind of evidence and the field patterns themselves. Of course, there were historically more woods and trees, as I was able to show in a study of the parishes of Caerhun and Llanbedrycennin in the Conwy valley in the late 1990s – with settlements bearing such names such as *coed* 'wood', *llwyn* and *gelli* 'grove', or *goitre* 'homestead in a wood', especially in the tributary valleys of the Conwy where woodland had diminished but not disappeared by the nineteenth century. Virtually every upland region of England and Wales is rich in similar kinds of archaeological remains, testament to a region's changing land use history and, as such, worthy of preservation.

The concept of 're-wilding' came again to the fore in the 1990s, but this time as a rather better thought out approach. Essentially this involves the re-introduction of native animal species that are no longer present, plus the restoration of the habitats necessary for their survival. One gets the impression that over the last few years the emphasis has definitely been upon the re-introduction of animals rather than an emphasis upon the landscape. It is clear that any such moves would require careful management and since then various projects and experiments have tested the water so that further steps can be controlled. The idea that minimal human intervention should leave nature in control might just be a possibility in other parts of the world but not in Britain, and cultural implications always deserve consideration. Indeed, it is widely recognised that the ubiquity of human disturbance forces us to 'confront the fact that we cannot have wilderness that is truly wild or natural' (Cole, 2001, cited by Hodder and Bullock, 2009, 41). However, large-scale core wilderness areas with connecting corridors might still be achievable in the long run if local support could be gained.

Paul Lister's hopes for the re-introduction of such species as moose, brown bear, elk, wild boar, lynx and wolves on his estate in Scotland have so far proved highly contentious (e.g. Mountaineering Council of Scotland (MCofS), n.d.) and for most of Britain it would indeed be a dramatic reversal of our country's history. The white-tailed eagle has been successfully re-introduced on certain isles off the west coast of Scotland but rejected in Suffolk and currently beavers are being re-introduced – but carefully monitored – on the Allandale estate, also in Scotland. Arguments have been presented for the re-introduction of the lynx, one of the most endangered European mammals, and it has been estimated that this country could support about 450 lynx (Hetherington, 2008). Lynx mostly take deer but sheep would, for safety, have to be pastured some distance away from woodlands. Some of our native animals (i.e. those present after Britain had been severed by rising sea levels from the Continent) were lost at an early date – the aurochs and elk, for instance, seem to have virtually disappeared during the Bronze Age and the brown bear much later, probably in the early medieval period, but the beaver, lynx, wild boar and wolf were still present in medieval times, the wolf surviving in Scotland until 1743 and slightly longer in Ireland (Yalden, 2003). The beaver and wild boar were hunted out but the latter has returned from escaped stock, as in the Gloucestershire Forest of Dean. Some other mammals have experienced diminishing numbers but the polecat is recovering in numbers, especially in Wales.

From a cultural point of view the concept of 'wilderness' is attractive to some who relish the 'appearance' of wildness and a sense of remoteness – but there are always others who oppose landscape intervention of this kind for a variety of reasons – woods are seen as 'savage' and 'threatening'; they give rise to the fears expressed in fairy tales and mythology. As early as the Anglo-Saxon period, Bede expresses the perceived difference between the safety of the 'home' and the dangers waiting outside:

In the midst [of the banqueting hall] there is a comforting fire to warm the hall; outside, the storms of winter rain or snow are raging. This sparrow flies swiftly in through one door of the hall, and out through another. While he is inside, he is safe from the winter storms; but after a few moments of comfort, he vanishes from sight into the wintry world from which he came. (Bede, *Historia Ecclesiastica* II.13: Sherley-Price 1968, 127).

Here Bede is likening the passage of the sparrow to the life of man, but the dangers of the 'outside' are obvious and throughout the early medieval and medieval period wilderness in literature and legend is regarded as a place of demons, unknown perils and uncertainty (Neville 1999, 127; Hooke 2010a, 69-75).

Landscapes managed for ecology are not necessarily the (to some) tortured landscapes of Renaissance gardens or even the manicured lawns of later garden designers – 'wild' landscapes were not to be appreciated until the idea of 'romantic' landscapes raised its head with a new body of artists later in the eighteenth century: Wilson's *Cader Idris*, for instance, painted in the 1760s, depicts a rough landscape of primitive simplicity, a retreat from an ever more complicated world. The attraction of wild landscapes was further expressed in the writings of such people as John Muir in the later nineteenth century and early twentieth century (e.g. Muir, 1911). But still, for some, 'wild' landscapes are not necessarily producing the 'managed' landscapes which imply order and civilisation, the tidy' landscape of suburbia. And some would argue that they represent 'abandoned wildernesses' as opposed to the preferred landscapes of agricultural productivity – as Arthur Gibbs in his *A Cotswold Village*, expressed his idea of the rural idyll. His favoured view was of

... a wide expanse of undulating downland, divided into fifty-acre fields by means of loose, uncemented walls of grey stone. The grass is green for the time of the year, and scattered about are horses, cattle, and sheep, contentedly nibbling the short fine turf (Gibbs, 1868–1899/1988, p. 98).

It has been said that the English prefer a countryside that is *'tamed and inhabited, warm, comfortable, humanized rather than wild'* (Lowenthal and Prince, 1965, 190). To many today, it is not only the appearance of the farmed countryside that would render it attractive but the fact that it was producing food, bio-fuel or any other economic benefit.

Whatever changes are made to restore former habitats would obviously have considerable impact on the landscape. Re-wilding may represent a possibility where large tracts of open countryside survive, as in parts of Scotland, but elsewhere will probably have to be restricted to rather smaller areas. One has to approach the subject from a number of viewpoints and one would hope that these might include the historical as well as the ecological.

Historical landscapes are more than mere ecosystems; they illustrate ways in which man has adapted wild nature for his own use in ways that have been sustainable for generations. While future changes in land management and farming are inevitable it will be a challenge to accommodate these while preserving – and actually improving – the habitats available for our native fauna and flora.

Traditional landscapes

If re-wilding is accepted as an aim for some places, no single era can assume any immediate right to supremacy as the preferred objective, for change has contributed to the character of the landscape we see today. The landscape has never been static and one might question just what kind of landscape we wish to conserve, and for whose benefit, but the historical development of the landscape needs to be fully understood. Our flora and fauna have indeed survived and thrived in the *traditional* landscapes of Britain, produced by man's land use practices over thousands of years, and such landscapes contribute vastly towards the maintenance of 'Countryside Character' as well. It is not just the animals of the 'wilderness' we need to consider but our general fauna, especially as we appear to be producing increasingly damaged habitats. Insect life is jeopardised by over-reliance upon the widespread use of insecticides and many bird species are diminishing in number as food supplies are reduced; some small mammals are equally endangered. Thus problems arise not only from competing introduced species such as mink and coypu, but from present-day land use practices. Traditional landscapes are potentially just as, if not more, important than 'wilderness' and commendable moves towards the conservation maintenance of such landscapes have been taken under the Stewardship and later Farm Environment schemes, largely in response to the vast changes that took place in the latter half of the twentieth century. Within them trees and woods often play a significant role but the role of man has also left evidence that is of historical significance.

- Lowland heath was one such 'traditional landscape', much of which was destroyed in Dorset, for instance, by programmes of conifer planting after the two World Wars. Ironically, military usage helped to preserve this valuable wild-life habitat in some areas, as on the tank ranges to the north-east of East Lulworth. Yet, there have sometimes been problems with heathland restoration – the scraping away of topsoil can destroy the archaeological evidence of flint scatters or other prehistoric remains. Elsewhere, too, other open habitats and 'unproductive scrub' have been converted to productive plantations which generally support much more limited ecosystems. Plantations are not necessarily 'bad', however: populations of hen harriers, owls, sparrowhawks and crossbill, may increase – but they do create a very different kind of countryside, only occasionally or temporarily provided with the open areas that encourage many other species, and cannot match deciduous woodland in this respect.

- Open moorlands also are not secure from change. Upon the flanks of upland hills and on infertile granite or similar outcrops in the lowlands, moorlands were greatly extended in prehistoric times, especially as grazing was extended from the Bronze Age onwards, with cattle being a major sign of wealth. Tree regeneration was hampered and deteriorating climatic conditions at the end of the Bronze Age further damaged fragile soils. In many areas there was a change from a tree level as high as 700–800 metres to the open barren views of today; leaching or peat formation prevented further tree growth. However, the moorlands became a habitat for such birds as the merlin and hen-harrier which could more easily catch their prey over open ground. With the predatory birds targeted by nineteenth- and twentieth-century gamekeepers, anxious to protect their black grouse for their shoots, many have become threatened species and the dangers are not yet over. It has been shown, however, how raptors can help to keep game bird populations healthy by removing ill and infected specimens (Davies, 2005).

 There are other conflicts: today conservationists welcome the presence of 'wild' ponies such as the Exmoor and Dartmoor breeds, but these animals are not really 'wild' and farmers, who now derive little economic benefit from their presence, are advocating culling young foals to avoid the cost of winter provisions. The animals help to keep the gorse – no longer needed for roofing *etc* – from invading open habitats.

- The extension of ploughland, again stimulated by wartime experiences and made possible by the addition of vast amounts of chemical fertilisers, irrevocably changed much of our chalk downland – again Celtic field systems that had survived for over 1,000 years were destroyed by a few ploughings.

 Other traditional farmed landscapes have suffered considerable decline over the last fifty years or so. Indeed, open-field landscapes are now mere fragments following eighteenth-century enclosure. However, the grass baulks of some of these fragments, as at Forrabury in Cornwall, still carry wild flowers, as do ancient grassland pastures, many of which arose from Tudor enclosure; many of these species-rich old grasslands have now been ploughed up. Over 63% of our old orchards, too, have been grubbed up since the 1950s leading to pollen loss which historically has helped to maintain insect and bee populations.

- Our water meadows were an essential way of providing hay for winter feed throughout history.

Although advanced methods of irrigating them were a relatively late development, these were aimed at stimulating the early growth of grass for grazing sheep. The meadows, which would originally have been subjected periodically to natural flooding, also conserved a rich flora. However, they have been much encroached upon by building and roads, the latter frequently choosing to follow relatively flat valleys. Brian in the early 1990s (Brian, 1993) showed how our common meadows had been decimated by such changes and even today the Lugg Meadows once pinpointed as the chosen route for a Hereford bypass – are not entirely safe. The loss of our wild flowers can only have had a detrimental effect upon bee populations, essential for pollination. Some also still show evidence of the channels that represent attempts to irrigate or 'flood' them, mainly in western and southern England constructed in the seventeenth and eighteenth centuries (Williamson, 2002, 59-62).

- Everyone is aware of hedgerow loss – hundreds of miles of ancient hedgerows have been removed to make way for extended arable farming with large machines. The patterns of ancient hedgerows were a significant feature of the historical character of many regions, not only fossilising field systems which in some areas can be traced back to Roman times, but also acting as valuable corridors for wildlife and providing homes for nesting birds. But even here there are caveats – while few would question their benefit as wildlife corridors, deliberate hedgerow creation has its drawbacks. If one knows the historical character of the countryside there are some regions that have been open arable for well over 1,000 years – such as the arable lands of parts of Cambridgeshire – and here the introduction of hedgerows would be historically quite wrong. Equally beneficial results might be achieved with unsown field margins, beetle banks or patches left for wild plants and grasses.

- Wetlands, once important for fishing and fowling and the gathering of rushes and reeds for, amongst other uses, roofing thatch, have often been destroyed by being drained for agriculture. This has been particularly detrimental to our wild bird populations and at an early stage led to the loss of species such as the stork, crane and spoonbill. However, the spoonbill, as a bird migrating to the UK in summer, successfully nested at Martin Mere in Lancashire in 1999 and is an occasional visitor (WWT Martin Mere, 2010) while the crane is being re-introduced on the Somerset Levels and Moors (RSPB, 2011). In the Fenlands, extensive reclamation followed the adoption of wide-scale schemes often first carried out by Dutch engineers in the seventeenth century. Today an attempt is being made to conserve or re-create area of fenland (Figure 1), often

Figure 1. Carr woodland in north Warwickshire (Photograph D. Hooke).

Figure 2. Conifer plantations in Cwmsylfaen near Bontddu, Gwynedd (Photograph D. Hooke).

associated with areas of willow and alder carr, largely for the benefit of bird populations, as at Wicken Fen in Cambridgeshire.

- Upland landscapes are of many kinds but indiscriminate grazing, as encouraged some years ago by subsidies based upon numbers of stock kept, not only destroys trees but damages variegated grassland, suppressing the ground flora: the number of sheep increased nearly fourfold in the twentieth century. With some 25% of the Welsh upland affected by the spread of conifer plantations since 1945 this has meant increased pressure on the remaining open land (Green M. 2003, 408; Wildlife Trusts, 1996) (Figure 2). Further, 'improvement' by the drainage and reseeding of upland pastures further undermines the historical character of the countryside as well as being destructive to the richness of ground flora.

Upland landscapes are indeed 'on the edge' of change. With upland farming providing such poor returns it has been suggested that ecotourism might be a better source of finance. Certainly a decline in sheep numbers would be ecologically beneficial and there is undoubtedly scope for the extension of woodland in upland valleys. But there is also a need for ecotourism to be carefully managed if unsuitable activities are not to take place.

Wood-pasture landscapes

The author's specific interest lies with wood-pasture landscapes. Many upland pastures still show traces of an earlier wood-pasture usage and are generally species-rich (Figure 3) but many wood-pasture regions were also characteristic of lowland Britain (Figure 4).

This is a type of landscape that does not fit readily into modern farming but is one of our most treasured traditional landscapes. From at least the late Iron Age into the early medieval period wooded regions played an important economic and social role. The pasturing

Figure 3. Relict wood-pasture landscape in Dovedale, Derbyshire (Photograph D. Hooke).

Figure 4. A wood-pasture scene in Sutton Park near Birmingham (Photograph D. Hooke).

of domestic stock, often initially driven for considerable distances to their summer pastures, was a basic feature of the rural economy. The woodland was thus maintained as open in character but well scattered with large native trees, especially those that survive well in such conditions – like the oak, the young shoots of which are unpalatable to stock and which can grow again from a deep root once the top growth has been bitten-off (Rackham, 2003, 293). The distribution of oak – and ash, which readily re-grows if stocking numbers are diminished – can be mapped from early medieval place-names and charters and clearly shows marked concentrations in the regions known to have been well-wooded areas of seasonal pasture in pre-Conquest times (Hooke, 2010a, 192 Fig. 14, 193-200).

The pig was perhaps the most important animal pastured in this way, although cattle, horses, sheep and even goats are mentioned in contemporary documents. The fact that the pigs rooted around the trees helped to bring in light

and ensure good crops of acorns (Green, 2010, 57). In the south of England, beech-mast was an equally important source of seasonal food. Pre-Conquest charters offer the earliest detailed documentary accounts of this practice, especially for the Weald of south-eastern England (Hooke, 2011). Here domestic animals – pigs, cattle/plough-beasts, sheep, horses or goats were driven annually from estates in the surrounding lowlands to seasonal pastures called dens. Sometimes information is also provided about the numbers of pigs involved – like the 120 pigs and 50 cattle pastured in two dens belonging to estates held by Christ Church, Canterbury (S 323). Domesday Book records that the Warwickshire estate of Stoneleigh in its amassed woods had pasture for 2,000 pigs (Plaister, 1976, 1,4).

Forests after the Norman Conquest helped to preserve deciduous woodland across much of England; these maintained populations of deer, wild boar and other woodland animals, the fallow deer being re-introduced in large numbers. The use of seasonal pasture was kept alive in the Norman forests, even if sometimes it led to conflict, – the open nature actually helping huntsmen to follow their quarry. Neither should the social role be forgotten – although hunting was an elitist activity it paradoxically sustained those of lower status in the community. Real conflict occurred when woods were increasingly taken into private ownership, as on the Paget estates on Cannock Chase in Staffordshire in the eighteenth century, referred to in my previous conference paper on 'Early wood commons and beyond' (Hooke, 2010b). Here, attempts to enclose coppices to provide wood for the family's ironworks reduced the commoners' rights to take loppings from trees and their rights of pasture for their stock, leading to riots in the sixteenth century (Harrison, 1999, 103). Riots also occurred when enclosure affected the remaining open commons in the eighteenth and nineteenth centuries, as at Ogley Hay in south Staffordshire. This was one of the small administrative divisions known as hays that had survived the breakup of the former Cannock Forest, but following enclosure in 1838/39 the access roads used by surrounding communities to take their animals into the woods were deliberately stopped up, leading to unrest. Patches of former forests and chases which escaped desecration at the hands of eighteenth- and nineteenth-century agricultural improvers may on occasions still be blessed with wood-pasture landscapes.

Woodlands are rich in archaeology. On occasions they have apparently re-grown over earlier landscapes – linear dykes are found within Wychwood in Oxfordshire and at Blunt's Green in the Warwickshire Arden which appear to represent Iron Age enclosures constructed close to territorial frontiers. Trees have colonised abandoned Iron Age hillforts in the Welsh Borderland, and at Welshbury hillfort, in the Forest of Dean, the limes are probably growing from a rootstock as ancient as the earthworks themselves. In northern Hampshire, in the woods of Faccombe and Crux Easton, it is still possible to trace the so-called 'Celtic' field systems that were in use in late Iron Age and Roman times; these were abandoned in post-Roman times and the woods became important areas of royal game reserve (Hooke, 1988). Trees soon move in if fields or buildings are neglected, as wild nature regains control: thorns rapidly colonise abandoned fields and pastures and trees sprout on crumbling walls, like the gnarled yews that grow around and through the walls of Craswell Priory in Herefordshire.

Other archaeological relics reveal former woodland usage: woodbanks can be traced which are testament to changing management, as in Sutton Park near Birmingham. Here some of them bounded the hollins which were a valuable source of leaf fodder in the middle ages. Since coal measure rocks are usually infertile, these have often remained wooded in the midland region. In the Forest of Dean, in

Gloucestershire, the coal measures overlie iron ore beds that supported ironworking by late Iron Age times and continued use of these iron resources has often left a landscape of heavily disturbed rough ground within woodland, partly arising from the mining of iron from shallow outcrops and eroded caves systems (for the origin of such scowles, see Gloucestershire City Council, 2004, 2008), plus the associated features of charcoal burning platforms. The iron ore was generally roasted prior to smelting to remove moisture and impurities and was then refined by further heating in a bloomery which required about two acres of wood annually for each ton of iron produced (Cleere and Crossley, 1985, 100). The charcoal-fired blast furnace replaced the bloomery as continental technology was introduced into England in the mid-fifteenth century and by the mid-seventeenth century Dean had the greatest concentration of ironworks in the country with 20 blast furnaces in the region (Riden, 1993); it was not until 1795 that coke-fired furnaces were introduced at the Cinderford Ironworks, so plentiful were the supplies of charcoal. In Dean, the Weald of southeast England and other early iron-working regions, the charcoal-burning areas may be revealed by earthen platforms, still often floored with charcoal, that are often connected by systems of trackways. The industrial features that were located close to these supplies of charcoal – the bloomeries, blast furnaces and forges – have often left significant archaeological remains, added to which are the hammer-ponds or their dams and leats, wheel-pits, masonry, and quantities of slag and cinder. In some woods, coal mining has given rise to both early bell-pits and later features associated with shaft mining. Built by people who frequently combined mining with small-scale farming, cottages were often built around the edges of woodland commons in the post-medieval period, as in Dean, giving rise to straggling hamlets or isolated settlements, some now long abandoned but still traceable on the ground. These and other indicators of ancient crafts, such as sawpits, make woodland regions vulnerable areas for any extension of the woods.

Wood-pasture landscapes have often been conserved in historic parklands, as at Staverton in Suffolk, and trees were often pollarded to encourage the growth of timber out of the reach of grazing animals, giving rise to some of our most valuable veteran trees. Today, the importance of managing these pollard trees, so much a feature of ancient wood-pasture, is fully recognised. Parks are actually some of our most precarious landscapes and have undergone change throughout history. Medieval parks were initially game reserves, with deer kept for hunting and a source of venison, but as the fashion began to have them as an ornamental feature around a large Tudor mansion so they became expressions of good taste, beauty and wealth. Parkland design changed with fashion taste but the 'natural' landscapes favoured by Brown and Repton preserved something of their earlier appearance – at Moccas in Herefordshire the ancient pollards were retained by Brown, possibly inherited from an earlier existence within the Forest of Dorstone (Figure 5). Many parks were made, however, over former farms and fields; in an otherwise praiseworthy wish to replace trees as ornamental features in their own right, I have seen the remains of deserted medieval villages, with their house platforms and tofts, almost totally destroyed by injudicious planting.

Figure 5. Old oak pollards in Moccas Park, Herefordshire (Photograph D. Hooke).

Woodland management

Both upland and lowland woods were heavily planted with conifers after the two World Wars in an attempt to make Britain more self-reliant and less dependent upon imported materials, leading again to the loss of deciduous woodland and wood-pasture. While conifer plantations may support their own kind of wildlife, including the goshawk and some species of owl, and may eventually revive mycorrhiza in the soil, the extension of native deciduous woodland seems to be the preferred objective. Not only does this support a rich wildlife but people like deciduous trees:

Deciduous trees please the English because they are delicately patterned, softly outlined, varied in form and color, scumbled in texture, seasonal in foliage, tolerant of undergrowth, and generally older than conifers.

Whereas

Conifers are considered gloomy, harsh, and oppressive, partly because many of them are strictly commercial (Lowenthal and Prince, 1965, 197).

In Ennerdale valley, Cumbria, native woodlands are being allowed to spread to promote the objective of a wilder landscape there and Galloway cattle have replaced sheep. The Brecon Beacons Management Plan draft (2009) also noted how:

The point is fast approaching whereby what biodiversity remains will no longer be sufficient to provide a sustainable future for both habitats and species. What remains today is only a fraction of what was here in the past. (Brecon Beacons National Park (BBNP), 2009, 59).

As result it is recommended that, while commercial forestry must continue, and can complement the open landscapes of unimproved upland grazing at higher altitudes, the lower valley native trees should be allowed to expand further onto the higher slopes where they are already an existing feature, and also to migrate into the commercial plantations with additional broadleaf planting. In the Mynydd Du Forest, broadleaf planting should increase from 7% of the woodland cover to some 33% by a combination of felling and replanting and natural regeneration management (BBNP, 2011, 102).

If woods are not pastured – or if the effects of pasture are not deliberately copied – then there is a danger that they become a tangle of trees, bracken and bramble. One area of woodland, Lady Park Wood in the Wye Valley, has been kept with the minimum of intervention and has remained relatively open through natural tree fall and browsing by deer, but the latter, given that no higher carnivores survive today, are now having to be culled (Peterken, 2005) so that no real 'natural' habitat seems possible today. By removing predators, deer may now increase in number so as to cause considerable tree damage.

In general, historical management methods of managing woods have also often faded away – the creation of varying habitats by coppicing, for instance, has been neglected, to the detriment to many species. Coppices were of enormous value to iron manufacturers in the seventeenth century, as in Dean or around Coalbrookdale, especially producing wood for the charcoal furnaces; besides they produced a wide range of usable wood for hurdles, building *etc* and other commodities such as hazel nuts. The regular cycle of light and shade, together with the grazing being restricted when coppices were first cut, favoured such woodland plants as wood anemones, bluebells and foxgloves; the glades and scrub were favoured by nesting birds and insects together with many species of butterfly. In the forest of Wyre on the Worcestershire/Shropshire border pigs are again being introduced in Wimperhill Wood to clear scrub from part of a (possible) prehistoric enclosure (ex inf. Adam Mindykowski, Worcestershire Archaeology Unit) (Figure 6).

Figure 6. Pigs being pastured in Wimperhill Wood, Forest of Wyre (Photo Adam Mindykowski).

There are many present-day schemes for managing woodlands and heathlands by pasturing stock – whether the animals are Longhorn cattle, as in Windsor Forest or Epping Forest, or, on the Malvern Hills on the Herefordshire/Worcestershire border, where hardier breeds are required, Highland or Belted Galloways (sheep, eating shorter grass, are also put onto the hills to complement the cattle grazing). Elsewhere, as in Wyre, pigs are used for selected purposes.

It is widely recognised today that woodland has an added recreational value, a concept that has been taken on board by such projects as the National Forest and various Community Forests and may be a strong feature in most upland reafforestation schemes. In all of these, it is recognised that woodland management should ideally incorporate pasturing by a range of animals. Even if wood-pasture can only be sustained in limited regions, such controlled grazing remains essential if this type of traditional woodland landscape is to be conserved.

Conclusions

Re-wilding on a large scale for the introduction of now extinct species may have only limited potential over much of Britain but the re-instatement or conservation of traditional landscapes has a major role to play in both preserving the habitats of our native fauna and flora and also in preserving the regional character of our countryside. All attempts to manage the landscape should, however, pay close attention to man's contribution towards creating these landscapes in the first place and ensure that any surviving historical evidence is not destroyed. In a situation in which many habitats are becoming degraded and where the quality of landscape is also being diminished, the re-creation of treescapes, especially the kind of open woodland that once characterised wood-pasture regions, has much to offer from almost every angle: timber resources, beneficial ecosystems and wildlife habitats, and places for recreation or personal wellbeing. In them animals, man and nature combine to produce a rich milieu of both biodiversity and beauty.

Bibliography

Bede. *Historia gentis Anglorum ecclesastica*, see Sherley-Price, L., below.

BBNP (2009) *Brecon Beacons National Park Management Plan 2010–2011*. Draft Version 2, http//:www.breconbeacons.org/the-authority/planning/strategy

BBNP (2011) *Brecon Beacons Management Plan 2010–2011*, http//:www.breconbeacons.org/the-authority/planning/strategy

Brian, A. (1993) Lammas meadows. *Landscape History*, **15**, 57-69.

Cleere, H.F. and Crossley, D. (1985) *The Iron Industry of the Weald*. Leicester University Press, Leicester.

Cole, D.N. (2001) Management dilemmas that will shape wilderness in the 21st century. *Journal of Forestry*, **99**, 4-8.

Davies, R. (2005) Predators and the profitability of grouse moors. *British Wildlife*, **16(5)**, 339-47.

Gibbs, J.A. (1868-99) *A Cotswold Village*. Repr. 1988, Allan Sutton Publishing, Stroud.

Gloucestershire City Council Archaeology Service (2004) *The scowles of the Forest of Dean*. http://www.gloucestershire.gov.uk/utilities

Gloucestershire City Council (2008) '*Scowles*'. http://www.gloucestershire.gov.uk/index.

Green, M. (2003) The Welsh uplands – past, present and future. *British Wildlife*, **14(6)**, 403-12.

Green, E.E. (2010) The importance of open-grown trees – from acorn to ancient. *British Wildlife*, **21(5)**, 334-8.

Harrison, C. (1999) *Fire on the Chase: rural riots in sixteenth-century Staffordshire*. In: Morgan, P. and Phillips, A.D.M (eds.) *Staffordshire Histories. Essays in Honour of Michael Greenslade*. Staffordshire Record Society & Centre for Local History, University of Keele, Keele, 97-126.

Hetherington, D. (2008) The history of the Eurasian lynx in Britain and the potential for its reintroducton. *British Wildlife*, **20(2)**, 77-86.

Hodder, K.H., and Bullock, J.M. (2009) Really wild? Naturalistic grazing in modern landscapes. *British Wildlife*, **20(5)**, 37-43.

Hooke, D. (1988) *Regional variation in southern and central England in the Anglo-Saxon period and its relationship to land units and settlement*. In: Hooke, D. (ed.) *Anglo-Saxon Settlements*. Basil Blackwell, Oxford, 123-52.

Hooke, D. (1997) *Place-names and vegetation history as a key to understanding settlement in the Conwy valley*, In: Edwards, N. (ed.) *Landscape and Settlement in Medieval Wales*. Oxbow Monograph 81. Oxford, 79-95.

Hooke, D. (2003) *Place-names and land use in coastal Ardudwy, with comparisons with the Conwy valley in north Wales*. In: Unwin, T. and Spek, T. (eds.) *European Landscapes: from mountain to sea*. Huma Publishers, Tallinn, Estonia, 139-45.

Hooke, D. (2010a) *Trees in Anglo-Saxon England: Literature, Lore and Landscape*. Boydell Press, Woodbridge.

Hooke, D. (2010b) Early wood commons and beyond. *Landscape Archaeology and Ecology* **8(1)**, 107-20.

Hooke, D. (2011) *The woodland landscape of early medieval England*. In: Higham, N.J. and Ryan, M.J. (eds.) *Place-Names, Language and the Anglo-Saxon Landscape*. Boydell Press, Woodbridge, 143-74.

Lowenthal, D. and Prince, H.C. (1965) English landscape tastes. *Geographical Review,* **55(2)** 186-222.

MCofS (n.d.) Mountaineering Council of Scotland, '*Position statement on Alladale Project*', http://www.mcofs.org.uk/assets/access

Muir, J. (1911) *My First Summer in the Sierra* (London). Repr. in The Eight Wilderness-Doscovery Books (1992) Diadem Books, London.

Neville, J. (1999) *Representations of the Natural World in Old English Poetry*. Cambridge University Press, Cambridge.

Peterken, G.F. and Mountford, E. (2005) National woodland reserves - 60 years of trying at Lady Park Wood. *British Wildlife*, **17(1)**, 7-16.

Plaister, J. (1976) *Domesday Book, 23, Warwickshire*. Phillimore, Chichester.

Rackham, O. (2003) *Ancient Woodland, its History, Vegetation and Uses in England*. New edn. Castlepoint Press, Dalbeattie, Kirkcudbrightshire.

Riden, P. (1993) *A Gazetteer of Charcoal-Fired Blast Furnances in Great Britain in Use since 1660*. Merton Priory Press, Cardiff.

RSPB (2011) *The great crane project*. http://www.rspb.org.uk/supporting/campaigns/greatcraneproject/project.aspx

Sawyer, P.H. (1968) *Anglo-Saxon Charters, an Annotated List and Bibliography*. Royal Historical Society, London.

Sherley-Price, L. (ed. & trans.) (1968) *Bede. A History of the English Church and People*. Penguin Books, Harmondsworth.

Wildlife Trusts (1996) *Crisis in the Hills – Overgrazing in the Uplands*. The Wildlife Trusts, Lincoln.

Williamson, T. (2002) *The Transformation of Rural England. Farming and the landscape 1700–1870*. University of Exeter Press, Exeter.

Wildfowl and Wetlands Trust Martin Mere (2010) *Saving wetlands for wildlife and people*. http://www.org.uk/visit-us/martin-mere/news

Yalden, D.W. (2003) Mammals in Britain – a historical perspective. *British Wildlife*, **14(4)**, 243-51.

Smuggling and surviving in the uplands: a landscape builder of grazing and cattle on the Portuguese and Spanish Borders in the nineteenth century

Cristina Joanaz de Melo
Sheffield Hallam University; post-doctoral grant from FCT, Portugal.

Summary

This paper deals with the importance of the strategy developed by the highlanders to keep their flocks intact throughout the second half of the nineteenth century in the Portuguese uplands bordering Spain. The strategy occurred within the climatic context of torrential floods and subsequent devastation. The analyses will then focus on the extent that the success of highlanders in avoiding cattle losses, because they were away from the flood waters, would have triggered competition for the pastures on the slopes, which were now desired by the lowland agrarian landowners. The latter, being unable to legitimately expel the secular occupants, attempted that action by making the highlanders guilty of one crime: smuggling cattle. This attitude would justify a strong intervention by public authority in the uplands decreeing the restriction of the highlanders' rights over the common lands. Eventually this would lead to the highlanders being pushed away from the alternative pasturing system and the lowlanders being assured food for their flocks the year round namely during winter flooding and summer drought.

Introduction

After the cycle of torrential devastation which occurred in Portugal in 1854 and 1858, areas considered to be of low agrarian value acquired a higher significance for lowland farmers. In the torrential downpours of the 1850s, unlike the situation in the valley bottoms and plains, where meadows and cultivated fields were devastated, flocks and vegetable crops did not suffer the same degree of loss on the slopes and summits of the uplands.

Thus, the highlanders' economic system appeared to be better prepared to overcome hydrological natural hazards, such as torrential downpours, than the system carried out in the lowlands. Such a difference in economic response due to the effects of heavy rains and flooding in the territory were noticed by politicians, as they were part of the agrarian elite. The cattle raising system of the highlanders was clearly more efficient in facing the impacts of the hydrological hazards in the territory than the ones followed in the lowlands. The slopes, even holding weak arable soils could be seen with new appeal to raise cattle.

Hence, despite their renewed interest in the potential pasture areas on the slopes and summits, the wealthier landowners had to overcome many obstacles to access to them. As in other European regions, it could be expected that there would be strong opposition from the highlanders to having their commons occupied by wealthy farmers from the lowlands. Once upland communities had secular rights over pasturing they could not simply be pushed away. Even any attempt to implement a state-led public regime for the management of natural resources would present a major challenge for the administrative and police bodies in the districts.

Portuguese parliamentarians were well aware that the equivalent attempts to impose an administrative regime to convert pasture to forest on the slopes and the summits of the French Pyrenees had not been accomplished in the best way in France. Indeed, these attempts resulted in very heavy conflicts between the local population and the state officers, in 1828 and again in 1846. Therefore it was obvious that another legal path had to be followed in Portugal.

One alternative was to challenge the legitimacy of the highlanders' way of life and their trading practices. It was reasoned that there could then be action taken under the main duty of executive power to restore order or legality. A criminal activity allegedly practiced by the cattle producers in the mountains was found. In 1860, highlanders were believed to be smuggling cattle across the inland border with Spain. Therefore it was decided that a wider and stronger surveillance should be carried out in that area to gather evidence about the situation. Linking the issue of the highlanders' cattle raising activities with the crime of smuggling in the parliamentary debate in 1860 might have a two-fold outcome. As well as highlighting the need to police the highlanders' agrarian activities and trade, it could also enable the cattle producers to be pushed aside and justify a legal transfer of land and land-use to other landowners.

Primary constraint and incentive to pasture uses and management: geography

Bells clanging and sheep running in the fields could be pictured as an old memory of the past countryside. However, in nineteenth-century Europe, more than a relic image of the Romantic period, rearing cattle represented a major activity in a wide range of rural landscapes.

A considerable number of studies about the management of commons have shown that raising cattle was an activity held by a wide range of economic and social agents. Historiographically, its relevance throughout the Modern period and across the nineteenth century has been tested as well, across a vast geographical area within Europe. This has covered both the United Kingdom and continental regions such as the

North Western, Circum-alpine chain, the North Mediterranean and the Iberian Peninsula.

Up until about two decades ago, the historiographies of the commons and forest management tended to dichotomize cattle rearing both socially and geographically. According to this vision, powerful economic landlords would keep the most fertile pastures for their flocks while highlanders would shepherd cattle on poorer soils in the upland slopes.

More recently, within the last decade, studies have shown that these sharp divisions between the social actors and geographical areas have become blurred. It has been carefully stressed that there is a vast palette and quality of natural resources which are unequally distributed both in the lowlands as well as in the uplands. This is apparent in a range of different territories including within the British Isles, North Western Europe, the alpine region and the Iberian Peninsula. Furthermore, the variety of natural stages within ecosystems would determine diversity of the commons economies as well as of the practices on the recollection, uses, regulations and management of untamed wild flora. At the same time, different cultures could and did end up developing similar economic behaviours.

This new trend in commons research takes into consideration a complex set of factors, geographical, cultural and political which explain the plurality of practices taking place in the management of the commons. The characteristics of the terrain inside political boundaries, the soil thickness of the slopes, the hydrology and snow distribution over the topography, the altitude and the finally atypical weather conditions throughout the year are all contributory factors towards the contraction or enlargement of the areas for shepherding.

Obviously, the geomorphological characteristics of the land inside political borders would clearly determine access to the kind of pastures existing within these boundaries. It is easy to understand that independently from the wealth of the farmers, for instance, in the Helvetian Confederation the struggle for the meadows in the slopes would take place among the uplands, while in Holland, flocks and herds would be raised in the lowlands. Yet in the second half of the nineteenth century in France, Spain or Portugal, territories which encompass a vast range of landscapes, similar competition for cattle raising areas could take place in the lowland plains as well as in the mountain regions, mostly in meadows which weren't farmed for arable crops.

It has been extensively documented, in the nineteenth century in France and in Portugal that there were parliamentary debates around the theme of the legitimacy of the landowners from the lowlands to occupy the pastures of the commons both in the plains and in the highlands.

Within the liberal new legal order within these countries (abolishing Ancient Regime rights), the new framework, which endorsed equal opportunities to accessing public land, had opened up the possibility for other farmers to claim access to the upland pastures, besides the traditional community of shepherds. Historiographically, it has been shown in some cases, that cattle growers were interested in pastures in both the lowlands and at higher altitudes, in order to assure food for their cattle throughout the year.

The upland pastures had actually been managed for centuries, since the Middle Ages, from the Spanish Pyrenees through the Central Chain across Portugal and Spain and down to Béticà. Nonetheless in the nineteenth century, in Spain, these *Mesta* privileges were taken back. Transhumance was not a problem in itself but granting low-level pastures in summer as well as in winter could be avoided by using pastures at different altitudes ie. in the mountainous regions.

However, the relationship between the lowlands and uplands was not simple. A set of questions springs to mind when trying to understand the motives of the wealthy farmers in the lowlands. Who would really be interested in investing in areas subject to the impact of natural hydrological hazards? Who would be interested in investing in risky areas of annual erosion brought about by the impact of torrential rains, falling annually in winter and spring? Then, what altitude would individual wealthy farmers be prepared to use to assure pasture would continue in the uplands as opposed to what the existing groups of shepherds would be prepared to use, at what height and fertility of the soil? Would it be cost effective from the point of view of both the land and also their cattle movement across such a wide range of territories? Secondly, what were the odds of obtaining free permits to explore public land in the mountains and compete successfully with existing highland communities of shepherds, especially after the failed attempts of the public services to forest the summits? Thirdly, why would they explore such a difficult alternative if the lowlands were richer than the upland pastures? Even wet lands, the moors, swamps or marshlands could be converted into artificial meadows.

A further question presents itself, why were they making a claim on for what at first glance seemed to be the most difficult option? Why,. if these wealthy farmers were living in areas of richer soils, either arable farming or rearing cattle near to areas of major concentrations of population which would be better for trade and easy transport of goods, would they be looking to expand into the uplands?

A crucial element for the understanding of this apparently similar problem in so many '*upland*' regions across the European Mountain chains lies in the meaning attached to the words '*uplands*' or '*highlands*' in each region. The same expression is being applied to a quite different spectrum of landscapes. It seems to me that both altitude and latitude matter in order to explain the different reactions and uses of lowland farmers to their regional uplands across Europe.

Altitude, weather behaviour and water erosion impact

The term 'uplands' in the Pennines of England, in the Alps or in the Central Chain on the Iberian Peninsula describe different environments of flora, pedology, hydrology and erosion impacts upon the slopes. Hydrological factors linked to the steepness of the topography and the altitude of the valleys were features that might have influenced specific economic systems. In the uplands, these would be based on cattle and sheep rearing, dairy products and perhaps also in a higher fibre diet of dry fruits and a wide variety of nuts, rather than in cereals which constituted the default diet in the lowlands.

In areas where the altitude varies from sea level to 4,500m asl in the Mont Blanc region of the French and Italian Alps, or up to 3,500m asl in the Bética in Spain, the word '*uplands*' hardly means the same as in continental Portugal where the highest peak of Serra da Estrela rises to 2000m asl. These differences in altitude have different consequences in terms of weather conditions and hydrological performance.

The mountains of Portugal don't have perpetual snows. This results in the projection of flooding incidents in Portugal to be normally expected to be within a specific period, November and February, each year. To some extent, as it will be further examined below. It might also explain why in Portugal when the length of the rainy season increased, in the years between 1854 and 1857, from October to May, and then again in 1859 to 1861, the population and the rulers were just not culturally prepared to deal with weather conditions that were thought to be exceptional, of short duration and not repeatable.

Whilst, in other countries where some of the mountain ranges are higher, such as France, Italy, Germany, Austria or Switzerland, the seasonal water-flow is likely to last longer with summer pastures available at higher altitudes but in more difficult conditions of access than in Portugal.

In the Pyrenees, the Alps or the Bética, the drainage patterns drive strong flows of water into the lowlands, twice a year. The river margins and adjacent lands and the plains are charged with two seasons of floods: devastating mudflows during the winter, the period of both torrential rains and snow, and again in the spring, due to the melting of snow and ice cover from the mountain slopes.

In this sense I will be put forward the argument that the lower altitude of the headsprings in the Portuguese mountains (up to 2000m asl), the lack of perpetual snow on the summits, leads to a band of vegetation above the altitude of the torrential waters' destructive impact which contain leaf shedding trees with rich nutritional fruits or nuts, such as *Castanea sativa*, between 900m asl and 1500m asl[1], would enable cattle and people to survive more easily than in the higher altitudes. Cattle would live in new or renewed pastures and the highlanders diet of animal proteins, vegetable and fruits would be different from the cereal based diet of the lowlands.

Across Europe between 1850 and 1855, there was a short cycle of heavier than average rainfall. This exacerbated the trend in Portugal where an increase in average rainfall had begun at the beginning of the century. Since the early 1800s, in Portugal, precipitation had been increasing with rolling average values of annual precipitation in the second half of the century significantly higher than ones measured at the start. The peaks of rainfall during the 1850s were much higher than in the 1800s. (See Table 1. and Figures 1 and 2). From qualitative data it appears that the summers of 1854 to 1858 and again in the 1860s were "*quite warm*"[2].

Although there are no accurate data from the time about the effects of the warmer temperatures, one might presume that steady wet weather and heat could have produced more fertile pastures at higher altitudes where previously such a quality of grass had never been expected to develop. Furthermore, such a set of atypical conditions developing in a relatively short time, might also have encouraged shepherds to move higher up into the mountains. Thus they would have avoided their flocks being affected by either flooding or the effects of the heat at lower altitudes in the mountains or on the lowland plains.

All of these hypotheses and questions emerged from two episodes which I have studied and which appear to me to have unsatisfactory explanations. The first episode centres around the apparent 'oddness' of the statement from the Civil Governor of the Guarda, one of the highest and poorest regions of the country in 1856. He asserted that the area under his responsibility had no problems with food supply. This was in marked contrast to most of the rest of the country. In that year the country was dominated by a famine amongst the population at all levels and agriculture crises all over the country. Guarda happened to be the only District where administrative officers did not report a severe crisis. The second episode which drew my attention to the Guarda region's food production occured four years later, in 1860. Here some members of the national parliament raised concerns about the apparanet cattle smuggling over the inland border with Spain. This enquiry was centred precisely in the correspondent area of mountains of the Guarda District.

The question lies in understanding why that it was only by 1860 that politicians raised their concerns about smuggling in the mountains. Or at least expressed them more strongly than in the previous decades, when the problem was known to have existed in that region of the country since the eve of time? Was the reason for their interest that the parliamentarians were looking to reduce the illegal smuggling activity, and use this potential food reserve as a preventive measure against future famine? Or, did they want to acknowledge the success of raising cattle in the uplands? Whereas in the lowlands, floods had severely damaged pastures and flocks, in the past six years of heavy rainfall leading to shortages of food, the upland region had appeared to escape. Smuggling might have become then a precious indicator of an economically successful practice of cattle rearing in the mountains, which had been unexpectedly brought to light within a framework of more general agricultural, health and economic calamities in the rest of the country.

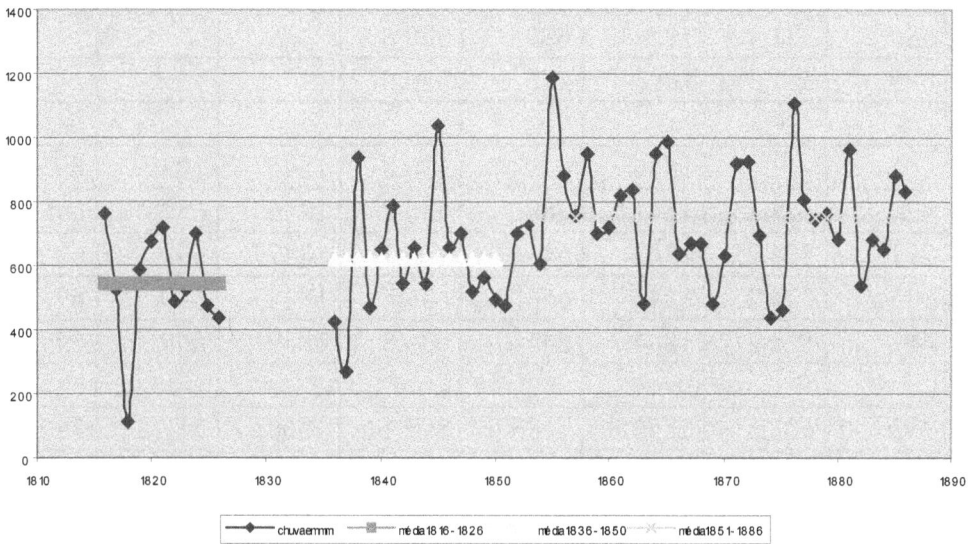

Figure 1. Average rainfall between 1816-1826, 1836-1850, 1851 1886 over the curve of absolute annual values[3].

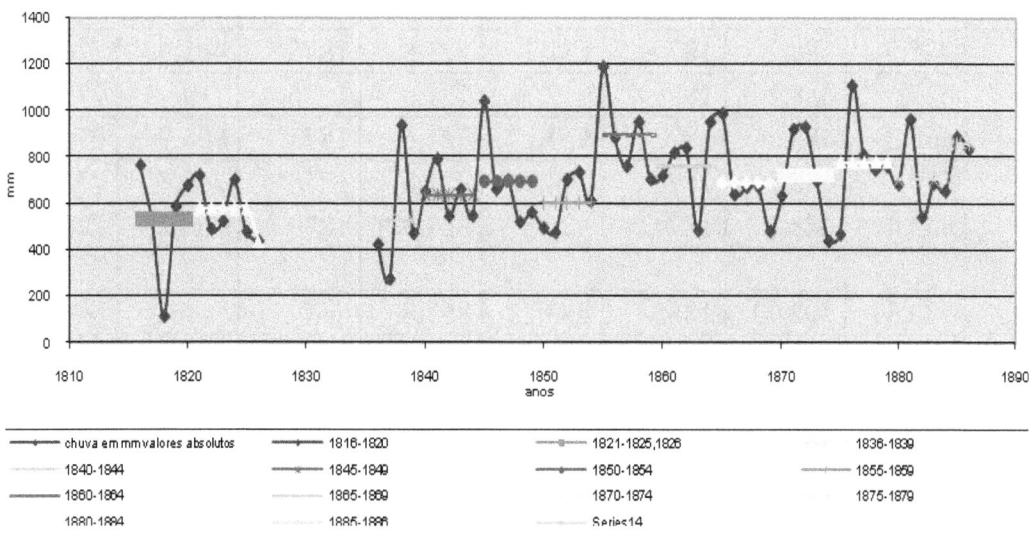

Figure 2. Average rainfall in annual absolute values and for periods of five years between 1816 and 1886.

Table 1. Annual absolute values of rain fall and average for periods of five years, in millimetres. (1816 to 1886)[4]

Years	Rain in mm.	5 yrs average mm.	Years	Rain in mm.	5 yrs average mm.	Years	Rain in mm.	5 yrs average mm.
1816	762	531,4	1821	718	580,6	1826	436	436
1817	524	531,4	1822	487	580,6	1827-1835	-	-
1818	111	531,4	1823	523	580,6			
1819	585	531,4	1824	699	580,6			
1820	675	531,4	1825	476	580,6			
-	-	-	1840	649	636,8	1845	1039	695,2
1836	422	524,25	1841	789	636,8	1846	659	695,2
1837	271	524,25	1842	543	636,8	1847	699	695,2
1838	935	524,25	1843	658	636,8	1848	519	695,2
1839	469	524,25	1844	545	636,8	1849	560	695,2
1850	493	601,6	1855	1186	895,14	1860	717,2	760,56
1851	474	601,6	1856	880,2	895,14	1861	817,3	760,56
1852	700	601,6	1857	758,3	895,14	1862	836,4	760,56
1853	732	601,6	1858	949,9	895,14	1863	481,3	760,56
1854	609	601,6	1859	701,3	895,14	1864	950,6	760,56
1865	985,9	688,2	1870	631,3	721,6	1875	465,6	776,64
1866	637,5	688,2	1871	917,7	721,6	1876	1106,9	776,64
1867	668,2	688,2	1872	927,2	721,6	1877	806,9	776,64
1868	670	688,2	1873	694,3	721,6	1878	743,6	776,64
1869	479,4	688,2	1874	437,5	721,6	1879	760,2	776,64
1880	680,5	702,92	1885	883,7	857,8			
1881	960,4	702,92	1886	831,9	857,8			
1882	538,4	702,92						
1883	684,2	702,92						
1884	651,1	702,92						

Presented in: Melo, Cristina Joanaz de, Contra Cheias e Tempestades: Consciência do Território, Debate Parlamentar e Políticas de Águas e de Florestas em Portugal 1852-1886, 2010, Unpublished PhD thesis, European University Institute, Flornce.

Stormy weather and flooding: the knights of the Apocalypse

In Portugal, the 1850s were beset by a set of hazards which led the country into a desperate material, economic and social environment. The impact of weather conditions provoked an Armageddon-like picture of floods, famine, diseases, death and conflicts. It started with unexpected flooding in the winters of 1852 and 1853, at a regional level in the largest river catchments of the Tagus and Mondego rivers resulting in crops being severely damaged. This localised framework of natural disaster developed into a general state of increasing public calamity over the subsequent four consecutive years, 1854-1857, and then repeated between 1859 and 1861.

The crises in agriculture, economic, social and public health were more profound in the autumn and winter of 1854-55, due to unexpected torrential rains which led to flooding of farmed lands. This devastation continued and was further exacerbated in 1856 when the country was subject to a similar weather and hydrological pattern.

In Portuguese contemporary literature of the 1800s, the year 1856 became known as the most horrendous year of the century. It recorded the worst harvest known for the whole century[5]. A repetition of the climatic scenario of 1854-55 in 1856, saw for the third consecutive year heavy rains and torrential floods across pastures and cultivated fields in the lower lying areas causing extensive damage. As a result, cereal production was scarce and the potential for recovery was worsening as the amount of seed left for new plantations, had drastically diminished. This drove the country's population into a general state of poor nutrition and famine[6].

Within this context, the Portuguese rulers decided to evaluate the real dimension of food scarcity and also the capacity of the public bodies to distribute provisions amongst all the population. The government ordered the public administrative regional service to compile a survey looking at cereals and farming production. The information sought to cover all the territory. Civil Governors were urged to describe the economic, social and health situation of their District as part of the survey. Replying to this survey, the Civil Governor of the Guarda (as previously mentioned), reported a scenario of no concern either with food production as a whole or with its distribution[7].

Set against the general framework of famine, pest, pain and death across the country as a whole, the information provided for the Guarda district painted a completely different picture. Although if it had provided detailed information about what kind of goods would be available to feed the population, this testimony would probably have unburdened the immediate concerns of the Central Power upon this region. Furthermore, it revealed an unexpected economic autarchy in the highest inland mountains of the territory - Serra da Estrela-, which suffered from scarce transport facilities and difficult access to the expected fruitful markets of the Portugeuse lowlands, with a higher population to trade with.

Albeit that this area seemed to be under control, the following years of 1857-58 saw a deepening crisis across the rest of Portugal. Due to under nutrition and the wet and warm weather, epidemics such as yellow fever, typhus and *cholera morbus* became widespread all over the country. The crisis had reached its zenith. In Lisbon, the capital, these diseases were solely responsible for killing between 7% and 10% of the population[8].

By 1857, the impact of the weather conditions including floods seemed to have created a *status quo* of public calamity around agriculture, economy and health. Flood prevention measures in the uplands to mitigate against the effects of flooding were perceived as crucial. In 1857 an attempt was made by the Head of the National Government to implement public forestry and water regimes.

Hazards control: a failed legal attempt

In 1857, the Marquis of Loulé, uncle of the King D. Pedro V, and head of the Government brought forward legislation to implement a public forestry regime across Portugal encompassing land under all forms of ownership: state, common and privately owned.

Using the colonial dimension of a similar project presented to the deputies in 1849 (which had never been discussed in that forum) his goal was to create a statute that would allow public intervention in areas of natural risk, which had been subjected to damage from the torrential flooding. According to his project the goal would be achieved by afforestation projects along river margins, in swamps, on hillsides and in the upper reaches of the mountains. State institutions would carry out all the tasks of afforestation as well as the management of these new woodland plantations[9].

The draft bill was presented to parliament by the Head of the Government on the 5th of March 1857, published in the official newspaper ten days later, but it was never put on the agenda for parliamentary discussion. It was completely ignored by the parliamentary bodies in 1857 and throughout the period until the end of the Monarchy in 1910.

If this bill had been approved, it would have had a profound effect on property of a private nature, both individual and collective. Neither the elected deputies who would have been amongst the biggest contributors of land, as they were in the majority landowners, nor rural communities and municipal authorities would have been in favour of such a take over of their lands by the central administration. In the 1850s the collective view of the representatives, notwithstanding that they were aware of the benefits of a forestry regime to protect lands, was that they did not support any action towards plantations of trees nor for the reinforcement of State institutions, like a national forestry service or even less the forestry regime. For them, any amount of budget allocated for forestry actions would mean taking away public funds from other investments which they deemed much more important, such as transport infrastructure which they thought would serve to distribute agrarian goods and promote trade more easily[10].

On one hand the agrarian sector was not interested in the reinforcement of the public forestry sector while on the other hand, Guarda's Civil Governor made it clear that there was already sufficient local control in the highlands from the municipal authorities. And, they intended to keep that same regional administrative *status quo*. Therefore showing that the uplands were under tight control might have been seen as an intentional strategy to be followed by the Civil Governor of Guarda, while describing the economic performance and social control of the district.

No conflicts, no economic problems, then, no need for state control

In the 1856 report, the Civil Governor of Guarda confirmed quite clearly to the Minister of Public Works that the District under his administration wouldn't need help of any kind from Central Government. He reinforced the fact that both social and economic agencies were under the control of the municipal authorities. Furthermore, he testified to the absence of conflicts over land management in the region because there were no common land. All the land was managed under private or direct municipal administration. Thus, a syllogism could be deduced: because there were no commons and no conflicts would arise between the landowners and the highlanders, therefore Central Government didn't have to worry about the Guarda region[11].

This declaration seems to acquire extraordinary meaning for Guarda, precisely in 1856, when Central Government had shown an interest in it. This district, located in the highest mountains of the country, had for centuries from the Middle Ages onwards been an area where cattle rearing had been carried out by the highland communities.

The Portuguese law passed on 13th August 1832 specified that the summits of mountains were to be regarded as national property and come under state administration[12]. The same act ruled that the state had an exclusive duty and right of surveillance over national properties. Whilst it hadn't been changed since its enactment this law was not being enforced by the mid 1850s. Thus, in 1856, Central Government was entitled to act upon those territories defined as national property and as a consequence of the legislation, this included part of the mountains of Serra da Estrela in Guarda.

However, the 1832 legislation did not specify the altitude at which *summits* would be defined. This imprecision could lead to discussions about how state property in the mountains could be classified and about which areas the state would be entitled to intervene in. Indeed in the following year, 1857, neither the private landowners nor the local municipal powers showed any intention of supporting an increase of State power over the mountains. They chose to ignore the bill of law that proposed the definition of what would come under the public domain across the country.

From this opposition to state control, it could be deduced that farmers from the lowlands may also face major difficulties in their attempts to compete for the pastures in the mountain areas, because of the locally established administrations. Independently of the debate about the altitude above which summits would be defined, regional control was already being implemented. However, if the state took control only over its notional properties on the lower summits, it could still have been worthwhile for the lowland farmers to explore other pastures that might serve their agrarian interests.

Eventually, the rural elite would have a better chance to manage and use these territories perhaps under some legal act of concession, agreed between them and the municipal administrations. Presumably though, these economic agents would be more interested in negotiating with the state rather than dealing with municipal powers. Hence in order to induce Central Government to implement stronger control over those landscapes, a political solution to achieve this goal had to be found.

On the other hand, in the 1850s, the local district and municipal powers had no interest in calling attention to what could become a flourishing activity in the uplands: cattle rearing. Up until then, they had been quite independent from state controlled taxation. However, both in 1856 and again in 1860, the highland economy and strategies to prevent cattle losses proved to be able to overcome the impact of natural hazards. Altitude was probably the key to the successful performance of these strategies.

The importance of pastures on the slopes above the watershed

Whilst between 1854 and 1857, torrential rain had almost become a pattern in the Portuguese lowland valleys and plains, in 1858 a more normal weather cycle prevailed. A short period of rain and a dry summer along with improved hygiene, led to the contraction of disease epidemics and improved agricultural production. Nonetheless the reprieve was short-lived. In 1859 and 1860, albeit on a smaller scale, torrential floods returned and damaged agricultural production as in previous years.

In the winter of 1860, a parliamentary debate took place which accused the Government of not being able to deal properly with the situation[13]. This happened independently of which political group was in Government or in opposition. The scandal was even greater because whilst the population was starving in some areas, cattle and meat smuggling was being developed freely across the inland borders with Spain[14].

This happened to be the same region, Guarda, that in 1856 had claimed not to have suffered from food shortages. Again the economy of the highlands was mentioned as being able to survive these extreme weather impacts and flooding disasters. What characterised it then?

The District of Guarda located in Serra da Estrela was one of the biggest wool producers and had been granted crown support since the eighteenth century for raising flocks. By the 1750s the Prime Minister, Marquis of Pombal, had promoted the woollen industry in the Guarda area which he had also realised was very rich in hydrological resources[15].

Profiting from good natural conditions for sheep rearing and sources for hydrological energy, textile factories had been built inside the steeply draining valleys. The woollen textile industry had then been encouraged and favoured in theses areas of natural capacity. Still, enmeshed in the middle of this topography, when the heavy rains and downpours increased enormously in the 1850s, both the sheep pastures and industrial mills suffered from the impact of the torrential rainfall.

Unlike the livestock, the industrial mills and dams could not be transported further up the valleys to avoid being damaged or drowned. This almost absurd comment is in itself the key to understanding the truthful statement made by the Civil Governor of the Guarda District in 1856 about their food autarchy. Because the population was able to move food away from the natural hazards, they did not experience shortages of food and other economic goods such as: leather, meat and dairy products that could be traded.

In other words, in the context of torrential floods, the risk of cattle loss was reduced in the uplands compared to that in the valleys and fertile lowlands, where there was no spare land for landowners to move their livestock into. The size of the landholdings, their judicial regime, territorial divisions and topographical characteristics doomed the plains to flooding and the agrarian economy was left with no alternative resources in the lowlands.

However, in the uplands there was an alternative to flooding and this was to go higher into the mountains. Living in the highest place in the country, where population was also scarce and already living on a mountain-products based diet, it was possible for local inhabitants and their authorities to efficiently collect and distribute resources which would cover Guarda's food supply[16].

As long as they could live at the altitude line for nut trees[17], they could rely on their pastures and nutritional fruits. The Serra da Estrela had woodlands of chestnut trees. Eventually due to the weather pattern across the decade of 1850s and without being subjected to torrential flows, the organic cover of the ground could be increased with enough humidity and warm temperatures in the summers to aid the decomposition of the moist leaves. Pastures could also be burnt in winter to allow fresh vegetation to erupt in the following season.

Actually, during 1856 to 1860, the population of Serra da Estrela might have just been repeating what their ancestors had been practising for centuries in the uplands. In a transhumance regime from the South to the North of the Iberian Peninsula, changing from winter to summer pastures, they had learnt how to survive on cattle and dairy products as well as profiting from other mountain food resources from bushes and woodlands. They would have learnt how to overcome torrential rains in the uplands better than the population in the cultivated lowlands.

In the early 1860s, whilst the richest agrarian and economic areas were facing an apparent endless cycle of economic and food crises, which kept increasing through physical causes, the uplands provided enough resources for the highland population to survive. Whilst the landowners on the plains were suffering losses of their flocks and raw material for the wool industry, the highlanders had developed a strategy for surviving the torrential floods. Therefore, summits and slopes at high altitudes presumably previously taken as risky areas for investing in flocks by these landowners, might have now become more attractive as an alternative.

However a problem remained before it would be possible for them to occupy the uplands and its commons. This problem was the property rights and ownership of the slopes and summits. In my view, three factors played a crucial role in finding a political target that would serve private interests without jeopardizing private property rights. Landowners had rejected the idea of supporting the enlargement of the public domain as this would set a very risky precedent over property rights. Thus, in a very subtle way, in the 1850s and 1860s, an investigation into smuggling in the inland mountains served also to get information about the mountains, the living conditions of livestock, sheep production and the meat trade.

Smuggling as a gateway to collect information about pastures in the uplands

The smuggling issue was approached in 1860, in the Portuguese Deputies' Chamber under a renewed context of torrential rains and the destruction of cultivated lands[18]. It had been alleged that hundreds or even thousands of head of cattle heads were being taken off to Spain, preventing Portugal from having access to this food supply. Adding to this shocking offence, the illegal activities produced income for the shepherds who then avoided paying taxes on this profitable activity to the State[19].

Apart from the exaggeration in numbers that picture was – for the highlanders- an unproblematic truth. As Conceição Martins has shown in the Portuguese case[20], in the nineteenth century neither the upland communities nor the shepherds had any real understanding of the concept of "smuggling". Under their way of life they did not think they were taking any illegal action. On the contrary they were simply repeating what had been traditionally practiced for centuries in their region.

The second non-problem was the concept and location of the "border". Firstly, politicians were raising the problem of crossing a line that hadn't yet been drawn or even officially established. The surveys for mapping the country on which the border would be designed, would not be finished until 1884[21]. Consequently the border was a notional idea of frontier that was not even set down in any administrative tool. This un-identified line which animals were being crossed over was then at the heart of the "smuggling" question denounced in parliament. This was actually, in my view, hiding the real aim of the discussion, namely provoking a scandal in order to obtain reliable information about what was really going on in the highlands, as the Civil Governor appeared to be stating controversial information.

Indeed the smuggling issue became an element of pressure and maybe an accelerating factor in promoting a survey on cattle production which was undertaken a decade later. In the early 1870s, the first census on cattle rearing was carried out across the country[22]. In the case of Portugal this information was juxtaposed with the geographic map (1865)[23] and report on the recognition of territorial information and mapping for geological minerals which had been finished in 1867[24].

Initially put in motion to evaluate the areas for urgent afforestation, this report included a map for forestry and water distribution, uncultivated land (not cereal production)[25] and by default the cultivated area. In its final conclusion, it revealed that out of 9,000 hectares, 5,000 were cultivated. It also gave information about the extensive areas of wetlands and usable slopes that could be converted to natural pastures. The authors of the report strongly recommended investment on cattle both for the wetlands as well as in some of the upland areas[26].

In the following years of that decade the most relevant agricultural journals often explored the subject of cattle rearing and drainage works while in the two preceding decades they had been scarcely an object of scientific articles[27].

Thus, by 1873, when the survey on cattle distribution was published, the core of the inquiry was more than anything about trying to split the information by regions. Its primary concern was not to evaluate smuggling but internal production. Nonetheless the report produced a rough estimate of the cattle data, as highlighted by the authors[28].

The records had been collected under extensive fieldwork. But despite this, the survey was extremely inaccurate. The farmers and shepherds especially in the mountains thought that the surveyors were tax collectors, therefore, they lied extensively about the number of animals in their ownership[29].

In the end the cattle survey provided information about the locations in which to invest and in which species of cattle. It became a tool for more efficient state financial control over the cattle trade and subsequently stricter control over shepherds' activities in the highlands as well as reducing excessive local municipal intervention on this sector. But ultimately, the issue which had provoked discussion about the need for the inquiry regarding the cattle situation, ie. smuggling, was the one for which there were almost no records in the report.

Smuggling across the Portuguese Spanish border was in the end not the real question but a mere excuse to investigate the economic interests of the highlands to provide information for other economic and social agents to invest there.

Although it had limitations, this document provided useful information to some of the Central Administration's questions about cattle rearing. From the economic point of view, it produced an image of the distribution of different species of livestock across the country. It suggested which regions would be better for investing in cattle and sheep production and also considered which wetlands and uplands could and should be converted to grassland and pastures (confirming mostly what had been suggested in the report of 1867).

A conclusive suggestion: torrential floods encouraged economic activity higher in the uplands

Against the backdrop of the torrential floods of mid-nineteenth-century Portugal, the highlanders were forced to find a further strategy for their flocks' survival in the highlands. These floods provoked more human intervention in the mountains that extended the cover of green at higher altitudes. This was fuelled by both the highlanders themselves and through private and public investment. This exploitation was probably noticed by the powerful agrarian sector interested in those pastures as an alternative to their flooded ones in the lowlands. Given this new interest from lowland owners, at least in them thinking whether investing in these areas would be worthwhile in responding to an emergency situation; and the absence of taxation over the livestock trade and meat production, this exploitation appeared to be a good route towards bringing the subject forward for parliamentary debate. In order to get decisions taken on this subject, this economic group exerted pressure for greater attention to be paid from Central Government in order to control activities in the uplands. This resulted in the collection of environmental and economic data about the area in question.

As with Portugal, the cycle of torrential downpours across the different mountain ranges in other European countries had also probably encouraged the use of higher pastures. In the long run, the afforestation of slopes and summits at the altitudes of the watershed and above (which was promoted by central administrations) would eventually produce new green cover in what used to be areas that were above the snowline.

Once state policies for afforestation of the summits were attempted in one country there was as an almost domino reaction across the Alps, as Joseph Bruggmeir suggested, with national laws for afforestation in France in 1860, Switzerland 1876, Italy 1877[30] and Austria 1884[31]. To which might be added the Portuguese case with the law for coastal protection in 1872 and for the mountain tops in 1884[32], as well as in Spain with the national law for afforesting mountains in 1877[33] and estuaries and the coastal area in 1882[34].

What previously would have been thought of as a risky investment for landowners, who had developed drainage schemes on moorland and irrigate arid lands in the lowlands[35], might now be promoted in the uplands as was the case of Switzerland where lowlands are scarce.

Christian Pfister has demonstrated that afforestation of the Helvetian uplands in the 1870s took off in response to the impact of torrential rains, mudflows and inundations in the valleys[36]. By stimulating the process of afforestation it would be likely that following the natural course of autumn and winter, organic cover would increase and occur further up in the mountains.

In the first half and in the mid-nineteenth century, in the Alps, Pyrenees, Central Iberian Chain and Sierra de Granada, wet weather and warmth combined with long periods of rain from Autumn to Spring, might have not just produced extensive erosion. It may also have stimulated a renewal and creation of new safe environments against natural hazards in areas above the heads of the rivers, among the slopes which were still covered by natural forest and could accumulate sufficient humus to develop grazing.

What I am then suggesting, but which would require a thorough investigation and analysis from a comparative perspective, is that beyond the Portuguese case, the wet weather context of the nineteenth century might have produced significant changes in the traditional pastured landscape by greening the uplands at a higher altitude than before. Weather conditions might have naturally changed the upland pasture landscapes, later managed and improved by cattle farmers.

In other words torrential floods strengthened the renewal of pasture landscapes at higher altitudes in the uplands than before. The actions of afforestation taken to prevent the impact of torrential flooding brought attention to the pastures in the uplands which might have helped to promote a political argument for more state control over the uplands. This ultimately meant opening a door for the privatisation of pastured uplands[37].

Notes

1. Map and official report on the afforestation of the country in 1867, *Relatório da Arborização Geral do País*, Lisboa, Imprensa Nacional, 1868.

2. Soares, Rodrigo de Morais, "Chronica Agrícola de 5 Novembro de 1863, in *Archivo Rural*, Vol VI, pp.248-251; *Idem, Ibidem*, vol. IX, 1866, p. 135; *Idem, Ibidem* "Chronica Agrícola", in *Archivo Rural*, vol. X, 1867, p. 189

3. The data were collected from difference sources and compiled together in order to produce an annual value. The values between 1816 and 1855, come from Franzini, Marino Miguel, "Mappa geral da primeira serie de observações feitas em Lisboa, acerca das chuvas que caíram desde o ano de 1816 até Julho de 1826; Segunda serie de observações, que começam em março de 1835 e findam em 1855", precedidos de várias considerações sobre o assunto, in *Diario do Governo* n.º 59, de 11.3.1859. There are no published data for 1817-1835. The data for 1856-1875 have been taken form : *Annaes do Observatório do Infante D. Luís.Resumo das Principais Observações Meteorológicas executadas Durante o Período de 20 Annos Decorridos Desde 1856-1875*, Lisboa Imprensa Nacional, 1877. Os dados relativos aos período de 1876 a 1886, dos relatórios anuais do observatório do Infante D. Luís, *Annaes do Observatório do Infante D. Luís*,1876-1886 *XIX*, Lisboa Imprensa Nacional.

4. *Idem, Ibidem*, para todos os dados.

5. Reis, Jaime "A «Lei da Fome»: As Origens do Proteccionismo Cerealífero (1889-1914)" in *O Atraso Económico em Perspectiva Histórica: Estudos Sobre a Economia Portuguesa na Segunda Metade do Século XIX (1850-1930)*, Lisboa, Imprensa Nacional Casa da Moeda, 1993, pp.33 85.

6. Melo, Cristina

7. "Relatório da Sociedade Agrícola da Guarda" in *Boletim do Ministério das Obras Públicas Commércio e Indústria*, Abril 1856, Lisboa, 1856, pp. 208-219.

8. Leite, Joaquim da Costa, "População e Crescimento Económico" in *História Económica de Portugal*, vol. II, O século XIX, (org. Pedro Laíns e Álvaro Ferreira da Silva), Lisboa, Imprensa de Ciências Sociais, 2005, pp. 43-77

9. Duque de Loulé, Projecto de Lei para um Código Florestal, 17.03.1857, *Diário do Governo (Diary of the Commons)*, Março 1857, p. 319.

10. Joanaz de Melo, Cristina, *Contra Cheias e Tempestades: Consciência do Território, políticas de águas e florestas no século XIX em Portugal 1851-1886/ Against Floods and Tempests: Awareness of the Territory, water and forest policies in Portugal 1851-1886*, Unpublished PhD thesis, European University Institute, Florence, 2010.

11. "Relatório da Sociedade Agrícola da Guarda" in *Boletim do Ministério das Obras Públicas Commércio e Indústria*, Abril 1856, Lisboa, 1856, pp. 208-9.

12. Lei de Extinção dos Bens da Coroa e Ordens, de 13 de Agosto de 1832.

13. Joanaz de Melo, Cristina, Contra Cheias e Tempestades: Consciência do Território, políticas de águas e florestas no século XIX em Portugal 1851-1886/ Against Floods and Tempests: Awareness of the Territory, water and forest policies in Portugal 1851-1886, Unpublished PhD thesis, European University Institute, Florence, 2010

14. 18.05.1860, Diário da Câmara dos Senhores Deputados/ Diary of the Commons, Maio de 1860.

15. Macedo, Jorge Borges de, *A Situação Económica no Tempo de Pombal: alguns Aspectos*, Lisboa, Moraes, 1982.

16. Censos de 1864, 1878 e 1890: http://censos.ine.pt/xportal/xmain?xpid=INE&xpgid=censos_historia_pt

17. Franco, João do Amaral, *Nova Flora de Portugal (Continente e Açores)*, Vol. I, Lisboa, Sociedade Astória Lda., 1979; *Idem, Nova Flora de Portugal (Continente e Açores)*, Vol. II, Lisboa, Sociedade Astória Lda., 1984.

18. *Annaes do Observatório do Infante D. Luís. Resumo das Principais Observações Meteorológicas executadas Durante o Período de 20 Annos Decorridos Desde 1856-1875*, Lisboa Imprensa Nacional, 1877; "Inundações no Rio Tejo", *Boletim do Ministério das Obras Públicas Commércio e Indústria*, vol. 12, Lisboa, Imprensa Nacional, 1856, pp. 469-503; "*O Conselho das Obras de Arte Para a Quarta secção do Caminho de Ferro de Leste*" in Boletim do MOPCI, nº 4, Abril, Lisboa, Imprensa Nacional, 1865, pp. 508-510; Alarcão, D. José "A Falta de Águas Potáveis e de Irrigação" in *Revista Agronómica*, Tomo II, Terceira série, 1864, pp. 45-48; Alarcão, D. José de "Cultura dos Baldios Pela Arborização" in *Revista Agronómica*, Terceira série, Tomo III, 1865, pp. 221-225;Chelmicki, José Carlos Conrado "Relatório Sobre o Traçado de um Caminho de Ferro pela Beira" in *Boletim do Ministério das Obras Públicas Commércio e Indústria*, nº 1, Janeiro, 1860, Lisboa, Imprensa Nacional, 1860, pp. 71-74;Couceiro, José Anselmo Gromicho, "Relatório Sobre o Resultado do Reconhecimento do Terreno Entre o Caminho de Ferro do Norte e a Fronteira de Leste, a Fim de Conhecer a Possibilidade de Uma Linha Férrea Nesta Direcção" in *Boletim do Ministério das Obras Públicas Comércio e Indústria*, nº 1, Janeiro de 1860, Lisboa, Imprensa Nacional, 1860, pp. 74 75.

19. 18.05.1860, *Diário da Câmara dos Senhores Deputados/ Diary of the Commons*, Maio de 1860.

20. Martins, Conceição Andrade," A agricultura" in *História Económica de Portugal 1700-2000*, vol. II, Org. Pedro Laíns e Álvaro Ferreira da Silva, Lisboa, ICS, 2005, pp. 221-258, p. 22.

21. Branco, Rui Miguel C., *O Mapa de Portugal. Estado, Território e Poder no Portugal de Oitocentos*, Lisboa, Livros Horizonte, 2003.

22. Devy-Vareta, Nicole, "A Floresta em Mapas" in *Geografia de Portugal*, Vol. I, Coordenação de Carlos Alberto Medeiros, Lisboa, Círculo de Leitores, 2006, pp.108-114.

23. *Relatório da Arborização Geral do País*, Lisboa, Imprensa Nacional, 1868

24. Radich, Maria Carlos, Alves, A.A. Monteiro *Dois Séculos de Floresta em Portugal*, Lisboa, edições CELPA, 2000.

25. *Relatório da Arborização Geral do País*, Lisboa, Imprensa Nacional, 1868.

26. *Archivo Rural, Jornal de Agricultura, Artes e Sciências Correlativas*, Lisboa, 1854-1876; *Boletim do Ministério das Obras Públicas Comércio e Indústria*, 1853-1868, Lisboa, Imprensa Nacional; *Diário da Câmara dos Senhores Deputados*, 1852 -1861; 1869-81, Lisboa, Imprensa Nacional; *Diário de Lisboa*, 1861-1869, Lisboa, Imprensa Nacional, *Revista Agrícola*, 1866-1876, Lisboa; *Revista Agronómica*, 1858-1864, Lisboa

27. Ministério das Obras Publicas Comércio e Industria, *Recenseamento Geral dos Gados no Continente do Reino de Portugal em 1870*, Lisboa, Imprensa Nacional, 1873

28. *Idem*.

29. Sansa, Renato, "Il Mercato e la Legge: la Legislazione Forestale Italiana, nei Secoli XVIII e XIX," in *Ambiente e Risorse Nel Mezziogiorno Contemporâneo*, a Cura di Piero Bevilacqua, e , Gabriella Corona, Roma, Meridiana Libri, 2000.

30. Bruggemeier, Josef-franz, "New Developments in Environmental History" in *Proceedings, 19th International Congress of Historical Sciences*, Oslo, 2000.

31. *Regulamento da Administração das Matas 1824, Lisboa*, Impressão Régia, 1824; "Regulamento da Administração das Matas de 11 de Maio de 1872", in *Diário do Governo*, nº 111, 22 de Maio de 1872; *Regulamento Para a Administração Geral das Matas do Reino Aprovado por Decreto de 7 de Julho de 1847*, Lisboa, Imprensa Nacional, 1862; *Regulamento Para a Execução da Lei de 6 de Março de 1884 Aprovado por Decreto de 2 de Outubro de 1886*, Lisboa, Imprensa Nacional, 1887

32. Laso, Maria-Pilar; Bauer, Erich "La Propriedad forestal en España" in *Revista de Estudios Agrosociales y Pesqueros*, n.200,Vol. I, Ministério de Agricultura, pesca y Alimentación, Madrid, 2003, pp. 297-343.

33. Calvo Sánchez, Luis, *La Génesis Histórica de los Montes Catalogados de Utilidad Pública (1855-1901)*, Madrid, Ministério de Médio Ambiente, Direccion General de Conservación de la Naturaleza, 2001.

34. Shaw-Taylor, Leigh, "The Management of Common Land in the Lowlands of Southern England circa 1500 to circa 1850" in *The Management of Common Land in North West Europe, c. 1500-1850*, n°8, Brepols, 2002, pp.59-86; Smout, T. C., *Nature Contested: Environmental History in Scotland and Northern England Since 1600*, Edinburgh, Edinburgh University Press, 2000; Vivier, Nadine, "The Management and use of Commons in France in the Eighteenth and nineteenth Centuries" in *The Management of Common Land in North West Europe, c. 1500-1850*, n°8, Brepols, 2002, pp. 143-173; Warde, Paul, "Common Rights and Common Lands in South West Germany, 1500-1800" in *The Management of Common Land in North West Europe, c. 1500-1850*, n° 8, Brepols, 2002, pp. .15-32; Winchester, Angus, J. L., "Upland Commons in Northen England" in *The Management of Common Land in North West Europe, c. 1500-1850*, n°8, Brepols, 2002, pp.33-58.

35. Pfister, Christian, *Das Klima der Schweiz von 1525-1860 und seine Bedeutung in der Geschichte von Bevölkerung und Landwirtschaft / Christian Pfister Band 1 Klimageschichte der Schweiz 1525-1860*, Bern ; Stuttgart : Paul Haupt, 1984.

Woods, Trees and Animals: a South Yorkshire Historical Perspective

Melvyn Jones
Sheffield Hallam University

Introduction

Stock rearing and woodland management went hand in hand in the past in South Yorkshire in deer parks, on wooded commons and in coppice woods. And this strong relationship is well documented over the last 1,000 years.

Silva pastilis in South Yorkshire at Domesday

If we take at face value the results of William the Conqueror's great national survey of 1086, then woodland cover had been drastically reduced by the late eleventh century and the countryside was not covered by the boundless wildwood of people's imagination. Rackham has calculated that the Domesday survey of 1086 covered 27 million acres of land of which 4.1 million were wooded, that is 15 per cent of the surveyed area. His figure for the West Riding of Yorkshire is 16 per cent (Rackham, 1980, p.111). My own calculation for South Yorkshire is just under 13 per cent (Jones, 2009, p. 8). By way of comparison, woods today, including plantations, cover just over six per cent of the region. What this means is that in the eleventh century, South Yorkshire was relatively sparsely wooded even by today's standards.

Domesday woodland in South Yorkshire was described in four main ways: as *silva, silva modica, silva minuta* and *silva pastilis*. *Silva* is simply woodland; the meaning of *silva modica* is not clear; *silva minuta* is coppice; and *silva pastilis* is wood pasture. Of the 111 manors in which woodland was recorded, 102 had wood pastures and seven had coppices (Figure 1). All seven occurrences of coppice woods were in the eastern half of the region, two in the eastern part of the Coal Measures (at Little Houghton and Barnburgh) and five on the Magnesian Limestone (at Adwick-le-Street, Hampole, Marr, High Melton, and a manor incorporating land at Sprotbrough, Cusworth and Balby). On the other hand, although wood pastures were found throughout South Yorkshire they were very extensive and the only type of woodland found in the Millstone Grit country and throughout most of the Coal Measures.

Wooded commons

Silva pastilis in the form of wooded commons continued to be a widely distributed type of land use until at least the mid-eighteenth century in the central third of South Yorkshire. The wooded commons were in great contrast to the moorland commons of the Dark Peak zone in the extreme west and the

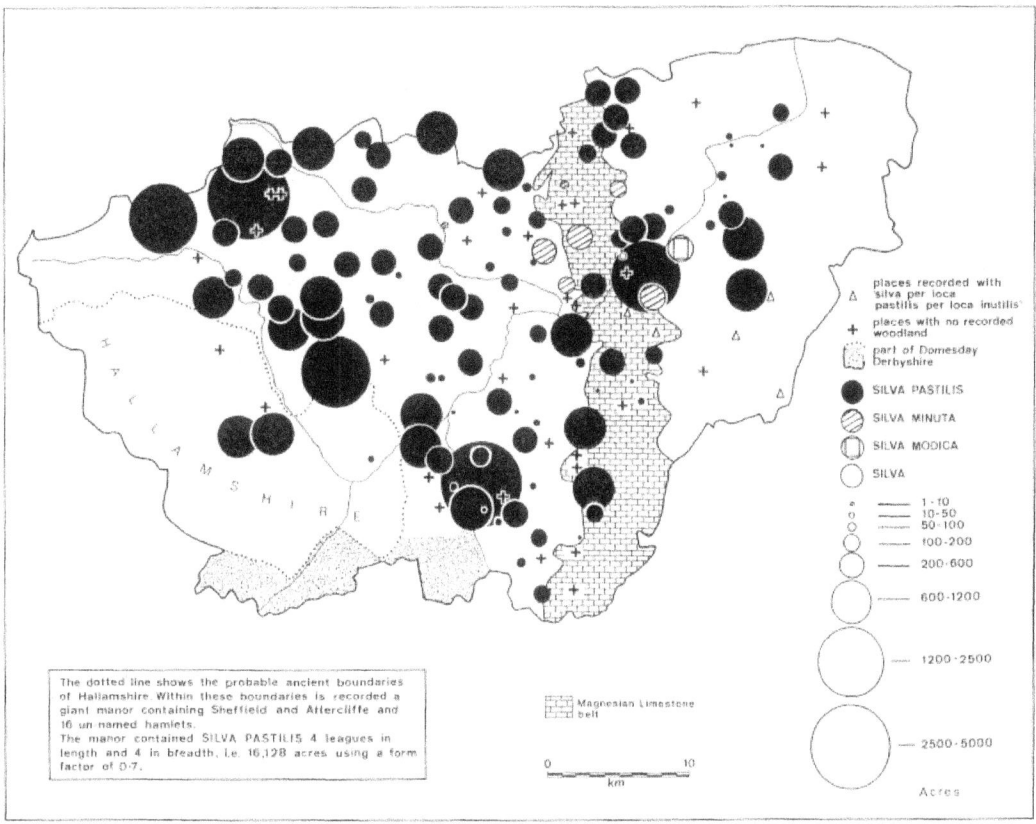

Figure 1. Woodland in South Yorkshire at Domesday.

marshland commons of the Humberhead Levels in the east. Wooded commons were unfenced woods in which underwood and timber were harvested but in which the animals of commoners, i.e., those who had certain rights on the common land of a manor, were allowed to graze freely. Commoners usually also had the right of the underwood and dead wood but the timber trees usually belonged to the lord of the manor. In the manor of Sheffield as late as 1637 there were 21,000 acres of common land, much of it wooded (Ronksley, 1908).

The first record of a wooded common in South Yorkshire after the Domesday survey was in 1161 when the monks of the abbey of St Wandrille (who built Ecclesfield Priory) were given permission by the lord of Hallamshire, Richard de Louvetot, to pasture their flocks from January to Easter, their swine in the autumn, and to take dead wood in a large wood stretching from Birley Edge down to the River Don all the way from Wardsend to Oughtibridge. In an undated charter of about 1297 Thomas de Furnival, the lord of the manor of Hallamshire made a number of grants of common in the largely uninhabited uplands and river valleys in the western part of the manor. He gave to the men of Stannington, Morewood, Hallam and Fulwood the right of herbage and foliage (to gather green and dead wood) throughout his forest of Riveling (i.e. Rivelin Chase, his private hunting forest) all the way from Malin Bridge at the confluence of the rivers Rivelin and Loxley to Stanage Edge at a height of more than 1,421 feet (435m) more than seven miles (11 km) to the south-west. In an inquisition *post mortem* of 1332 on the death of Thomas de Furnival it was recorded that his properties in the manor of Sheffield included pastures in among other places 'Greno, Billy Wood, Ryvelyngden and Baldwinhousteads' (Curtis, 1918). Ryvelyngden was the valley of the Rivelin occupied by his private hunting forest which continued in part to be wood pasture until the Parliamentary enclosures but by 1600 the other three, Greno Wood, Beeley Wood and Bowden Housteads Wood, were all enclosed coppice woods. But some wood pastures continued in existence for more than two centuries longer.

There are graphic descriptions of a number of wooded commons in the late seventeenth and early eighteenth centuries. In 1650, Loxley Chase was referred to as 'one Great wood called Loxley the herbage common and consisteth of great Oake timber'. About ten years earlier, another wooded common, Walkley Bank, was said to have 'a great store of rough Oake trees & some Bircke (birch) woods'. In the same year Stannington Wood, formerly part of Rivelin Chase and which covered 217 acres (88 ha) in 1637, was said to consist of 'pt of rough Timber and part of Springe wood'.

Perhaps the best documented and interesting of the few surviving former South Yorkshire wooded commons is Loxley Common and the coterminous Wadsley Common. The area in question covers the valley side to the north of the River Loxley with Loxley Edge, a sandstone escarpment outcropping in the eastern half of the site and with a boulder-strewn slope below it. Loxley Common is variously referred to in historical documents as Loxley Common, Loxley Chase and Loxley Firth. Loxley Common was mentioned in a late thirteenth century document in which Thomas de Furnival, the lord of Hallamshire, granted common rights to the inhabitants of the area. In the inquisition *post mortem* in 1332, on the death of Thomas de Furnival, it was recorded that the pannage of the woods (*pannagio boscorum*), i.e. the pasturing of pigs on acorns, at 'Rivelyngden and Lokesley' was worth forty shillings (Curtis, 1918, 41). Just over 300 years later in 1637 it was recorded in John Harrison's survey of the manor of Sheffield as 'A Common Called Loxley wood & ffirth' and covered 1,517 acres (Ronksley, 1908, p. 336). In 1650 the common was referred to as 'one Great wood called Loxley the herbage common and consisteth of great Oake timber'. Two old oak pollards still survive on the site (Figure 2).

Medieval deer parks

Medieval deer parks were symbols of status and wealth. In South Yorkshire they were created by the nobility and they were also attached to monasteries. There were also two royal deer parks:

Figure 2. Oak pollard on Loxley Common.

Conisbrough Park, formerly the property of the de Warenne family that reverted to the Crown in the fourteenth century and Kimberworth Park that became Crown property for a period in the late fifteenth century. As all deer were deemed to belong to the Crown, from the beginning of the thirteenth century landowners were supposed to obtain a licence from the king to create a park, although this appears not to have been necessary if the proposed park was not near a royal forest. The medieval parks at Conisbrough and Sheffield predated the issuing of royal licences and so must have been of twelfth century or even earlier, possibly Saxon, origin.

The crown issued rights of free warren which gave a landowner the right to hunt certain animals – such as game birds, hare, fox, badger, wild cat, polecat and pine marten – within a prescribed area. This was often the forerunner to the fencing of demesne land to create a deer park. Searches of parish histories, principally Hunter's two-volume *South Yorkshire*[1] reveal that more than eighty grants of free warren were given in the medieval period in South Yorkshire and that in nearly a third of the cases, a deer park is known to have been subsequently created.

Nationally the great age of park creation was the century and a half between 1200 and 1350, a period of growing population and agricultural prosperity. Landowners had surplus wealth and there were still sufficient areas of waste on which to create parks. In South Yorkshire the majority of grants of free warren, which as already noted were often the forerunners of the creation of deer parks, were given in the period from 1250 to 1325 when forty-four grants were made. Significantly, no grants of free warren were given for thirty years following the Black Death (1349), but then there were twenty-one grants between 1379 and 1400. The last known medieval royal licence to create a deer park was given in 1491-92 when Brian Sandford was granted permission to create a park at Thorpe Salvin. This grant is also notable for the fact that it was accompanied by a gift of twelve does from the king's park at Conisbrough 'towards the storing of his parc at Thorp' (Jones, 1996). The last-known local licence was granted to the 2nd Viscount Castleton in 1637 by King Charles I to create a deer park at Sandbeck (Figure 3). The licence states that Viscount Castleton was given permission to make separate with pales, walls or hedges 500 acres or thereabouts

Figure 3. Royal licence to create a deer park at Sandbeck Park, 1637.

of land, meadow, pasture, gorse, heath, wood, underwood, woodland tenements and hereditaments to make a park where deer and other wild animals might be grazed and kept (Rodgers, 1998).

The deer in medieval parks were carefully farmed (Birrell, 1992). Besides their status symbol role the main functions of parks were to provide for their owners a reliable source of food for the table, supplies of wood and timber, and in some cases quarried stone, coal and ironstone. They were, therefore, an integral part of the local economy. Besides deer, hares, rabbits (also introduced by the Normans and kept in burrows in artificially made mounds) and game birds were kept in the medieval parks of South Yorkshire. Herds of cattle, flocks of sheep and pigs were also grazed there. Another important feature were fish ponds to provide an alternative to meat in Lent and on fast days.

To use the modern term a deer park was also usually part of the manorial 'forestry' operation. Although there are records of parks without trees, deer parks usually consisted of woodland and areas largely cleared of trees. The park livestock could graze in the open areas and find cover in the wooded areas. The cleared areas, called launds or plains, consisted of grassland or heath with scattered trees (Figure 4). The king's park keeper at Conisbrough Park in the second half of the fifteenth century was referred to in a document written in French as *Laundier et Palisser de n're park de Connesburgh*, i.e. keeper of the unwooded areas and the park boundaries at our park at

Conisbrough (Hunter, 1828). Many of the trees in the launds would have been pollarded, i.e., trees cut at least six feet from the ground leaving a massive lower trunk called a bolling above which a continuous crop of new growth sprouted out of reach of the grazing deer, sheep and cattle. In the launds regeneration of trees was restricted because of continual grazing and new trees were only able to grow in the protection of thickets of hawthorn and holly. Some of the unpollarded trees might reach a great age and size and were much sought after for major building projects.

The woods within deer parks were managed in different ways. Some woods were 'holted', i.e., they consisted of single-stemmed trees grown for their timber like a modern plantation. Most park woods were coppiced and were surrounded by a bank or wall to keep out the grazing animals during the early years of re-growth. Later in the coppice cycle the deer would have been allowed into the coppice woods. There were also in South Yorkshire's deer parks, separate woods or special compartments within coppice woods in which the dominant tree was holly and which were called holly hags. In Tankersley Park an engraving of $c.1730$ shows two holly hags (Figure 4). The holly was cut in winter for the deer and other park livestock. I return to the subject of holly hags below.

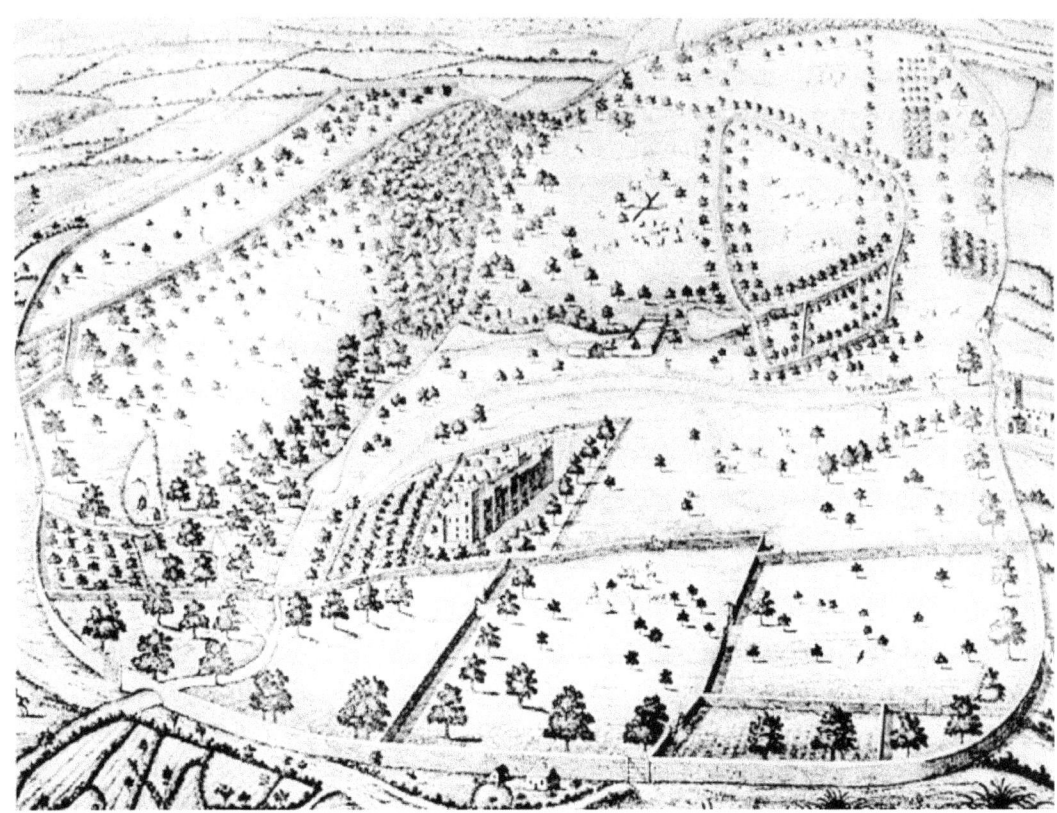

Figure 4. Tankersley Park c **1730.**

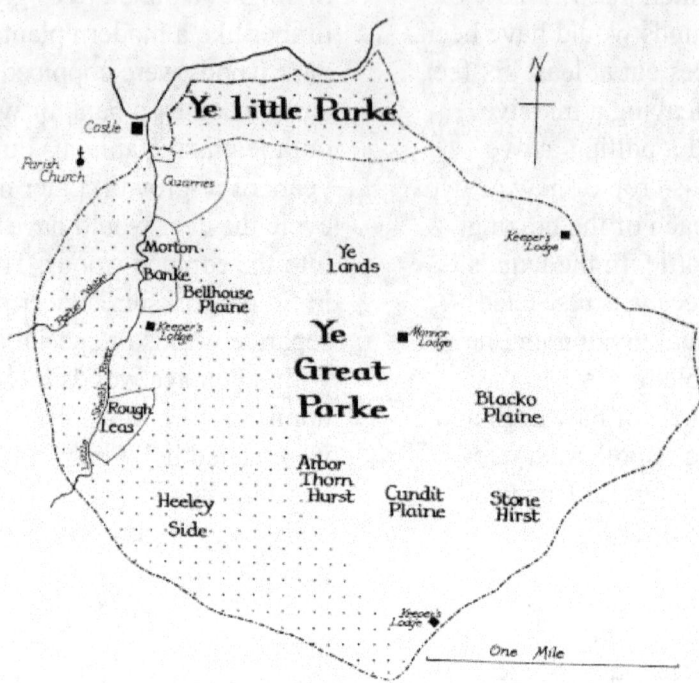

Figure 5. Sheffield Park, 1637, based on the description in Harrison's survey of the manor of Sheffield.

Sheffield Park is particularly well documented and a clear picture emerges of the woods and trees within it and the way they were used in the medieval period. This deer park, which at its greatest extent covered 2,462 acres (nearly 1,000 hectares) and was eight miles (13 kilometres) in circumference, came right up to the eastern edge of the town of Sheffield (Figure 5). Harrison in his survey of the manor of Sheffield in 1637 named the various parts of the park including some with woodland names including Arbor Thorn Hirst and Stone Hirst (*hyrst* = a wooded hill) but they would only have been covered with scrub woods of hawthorn and holly. The cleared areas within the park are also precisely named in Harrison's survey: 'ye Lands', 'Cundit Plaine', 'Blacko Plaine' and 'Bellhouse Plaine'. Ye Lands is probably a corruption of laund. These launds or plains contained large aged oak trees in the seventeenth century, that would have already been very large trees two or three hundred years earlier in the late medieval period. They were described in great detail by John Evelyn in his book *Silva*, first published in 1670. Evelyn said that in 1646 there were 100 trees whose combined value was £1,000. He described one oak tree in the park whose trunk was thirteen feet in diameter and another which was ten yards in circumference. He also described another massive oak that when cut down yielded 1,400 'wairs' which were planks two yards long and one yard wide and 20 cords from its branches. A cord was a pile of wood four feet high, four feet wide and eight feet long. He described another oak, that when felled and lying on its side was so massive that two men on horseback on either side of it could not see each other's hat crowns. On Conduit Plain (the Cundit Plaine of Harrison's 1637 survey), Evelyn reported that there was one oak tree whose boughs were so far spreading that he estimated (giving all his calculations) that 251 horses could stand in its shade (Evelyn, 1706, pp. 229-30).

These mighty veteran and ancient oaks had had a multiplicity of uses for centuries. When felled they provided not only timber for building projects, but also charcoal (from their branches), and wood for a multiplicity of crafts and industries. Standing, live, veteran oak trees also had an important function. These open-grown enormously-branched trees (the one on Conduit Plain described by Evelyn had branches extending for 15½ yards (14m) in every direction) produced, unlike most woodland grown oaks, burgeoning crops of acorns. These not only provided the food for fattening pigs during the pannage season but also for keeping the deer population in good heart in preparation for the long winter.

A 'Feet of Fines' document of 1268 and mid-fifteenth century manorial rolls give glimpses of the uses to which wood and timber in Sheffield Park were put in the late thirteenth and mid-fifteenth centuries respectively. A Feet of Fines document was one relating to a judgement on a title to land. This one relates to the dowry of Berta, the widowed wife of Thomas de Furnival, lord of Hallamshire (Thomas, 1924). The judgement stated that Berta de Furnival had rights to a third of the income from certain activities in the park. This income included that derived from pannage and herbage. Herbage (also known as agistment) was the renting of grazing space for cattle, sheep and horses and pannage (*pannagio porcorum*) was the autumnal grazing of pigs on fallen acorns.

The manorial roll of the 1440s (YAS, 1921), shows that besides its role as a food larder for the lord, the park in the mid-fifteenth century supplied firewood for the castle, timber for building repairs at the castle stables and the chapel in the castle. Pollarded oaks were also felled to make scaffolding and hurdles for repairs at the castle. Oaks in the park were felled to make posts, rails and palings for fencing the castle garden. Income was also derived from allowing holly trees to be cropped (for fodder), from the pannage of pigs, the sale of felled trees and a parcel of underwood, and from charcoal made from the branches of trees where they were being cleared to make a new pasture.

Between the late fifteenth and eighteenth centuries many medieval deer parks either changed their function and hence their appearance, or, more commonly, disappeared altogether. Well-wooded parks often simply became large coppice woods. Examples of the reversion to managed woodland in South Yorkshire are Cowley Park, Hesley Park, Shirecliffe Park, Tinsley Park and what are now Ecclesall Woods.

Holly hags

Holly hags, special woods of holly, have already been mentioned in connection with feeding deer in deer parks in winter but they were once also features of the wider farming countryside where they were used as fodder for sheep until at least the eighteenth century. The use of holly for winter fodder was recorded in the Conisbrough manorial rolls in 1319 when two people were fined for cutting holly for feeding to their animals (CCR c/1/8-15 and c/1/8-31). Another medieval record was in the Sheffield area in 1442 when the Lord of Hallamshire's forester at Bradfield noted in his accounts payment for holly sold for animal fodder in winter (Thomas, 1924, 74). John Harrison in his survey of the Manor of Sheffield in 1637 recorded 27 separate 'Hollin Hagges' that were rented by farm tenants from the Earl of Arundel (Ronksley, 1908, pp. 32-33). The use of holly as fodder in the Sheffield area was also graphically described by two early diarists. In 1696 Abraham de la Pryme wrote that:

In south-west Yorkshire at and about Bradfield and in Derbyshire they feed all their sheep in winter with holly leaves and bark, which they eat more greedily than any grass. To every farm there is so many holly trees ... care is taken to plant great numbers of them in all farms hereabouts.

(Surtees Society, 1870)

Twenty-nine years later in 1725 a party headed by the Earl of Oxford travelled through Sheffield in a south-easterly direction across an area of common land still called Birley Moor and Hollinsend. It was noted that they travelled:

... through the greatest number of wild stunted holly trees that I ever saw together. They extend themselves on the common for a considerable way. This tract of ground that they grow upon is called the Burley Hollins... [They have] *their branches lopped off every winter for the support of the sheep which browse upon them, and at the same time are sheltered by the stunted part that is left standing.*

(Historical Manuscripts Commission, 1901)

That holly was considered a valuable crop and had to be protected is illustrated by an entry in the accounts of the Duke of Norfolk's woods in the early eighteenth century. In the winter of 1710 the Duke of Norfolk's woodward noted in his accounts that he had paid Henry Bromhead 'for him and horse going 2 days in ye great snow to see if anyone croped holling'(ACM S283). The impression given is that Bromhead would have had a blunderbuss over his saddle!

Bull Wood, a deer park holly hag at Tankersley, still exists. Writing in 1977, two local researchers, Spray and Smith, believed that there were at least the remains of five holly haggs in the country to the west of Sheffield. They mention Fox Hagg and Coppice Wood in the Rivelin valley, the holly bushes still surviving at Holly Edge and at Holly Busk near Bolsterstone and a location near the edge of Loxley Common at grid reference SK 308905 (Spray and Smith, 1977).

Agistment

Tenants' animals were allowed access to coppice woods for grazing on the woodland grasses and herbs once the coppice was well grown and beyond possible damage from browsing animals. There are records of horses and cattle being grazed in local coppice woods. The practice was known as agistment or herbage. Two records demonstrate the importance of only allowing grazing animals into coppice woods that were well grown. In 1710, for example, Joseph Ashmore, the Duke of Norfolk's woodward, charged himself two shillings for 'My Mare & fole in Woolley Woods this Spring a month' adding, just to make it absolutely clear that he was not contravening the normal custom, 'its old Cutt' (ACM S283). Eight years later in 1718 the vicar of Ecclesfield, just after coppicing had taken place in Greno Wood, was paid twopence for giving notice to tenants at a Sunday service that they should 'take care that their cattle do no longer Continue to Graise in Greno Wood for Spoyling ye young sprouts' (ACM, S283).

Animals were likely to stray from pastures and commons into neighbouring coppice woods. When detected they were impounded and the owner fined. In 1718, Enoch Moor was fined one shilling when nine of his sheep were pounded out of Greno Wood and in 1720 two men were paid three shillings and sixpence for their trouble in 'pounding 5 sheep belonging to Mr Watts that was trespassing in Little Hall Wood (ACM S283). The village pinfold in which these animals would have been impounded still survives in Grenoside village.

Postscript: Snigging

There is another type of record of the relationship between animals and woodland management in South Yorkshire. Records of coppice management in the period from 1600 to 1850 regularly mention the use of

Figure 6. Snigging in Woolley Wood, Sheffield in 2006.

horses in the management of the woods. The term used for the work that horses did was **snigging**, sometimes also known as **tushing**. And in recent years the practice has been re-instated to protect the ground flora and archaeology when group felling and thinning are taking place in Sheffield and Rotherham's ancient woods (Figure 6).

References

ACM (Arundel Castle Manuscripts) in Sheffield Archives.

Birrell, J. (1992) Deer and Deer Farming in Medieval England. *The Agricultural History Review*, **40**, 112-126.

CCR (Conisbrough Court Rolls) in Doncaster Archives.

Curtis, E. (1918) Sheffield in the Fourteenth Century: two Furnival Inquisitions. *Transactions of the Hunter Archaeological Society*, **1**, 31-53.

Evelyn, J. (1706 edition) *Silva or a Discourse of Forest Trees*. pp. 229-230.

Historical Manuscripts Commission (1901) Lord Edward Harley's (later Earl of Oxford) *Journies and tours in the eastern counties 1723-1738*. Portland Mss, Volume 6.

Hunter, J. (1828-31) *South Yorkshire: the History and Topography of the Deanery of Doncaster*. 2 volumes, J. B. Nicols and Son, Volume 1, p.114.

Jones, M. (1996) *Deer in South Yorkshire: an Historical Perspective*. In: Jones, M., Rotherham, I.D. and McCarthy, A.J. (eds.) *Deer or the New Woodlands?, The Journal of Practical Ecology and Conservation*, **Special Publication, No. 1**, 11-26.

Jones, M. (2009) *Sheffield's Woodland Heritage*. 4th edition, Wildtrack Publishing, Sheffield.

Rackham, O. (1980) *Ancient Woodland; its history, vegetation and uses in England*. Arnold.

Rodgers, A. (1998) *Deer Parks in the Maltby Area*. In: Jones, M. (ed.) *Aspects of Rotherham: Discovering Local History, Volume 3*, Wharncliffe Publishing, Barnsley. p.20.

Ronksley, J.G. (ed.) (1908) *An exact and perfect Survey of the Manor of Sheffield and other lands by John Harrison, 1637*. Robert White & Co.

Spray, M and Smith, D.J. (1977) The rise and fall of holly in the Sheffield region. *Transactions of the Hunter Archaeological Society*, **10**, 239-51.

Surtees Society (1870) *The diary of Abraham de la Pryme, the Yorkshire antiquary*, Surtees Society, Volume **54**.

Thomas, A.H. (1924) Some Hallamshire Rolls of the Fifteenth Century. *Transactions of the Hunter Archaeological Society*, 65-79, 142-158, 225-246 and 341-360.

Yorkshire Archaeological Society (YAS) (1921) *Feet of Fines for the County of York 1218-1231*. Record Series, Volume LXII.

What was the pre-Neolithic landscape like and is it a relevant template for modern conservation?

Keith J. Kirby
Natural England

Introduction

The structure and composition of a natural landscape is of interest in its own right, but to what extent is it relevant to current and future conservation, particularly in a highly modified cultural landscape, such as England?

When was the landscape last natural?

The first challenge is to consider when past-natural conditions may last have existed over the majority of the country: the latest period, and the one adopted by Vera (2000) and others, is probably the pre-Neolithic period, about 6,000 years ago (in England), before farming became widespread. There were humans present before that and there are arguments that the impact of Mesolithic hunters on game populations might have been sufficient to lead to significant changes to vegetation. However, humans then could be considered as acting like other top predators, whereas the change to a more settled existence introduced major new elements to the landscape.

The pre-Neolithic landscape was itself only one stage in the evolution of the vegetation cover of Britain after the last glacial period (Godwin, 1975) and even without human intervention, the landscape would have continued to change. The landscape would not have been uniform across the country; variations in local climate and soils strongly determine species patterns today (e.g. Rodwell, 1991) and are likely to have been more significant in their impact before human management was imposed upon them.

So there was not one 'natural landscape' but many, depending on what time period we choose and where in the country we look.

Sources of information

The most used sources of information for past landscapes are pollen records, but other direct evidence comes from more substantial plant remains, up to whole tree trunks such as are ploughed up in the Fens; remains from invertebrates such as beetles or chironomid midges; soil deposits etc. Indirect evidence may come from analogies with modern or historic records, extrapolations from modern species ecology or models. Each of these approaches has its limitations; they may be incomplete and irregularly distributed in time and space, but taken together they can suggest what the pre-Neolithic landscape in England was like.

A tree-ed but was it a wooded landscape?

The pollen and invertebrate records indicate a shift from vegetation that was predominantly open in the immediate post-glacial period to one where broadleaved trees become more abundant in the pre-Neolithic period. 'Open' indicators do not completely disappear, however, and the recent debate has been about what was the structure of this tree-ed landscape: was it more like closed forest as the matrix with patches of openness or largely open with patches of trees (Peterken,1996; Vera, 2000)? Were the main factors driving the dynamics of the system (assuming it was not humans) large herbivores, wind, flood, disease, fire *etc*? These are not necessarily linked – large herbivores could have been the key driver, but in a largely closed system; or there could have been open landscapes controlled by (say) fire in places.

The work that English Nature commissioned (Hodder *et al.*, 2005; Hodder *et al.*, 2009) and the literature seen since favours the largely wooded landscape with a limited role for large herbivores as drivers, rather than the temperate savannah hypothesis (Vera, 2000). Mainly closed woodland seems to me to be more consistent with the direct evidence from pollen and sub-fossil invertebrates. It also seems more likely given the recent work on the ecology of the aurochs (van Vuure, 2005) and the experience of predator re-introduction in Yellowstone National Park (e.g. Ripple and Beschta, 2003, but see also Kauffman *et al.*, 2010).

One major argument for the savannah hypothesis has been that it could explain how oak (*Quercus* spp) maintained itself in the face of more shade-tolerant competitors such as beech (*Fagus sylvatica*). However, there are alternative explanations to the grazing option, such as the slower spread of beech from post-glacial refuges in southern Europe; in addition in Epping Forest and the New Forest beech in fact increased under the wood-pasture management that is seen as the analogue for natural temperate savannahs (Tubbs, 1986).

So my current view is of a varied landscape in both composition and structure, with open ground and large herbivores, but one that would have looked predominantly wooded.

But what is the relevance to modern English conservation?

In many parts of the world the 'natural' landscape or wilderness is, at least nominally, the template for nature conservation. The aim is to reduce or remove as much human impact as possible. However, English landscapes are not anywhere near 'natural' – they are cultural (Rackham,1986); the product of a period of human modification as long as that between the retreat of the ice and development of

Neolithic cultures. The habitats that we value (Ratcliffe, 1977), including coppice woods and wood-pastures, as well as meadows and heaths, are mostly the remnants of pre-industrial farming and forestry.

Many of the species we value were present in the pre-Neolithic period but their abundances and the assemblages in which they occur will often have changed, partly as a consequence of human intervention, but also because of ongoing 'natural' change. There have been species extinctions, but other species, some of them introductions, have thrived on the farmland created (e.g. brown hare, cirl bunting). Large and medium sized herbivore populations have been largely controlled by humans.

Our conservation template for the last 150 years has been largely based on a view of the countryside as it was experienced by the founding fathers and mothers of modern conservation; or as a gross simplification, as it appears in the background to pre-Raphaelite paintings. Is such a template still useful for the twenty-first century and if not what should supplement it?

The problems of maintaining traditional farming and woodland habitats are well-known.

- The social and economic systems that led to their creation have broken down and frequently can only be mimicked by public subsidy because people do not wish to live a peasant life-style. We pay farmers to put more stock on to abandoned commons and wood-pastures; we pay other farmers to reduce stock numbers on upland bogs.

- Biotic conditions have changed. The rabbit population, which maintained close-cropped downland on sites even after the sheep had been removed, crashed in the 1950s and scrub started to spread; since the 1970s deer populations in woods have increased with major impacts on the composition of both plant and animal communities, but also making coppicing and other forms of woodland management more expensive.

- The physical environment has changed with increased levels of nitrogen deposition and increasing evidence for impacts of climate change.

To some extent therefore we have to adapt the late Victorian countryside template as the basis for our conservation and accept that we will develop new cultural landscapes. In many places what we seek to achieve will be analogues of the past traditions, albeit there are moves to work on a larger scale, as indicated in the Lawton Report and the Natural Environment White Paper. Is there also scope for more radical approaches, such as the Dutch have adopted at Oostvaardersplassen (Vera, 2009), where fixed targets for habitats or species are abandoned in favour of seeing what happens if human influences are removed as far as possible? If so what role would large and medium-sized herbivores have in such systems (Hodder *et al.*, 2005)?

Adopting a 'rewilding' approach implies accepting change and unpredictable outcomes (Hughes *et al.*, in press). The habitats and species assemblages will not necessarily bear much resemblance to those of traditional land management systems, but neither may they resemble the pre-Neolithic landscape. A 'rewilded' landscape is likely to consist of a mosaic of different habitats, but we cannot predict or prescribe at what scales and what proportions the different elements might have. Species may be lost or gained which could create a dilemma for conservation managers.

Large herbivores are seen as an important element of 'rewilding' both as part of natural ecosystems in their own right, but also because of their impact on the landscape (Hodder *et al.*, 2005). Depending on the circumstances this may mean just allowing more free ranging of domestic stock, to ideas for developing feral herds as at Oostvaardersplassen. The advantages of using domestic stock are that they are easier to manage and the system may still just come within the scope of agri-environment funding. Feral herds present more difficulties in terms of how they are treated with respect to animal welfare legislation.

The choice is yours

In all rewilding projects in England some human intervention will be unavoidable for legal or political reasons (Kirby, 2009), even if only at the edges; so in practice 'rewilding' is just another form of cultural landscape management. Therefore future conservation may be based around three different sets of templates:

- 'traditional' – where the aim is to maintain past habitats and species assemblages through mimicking past land uses such as coppice, hay meadow management etc;

- 'targeted habitat/species management' – where we deliberately manage for a particular habitat or species assemblage, but this may not follow traditional practices; rideside management for butterflies in high forest might be an example of this;

- 'natural development/rewilding' – where we decide to allow change (within broad limits) in response to different processes such as free-range grazing, flooding *etc*.

What the balance is between these three approaches will be for future conservation managers and policy makers to debate. Rewilding areas will need to be justified on the basis of what they can contribute to future habitat and species conservation, as well as to other ecosystem service provision (including spiritual values). They will not be the same as pre-Neolithic landscape, but we may be able to use such areas to test hypotheses on what such landscapes were like and how they functioned.

Acknowledgements

My thanks to Kathy Hodder, Paul Buckland and James Bullock who carried out the study of naturalistic grazing for Natural England; and to Frans Vera for stimulating this debate.

References

Godwin, H. (1975) *History of the British flora* (second edition). Cambridge University Press, Cambridge.

Hodder, K.H., Bullock, J.M., Buckland, P.C. and Kirby, K.J. (2005) *Large herbivores in the wildwood and modern naturalistic grazing systems.* Peterborough: English Nature (Research Report 648).

Hodder, K.H., Buckland, P.C., Kirby, K.J. and Bullock, J.M. (2009) Can the pre-Neolithic provide suitable models for re-wilding the landscape in Britain? *British Wildlife*, **20**, (supplement) 4-15.

Hughes, F.M.R, Stroh, P.A., Adams, W.M., Kirby, K.J., Mountford, O. and Warrington, S. In press. Monitoring and evaluating large-scale, 'open-ended' habitat creation projects: a journey rather than a destination. *Journal of Nature Conservation.*

Kauffman, M.J., Brodie, J.F. and Jules, E.S. (2010) Are wolves saving Yellowstone's aspen? A landscape-level test of a behaviourally mediated trophic cascade. *Ecology*, **9**, 2742-2755.

Kirby, K.J. (2009) Policy in or for the wilderness? *British Wildlife*, **20**, (supplement) 59-63.

Peterken, G.F. (1996) *Natural Woodland: ecology and conservation in northern temperate regions*. Cambridge University Press, Cambridge.

Rackham, O. (1986) *The History of the Countryside*. J.M. Dent, London.

Ratcliffe, D.A. (1977) *A nature conservation review.* Cambridge University Press, Cambridge.

Ripple, W.J. and Beschta, R.L. (2003) Wolf reintroduction, predation risk, and cottonwood recovery in Yellowstone National Park. *Forest Ecology and Management*, **184**, 299-313

Rodwell, J.S. (1991) *British plant communities: I woodlands and scrub.* Cambridge University Press, Cambridge.

Tubbs, C.R. (1986) *The New Forest*. Collins, London.

Van Vuure, C. (2005) *Retracing the Auroch*. Pensoft, Sofia-Moscow.

Vera, F.W.M. (2000) *Grazing Ecology and Forest History*. CABI International, Wallingford:Oxford.

Impacts of herbivory on vegetation dynamics in the New Forest

Adrian Newton
Bournemouth University

Introduction

The New Forest provides an exceptional opportunity to understand the interactions between grazing animals, people and wooded landscapes, having developed as an ecological system under the influence of large, free-ranging herbivores, including deer and livestock. The present character of the vegetation is strongly dependent on its history as a medieval hunting forest, and the survival of a traditional commoning system since late medieval times. Situated on the south coast of England in the counties of Hampshire and Wiltshire, the New Forest is today the largest area of semi-natural vegetation in lowland England, and includes large tracts of heathland, valley mire and ancient pasture woodland, three habitats that are now fragmented and rare throughout lowland western Europe. The area was designated as a National Park in 2005. About 50% of the land area of the Park (the 'Open Forest') is covered by unenclosed vegetation, on which more than 7000 ponies, cattle, donkeys and pigs are currently depastured by local commoners.

Impacts of herbivory

This presentation will examine the impacts of herbivory on vegetation dynamics in the New Forest, first by profiling the research undertaken in the area over the past four decades. Results from a recent field survey, involving a systematic assessment of browsing impacts in all of the New Forest's woodlands, will also be presented. Data obtained during this survey have been used to parameterize a spatially explicit model of vegetation dynamics (LANDIS II), which enables the interactions between animals, vegetation and human activity to be explored. This combination of modelling experiments and field data will be used to critically examine current ideas regarding the role of large herbivores in vegetation dynamics, with particular reference to Vera's cyclical theory of vegetation turnover. In addition, the resilience of the New Forest as an integrated social-ecological system will be considered, involving coupled interactions between people, animals and vegetation. Results highlight that over the long term, coupled social-ecological systems such as the New Forest can be highly resilient to major internal and external shocks, despite being highly dynamic. This resilience depends on maintaining adaptive capacity in social structures and institutions as well as environmental processes.

Legacies of livestock grazing in the forest structure of Valonia oak landscapes in the Eastern Mediterranean

Tobias Plieninger[1], Harald Schaich[2] and Thanasis Kizos[3]

Ecosystem Services Research Group, Berlin-Brandenburg Academy of Sciences and Humanities[1], Institute for Landscape Management, University of Freiburg[2], Department of Geography, University of the Aegean[3].

Introduction

Since the 1960s, most dryland ecosystems of the Mediterranean Basin have experienced a comprehensive land-use transition from complex and multifunctional agrosilvopastoral land-use systems to simplified and intensified forms of livestock husbandry and agriculture (Naveh, 1982; Pinto-Correia and Vos, 2001; Hill *et al.*, 2008) Intensified livestock husbandry is believed to shift rangeland ecosystems from equilibrium states and to initiate degradation processes (Iosifides and Politidis, 2005; Röder *et al.*, 2007; Röder *et al.*, 2008). In the Eastern Mediterranean, overgrazing has resulted in the removal of soil cover and the domination of undesirable plants, mostly *Sarcopoterium spinosum* (Bakker *et al.*, 2005). These processes have been exacerbated by changes in the spatial configuration of grazing, which is now largely uncontrolled, continuous and all-season (Giourga, Margaris and Vokou, 1998). A remote-sensing survey showed that, between 1977 and 1996, 40% of rangelands on Crete (Greece) suffered declining vegetation cover in consequence of increased grazing pressure (Hostert *et al.*, 2003). However, grazing pressure is highly heterogeneous, so that over- and under-grazing can be observed even in immediate proximity of each other (Röder *et al.*, 2007). Both over- and under-use can modify ecosystem structure and functions, as Mediterranean drylands are tightly coupled human–environment systems (Aranzabal *et al.*, 2008; Röder *et al.*, 2008). For example, a comprehensive cessation of livestock may involve loss of biodiversity and devastating wildfires (Papanastasis, 2009).

(Agri-)silvopastoral woodlands are common Mediterranean vegetation complexes. They have been shaped by human uses and correspond to different stages of regressive succession of the Mediterranean climax forests, which have virtually disappeared (Scarascia-Mugnozza *et al.*, 2000). Many of these complexes can be considered 'legacies' of past land uses. Land-use legacies persist and continue to influence ecosystem structures and functions, though former uses may have been abandoned decades or centuries ago. Land-use legacies express themselves in diverse ecological phenomena, ranging from biodiversity, vegetation structure, and soil properties to biogeochemical cycles (Foster *et al.*, 2003). The legacy of traditional grazing and cultivation practices in Mediterranean woodlands is not well understood, but it is assumed to manifest itself in elevated morphological plasticity, stress tolerance, and ecological resilience (Bergmeier, 2008). Traditionally, silvopastoral woodlands have delivered a large variety of ecosystem goods, including firewood, charcoal, food for humans and animals, gums, resins, dyes, pharmaceuticals, cork, and aromatic plants. Moreover, they provide intangible ecosystem services, such as soil protection, stabilization of soils, reduction of water runoff in mountainous and hilly watersheds, maintenance of landscape beauty, and microclimate amelioration (Palahi *et al.*, 2009; Scarascia-Mugnozza *et al.*, 2000). Loss of resilience in the silvopastoral systems in the Western Mediterranean has been expressed in a geographically widespread and profound lack of tree regeneration, accompanied by a gradual ageing and dieback of existing forest stands (Moreno and Pulido, 2008).

Silvopastoral woodland dominated by *Q. macrolepis* Kotschy is a particularly under-studied type of oak woodland (Figure 1). In consequence of conversion of forests to agricultural land, illegal lumbering, overgrazing and forest fires, *Q. macrolepis* stands have become marginal and fragmented into small-forested units or isolated individuals in various locations (estimated remaining area in Greece:

Figure 1. Different types of silvopastoral oak woodlands in Filia municipality, Greece:

a Open stands established on formerly arable terraces, situated close to the village.

b dense oak stands on steeper slopes at the outskirts of the village.

c stands heavily infested by *sarcopoterium spinosum*.

29,600 ha; Pantera *et al.*, 2008). *Q. macrolepis* is frequently mixed with *Q. pubescens* Willd. and *Q. cerris* L. Being one of the few deciduous oak species in the Eastern Mediterranean zone, *Q. macrolepis* is being increasingly appreciated as a means for desertification control, for its ability to survive after wildfires and to thrive under conditions unfavorable to other oak species, and for an acorn mast that can support both wild fauna and domestic pigs (Pantera *et al.*, 2008). Since the European Union has declared *Q. macrolepis* forests to be a natural habitat type of community interest (Habitat Directive 92/43EEC), efforts to protect, manage, and expand their populations by afforestation are underway. The overall aim of the following landscape-level study is to contribute towards conservation efforts by investigating land-use history, monitoring forest structure and regeneration of *Quercus* woodlands, and modeling ecological and management factors that determine habitats for oak regeneration on Lesvos Island, in the Eastern Aegean (Greece). In particular, we aim to answer the following research questions:

- What land-use changes have taken place since the early twentieth century that may be influential on silvopastoral oak woodlands?

- Does forest structure (especially long-term regeneration and short-term recruitment of *Q. macrolepis* and accompanying oak species) reflect local land-use legacies?

- How are patterns of oak regeneration related to current grazing intensities, environmental site characteristics, and over- and under-storey plant community structure?

Materials and methods

Study Area

As study sites (Figure 2), we selected silvopastoral oak woodlands in the municipality of Filia (39° 15' to 39° 20' N, 26° 05' to 26° 10' E; 2,190 ha area) in North-Central Lesvos Island. The area covers the valley of a small seasonal stream, and the village is located on a small plateau upwards from the outlet of the stream. The three hills that form the valley are 466 m, 682 m, and 785 m high; with the exception of the plateau and the pocket plain in the outlet of the stream, the area is sloping and steep. Soils are stony, shallow, and severely eroded, described as Typic Yerochrept, Lithic Xerochrept, and Lithic Xerorthent. Typical for the Mediterranean region, the climate shows a strong seasonal variation of rainfall and high oscillations between minimum and maximum daily rainfall. Mild, humid winters alternate with hot and dry summers, with a mean annual air temperature of 17.7°C and an average rainfall of 670 mm.

Figure 2. The Study Area

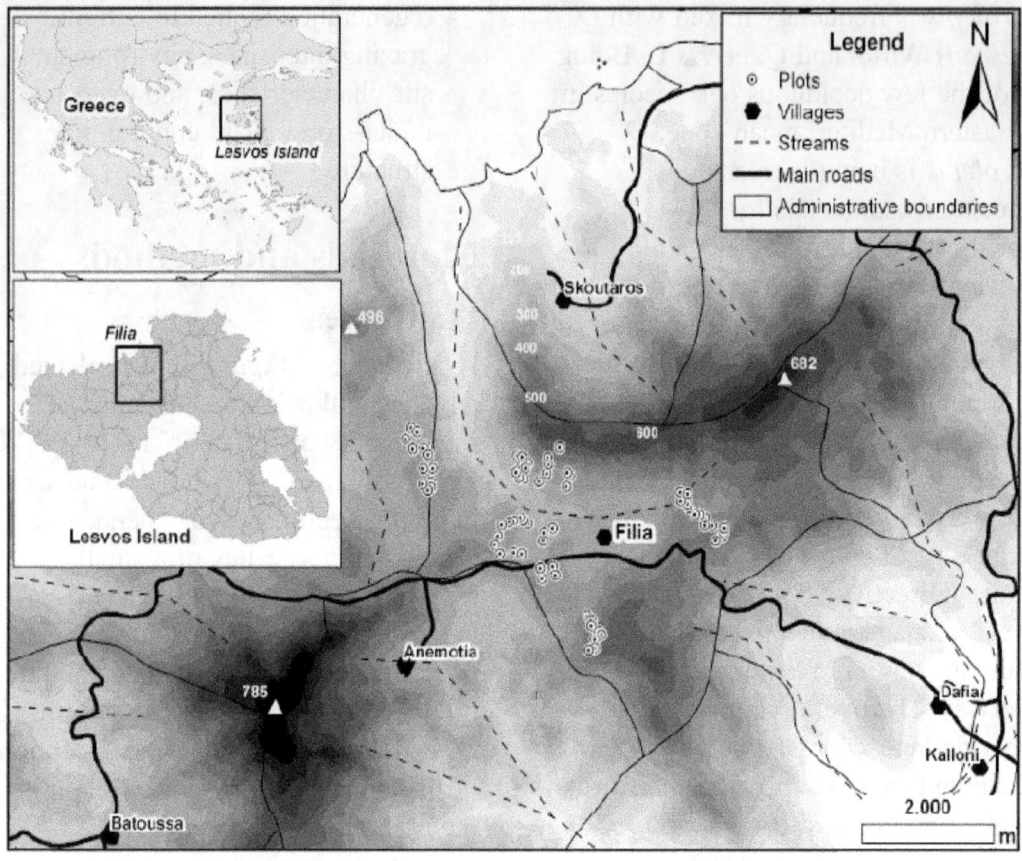

Land-use statistics

Statistical information on land use and livestock for the Filia municipality was derived from the official data of the census for agriculture and animal husbandry, available at the settlement level from 1961 on (ESYE, 1964, 1978, 1994, 2003). Earlier data, not available at settlement level, were taken at the level of the entire island (ESYE, 1958; GSYE, 1934). In Greek agricultural statistics, cultivated area includes arable land, vines, tree crops and fallow, while the Utilized Agricultural Area (UAA) includes both cultivated and grazing lands.

Field measurements of forest structure and oak regeneration

As the sample for this study, we selected seventy parcels of silvopastoral woodland (see Figure 2). The parcels included in each cluster were identified by a random-walk procedure (Kent and Coker, 2000) in May and June 2009. We placed our sampling plot in the centre of each parcel, with the criterion for a plot to enter the sample being the presence of at least one mature *Q. macrolepis*, *Q. pubescens*, or *Q. cerris* individual within a maximum distance of 15 m around the focus. Each plot consisted of three concentric circles. Mature trees were recorded within a 15 m radius (area: 706.9 m²), saplings and shrub species within a 5 m radius (area: 78.5 m²); and seedlings within a 2.5 m radius (area: 19.6 m²).

For the analysis of forest stand structure, the number, species, and diameter at breast height (DBH) of all woody plants ≥10 cm DBH were recorded within the outer circle. The frequencies of stems in 5 cm diameter classes were determined for the three oak species in each plot. Size-class frequency diagrams were evaluated to indirectly assess long-term regeneration, as recruitment failure translates into 'gaps' in the current age structures of tree populations (Ramírez and Díaz, 2008). Short-term recruitment was assessed directly by measuring two juvenile life stages of oaks delimited by size: seedlings (base diameter < 1 cm) and saplings (base diameter: 1 cm to <10 cm). These were used as an indication of recent recruitment, while long-term regeneration was assessed by means of the size structure of adult oak populations. We counted the number of all saplings of the three oak species within the 5 m radius. For each sapling, we measured base diameter of the main stem, height, and the number of stems in cases of stem aggregations. Within the inner circle, the numbers of both individuals and aggregations of oak seedlings were counted.

Cover of canopy, shrubs (separately for each species), forbs, rocks, litter, and bare soil were estimated by the step-point method (Evans and Love, 1957). Ground and canopy cover was noted down for 100 points, situated at one-step intervals in a fifty-step transect perpendicular to the slope and another fifty-step transect parallel to contours. Short-term grazing intensity was estimated by counting the number of observations of faeces pellets along the steps of the two transects and is also expressed in percent of observations. Presence of shrub species within the 5 m radius was also noted down.

We applied bivariate logistic regression to explore simple patterns of oak recruitment and thus potential drivers among site conditions, vegetation structure, and grazing intensity parameters. The presence on a plot of at least one seedling or sapling (coded as 1) or no presence at all (coded as 0) was used as the dependent variable. An array of continuous parameters describing site conditions, vegetation structure, and livestock grazing were used as independent variables.

Results

Land-use change

In the early twentieth century, most of the cultivated area on Western Lesvos was covered by cereals and arable crops, followed by olives and vines. An increase in cultivated land followed the population increases of the 1930s and 1940s, up until the 1950s; in the Mithimna district, where Filia is located, this increase led to arable land taking more than 70% of the cultivated area, 26% of which was in areas with 'scattered trees' (EYSE, 1958). After 1961, the Utilized Agricultural Area in Filia increased slightly, due to the increase of grazing lands by 44% and that of tree crops (practically speaking, olives) by 81% until 2001 (Table 1). All arable uses – which were associated with extensive terracing to accommodate ploughing – have decreased, practically disappearing from the 1991 and 2001 statistics. The period from the 1950s to the 2000s has been characterized by a more than twofold increase in the sheep population, while the number of sheep farmers has sharply decreased (Table 1). Even more dramatic livestock increases are to be found for the whole of Lesvos. In 1918 the total number of sheep was 70,000, a figure that remained more or less constant until the 1950s, when it went up to 93,000; but after that the sheep population effectively tripled on the island (Figure 3).

Forest structure

In total, 1,312 trees ≥ 10 cm DBH belonging to fourteen species were recorded. *Q. macrolepis* (44.4% of all trees) and *Q. pubescens* (30.1%) were by far the most frequent tree species. Total tree densities ranged from 28.3 to 820.5 trees ha^{-1}. Basal area extended from 2.2 to a maximum of 24.6 m² ha^{-1}. Between one and seven tree species ≥ 10 cm DBH were found within one plot, resulting in a mean of 3.4 species ($\pm$ 1.4) per plot. In total, twenty-four woody species (above and below 10 cm DBH) were recorded (Table 2). Forest cover was significantly related to litter cover (Spearman's $r=0.720$, $p<0.001$, $n=70$) and bare soil cover (Spearman's $r=-0.443$, $p<0.001$), but unrelated to shrub and forbs cover. In contrast, shrub and forbs cover were correlated negatively (Spearman's $r=-0.457$, $p<0.001$, $n=70$).

Table 1. Farm and land-use statistics for Filia village

	1961	1971	1991	2001
Farms (n)	404	322	196	192
Utilized Agricultural Area (UAA) (ha)	1968.1		1990.6	2129.4
Cultivated land (ha)	888.5	951.3	503.5	571.3
Arable land (ha)	256.5	56.1	4.3	3.9
Fallow (ha)	295.6	528.4		0
Tree crops (ha)	302.7	343.1	479.1	549.9
Grazing land (ha)	1079.6		1487.1	1558.1
Farms with sheep (n)	177	166	111	101
Sheep (n)	3971	6846	6886	8064
UAA / farm (ha)	2.2	2.9	10.2	11.1
Average plot size (ha)	0.55	0.78	2.00	2.26
Plots per farm (n)	4.0	3.8	5.1	4.2

(sources: ESYE, 1964, 1978, 1994, 2003)

Figure 3. Number of sheep and number of sheep farms on the Aegean Islands and Lesvos, 1950-2001 (sources ESYE 1958, 1964, 1978, 1994, 2003)

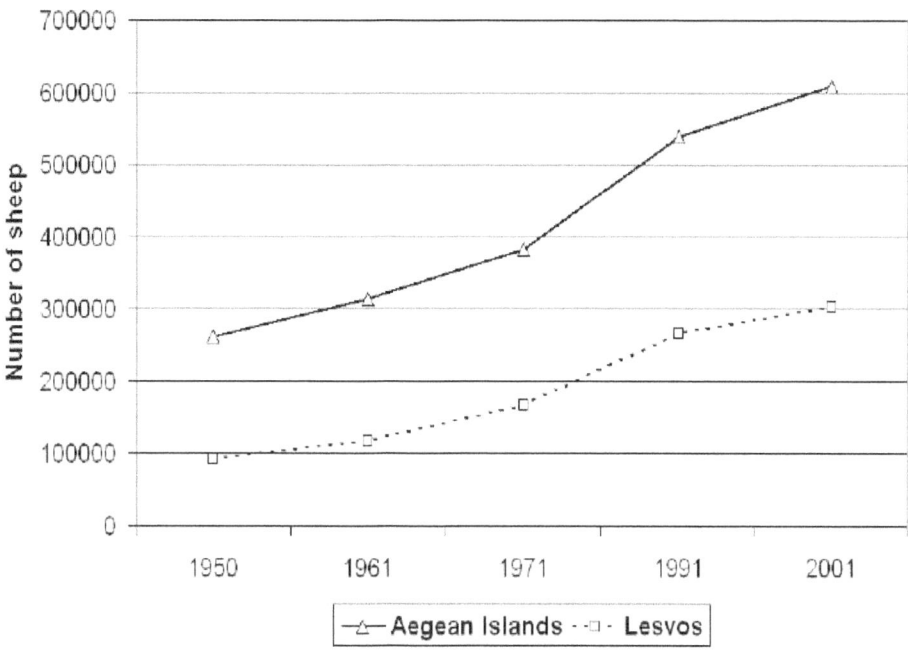

Long-term regeneration of oak populations

The three populations of oaks were composed of 583 *Q. macrolepis*, 395 *Q. pubescens*, and 150 *Q. cerris* trees. Of these, 80.8% (*Q. macrolepis*), 80.3% (*Q. pubescens*), and 71.3% (*Q. cerris*) were composed of one major stem, whereas 19.2%, 19.7%, and 28.7% were multi-stemmed associations, indicating coppice-like stand structures with a high extent of vegetative regeneration. *Q. macrolepis* populations showed an inverse J-shaped distribution (Figure 4). Among all mature oaks recorded, the 10 cm and 15 cm size classes were most frequent, comprising on average 61.1% (*Q. macrolepis*), 52.1% (*Q. pubescens*), and 62.5% (*Q. cerris*) of all trees. In *Q. pubescens* and *Q. cerris* stands, the 15 cm class was more strongly represented (26.5% and 34.9%) than the 10 cm class (25.6% and 27.6%), indicating a potential transition from an inverse J-shaped towards a bell-shaped size distribution.

Short-term oak recruitment

All in all, 353 oak seedlings were counted in the sampling plots, of which 276 could be categorized as isolated shoots and seventy-seven as seedling aggregations. Seedlings were absent from 31% of the plots. In those plots where seedlings occurred, densities ranged from 509.2 to 20,366.8 seedlings ha^{-1} (mean: 2,567.7, S.D.: 4,080.2). We counted 163 oak saplings in the seventy plots, with sapling densities ranging from 127.3 to 4,456.3 saplings ha^{-1} (mean: 296.5, S.D.: 605.7), where they occurred at all. Oak saplings were completely absent from 44% of the

Table 2. Overall occurrence of woody plants in the 70 plots, cover of woody species (where present), and density and basal area of the tree layer (>10 cm DBH, where present) (mean values ± S.D.)

Species	Woody Plant presence	Shrub Cover (%)	Tree Density (N ha^{-1})	Basal Area (m^2 ha^{-1})
Asparagus acutifolius L.	57%	1.62 ± 0.77		
Ballota acetabulosa (L.) Benth.	36%	2.44 ± 1.60		
Cistus creticus L.	41%	15.26 ± 14.36		
Crataegus monogyna Jacq.	21%	1.00 ± 0.00	14.10 ± 0.00	0.29 ± 0.07
Fraxinus ornus L.	1%		42.40	2.77
Juniperus oxycedrus L.	1%		14.10	0.20
Lonicera etrusca Santi	4%			
Olea europaea L.	24%	2.50 ± 0.71	22.20 ± 13.28	1.53 ± 1.36
Origanum vulgare L.	31%	1.40 ± 0.89		
Phillyrea latifolia L.	51%	2.00 ± 1.73	32.27 ± 34.62	0.70 ± 0.74
Pinus brutia Ten.	3%		14.10	4.77
Pistacia terebinthus L.	27%		14.10 ± 0.00	0.20 ± 0.09
Prunus domestica L.	51%	2.53 ± 2.62	29.28 ± 21.12	0.46 ± 0.38
Prunus dulcis (Mill.) D.A.Webb	1%		14.10	0.35
Pyrus amygdaliformis Vill.	49%	1.80 ± 0.84	30.53 ± 20.71	0.83 ± 0.59
Pyrus communis L.	4%		33.00 ± 21.64	1.23 ± 0.49
Quercus cerris L.	36%	1.00 ± 0.00	85.84 ± 77.63	3.83 ± 2.93
Quercus coccifera L.	7%	1.33 ± 0.58		
Quercus macrolepis Kotschy	87%	1.39 ± 0.51	135.21 ± 126.07	5.78 ± 4.56
Quercus pubescens L.	91%	1.00 ± 0.00	87.30 ± 89.15	4.23 ± 3.61
Rosa canina L.	9%	1.00		
Rubus sp.	4%	2.00 ± 1.73		
Ruscus aculeatus L.	3%			
Sarcopoterium spinosum L.	46%	15.31 ± 11.67		
Woody plants total	100%	12.69 ± 14.64	265.16 ± 166.24	11.34 ± 4.85

Figure 4. Size structure of mature *Quercus* species stands. (mean ± S.D.)

a *Q. macrolepis*
(n = 61)

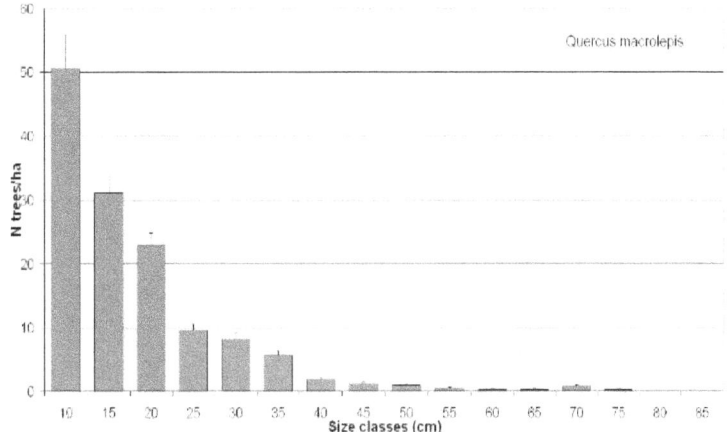

b *Q. pubescens*
(n = 64)

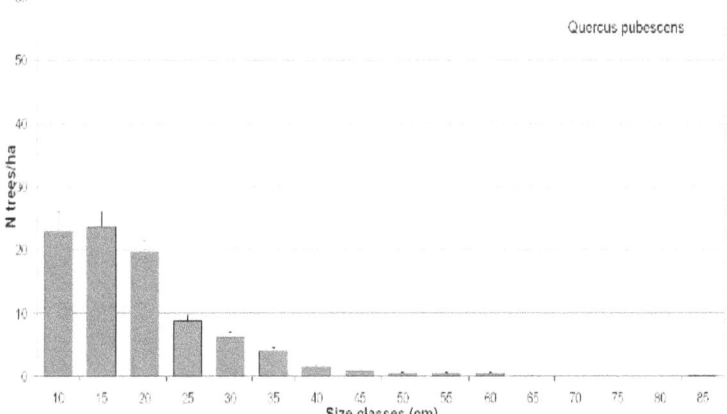

c *Q. cerris*
(N = 25)

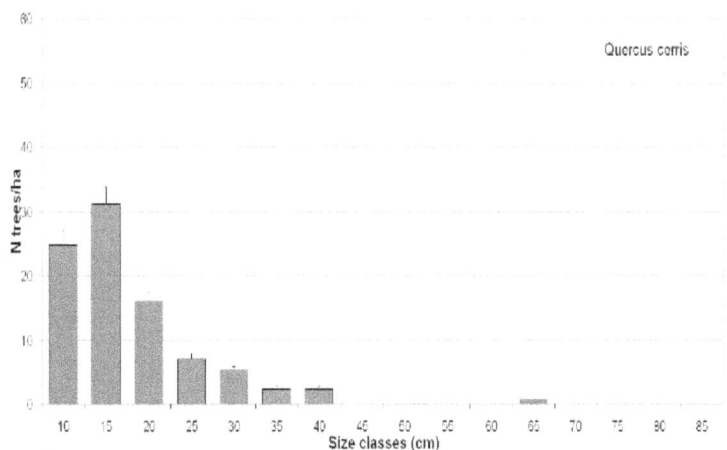

Figure 5. Percentage of plots containing 0 individuals, 1-5 individuals, 6-10 individuals, and >10 individuals of oak seedlings and saplings (n=70)

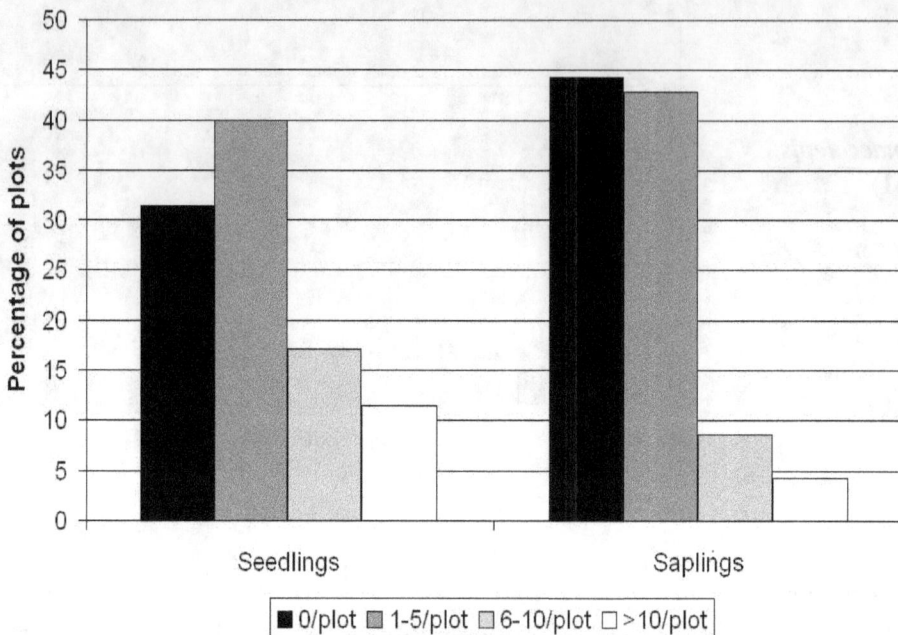

Table 3. Results of bivariate logistic regression analysis testing for effects of site parameters, vegetation structure, and livestock grazing on oak seedling and sapling occurrence (n=70). n.s.: p≥0.05. r indicates Nagelkerke R^2 as measure of goodness of fit

	Seedlings			Saplings		
	sign	R^2	p	sign	R^2	p
Site Conditions						
Slope			n.s.			n.s.
Northness			n.s.			n.s.
Bare soil	−	0.105	0.028			n.s.
Rock cover			n.s.			n.s.
Vegetation Structure						
Forest cover	+	0.249	0.001	+	0.259	0.001
Quercus sp. density	+	0.094	0.048	+	0.273	0.001
Quercus sp. basal area	+	0.156	0.011	+	0.242	0.001
Woody plants richness	+	0.105	0.026	+	0.319	<0.001
Shrub cover			n.s.			n.s.
Herbaceous cover			n.s.	−	0.119	0.015
Litter cover	+	0.139	0.017	+	0.211	0.003
Livestock						
Dung frequency	−	0.106	0.025	−	0.138	0.015

Table 4. Results of χ^2 tests for the relationship between the occurrence of dominant shrub species and oak seedling and sapling occurrence (n=70). n.s.: p>0.05

	Seedlings			Saplings		
	sign	R^2	p	sign	R^2	p
Asparagus acutifolius			n.s.	+	7.72	0.005
Cistus creticus	+	4.62	0.032	+	18.66	<0.001
Phillyrea latifolia			n.s.			n.s.
Pyrus amygdaliformis			n.s.			n.s.
Sarcopoterium spinosum			n.s.			n.s.

plots (Figure 5). Sapling stem diameters ranged widely: from 1 cm to a maximum of 21 cm (mean: 4.44 cm, S.D.: 4.76 cm). This distribution was skewed, with 47.2% of oak saplings being in the 1 cm size class.

Influences of grazing and other ecological factors

The occurrence of oak seedlings and saplings was significantly associated with several site, vegetation, and management parameters (Table 3). Dung frequency was negatively associated with both size classes. Forest cover, density and basal area of oak stands, woody plant richness and litter cover showed significant positive relationships for both seedlings and saplings. We did not detect any significant associations (threshold: p<0.05) for slope, northness, rockiness, or shrub cover. Seedlings were negatively related to bare soil, saplings were negatively related to herbaceous cover. Occurrence of *Cistus creticus* shrubs was significantly and positively associated with both seedlings and saplings. *Asparagus acutifolius* was positively associated only with saplings. Associations with other shrubs were insignificant (Table 4).

Discussion

Land-use transition

Available statistical data on land-use and human population changes reveal the great rupture that most Mediterranean land uses experienced from the 1950s to the 1970s (Pinto-Correia and Vos, 2001): A complex and multifunctional agrosilvopastoral land-use system was simplified into a pure livestock-raising system. In landscape terms, the former mosaic of terraced arable land, tree crops, and pastures was replaced by more homogeneous grazed woodland. The abandonment of cereal cultivation was especially widespread on the terraces in the hill and mountain zones of the study area (Papanastasis, 2007). In a wider context, this land-use transition can be interpreted as a regional specification of a global land-use trend: from subsistence agriculture and small-scale farms towards intensive agriculture (Foley *et al*., 2005). The transition is the result of several parallel social and economic developments. The opening of local markets to competition from more productive areas had made most extensive cultivation of the Aegean islands unprofitable since the 1950s (Papanastasis, 2007). A rural exodus reduced the population of the study area by more than 60% (1940s-2000s) and the number of farms by around 50% (1960s-2000s). However, an increased nationwide demand for dairy and meat products provided a powerful incentive for intensified livestock raising in the 1970s and 1980s. European agricultural policies that granted *per-capita* subsidies for sheep and goats in the 1980s and 1990s additionally contributed towards increasing herd sizes. However, the current ongoing intensification of livestock husbandry cannot be attributed to any of these factors, since European agricultural policies have been reformed and the demand for milk and meat products is now being satisfied by cheaper imports. Rather, it seems to be the consequence of the reduced profitability of animal production: those that choose to keep their herds face diminishing per-head profit (if any) and increasing dependence on imported feed. To maintain total revenues, these farmers have been tending to further increase their herds and, thus, have more and more decoupled livestock raising from the land (Beopoulos and Vlahos, 2004; Iosifides and Politides, 2005). In consequence, a standardized and largely uncontrolled form of land use has been introduced, while cultural legacies and localized ecological knowledge have been lost (compare Hostert *et al.*, 2003; Röder *et al.*, 2007 for similar insight found for Northern Greece and Crete).

Land-use legacies in forest structure and regeneration

In this study we asked whether the land-use transition outlined above has left specific legacies in terms of forest vegetation patterns, as these have also been found in deforestation-reforestation sequences elsewhere (Foster, 1992; Bellemare, Motzkin and Foster, 2002; Foster *et al.*, 2003). In general, legacies may be imprinted on several components of forest structure: First, tree species composition may be modified compared to ancient forests (Hermy and Verheyen, 2007). Second, agricultural legacies may leave biotic and abiotic characteristics, such as multiple-stemmed trees, whereas elements of ancient forests, such as large trees, dead snags, and uproot mounds and pits, are rare (Foster *et al.*, 2003). Third, and most importantly, agricultural abandonment may generate specific age and size structures of forests (Marks and Gardescu, 2001). We recorded many species and elements in our plots that bear witness to an agrosilvopastoral past, for example cultivated tree species such as *Olea europea*, *Prunus domestica*, *Pyrus communis*, and *Prunus dulcis*. Indeed, even the wide distribution of *Quercus macrolepis* can be considered an enduring land-use legacy, as oak populations were deliberately expanded by humans at the end of the nineteenth century to use oak cupula for extraction of tanning agents (Bergmeier, 2008).

Frequent terraces (Figure 1a), threshing floors, stone walls, farm infrastructural elements and a proportion of 19% to 29% multi-stemmed mature trees present further evidence of past land uses.

We have documented a major land-use legacy in the diameter structures of silvopastoral oak woodlands, which we interpret as an indicator for long-term regeneration: The size-structure of the *Q. macrolepis* population is similar to the inverse J-shaped distribution typical for natural Mediterranean oak forests (Pulido, Días and Hidalgo de Trucios, 2001). Assuming a close relationship between tree rings and diameter – as has been demonstrated for *Q. ilex* stands in the Mediterranean for homogeneous environments (Pulido, Días and Hidalgo de Trucios, 2001) – the population structures of both oak species correspond to those of natural multi-age forest stands. A positively skewed age distribution indicates continuous recruitment with a constant mortality rate of mature individuals, resulting in long-term persistence of the tree populations in the absence of exogenous disturbance (Oliver and Larson, 1996). The size distribution of the studied oak populations suggests that the traditional land-use system has supported continuous regeneration. Our data further show that short-term recruitment, as determined by seedling and sapling counts, is highly variable, but generally low in relation to adult oak densities. In conclusion, the legacy of the land-use transition that we studied becomes evident in a major discrepancy between the successful long-term regeneration (as indicated by size-structure analysis) and the less successful short-term recruitment of oaks. Oak trees are mere legacies of the former, rather than active components of the current, land-use system.

Grazing and other ecological factors related to recruitment

Both oak seedlings and saplings are in consistent negative association with dung frequency, confirming the barrier that grazing can impose on oak regeneration. The significant impact of grazing on regeneration of *Q. ithaburensis* – a near relative species to *Q. macrolepis* – has been demonstrated by a study in Israel (Dufour-Dror, 2007). In a comparison between a grazed and an ungrazed oak stand, the densities of seedlings were 61% and of sapling 67% lower in the grazed treatment. A similar relationship has been found for *Q. ilex* in South-East Spain (Cierjacks and Hensen, 2004). This finding shows that the intensification of livestock grazing has been influential on forest regeneration and supports the view that Mediterranean vegetation is generally resilient against light and moderate grazing, but that impacts increase sharply beyond a certain threshold of grazing intensity (Plieninger, 2007; Köchy *et al.*, 2008). Recruitment of oak seedlings and saplings is also related to determinants such as forest cover, adult oak density and basal area, woody plant richness, and litter cover. A relationship of basal area with occurrence or density of recruitment has also been found for other oak species in the Western

Mediterranean (Lookingbill and Zavala, 2000; Pausas *et al.*, 2006). On the one hand, this can be interpreted as an effect of the elevated acorn input from mature oaks. On the other hand, it could be a consequence of more favorable microclimatic conditions in terms of the radiation and soil moisture of dense stands. The association of higher seedling and sapling densities with elevated woody plant diversity is difficult to interpret. Both may be related to a common cause, such as livestock grazing, which may hinder oak recruitment and the establishment of grazing-sensitive woody species at the same time. Together with the finding that forest cover (and not only oak cover) is a significant variable, this indicates that mixed woodlands are appropriate or even better habitats for oak recruitment than monospecific oak woodlands. Litter cover seems to support recruitment by increasing soil moisture and, thus, water availability for oak seedlings (Espelta, Riba and Retana, 1995). Bare soil is negatively associated with seedling recruitment, while herbaceous cover negatively impacts sapling occurrence. Thus, it seems that seedlings are more sensitive to the adverse conditions of open microsites, such as livestock trampling and insulation, whereas saplings suffer more from the competition of herbs.

Conservation and management implications

Low recruitment rates and current land-use trends indicate that the long-term persistence of silvopastoral oak woodlands may be at risk.

Socioeconomic developments, such as increasing production costs (mostly due to high forage prices) and decreasing sales prices for livestock, have been leading to further increases in grazing intensities. An additional stress that will be testing the resilience of Eastern Mediterranean grazing systems is increasing drought conditions (as predicted by IPCC scenarios). The past decades have shown a gradual reduction in rainfall and a subsequent reduction of tree growth in the Aegean Islands (Körner, Sarris and Christodoulaiks, 2005). The predicted climate changes are likely to interact with grazing impacts, which may trigger a negative feedback cycle that increases soil erosion (Köchy *et al.*, 2008), reduces carrying capacity, and in the end undermines the capacity of rangelands to sustain ecosystem services (Körner, Sarris and Christodoulaiks, 2005). The inclusion of *Q. macrolepis* forests into the European Union's Habitat Directive as a habitat type of communal interest entails the ensuring of favorable conservation status through the formulation of a sound management plan. Our results suggest that oak regeneration can be enhanced by adaptive management of livestock grazing. For *Q. ithaburensis*, Dufour-Dror (2007) proposes a stocking rate limit of 0.7 livestock units ha^{-1}. Livestock management could also be improved by a controlled rotational system of grazing over several parcels and a seasonal steering of herds according to forage availability and depletion (Gutman *et al.*, 1999). A highly important task, however, will be to restore lost traditional knowledge on oak regeneration in cultivated and grazed landscapes through employing participatory approaches among resource users (Berkes, Colding and Folke, 2000). This knowledge may help to foster resilience by promoting appropriate resource usage and oak regeneration at the same time.

References

Aranzabal, I., Schmitz, M.F., Aquilera, P., Pineda, F.D. (2008) Modelling of landscape changes derived from the dynamics of socio-ecological systems - A case of study in a semiarid Mediterranean landscape. *Ecol Indic.*, **8**,

Bakker, M.M., Govers, G., Kosmas, C., Vanacker, V., van Oost, K., Rounsevell, M. (2005) Soil erosion as a driver of land-use change. *Agr. Ecosyst. Environ.*, **105**, 467-481.

Bellemare, J., Motzkin, G., Foster, D.R. (2002) Legacies of the agricultural past in the forested present: an assessment of historical land-use effects on rich mesic forests. *Journal of Biogeography*, **29**, 1401-1420.

Beopoulos, N., Vlahos, G. (2004) Exploitation of pastures in a sensitive natural environment: The case of Western Lesvos. *Adv Geoecol*, **37**, 183-194.

Bergmeier, E. (2008) Xero-thermophilous broadleaved forests and wooded pastures in the EU Habitats Directive: What is a favourable conservation status? *Berichte der Reinhold-Tüxen-Gesellschaft*, **20**, 108-124.

Berkes, F., Colding, J., Folke, C. (2000) Rediscovery of traditional ecological knowledge as adaptive management. *Ecol Appl*, **10**, 1251-1262.

Cierjacks, A., Hensen, I. (2004) Variation of stand structure and regeneration of Mediterranean holm oak along a grazing intensity gradient. *Plant Ecology*, **173**, 215-223.

Dufour-Dror, J.M. (2007) Influence of cattle grazing on the density of oak seedlings and saplings in a Tabor oak forest in Israel. *Acta Oecol*, **31**, 223-228.

Espelta, J.M., Riba, M., Retana, J. (1995) Patterns of seedling recruitment in West-Mediterranean *Quercus ilex* forests influenced by canopy development. *J Veg Sci*, **6**, 465-472.

ESYE (1958) Apotelesmata Georgikis Apografis tis Ellados 1950 (Results of the Agricultural Census 1950). National Print, Athens.

ESYE (1964) Apotelesmata tis Apografis Georgias - Ktinotrofias tis Ellados 1961 (Results of the Census for Agriculture-Animal Husbandry 1961). EYSE, Athens.

ESYE (1978) Apotelesmata Apografis Georgias - Ktinotrofias tis 14 Martiou 1971 (Results of the Census for Agriculture-Animal Husbandry of 14 March 1971). EYSE, Athens.

ESYE (1994) Apotelesmata Apografis Georgias - Ktinotrofias 1991 (Results of the Census for Agriculture-Animal Husbandry of 1991). EYSE, Athens.

ESYE (2003) Apotelesmata Apografis Georgias - Ktinotrofias 2001 (Results of the Census for Agriculture-Animal Husbandry of 2001). available at http://www.statistics.gr, accessed 20/10/09. EYSE, Athens.

Evans, R.A. and Love, R.M. (1957) The step-point method of sampling - a practical tool in range research. *J Range Manage*, **10**, 208-212. doi: 10.2307/3894015.

Foley, J.A., DeFries, R., Asner, G.P., Barford, C., Bonan, G., Carpenter, S.R., Chapin, F.S., Coe, M.T., Daily, G.C., Gibbs, H.K., Helkowski, J.H., Holloway, T., Howard, E.A., Kucharik, C.J., Monfreda, C., Patz, J.A., Prentice, I.C., Ramankutty, N. and Snyder, P.K. (2005) Global consequences of land use. *Science*, **309**, 570-574.

Foster, D.R. (1992) Land-use history (1730-1990) and vegetation dynamics in Central New-England, USA. *J Ecol*, **80**, 753-772.

Foster, D., Swanson, F., Aber, J., Burke, I., Brokaw, N., Tilman, D., Knapp, A. (2003) The importance of land-use legacies to ecology and conservation. *Bioscience*, **53**: 77-88.

Giourga, H., Margaris, N.S., Vokou, D. (1998) Effects of grazing pressure on succession process and productivity of old fields on Mediterranean Islands. *Environ Manage*, **22**, 589-596.

GSYE (1934) Georgiki kai Ktinotrofiki Apografi tis Ellados 1929 (Agricultural and Livestock Census 1929). Hellenic Republic, Athens.

Gutman, M., Holzer, Z., Baram, H., Noy-Meir, I. and Seligman, N.G. (1999) Heavy stocking of beef cattle and early season deferment of grazing on Mediterranean-type grassland. *J Range Manage*, **52**, 590-599.

Hermy, M. and Verheyen, K. (2007) Legacies of the past in the present-day forest biodiversity: a review of past land-use effects on forest plant species composition and diversity. *Ecol Res*, **22**, 361-371.

Hill, J., Stellmes, M., Udelhoven, T., Röder, A. and Sommer, S. (2008) Mediterranean desertification and land degradation: mapping related land use change syndromes based on satellite observations. *Global Planet Change*, **64**, 146-157.

Hostert, P., Röder, A., Hill, J., Udelhoven, T. and Tsiourlis, G. (2003) Retrospective studies of grazing-induced land degradation: a case study in Central Crete, Greece. *I J Remote Sens*, **24**, 4019-4034.

Iosifides, T. and Politidis, T. (2005) Socio-economic dynamics, local development and desertification in Western Lesvos, Greece. *Local Environ*, **10**, 487-499.

Kent, M. and Coker, P. (2000) *Vegetation Description and Analysis: A Practical Approach*. Wiley, New York.

Köchy, M., Mathaj, M., Jeltsch, F. and Malkinson, D. (2008) Resilience of stocking capacity to changing climate in arid to Mediterranean landscapes. *Reg Environ Change*, **8**, 73-87.

Körner, C., Sarris, D. and Christodoulaiks, D. (2005) Long-term increase in climatic dryness in the East-Mediterranean as evidenced for the island of Samos. *Reg Environ Change*, **5**, 27-36.

Lookingbill, T.R. and Zavala, M.A. (2000) Spatial pattern of *Quercus ilex* and *Quercus pubescens* recruitment in *Pinus halepensis* dominated woodlands. *J Veg Sci*, **11**, 607-612.

Marks, P.L. and Gardescu, S. (2001) *Inferring forest stand history from observational field evidence*. In: Egan, D. and Howell, E.A. (eds.) *The Historical Ecology Handbook*. Island Press, Washington D.C., pp 177-198.

Moreno, G. and Pulido, F.J. (2008) *The function, management and persistence of dehesas*. In: Rigueiro, A., Mosquera, M.R. and McAdam, J. (eds.) *Agroforestry Systems in Europe Current Status and Future Prospects*. Springer, Heidelberg, Berlin, New York, pp 127-160.

Naveh, Z. (1982) Mediterranean landscape evolution and degradation as multivariate biofunctions - Theoretical and practical implications. *Landscape Plan*, **9**, 125-146.

Oliver, C.D. and Larson, B.C. (1996) *Forest Stand Dynamics*. Wiley, New York, NY.

Palahi, M., Birot, Y., Bravo, F. and Gorriz, E. (2009) Modelling, Valuing and Managing Mediterranean Forest Ecosystems for Non-Timber Goods and Services. *EFI Proceedings*, **57**, European Forest Institute, Joensuu.

Pantera, A., Papadopoulos, A.M., Fotiadis, G. and Papanastasis, V.P. (2008) Distribution and phytogeographical analysis of *Quercus ithaburensis* ssp. *macrolepis* in Greece. *Ecol Mediterr*, **34**, 73-82.

Papanastasis, V.P. (2007) *Land abandonment and old field dynamics in Greece*. In: Cramer, V.A. and Hobbs, R.J. (eds.) *Old Fields: Dynamics and Restoration of Abandoned Farmland*. Island Press, Washington DC, pp 225-246.

Papanastasis, V.P. (2009) Restoration of degraded grazing lands through grazing management: Can it work? *Restor Ecol*, **17**, 441-445.

Pausas, J.G., Ribeiro, E., Dias, S.G., Pons, J. and Beseler, C. (2006) Regeneration of a marginal *Quercus suber* forest in the Eastern Iberian Peninsula. *J Veg Sci*, **17**, 729-738.

Pinto-Correia, T. and Vos, W. (2001) *Multifunctionality in Mediterranean landscapes - past and future*. In: Jongman, R.H.G. (ed.) *The New Dimensions of the European Landscape*. Springer, Dordrecht, pp 135-164.

Plieninger, T. (2007) Compatibility of livestock grazing with stand regeneration in Mediterranean holm oak parklands. *J Nat Conserv*, **15**, 1-9.

Pulido, F.J., Díaz, M. and Hidalgo de Trucios, S. (2001) Size-structure and regeneration of Spanish holm oak *Quercus ilex* forests and dehesas: effects of agroforestry use on their long-term sustainability. *Forest Ecol Manag*, **146**, 1-13.

Ramírez, J.A. and Díaz, M. (2008) The role of temporal shrub encroachment for the maintenance of Spanish holm oak *Quercus ilex* dehesas. *Forest Ecol Manag*, **255**, 1976-1983.

Röder, A., Kuemmerle, T., Hill, J., Papanastasis, V.P. and Tsiourlis, G.M. (2007) Adaptation of a grazing gradient concept to heterogeneous Mediterranean rangelands using cost surface modelling. *Ecol Model*, **204**, 387-398.

Röder, A., Udelhoven, T., Hill, J., del Barrio, G. and Tsiourlis, G. (2008) Trend analysis of Landsat-TM and -ETM+ imagery to monitor grazing impact in a rangeland ecosystem in Northern Greece. *Remote Sens Environ*, **112**, 2863-2875.

Scarascia-Mugnozza, G., Oswald, H., Piussi, P. and Radoglou, K. (2000) Forests of the Mediterranean region: gaps in knowledge and research needs. *Forest Ecol Manag*, **132**, 97-109.

The full version of this paper has been published as:

Plieninger, T., Schaich, H. and Kizos, T. (2011) Land-use legacies in the forest structure of silvopastoral oak woodlands in the Eastern Mediterranean. *Regional Environmental Change*. The original publication is available at http://www.springerlink.com/content/t415871550t77k86/ .

Creation of open woodlands through pasture: Genesis, relevance as biotopes, value in the landscape and in nature conservation in Southwest-Germany

Mattias Rupp
Albert-Ludwigs-University Freiburg

Introduction

Wood pastures (WP) are forbidden in Germany, but in certain places they can still be found by insiders. In the project *"Open woodlands through pasture"*, WPs have been searched for and examined to find out why this old land-use activity is kept alive and what effects it has on biodiversity. The spatial focus of the study is the federal state Baden-Wuerttemberg in South-western Germany.

The research was divided into three tasks: 1) Spatial research and classification, 2) interviews with stakeholders and 3) floristic and structural analysis to describe and compare the ecological situation of WPs and adjacent forests. The project is still ongoing (08/2008-09/2011) but this report presents the current state of play. Although the analyses are not yet finished, general conclusions can be drawn and preliminary results will be presented. A link to the final report will be posted in late 2011 on the homepage of the Institute for Landscape Management.

It has been possible to demonstrate that historical and modern wood pastures have little in common with each other. Nowadays WPs serve mainly as a functional element to support the farm business, the well-being of livestock and, when applied within the framework of a management concept, to increase biodiversity.

As described below, WP can trigger reserved or even antagonistic reactions against livestock owners. This form of agriculture can lead to misunderstandings and unnecessary clashes with the law. In light of these issues, it was agred that anonymity would be maintained and study locations will only be referred to at the regional scale.

Theoretical background

Spatial focus

The area of interest is the federal state of Baden-Wuerttemberg (Ba.-Wue.) in South-western Germany, as shown in figure 4. This has been determined in part by the project's financing through the *Stiftung Naturschutzfonds Ba.-Wue.* (Foundation for nature conservation). Furthermore, this state has a vivid agricultural history, including WP and as such it is expected that remnants of open woodlands remain there. The state's topography varies from lowlands with a Mediterranean-like climate to low mountain ranges with continental influences. This variety leads to five greater macrochores with 13 specific macrochores all together (www.lubw.baden-wuerttemberg.de).

Historical context of wood pasture

In Middle Europe, various factors led to the creation of open woodlands: shallow and dry or wet soils, physical disturbances (avalanches, fire), advanced age of climax-vegetation and agricultural influences. In Germany, WPs were commonly occurring biotopes, with regional specificities, over recent centuries (see Figure 1). However, due to the multifunctional uses of forests and intensified land-use, mainly during the Industrial Revolution, forests have been continuously over-cultivated and large areas went into decline, sometimes even to the point of devastation. Consequently, there was a need for sustainable forest management and in 1833 the "*Badische Forstgesetz*" (Forestry Law of Baden) implemented the concept of sustainability and strictly separated pastures and woodlands. Since then, keeping livestock in forests is forbidden and can be prosecuted (Liss, 1988; Sproßmann, 2009; Vera, 2000).

Emerging agricultural and technical inventions accelerated the division of forestry and agriculture. Open land could now also be used for keeping animals and to obtain fodder for winter. Hence, as livestock no longer needed to be herded in woodland, WP became a marginalised agricultural system, existing only in remote areas. Correspondingly, multifunctional forest use also changed. Coal emerged as a competitor to wood as an energy source, the production of glass and mining

Figure 1. Historical wood pasture in Germany with different influences on vegetation and landscape:
deceleration of natural regeneration, leaf and litter harvest, active herding.
Source: http://www.gymnasium-meschede.de, modified.

products could be outsourced and this downsized or even ended the local importance of these economies in South-western Germany (http://www.badische-seiten.de). These changes allowed the landowners to focus on timber forestry and hunting. The timber forests became the dominant type of forest. To keep the hunting business running for the upper-class and aristocrats, great efforts were undertaken to drive the rural population and their economic activities out of the forests (www.adelegg.de). These circumstances lead to the loss of semi-open biotopes with mosaic-like vegetation patterns.

Following the Second World War, many WP remnants were abandoned and succession took over or the biotopes were reforested as monocultures. A loss of biodiversity can be assumed based on the loss of these biotopes (Liss, 1988; Sproßmann, 2009; Vera, 2000).

Recent situation

Only a few WPs "survived" or were more recently established in Ba.-Wue. Relicts of WPs can be found on commons, remote areas of low mountain ranges and on unproductive soils or in some nature conservation projects. The purpose of wood pasture has changed totally from essentially feeding farm animals to keeping animals in a species-appropriate environment and supporting local biodiversity. Nowadays farmers, foresters and conservationists interact and create projects with the aims of preserving local breeds and supporting species and structural diversity.

Traditional livestock husbandry is applied using a modern approach. Common features such as careful handling on the pastures, a planned management and long periods of development are taken into consideration (see section 4).

Those who run WPs lament the significant lack of ecological information resulting from the fact that the wood pastures tradition was stopped 178 years ago. They note that in order to create open woodlands, *"the wheel needs to be reinvented"*.

Research questions and data acquisition

Spatial research

As the keeping of livestock in woodlands is strictly regulated in Germany, very few WPs are known or talked about and literature is virtually non-existent. To find WPs, telephone-research was conducted using the snowball principle. Nature conservationists and foresters in marginal areas were the most knowledgeable people to ask. However, although they may have known about WP, they were not always immediately willing to talk about it. Given concerns about misunderstanding and a possible clash with laws, they wanted to get to know the researcher personally before sharing information. A very important aspect of this research was therefore building confidence and visiting interviewees at their place of work. Once that had been agreed upon, the farmers shared further information or gave references to hidden WPs. Given that old breeds of farm animals are used in extensive agriculture, contacting breeder-clubs was an additional strategy for accessing information. Based on the proceeding work, the researcher's name was already familiar to prospective interview partners and the confidence built in the earlier phase of research eased communication. When the researcher rang the same people a second time and asked the same questions, also mentioning who he had met in the meantime, they were willing to provide information about more WPs.

Guided interviews

To obtain more detailed information from the practitioner's perspective, guided interviews were conducted. The stakeholders interviewed were farmers and their partners in administrations. The questions were structured according to the following guiding themes:

- Biotope tradition and land-use history.
- Land-use management.
- Vegetation and ecological effects.
- WPs in supra-regional context.
- Exchange of information and networking.
- Farms and their future.
- Possible conflicts and constructive criticism.

The interviews with practitioners took place indoors and on-site, as some farmers wanted to show the important features of their work "*in situ*". Sometimes the interviews were spread over two or even three meetings. In some cases detailed information was only disclosed after a certain period of confidence building at the second meeting as some practitioners feared accusations and fines. The contents were written down, as interviewees had requested that they not be recorded.

All administrators could be interviewed in their offices and the interview followed the pre-arranged chronology. Time for confidence building was rarely necessary due to the nature of their work, which usually included giving interviews. They did not fear misunderstanding to the same degree as the farmers did.

Plant-ecological fieldwork

The guiding question for this research was whether wood pasture has effects on the diversity of local plant species and the variety of spatial structures. Ecological side-effects were also of interest. During the growing seasons of 2009 and 2010, six WPs were examined (see Table 1). The sites were selected on the basis of the following features:

- Forest character with trees older than fifty years.
- Pasture-tradition of at least eight years to allow for the identification of floristic responses.
- Sites designated as pasture for at least the next ten years.
- Size of wood pasture greater than one hectare.

- Landscape work with machines only at the outset of projects and later just for safety reasons.

In some cases it was necessary to consider pre-existing pollution and to exclude some parts of the site (see Section 4. Structural Analysis).

Frequency method

Environmental conditions change abruptly at the fence between forest and WP. The frequency analysis as a punctual site-specific method was chosen to compare the floristic diversity between the two biotopes (Tremp, 2005). The following land-use classification characterised the present strata.

Table 1. Sites with pasture woodland and their features

Site Number and Location	Substrate	Altitude [amsl]	Livestock	Specific features	Period of pasture
1) Southern Black Forest	Gneiss	1,300	Cattle	1,000 years of pasture tradition, fens	1,000 years
2) Middle Black Forest	Gneiss, granite	485	Cattle	Traditional pasture hill, many woody species	at least 300 years
3) Northern Upper Rhine valley – sand dunes	Quartenary sediments, mainly sands	135	Goats, Sheep	Recently initiated project in pine forest on quaternary sand dunes, former military training ground.	8 years
4) Northern Upper Rhine valley – lower terrace	Quartenary sediments, mainly fine gravel	130	Goats, Sheep	Historical pasture wood, 300 year old beeches and oaks, former military training ground.	at least 250 years with breaks due to military activities
5) Middle Swabian Alb (Mittlere Kuppenalb)	Jura (Malm)	750	Cattle	Historical sheep pasture, rich seed bank.	9 years
6) Eastern Lohne-Valley (Swabian Alb)	Jura (Malm)	560	Goats, Sheep	Historical sheep trailing, vital *Juniperus*-forest.	20 years

These are:

- Dense forest (dF): Abandoned, ongoing forestry or protected forests.
- Light pasture woodland (WP).
- Formerly pasture woodland (fWP).

On each site and in each stratum criteria of homogeneity for landscape-, soil- and vegetation-structures were defined. In each stratum six plots were laid out at random. A plot covers one square metre divided into twenty-five squares with an edge length of twenty centimetres. For each square a list of species was compiled, they cover *spermatophyta* (seed plants), *pteridophyta* (ferns), *bryophyta* (mosses), *lycopsida* (clubmosses) and *lichenes* (lichens).

Structural method

Effects of livestock behaviour are evident in micro-topography, soil and vegetation composition, as well as the morphology of bigger plant individuals. In each stratum structures were registered vertically and horizontally by using a modified version of the step-point method (Evans and Love, 1957; Strauss and Neal, 1983). Each plot measured 2,500 m^2 with an edge length of fifty metres. Taking into account the size of the biotope, between one and three plots could be laid within it. This ensured that specific structural elements were recorded on 100 steps along two transects crossing each plot (one step equates to one metre). The structures were divided into the following groups:

Figure 2. Frequency method. Twenty-five species lists/m^2 were compiled in pasture woodland and in forests. Photograph: Oelke 2010.

Figure 3. Structural method. Four vegetation layers and 100 steps were compiled in pasture woodland and in forests. Photograph: Rupp 2010.

- **Direct effects**: Peeling, cropping on woody species, rubbing on soil and trees, defecation, losing fur in prickle plants, trampling.

- **Indirect effects**: Plant species with mechanical and chemical defence strategies, fructiferous species, habitual changes and decaying of woody species, reaction of fauna: breeding borrows in old/dead trees, presence of burrowing animals and anthills.

- **Anthropogenic effects**: tracks and paths, deposits, cultural remnants (boundary stones, buildings, fences, …).

Analysis and results

Spatial distribution and features

Fifty-one wood pastures were found in Baden-Wuerttemberg (see Figure 4). Based on the observations of the interview partners it is estimated that about the same number of WPs exist in marginalised regions. The presently known WPs display common features (combinations possible):

- All sites are situated in agriculturally and silviculturally unfavourable areas:

  - Higher altitudes of low mountain ranges (500 to 1,300 masl).
  - Steep slopes (inclines up to 35° and more).
  - Dry/sandy/fast drying or wet/boggy soils.
  - Quarries, stone pits, river banks.

- Traditional wood pasture areas, where no other land uses occur.

- Nature reserves.

- As yet no rivalry with other land uses.

WPs tend to cluster either in regions with a wood pasture tradition or in landscape conservation projects. Idealistic stakeholders initiate projects in their area of influence and attract further project partners.

Recently initiated pasture projects are conducted for the purposes of nature conservation, if possible combining plant species' protection and using endangered old breeds. There are two categories: 1) Reactivation of former WPs and 2) Conversion of dense forests into WPs to support local biodiversity and landscape elements with recreational character.

The size of the WPs is between 1.0 and 7.5 hectares. They are connected with grassland to allow the animals to roam. None of the WPs shows degradation as the possible stocking capacity is intentionally not attained. Only two types of land-uses exist side by side, pasture and timber extraction for household requirements.

Guided interviews

The following section presents an outline of statements extracted from twelve interviews with practitioners and six interviews with administrators. As these stakeholder groups interact, their statements will be blended into the section.

Biotope tradition and land use history

It is a common opinion amongst the stakeholders that modern WP should be orientated towards local conditions and be implemented as part of an ongoing land use management history. To avoid making WPs foreign bodies in the landscape, stakeholders use local breeds where possible and produce traditional products.

Land use management

"*Pure*" WP in an historical sense can no longer be conducted as the forest sites are too small to feed the livestock and the aims as such became totally different (see section 2). Consequently, WP always includes grassland and planned management is applied. Table 2 shows the main usage of modern WPs, the most important effects are underlined.

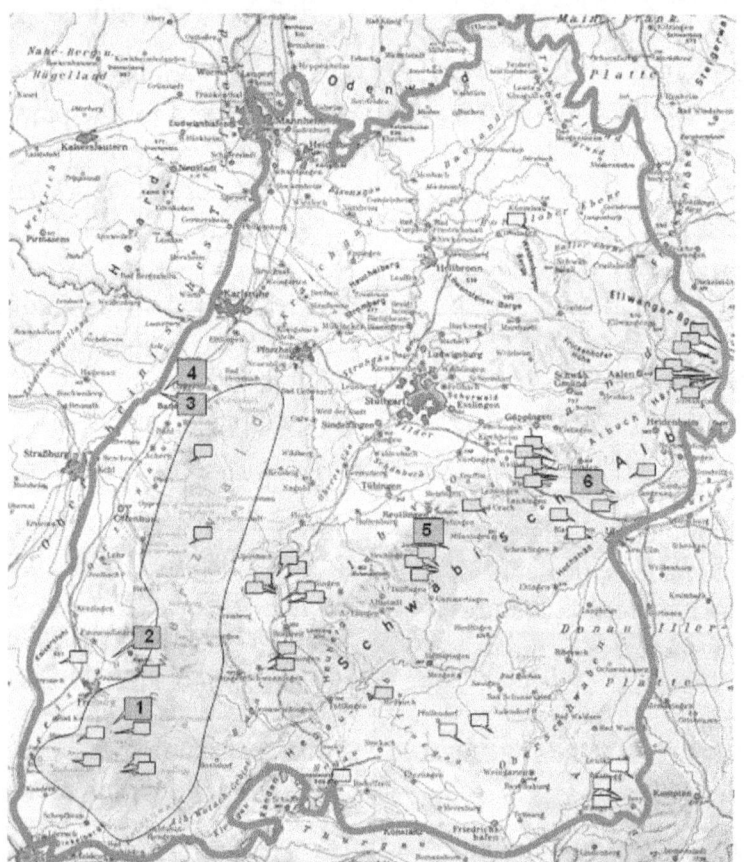

Legend			
	Site known, visited (10)		Site examined closely (6)
	Site visited, information gathered (35)		Region with traditional wood pastures. Many further sites expected

Figure 4. Schematic map of Germany, Baden-Wuerttemberg is highlighted in red. Source: http://www.gmk-net.de. Topographical map of Baden-Wuerttemberg with wood pastures found in the project. Source: www.dierke.de, modified.

The expenditure of human labour to keep a WP running is high. The requirements for daily controls and keeping the herd accustomed to the farmer and working in steep topography can be very demanding. In the case of accident, it can be difficult to reach or provide help in remote or mountainous areas. Furthermore, keeping wild animals separated from domesticated ones occasionally requires expensive measures.

Some projects use disturbance from farming livestock to create biotopes with increased structural diversity, which in turn can increase biodiversity (see section *structural analysis*). The pasture management is adapted to local desires and location conditions, which vary enormously between the sites. The difficulties are to accept slow progress due to natural processes and to secure long-time financing.

Vegetation and ecological effects

If woods are seen as shelters, hardly any effort goes into the development of biodiversity. When protection goals exist there are efforts to build up mosaic-like biotopes. The farmer`s primary motivation is the desire to create a site - rich in flowers and fructiferous shrubs - that reminds him of images from his adolescence. Management strategies are more or less appraised auto-didactically and are developed by learning about disturbance ecology and biodiversity in the farmers' leisure time. Administrators usually

Table 2. Structures, usage and effects of wood pastures.

Structures	Usage	Effects/benefits
Treestands, thickets	Shelter from heavy rain, hail, heat	No buildings needed, better air circulation than in stables, therefore less illnesses
	Retreating space during births and periods of social stress	Healthy calves and fawns, stress relief in the herd
	Free roaming between biotope structures	Training and building-up of solid social herd structures, better long-term handling, reduction of on-site accidents
Coniferous trees	Essential oils	Stress relief in the herd: reducing the burden of biting insects
Species rich in secondary phyto-chemicals	Bark and leaves as dietary supplement	Healthy animals, enormous reduction of endoparasites and illnesses
		High quality meat
Topography, vegetation structure	Training	Good muscle development, high quality meat
		Good muscle development → Uncomplicated births

want to enhance biodiversity by reactivating the seed bank where it exists. Another strategy is to lighten the canopy and to connect the wood to its surroundings. The side-effects are biotope structures that attract many species which are weak competitors. Observed changes are the increased germination of blossom bearing herbs, the presence of more insect species and consequently birds as well as associated fructiferous shrubs.

WPs in supra-regional context

WPs are not usually connected to each other and appear like islands in the agricultural or silvicultural landscape. If WPs develop successfully, only very few sites can be enlarged due to a lack of manpower, rights of ownership and the legal situation. That is why open WPs do not yet play an important role in nature protection, neither at the regional nor at the supra-regional scale. The stakeholders are aware of the importance of this land-use for biodiversity but as there is very limited knowledge about such biotopes, they cannot assess the value of their activities in comparison to other conservation projects.

Exchange of information and networking

As the judicial situation is restrictive, the current pastures are rarely made known. Usually the stakeholders are not connected to each other which means that an awareness of their work is reserved to a certain circle of insiders. Should the legal framework become more supportive they would seek a broader network of contacts and partners. The stakeholders complain that there is a lack of information and demand scientific support to obtain information about how to improve modern WPs to support biodiversity.

Farms and their future

Wood pasture does not provide the primary financial input into farm business. It does support the business as outlined above (see Table 2), however, these benefits only pay off over the long-term. Over these longer periods, broader political decisions, market conditions and other farm products determine the farm's future. In South-western Germany, remote areas face rural depopulation and farms are successively given up. It is very difficult to find successors. If local authorities integrate ecological pasture projects into a financially supported network of projects, farmers may be incentivised to continue the business. Furthermore, if farms specialised in funded projects for landscape conservation through pasture, the farms will exist as long our society is willing to pay for these ecological services

Possible conflicts and constructive criticism

The conflicts identified are shown in Table 3. Interview partners alluded not only to the conflicts themselves but also gave constructive ideas and comments about how to solve them.

Table 3. Conflicts, stakeholders, constructive criticism and proposals for solutions.

Stakeholders	Conflicts	Constructive criticism/proposals for solutions
Hunters	Simultaneous use of the site, hunting impossible	Effective time management
Hunters	Fences keep out game and complicate forestry	Modern fence systems allow wild animals and forestry vehicles to pass. Fence taken down following pasture period
Hunters	Livestock scares off game	Statement cannot be verified by farmers and administrators, scientific research should be conducted. Effective time management can help
Conservationists	Endangerment of protected species, e. g. orchids	Pasture management needs to be developed. A certain number of individuals will be destroyed, others will be gained. In the long run pasture creates supportive conditions
Conservationists	Change of present state	Change is inherent in any system. The conservation system should include processes, not only states
Foresters	Damage of trees (mechanically, through microorganisms)	Trees get damaged, but in WPs lucrative forestry will not be built up anyway. Damaged trees will provide habitat structures and support biodiversity. WPs could become part of forestry's commitment to sustain biodiversity at sites where reasonable
Foresters	Illnesses transferred between game and livestock	This can happen. Veterinary laws have to be considered, farmers should build necessary installations to avoid contact during risky times. If necessary, pasture should be stopped
Foresters	Restricted mobility due to fences, dogs to be kept on leash	In nature reserves and on agricultural production sites people are asked to stay on tracks and to keep dogs on a leash. That is common law and not specifically applied on WPs. The feeling of being restricted is subjective. One idea to address this issue is to offer information and guided trips over the site following the pasture period
Passersby, residents	Old dumping grounds found when animals scratch the ground	Local problem to be dealt with by local authorities
Passersby, residents	Landscape change considered as ugly	The initial state is accompanied by dramatic changes: motor-mechanical interventions and pasture. Vegetation needs time to build up suitable societies. Effective communication in advance and on the site can help understanding the changes
Livestock owners	Difficult legal situation, complicated applications for landscape conservation funding	Adapting forestry laws to local/regional circumstances would be beneficial. Alternatively, exceptional rules for biodiversity projects could be made in regions where forestry and extensive pasture are not competitors. Close cooperation between practitioners and administrators is helpful. Conservation activities should be supported over long time spans and directly managed by local administrators
Livestock owners	Sabotage, theft of livestock	In many cases fences and solar panels get destroyed by vandals. Now and then animals get tormented or stolen (sometimes remnants found at barbeque places), the more remote a site is, the more likely this may occur. There are no ideas how to stop these problems. Financial compensation after a case can be considered
Livestock owners	Litter thrown into the fields	As this problem is caused by a lack of awareness of the society, there is hardly any available solution besides legal restrictions. Only fencing off parts of the pasture that are close to parking grounds or meeting points can help the farmer
Livestock owners	Unleashed dogs and dog excrements	Dogs can harm the herd and kill animals. Prosecution and financial compensation needs to occur. High voltage fences with low wires can keep dogs away. Now and then cows defend the herd and can severely harm the dog

Plant-ecological fieldwork

Frequency analysis

Where surface water was present (streams, watering places) vegetation was nearly gone and the soil churned due to trampling. Such sites have not been covered by the frequency analysis. The stakeholders have followed the emerging succession with interest and expected benefits for amphibians as soon as the livestock moved on, but they also ensured that these sites maintained their small size.

The floristic comparison between grazed and non-grazed forests is shown in Table 4. The stratum with maximal species number is highlighted in grey. The analysis is conducted by comparing the strata`s species lists, first statistically and also by individual features. The floristic similarities are described by the Sørensen-coefficient. The frequency-analysis is in progress and will be published in late 2011.

In five sites the WPs contain the most species, up to more than double the number found in non-pasture

Table 4. Floristic comparison between wood pastures and adjacent forests

Site-No.	Stratum	Species number	Difference to max [number/percentage]		Sørensen-coefficient	
1	dF	25	34	57.63 %	(dF – WP)	S = 0.57
	WP	32	27	45.76 %	(WP – fWP)	S = 0.38
	fWP	59			(dF – fWP)	S = 0.38
2	dF	35	43	33.96 %	(dF – WP)	S = 0.32
	WP	78				
3	dF	53			(dF – WP)	S = 0.64
	WP	47	5	9.43 %		
4	dF	33	8	19.51 %	(dF – WP)	S = 0.46
	WP	41				
5	dF	39	52	57.14 %	(dF – WP)	S = 0.35
	WP	91				
6	dF	52	35	40.23 %	(dF – WP(J))	S = 0.56
	WP(J)	80	7	8.05 %	(dF – WP(P))	S = 0.45
	WP(P)	87			(WP(P) – WP(J))	S = 0.64

Legend
dF = dense forest, no grazing
WP = pasture wood, grazing
fWP = formerly pasture wood, no grazing
S = Sørensen-coefficient with 0 = max. difference, 1 = max. similarity
J = *Juniperus communis* wood, grazed
P = *Pinus sylvestris* wood, grazed

forests. The reasons can be found in better light-levels reaching the herb layer, reactivation of seed-banks and the input of seeds by farm animals and birds. Site number three, where the dense wood contains more species, is an exceptional case. The pastures' herb layers are densely covered with grasses such as *Agrostis capillaris*, *Brachipodium pinnatum*, *Deschampsia flexuosa* and brambles (*Rubus fruticosus* agg.). These species form a dense mat of roots and leaves and they dominate other species. Where goats manage to break this mat, sandy soil is exposed and only a few specialised plants, such as *Erophila verna*, can develop, on this meagre immature soil. Adjacent woods with mature soil support more species.

Site 1: The dF and the WP still show many similarities (S = 0.57), which might be caused by several decades of succession on the site with low grazing pressure. The WP differs obviously from the fWP, as does the dF (S = 0.38/0.38). The fWP unites three kinds of species: those which cope with conditions typical of dense forests; species that need light and cope with mechanical impacts; and species that cannot cope with disturbance. Some years after the grazing was stopped, this stratum is the most species-rich.

Site 2 and 5: dF and WP differ noticeably (S = 0.32/0.35). More light input to the ground activated the seed-bank and woodland species overlap with grassland species. Both sites show an outstanding amount of woody species, e.g. site two contains thirty-four woody species on two hectares!

Site 3 and 4: In site three, both strata still show many similarities as the canopies are fairly dense. The grazing pressure is too weak to change the forest character of the herb layer. It is intended that the pasture will continue for some years with more animals. Site four was grown over by *Robinia pseudoacacia* for some years. Pasture is beginning to push *Robinia* back and to change the herb layer slowly.

Site 6: Grazed and non-grazed areas differ (S = 0.56/0.45). Although a species-rich seed bank is estimated given the land use history, the floristic difference is not as strong as expected. *Bromus erectus* and *Brachypodium pinnatum* cover all strata densely and suppress other species. To widen the floristic spectrum in the pastures, high grazing pressure and strong mechanical influences on the root layer should be undertaken over a number of years.

In summary, mechanical opening of the canopy and associated pasture can change biodiversity. Usually the stakeholders act too gently as strong disturbance can be applied in the first years to allow weakly-competitive species to move in. Then the grazing pressure can be reduced gradually.

Structural analysis

The statistical data analysis is currently in progress; the results will be published in late 2011 (see Section 1). Initial results and peculiarities will be described here.

Direct effects from livestock:

Goats browse nearly every woody species, some species are particularly popular and become totally gnawed, e.g. *Euonymus europaeus* and *Fraxinus excelsior*. Less popular are *Acer* species. Cattle mainly eat young and sprouting woody species but do not browse as efficiently as goats. Cattle influence older trees by rubbing and leaning on them, they can even lighten up thickets by forcing themselves through. They do this predominantly in stands of coniferous trees to get the essential oils on their fur to protect themselves against biting insects. Sheep browse mainly sprouting woody species and gnaw young twigs but leave older parts. Due to their natural behaviour, sheep tend to prefer open land. If it is intended that they have an impact on the forest it is necessary to paddock them there.

The pasture-size offered determines the way the animals take on the species and how intensely they browse. If a lot of space is provided, the animals roam the area several times a day and browse here and there such that an overall consumption of individual trees or shrubs can seldomly be detected. When the animals are accustomed to being herded mainly on grassland, in the first year they do not use the given spectrum of fodder plants in a WP. Over the years, their behaviour changes and they eat plants which at the beginning were untouched. It was observed that over time cows start browsing *Prunus spinosa* shrubs in a similar manner to goats and even grazed stands of thistles.

It is estimated that a lack of minerals makes goats gnaw bark of massive *Pinus sylvestris* which have diameters of up to more than fifty centimetres, but in these cases only a small number of individuals are totally consumed. *Juniperus* can also be used. In spring, young leaves of *Betula* and *Frangula alnus* are preferred, mainly as a means against endoparasites.

The animals create paths and stick to them over the years. Consequently the pasture becomes rich in patterns of differing usage intensity. Goats and cattle create scrubbing spots on the soil where they cover themselves in dust. During the field studies droppings of variously advanced decomposition of wild animals (e.g. foxes) could be found there which indicated regular use of these spots to warm up or even to sleep.

Over the years regular defaecation in specific areas causes the growth of nitrophilous plants, especially on WPs with cattle. These plants grow densely and screen smaller animals from view. They also offer energy-rich fodder for both domesticated and wild animals. Mainly sheep but also cattle can lose fur on prickly plants like *Genista* and *Rubus* species. Scabby bark can also tear off hair. The wisps offer building material for nesting birds.

Indirect effects:

On wood pastures old trees are left to die. All stages of habitual changes and states of decomposition can be found on one individual, mainly from pioneer species as *Betula* and *Salix*. The tree

Figure 5. Cow hiding from biting insects; continuous use of shrubs starts to lighten them up. Photograph: Rupp 2010.

Figure 6. Torn out sheep's wool. Hair offers nest-building material. Photograph: Frankenhauser 2010.

offers a realm for xylobiontic organisms, leaking sap is used by many insects.

The mosaic-like pattern, decaying trees and increased invertebrate fauna attracts birds. They work as vectors and bring seed-banks of fructiferous woody species. Species like *Lonicera xylosteum*, *Sambucus nigra*, *Rosa* species or *Ilex aquifolium* can accumulate along paths, around exposed and decaying trees where droppings are preferentially left.

An increased presence of burrowing animals and anthills can be detected. We estimate, that the combination of more light and therefore warmth, nutrients from droppings, enhanced edaphic factors and a wider spectrum of plant species support the accumulation of geobionta. When dead wood is left lying it can become a nurse log and offer shelter for invertebrates. For instance, antlions (*Myrmeleontidae*) were found on two pastures.

The mosaic-like pattern is also built from plant species with mechanical and chemical defence strategies. *Prunus* and *Crataegus* species form thickets which can also contain *Ilex aquifolium*, *Rosa* and *Rubus* species. Plants with chemical defence strategies gather in more open sections and along paths. On site 1, the toxic *Gentiana lutea* increased its population enormously in the grazed area, in the other pastures for example *Thymus* species and *Oreganum vulgare* emerged at more dry spots.

Anthropogenic effects:

To initiate the lightly wooded character, trees are cut, often left or piled up and tracks are made. Around the gates cars compact soil, fodder is provided and the soil turns eutrophic. The animals can bring to light contaminated areas, deposits and cultural remains, such as overgrown boundary stones, old dumping grounds and military items, e.g. metal bars and training grenades (see Figure 7, Figure 8). Old barbed wire was found in all the pastures.

Figure 7. Historical boundary stone (1678) exposed due to goats creating a dust-bath. Photograph: Frankenhauser 2009.

Figure 8. Collapsing bunker and discarded metal. Photograph: Rupp 2010.

Where these items could not be removed and where they posed dangers they were fenced out.

Conclusions

In a three-year project, fifty-one wood pastures have been found in Baden-Wuerttemberg. The overview demonstrates that economically unattractive areas and nature reserves are the most suitable sites to establish this type of extensive agriculture. Wet soils and areas with operating forestry seem inappropriate and sites with endangered species require special handling. Wood pastures are managed using modern approaches and are not comparable to historically-known pasture systems. They offer structural elements that benefit the animals and therefore the farm business.

Amongst the sites, six have been examined closely. The field studies showed that they can gradually increase local biodiversity. Complications arise from the existing legal framework and lack of knowledge extending from the fact that wood pasture has been forbidden in the region for 178 years. Stakeholders ask for scientific support and legal adaptation. They also desire networking through different media and mentoring from a neutral actor e. g a university. Other problems occur in the confrontation between different stakeholder groups. However, effective communication and bottom-up strategies can address most of these in advance. WPs are not keeping farms running but they do enrich businesses. If the wish to maintain and develop wood pastures arises, the economic survival of farms must be guaranteed through broader political decisions and a favourable market situation for agricultural goods in general. As properly managed WP can increase biodiversity, it could be integrated within sustainability and biodiversity concepts in forestry, agriculture and landscape management.

References

Bünzel-Drüke, M. *et.al* (2008) *"Wilde Weiden"- Praxisleitfaden für Ganzjahresbeweidung in Naturschutz und Landschaftsentwicklung.* Bonn.

Conradi, M. and Plachter, H. (2001) *Analyse ökologischer Prozesse in Weidelandschaften und ihre naturschutzfachliche Beurteilung mit Hilfe skalendifferenzierter Strukturanalysen*: 132-146. In: Gerken, B. and Görner, M. (Eds.) Neue Modelle zu Maßnahmen der Landschaftsentwicklung mit großen Pflanzenfressern. Praktische Erfahrungen bei der Umsetzung. *Natur- und Kulturlandschaft*, **4**, Höxter, Jena.

Evans, R.A. and Love, M. (1957) The Step-Point Method of sampling. A practical Tool in Range Research. *Journal of Range Management*, **10**, 208-212.

Grossmann, H. (1927) *Die Waldweide in der Schweiz.* Zürich.

Kapfer, A. (1995) Der Einfluss der Beweidung auf die Vegetation aus der Sicht des Naturschutzes. In: Wieder beweiden? Möglichkeiten und Grenzen der Beweidung als Maßnahme des Naturschutzes und der Landschaftspflege. *Beiträge der Akademie für Natur- und Umweltschutz Baden-Württemberg*, **Band 18**, 27–36.

Liss, B.-M. (1988) *Versuche zur Waldweide- der Einfluss von Weidevieh und Wild auf Verjüngung, Bodenvegetation und Boden im Bergmischwald der ostbayerischen Alpen.* München.

Michels C. and Spencer J. (2003) Waldweide im New Forest. *LÖBF-Mittleilungen*, **04/03**, 53–58.

Sonnenburg et al. (2003) *Hutewaldprojekt Solling. Ein Baustein für eine Ära des Naturschutzes*. Höxter.

Sproßmann, H. (2009) Extensive Waldweide in Thüringen-Waldfrevel oder ein innovatives Landnutzungsmodell? *Forst und Holz*, **64(2)**, 32-37.

Strauss, D. and Neal, D. L. (1983) Biases in the Step-Point Method on Bunchgrass Ranges. *Journal of Range Management*, **36(5),** 623-626.

Tremp, H. (2005) *Aufnahme und Analyse vegetationsökologischer Daten. 1.* Auflage, Stuttgart.

Vera, F.W.M. (2000) *Grazing ecology and forest history*. CABI Publishing, Wallingford.

URLs (used in June 2011)

http://www.adelegg.de/default.asp

http://www.badische-seiten.de/schwarzwald/glastraegerweg.php

http://www.dierke.de

http://www.gymnasium-meschede.de/projekte/projekt12-04/anthropogene_einfluesse.htm

http://www.lubw.baden-wuerttemberg.de

Palaeoecological records of woodland history during recent centuries of grazing and management examples from Glen Affric, Scotland and Ribblesdale, north Yorkshire.

Helen Shaw and Ian Whyte

Lancaster Environment Centre, Lancaster University

Introduction

Future regeneration and management of woodlands rely on policy and practical decisions driven by cultural choices. What then is the role of historical knowledge? Whilst some argue that palaeoecological and historical knowledge is irrelevant due to the no-analogue climate and human land-use scenarios of the future, we would argue that historical knowledge always informs our cultural debate. However, it often lacks detail; forming a mere backdrop to decision making, or worse, provides *"myths"*, to coin a phrase of Smout (2000), through which rhetorical viewpoints can be argued. This paper presents the results from two areas where palaeoecological results have demonstrated the need for a closer understanding of ecological and management histories and argues that site specific palaeo-histories should, where possible, form a basis for understanding all sites subject to woodland regeneration and conservation.

What is palaeoecology?

Palaeoecology is the study of the ecology of the past and encompasses many methodologies, the commonest methods for understanding Quaternary and Holocene palaeoecology is pollen analysis. Pollen is dispersed widely in the environment and has a very resistant skin or exine which survives well in peat bogs and lake sediments. The stratigraphic nature of these sediments means that pollen preserved at a sequence of depths can be used to build up a picture of vegetation change through time.

Pollen analysis has been instrumental in developing our background knowledge of vegetation cover in our current interglacial. Since some dominant tree species produce large quantities of well dispersed pollen traditional palaeoecology has often focussed upon the major phases of post-glacial woodland development and the subsequent clearances of woodland by Neolithic and later human activities.

Results from pollen analyses have been challenged (e.g. Vera, 2000); there are biases in the pollen record and there is not a simple a linear relationship between the percentage of pollen counted and the percentage of plant cover. However, palaeoecologists are very aware of these biases and have increasingly taken steps to understand

and correct the pollen-vegetation relationship (e.g. Brostrom *et al.*, 2004, 2008). It is clear that with care in interpretation pollen can provide a useful tool in understanding past plant communities.

The idea from ecological climax theory, supported by pollen analysis, that the postglacial vegetation comprised a developing wildwood that was destroyed by human intervention, has been a major focus of arguments for rewilding projects and restoration targets. Following from Vera (2000) the structure of that wildwood has been keenly debated (e.g. Hodder *et al.*, 2005; Mitchell, 2005; Whitehouse and Smith, 2009). However, more importantly, the focus has relied on reinstating some previous vegetation state. Palaeoecology and palaeo-histories can, we argue, add more to our understanding of process in past vegetation. Importantly, change over the last few centuries is often very poorly understood. It is in the recent past that we can start to integrate environmental histories with palaeoecological data to understand in more detail the changes that have occurred and the human activities that may have contributed to that change.

Two examples from very different UK upland environments are presented and may help to challenge some preconceptions and to make us consider options for restoration.

The case study areas
Glen Affric

Glen Affric, the "*jewel*" of Scotland's woodland, lies in the north central pine zone (Forestry Commission, 1998) in the Scottish Highlands. Long a subject of conservation the aim is to expand the pine woodland. Woodland currently becomes patchy and grades to open heathland to the west in Glen Affric. This patchiness of woodland has been seen as recent degradation due to forestry activity and deer grazing. However, the idea of a former extensive pine woodland is debateable as highlighted in Smout's "*Myth of Caledon*" (Smout, 2000).

Pollen analyses show that woodland was long lived in the east; maintaining a continuous cover throughout the last 4,000 years of human land use (Shaw and Tipping, 2006; Froyd and Bennett, 2006). The woodland in the scattered stands to the west has recently spread from this core area (Shaw and Tipping, 2006) – with some stands expanding during the time that deer were at high numbers in the glen.

Pollen analysis can express woodland presence, and change through time but the reasons and drivers of that change are a matter of speculation. The longevity of the east-west boundary of woodland in Glen Affric however, implies an ecotone between east and west. Rainfall increases markedly to the west of the glen and the flatter blanket peat landscape is probably less conducive to pine growth. The pollen diagrams from the core pinewood zone also show that the forest was always mixed, with broadleaved trees such as birch and oak as well as pine.

Ribblesdale

In upper Ribblesdale in north Yorkshire the upland landscape is very different. The landscape is open heavily grazed pastoral land, much of it on limestone pavement. Here the influence of human land use is definite, producing pastoral landscapes which are iconic. However, traditional landscapes are understood to confer benefit to biodiversity with degradation in recent decades caused by Common Agricultural Policy (CAP) driven land management changes. In recent recognition of this the changing role of CAP away from production orientated payments and towards environmental benefits has provided an opportunity to reassess grazing levels through traditional land management. The investigation of the area through palaeo-historical analysis does, however, raise some questions about our views on the sustainability of traditional land management.

Palaeoecological results reveal a loss of variability in the landscape over centuries rather than decades (Shaw and Whyte, 2010). Here, although major woodland loss occurred in prehistory, patches of woodland, boundary trees and scattered scrub have previously contributed structural diversity in the landscape as illustrated by palaeoecological analysis, whilst documentary evidence reveals the loss of this wood as a resource in past centuries so that the diversity of human land-use was also reduced and traditional land management became less diverse and arguably less locally sustainable.

Although sheep and cattle have been "*at the core*" of the upland economy a diversity of farm enterprises and land usages as well as productive ecosystem services have been lost over recent centuries. This loss has been accompanied by a decline in the structural diversity of plant communities. Part of this loss has been of trees within the pastoral landscape, likely to be both small woodland areas and scattered field boundary trees and shrubs. The separation of pastoral land use within the CAP and woodland development within rewilding projects and forestry schemes is likely to continue to exacerbate this trend.

Conclusions

The application of pollen and historical analysis to areas where woodland restoration and traditional management are objectives for conservation initiatives demonstrates that we sometimes do not go far enough in our thinking and do not fully understand past process of change in vegetation, and the role of past human activity in their maintenance or degradation. Although large woodland restoration schemes have their place, within them we must not forget to allow for long-term processes, which may include periods of woodland loss and should include edges and open areas, whilst in pastoral landscapes, the unpopular scrub element may provide an important resource and was part of the traditional system. We argue that we need to pay more attention to small woodland areas, boundary trees and scrub within our plans for future land management.

References

Broström, A., Sugita, S. and Gaillard, M-J. (2004) Pollen productivity estimates for reconstruction of past vegetation cover in the cultural landscape of Southern Sweden. *The Holocene,* **14**, 371-384.

Broström, A., Nielsen, A.B., Gaillard, M.J., Hjelle, K., Mazier, F., Binney, H., Bunting, J., Fyfe, R., Meltsov, V., Poska, A., Rasanen, S., Soepboer, W., von Stedingk, H., Suutari, H. and Sugita, S. (2008) Pollen productivity estimates of key European plant taxa for quantitative reconstruction of past vegetation: a review. *Vegetation History and Archaeobotany,* **17(5)**, 461-478.

Forestry Commission (1998) *The Caledonian Pine Wood Inventory*. Forestry Commission. Edinburgh. (digital format available from Forestry Commission, Scotland).

Froyd, C. and Bennett, K. (2006) Long-term ecology of native pinewood communities in East Glen Affric, Scotland. *Forestry*, **79**, 279-291.

Hodder, K.H., Bullock, J.M., Buckland, P.C. and Kirby, K.J. (2005) *Large herbivores in the wildwood and in modern naturalistic grazing systems*. English Nature Research Reports 648 English Nature, Peterborough.

Mitchell, F.J.G. (2005) How open were European primeval forests? Hypothesis testing using palaeoecological data. *Journal of Ecology*, **93**, 168-177.

Shaw, H. and Whyte, I. (2010) Land management and biodiversity through time in upper Ribblesdale, North Yorkshire, UK: Understanding the impact of traditional management, *Landscape Archaeology and Ecology,* **8 (1)** and **8(2)**.

Shaw, H. and Tipping, R. (2006) Recent pine woodland dynamics in east Glen Affric, northern Scotland, from highly resolved palaeoecological analyses. *Forestry*, **79**, 331-340.

Smout, T.C. (2000) *Nature contested*. Edinburgh University Press, Edinburgh.

Tipping, R. (2008) Blanket peat in the Scottish Highlands: timing, cause, spread and the myth of environmental determinism. *Biodiversity and Conservation*, **17**, 2097-2113.

Vera, F.W.M. (2000) *Grazing ecology and forest history*, CABI publishing, Wallingford, Oxon.

Whitehouse, N. and Smith, D. (2009) How fragmented was the British Holocene wildwood? Perspectives on the "Vera" grazing debate from the fossil beetle record. *Quaternary Science Reviews*, **29 (3-4)**, 539-553.

Treescapes: Trees, Animals, Landscape and 'Treetime'

Luke Steer
Treescapes Consultancy Ltd.

Introduction

This paper has been prepared, not from the perspective of an academic landscape historian or ecologist, but from the perspective of someone trained in forestry and arboriculture, who was brought up on a farm and spends a lot of time in the uplands, mainly the Lake District and other parts of the UK but also the Alps, Karakorum in Pakistan, the Jammu and Kashmir Province of India, the Atlas Mountains in Morocco and the Julian Alps in Slovenia. In this paper I recount some of my observations and hypotheses.

We know that foresters go to great lengths to protect regenerating woodlands from herbivorous mammals. How then was it possible for much of the countryside to be covered in woods, pasture woodland and wood pasture, parkland, before people built walls, planted hedges or erected fences? Vera (2000 and 2002) puts forward an attractive hypothesis but it has not been accepted by all (Hodder et al., 2005; Kirby, 2003; Kirby, 2004; Mitchell, 2005; and Rackham, 2006).

Figure 1. Brothers Water in the Lake District. The ancient semi-natural woodlands are on the steep valley sides that are bouldery, have thin soils and are unsuitable for agriculture.

My observations are concerned primarily with heterogeneous upland landscapes, particularly their topography; aspect; slope angle; soil type, depth, fertility aeration and moisture retention; local climate; and bouldериness. I'm especially interested in Lakeland treescapes. The majority of the ancient semi-natural woodlands (ASNWs) in the Lakes are composed predominantly of sessile oak (*Quercus petraea* (Mattuschka) Lieblein) located on bouldery valley sides. There are also a few oaks in the intakes but the majority of the trees in these areas are ash (*Fraxinus excelsior* L.) and hawthorn (*Crataegus monogyna* Jacq.).

This paper is divided into six main sections:

1. a review of how site features affect where trees regenerate;

2. the factors that can lead to tree regeneration events – tree-time and tree and woodland cycles;

3. a discussion about human influences on treescapes;

4. the current situation in the Lake District;

5. some tentative recommendations for future tree planting; and

6. suggested further research.

Site features

Yalden (1999) tells us that plants and animals quickly colonised the British landscape after the end of the last Ice Age and soils started to develop. It seems logical to expect that areas with better soil ended up supporting lush vegetation whereas those with poor soil were sparsely colonised and this vegetation was often woody, unpalatable, or both. Generally most species of grazing herbivores prefer to feed on lush nutritious vegetation and only visit other areas when passing through from one feeding place to another, or for shelter and defence. Different species of browsing herbivores feed on woody and herbaceous vegetation in varying proportions (Mason and others, 1999; Thompson, 2004; Mason and Kerr, 2004; Vera, 2000). Wild animals also range over large areas. The impact that these animals had on the vegetation probably depended on their numbers; and their numbers would have largely depended on the winter carrying capacity of the landscape.

Work in Yellowstone National Park (for example, Beschta, 2005; Beschta and Ripple, 2010; Ripple and Beschta, 2006, 2007; and Ripple and Larson, 2000) indicates that when top predators – wolves in that instance – are re-introduced to an area, herbivorous mammal numbers are reduced and the remaining populations spend less time in any one place, and this allows woody vegetation to develop. When British woodlands developed, wolves and other predators, including humans, still roamed the landscape.

Work by the Forestry Commission (Mason *et al.*, 1999; Thompson, 2004; and Mason and Kerr, 2004) shows that tree seedlings are more likely to develop on infertile soils than fertile soils because of reduced competition from other vegetation. However, Fenton (2008) suggests that in Upland Scotland trees are more likely to grow on the fertile soils rather than infertile soils. Differences between these authors may not be related to soil fertility, but to its organic matter content. Fenton (2008) suggests that mor soil types, high in organic material, inhibit tree regeneration, whereas the other authors suggest that low fertility mineral soils, such as those dominated by sand, can enhance it.

I therefore suggest that many of our ASNWs developed under the influence of one or a number of factors including:

- low fertility mineral soils;
- soil prone to drought;
- steep slopes that were less easy for animals to traverse; and/or
- bouldery and craggy areas providing a natural barrier to large herbivorous mammals.

One or a number of these factors, when animal pressure was low enough, would have created suitable conditions for tree regeneration. Humans then '*allowed*' these woodlands to remain because alternative uses for the land, principally agriculture, were limited due to the low productivity of the soil or difficulty to harvest.

The Triglav National Park in Slovenia is like an extreme version of the UK Uplands with very steep-sided valleys. The prime agricultural land is in the valley bottoms while the valley sides are forested.

Figure 2. Triglav National Park, Slovenia - an extreme version of the UK Uplands.

High up in these valleys are some of the most beautiful alpine meadows and these were traditionally used for grazing cattle and producing hay. There are no manmade boundaries around these alpine meadows, the trees have branches down to ground level and there is little of interest for the animals within the forest matrix.

I was lucky enough to go on a walking holiday there a few years ago during which time it snowed. While walking along some snowy forest paths we noticed that they were covered with animal footprints but there were few footprints in the adjacent forest. I hypothesised that these paths may have been used by wild grazing animals when humans were still hunter gatherers and would follow them along these paths from alpine meadow to alpine meadow when hunting, similar to wolves following herds of large herbivores in North America or the big cats following their prey in Africa. The alpine meadows are generally in bowls where, over time, a depth of fertile soil has developed whereas, the soils in the forest are often thin or infertile and many are prone to either drought or water-logging.

I therefore suggest that the alpine meadows may have been open to a greater or lesser extent since the end of the last glaciation and before humans had a significant impact on the landscape and its ecology. When people started to farm and domesticate animals they would have continued to move

Figure 3. An alpine meadow in Slovenia. There aren't any fences between the grazed meadows and the forest matrix.

Figure 4. Triglav National Park, Slovenia. Numbers of grazing animals have reduced as the viability of agricultural businesses has become stressed in recent times. This meadow is being colonised by spiky shrubs, *Berberis vulgaris* L., and trees in its upper regions but the cattle are maintaining tightly grazed turf in its lower regions.

them from alpine meadow to alpine meadow along the same paths once used for hunting prey.

In the British Lowlands some of the woodlands that contain ancient trees are on poor soil – Sherwood and Staverton are on sandy soils, whereas others are on heavy clay soil that was hard to cultivate using traditional methods. Both Sherwood and Staverton are prone to drought but I expect that tree roots, particularly those of oak which dominate these woods, are able to grow deeper into the soil to obtain moisture than roots of competing vegetation.

Regeneration events

I suspect that in Britain, before people had a significant influence on its ecology, the landscape contained a range of terrestrial habitats from species-rich grassland grading into parkland with individual trees and copses, to woodland with glades. I imagine that the proportion of the land that was covered by grassland, wood pasture and woods would have slowly but continually fluctuated over space and time. Over time, trees within closed-canopy woodland would have died and, initially, the canopies of their neighbours would join to fill the gaps, but eventually glades would have opened. In some instances, these glades would have been kept open by grazing mammals, and the vegetation in them would have changed from shade-tolerant woodland vegetation to grazing-tolerant grassland vegetation. This would have increased the winter carrying capacity of the landscape for large herbivorous mammals and their numbers probably increased as a consequence.

This process would have continued until areas of closed-canopy woodland became pasture woodland and wood pasture or parkland.

Areas least suited to support grazing mammals might have continually remained as woodland but at their peripheries, over time, they would have expanded and contracted across the landscape and these fluctuations would have depended on tree age, health, and events that affected tree cover (such as infestations of insect pests, tree diseases, gales and fire), as well as tree regeneration events regulated by the population size of grazing animals.

At different periods along this gradation a collapse of the grazing animal population would have allowed a pulse of tree regeneration that, in certain areas, but more likely those with infertile mineral soil, would again have become closed-canopy woodland. The more severe the population collapse of large herbivorous mammals, the more extensive the tree regeneration.

Fenton (2008) suggests that in the Scottish Highlands the winter carrying capacity of the vegetation probably regulates numbers of large herbivorous mammals to a level sufficient to prevent landscape-scale woodland regeneration. I suggest that this indicates that something is required to reduce animal numbers sufficiently to allow tree or shrub regeneration. Potential influences that could have negative impacts on the population size of large herbivorous mammals are, to a greater or lesser extent:

- predation;
- low survival during one or a number of severe winters;
- animal diseases;
- animal parasites; or
- pests and diseases of food plants.

No doubt numbers of large herbivorous mammals would have fluctuated in both the short and long term. I suspect that generally they would have tended to increase in proportion to improving habitat as wooded areas thinned. Eventually, potentially a number of centuries after the previous mass tree regeneration event, animal numbers would have increased to levels where they would become vulnerable to a massive population collapse caused by animal disease, disease of their food plants, poor winter(s), parasites, or, more likely, a combination of these – a coincidence of factors.

Rabbits (*Oryctolagus cuniculus* L.) prevented tree regeneration at Silwood Park for decades if not centuries prior to the introduction of the virus that causes Myxomatosis (*Myxoma* spp.) in 1953. Myxomatosis caused catastrophic mortality of the rabbit population and by the late 1960s a new cohort of oaks had established (Dobson and Crawley, 1994).

During high animal populations their core feeding areas would expand into areas with sub-optimal vegetation and these habitats would 'degrade'. The canopy of aging woodland would thin over time as trees died and high animal numbers prevented regeneration. The opening of woodland canopies would have allowed increased levels of light to the woodland floor and consequently the vegetation would have altered from being dominated by woodland plants to becoming dominated by grazing-tolerant vegetation such as grasses and sedges. This alteration of vegetation would favour large herbivorous mammals and would increase the area's winter carrying capacity for them and, in turn, they would prevent tree regeneration.

Large herbivorous mammals often prefer to spend a disproportionate amount of time sheltering close to trees or in groups of trees, with the result of nutrient importation to those areas. Nettle (*Urtica dioica* L.), an indicator of soils with high fertility, is often found in and around groups of parkland trees for this reason. Enhanced soil fertility can have a detrimental effect on fungi that develop mycorrhizal relationships with tree roots and, in turn, their host trees. This leads to a further decline of the tree canopy and an improvement of the quality and quantity of the vegetation for large herbivorous mammals.

Large numbers of animals would have created soil and vegetation disturbance and, if then followed by a massive reduction in their population, would have created opportunities for tree regeneration. Population maximums of large herbivorous mammals, followed by crashes in their numbers that allowed a pulse of tree regeneration, would only have to have occurred once or twice within the lifetime of a tree to allow sufficient trees to regenerate and continue the presence of that species in the landscape; for oak this might be once or twice every 2-600 years or potentially longer.

At high population densities large herbivorous mammals would come into contact with each other more frequently and consequently increase the risk of spreading pests, parasites and diseases around the herd. Also, high numbers of animals may have increased the time they spent in areas where they had defecated and urinated and this, in turn, probably also increased the risk of spreading pests, parasites and diseases. Parasite populations, such as ticks and intestinal worms, could then increase and these are often vectors for diseases such as Lyme disease which can amplify their detrimental effects of the parasite on host vitality and population numbers.

After a crash in the numbers of large herbivorous mammals the remaining animals would have probably concentrated in areas with the most suitable and nutritious vegetation, rather than areas with poor soils and low quality food plants. Consequently trees were more likely to regenerate in areas with poor soils, due to reduced browsing and grazing pressure, and closed-canopy woodland would again develop in these areas. Within the closed canopy woodland the quality and quantity of vegetation utilised by large herbivorous mammals would have reduced and, at a landscape scale, the animal winter carrying capacity would also reduce. Closed-canopy woodland would have remained as long as the gaps created by tree death and failure could be closed by neighbouring trees but, eventually, this would not have been possible. Glades would form and the vegetation within them would have altered, so improving the quality and quantity of vegetation for large herbivorous mammals, and these would again have prevented further tree regeneration until their next population collapse. This would have created a treescape containing a limited number of cohorts of trees from separate regeneration events. I refer to this as the woodland regeneration cycle partly regulated by large herbivorous mammals. This cycle is summarised below.

- After a period of high animal numbers they decrease, potentially due to one or a combination of the following factors:
  - severe winter(s);
  - disease;
  - parasites; and
  - reduction in human population or the economic viability of farming.
- In a period of low animal numbers there is an episodic pulse of thorn and tree regeneration.
- Tree canopies expand and cast shade on ground vegetation which consequently changes from being dominated by grazing-tolerant grasses to shade-tolerant woodland vegetation. This produces less biomass of a lower feed quality than grazing-tolerant, light-demanding, grasses.
- Many decades pass with a relatively stable treescape. As trees die their neighbours grow to occupy their vacated canopy space.
- Woodland canopies eventually thin as trees die and the gaps are too large for neighbouring trees to fill. Grazing animals utilise these gaps and the vegetation changes from being dominated by shade-tolerant woodland plants, to grazing-tolerant vegetation. These gaps are maintained by grazing animals and extended as other trees die. This process increases the winter carrying capacity of the landscape for large herbivorous mammals.
- There are minor thorny shrub and tree regeneration events if animal numbers decrease by small amounts, potentially for the reasons listed above, but generally the landscape becomes increasingly open due to thinning woodland canopies and this leads to a generally upward trend in grazing animal numbers.
- Eventually there is a massive crash in animal numbers, due to one or a combination of the reasons listed above, and the remaining population concentrates in the areas most suited for grazing (good fertile soil and nutritious vegetation).
- And on goes the cycle.

With this model small frequent population crashes of grazing animals would create a more diverse tree age-class structure, whereas a long period without a significant crash in animal numbers would lead to a simplified tree age-class structure favouring long-lived light-demanding trees such as oak.

If numbers of grazing animals are insufficient to maintain glades in dense woodland, then shade-tolerant species could become established and the species make-up could alter to become dominated by these shade-tolerant trees, just as is happening today in enclosed oak woodlands where beech trees were introduced in the nineteenth century to 'enhance' the landscape.

High numbers of herbivorous mammals maintaining and enlarging open areas and large woodland glades would, when their populations collapsed, create conditions suitable for the regeneration of thorny shrubs and light-demanding tree species such as oak.

Human influence

Before people had a significant influence on the landscape trees and woods would have had a few thousand years to develop and it is likely that some of the trees were huge.

Anyone who has worked as a tree surgeon and felled large trees, even with a chainsaw, will know that it is hard work: but just imagine trying to fell and convert large trees with a stone axe? It is more likely that early humans concentrated their efforts on small trees and the branches of larger trees. Therefore, if we believe that Neolithic people colonized a country covered in closed-canopy forest, I suggest that it would probably have taken centuries, if not thousands of years, to clear it of trees.

We know that large herbivorous animals can maintain open or semi-open landscapes, such as the Serengeti and, according to Fenton (2008), Upland Scotland. As I mentioned earlier, foresters go to great lengths to exclude large herbivorous mammals from young woodlands because they can kill or damage high numbers of trees and render them useless as a timber crop.

For human populations to increase, they had to farm the landscape efficiently to provide sufficient food. In the uplands, apart from the valley bottoms, pasture is the most efficient use of the land for food production. Fenton (2008) suggests that historically domestic stock might have replaced indigenous herbivores to a greater or lesser extent but that they might not have altered the overall level of grazing, at least before 1700 AD. I suggest that the greatest challenges that humans had to overcome were:

- the limited winter carrying capacity of the area; and

- catastrophic collapses in animal numbers.

Wild animals might have ranged over large territories between their winter and summer grounds. Initially people mimicked this with the shieling system.

Later on they collected winter fodder: hay and '*tree-hay*' (leaves and branches of leaves) (Quelch pers. comm.); and '*stabled*' the cattle over winter to reduce their energy use and the amount of food required to keep them alive – this was a great innovation. More recently human inputs, such as lime and fertilisers, have increased the productivity of some areas of land and the practice of importing fodder and feed from other locations has also increased the number of animals that upland farms can support.

Enclosures might also have increased the number of animals that could be supported. I imagine that extensively grazed animals move from place to place in response to the quality and quantity of herbage and the amount of dung and urine in an area. Once enclosures were erected the animals could not move on and were forced to graze more intensively than if they were grazing extensively. Consequently the grass was probably grazed closer to the ground than in extensively grazed situations with low animal numbers.

At the time of enclosure many woodlands became '*fossilised*' within the landscape and their areas have not expanded since, although some have contracted or been lost as trees died, the woodland canopies thinned and grazing animals were encouraged to feed in them.

More recently veterinary science has allowed unnaturally high numbers of animals to be kept in close proximately to each other with a reduced risk of parasites and disease. I suggest that this allows unnaturally high numbers of grazing animals to be maintained

Figure 5. The enclosed nature of the Lakeland landscape.

without a collapse in the size of their populations and this prevents pulses of tree regeneration.

The current situation in the Lake District

Within Lakeland intakes most of the trees are ashes and hawthorns but there are some oaks with trunk diameters of 80-120cm at 1.3m. Using White (1998) these would be about 175 years old – so, was the last period of oak regeneration in these areas around 1836? I also have a section from a lapsed ash pollard that is 63cm in diameter and has 172 annual rings – it is therefore around that length of time since it was last pollarded.

One hundred and seventy five years ago was prior to the erection of many of the enclosures in the Lake District except for the ring-garth walls, sometimes referred to as the Head Dyke (Winchester, 2000) and the in-take walls of the sixteenth and seventeenth centuries. Observation indicates that there has been little oak regeneration within the intakes and fields since that time.

There are hawthorns in many of the Lakeland intakes that could indicate a period of reduced animal numbers. These are often said to date from the Great Depression of the 1930s. In the areas where these hawthorns grow there are few large-growing trees, except in a few areas that contain small numbers of ashes. I suggest that this indicates that generally the succession from hawthorn scrub to a landscape containing mature trees was arrested by an unnaturally quick increase in animal numbers. This might have been due to intensified agriculture during and after World War II.

There are many meadows within the Lake District that contain groups of trees growing on rocky knolls, mainly oak but some ash. I consider it unlikely that these would have established if the fields were grazed unless fences were erected around them but, as I haven't come across this in the literature, I consider it unlikely. More likely is that, at the time the trees colonised these knolls, the fields were hay meadows and the vegetation on the knolls was not harvested. The current practice of cutting grass early for silage and then grazing the aftermath now prevents tree regeneration in these areas. During the 2005 gales some of the trees on these rocky knolls blew over. If this trend continues trees on these rocky knolls will eventually disappear from our landscape.

There are areas of land in the Higher Level Stewardship (HLS) agri-environment scheme where thorny shrubs, gorse (*Ulex europaeus* L.), hawthorn and blackthorn (*Prunus spinosa* L.), and trees are regenerating in relatively large grazed enclosures. In some of these it appears that it is the slope angle that regulates whether the area is heavily grazed to a short turf or grazed infrequently enough to allow the thorny shrubs to become established and protect the tree seedlings sufficiently to allow them to grow large enough not to be damaged by farm stock.

In many grazed areas within the Lake District and other parts of Upland Britain tree regeneration is currently non-existent and the existing trees are ageing. Observation suggests that many of the trees in Lakeland fields and intakes may date from before the land was enclosed. Some of these blew over in the gales in January 2005. The number of trees within pasture is therefore reducing. Financial incentives for tree planting in pasture appear to favour woodland creation which is altering the ecology and landscape character. I suggest that, in some of the areas where woodlands have been established during the last 40 years, there may never have been closed-canopy woodland within historic times – indeed, some of these woodlands have been established on prime agricultural land close to farms and hamlets.

It appears to me that even though the agencies that offer financial grant aid to farmers and foresters are in the DEFRA *'family'*, there is a huge difference between their systems and the result is that in many pasture areas the available grants are inappropriate to maintain the traditional landscape character and ecology. What's more, the ancient semi-natural woodlands are invariably within enclosures, and are now unable to expand and contract as they once did.

Recommendations

1. Improve grant aid for planting individual trees and shrubs, or groups of trees and shrubs in upland pasture and intakes rather than establish woodland.

2. Carry out a site assessment prior to establishing trees in upland pastures and intakes, and establish them only in the least fertile or most naturally protected areas.

3. Do not establish woodland on prime agricultural land favoured by grazing animals. Instead, in these areas, establish trees individually or in groups with thorns.

4. Do not plant too many trees! Leave places to plant trees in fifty or one hundred years time.

Further Work

Further research could be carried out to ascertain the validity of the suggestions made in this paper. Certain features, such as aspect; slope angle; soil type, depth, fertility aeration and moisture retention; local climate; and boulderiness, could be assessed in a number of ASNWs and open areas. This information could be inputted into a Geographic Information System (GIS) to produce a computer model of where woodlands could be expected. The maps generated by the GIS could then be compared with actual woodland locations.

The GIS model could then be used to assess how these woodlands may alter under different grazing pressures. The

Macaulay Land Use Research Institute may have already carried out some work on this. It may also be possible to compare maps produced by the GIS model of potential woodland areas with historic maps.

Once a robust model has been developed it could be used to guide where tree and woodland establishment should be carried out and at what densities. This information could be used to prioritise where financial incentives for tree planting, in the form of grant aid, should be allocated.

As discussed above I suspect that in enclosed upland pasture landscapes the majority of the trees may pre-date the erection of the walls and hedges. I also suspect that their numbers are declining. I suggest that a tree survey should be carried out of trees in fields and intakes to assess how robust or vulnerable they are. This information could then be used to allocate financial incentives for tree establishment at appropriate densities.

Acknowledgements
I would like to thank Claire Nash of the Tree Bureau for her helpful comments about an earlier draft of this paper.

References
Beschta, R.L. and Ripple, W.J. (2010) Recovering riparian plant communities with wolves in northern Yellowstone, USA. *Restoration Ecology*, **86**, 391-403.

Beschta, R.L. (2005) Reduced cottonwood recruitment following extirpation of wolves in Yellowstone's northern range. *Ecology*, **86**, 391-403.

Dobson, A. and Crawley, M. (1994) Pathogens and the structures of plant communities. *Trends in Ecology & Evolution*, **Col. 9, No. 10**, 393-397

Fenton, J.H.C. (2008) A postulated natural origin for the open landscape of upland Scotland. *Plant Ecology and Diversity*, **1(1)**, 115-127.

Hodder, K.H., Bullock, J.M., Buckland, P.C. and Kirby, K.J. (2005) *Large herbivores in the wildwood and in modern naturalistic grazing systems.* English Nature Research Report 648, Peterborough, UK.

Kirby, K.J. (2003) *What might a British forest-landscape driven by large herbivores look like?* English Nature Research Report 530, Peterborough, UK.

Kirby, K.J. (2004) A model of a natural wooded landscape in Britain as influenced by large herbivore activity. *Forestry*, **77(5)**, 405-420.

Mason, B. and Kerr, G. (2004) *Transforming even-aged conifer stands to continuous cover management.* Forestry Commission Information Note 40, Edinburgh.

Mason, B., Kerr, G. and Simpson, J. (1999) *What is Continuous Cover Forestry?*, Forestry Commission Information Note 29, Edinburgh.

Mitchell, F.J.G. (2005) How open were European primaeval forests? Hypothesis testing using palaeoecological data. *Journal of Ecology*, **93**, 168-177.

Rackham, O. (2006) *Woodlands*. Collins New Naturalist 100, Harper Collins, London, UK.

Ripple, W.J. and Beschta, R.L. (2006) Linking wolves to willows via risk-sensitive foraging by ungulates in the northern Yellowstone ecosystem. *Forest Ecology and Management*, **230**, 96-106.

Ripple, W.J. and Beschta, R.L. (2007) Restoring Yellowstone's aspen with wolves. *Biological Conservation*, **138**, 514-519.

Ripple, W.J. and Larson, E.J. (2000) Historic aspen recruitment, elk, and wolves in northern Yellowstone National Park, USA, *Biological Conservation*, **95**, 361-370.

Thompson, R. (2004) *Predicting Site Suitability for Natural Colonisation: Upland Birchwoods and Native Pinewoods in Northern Scotland*. Forestry Commission Information Note 54. Edinburgh.

Vera, F.W.M. (2000) *Grazing ecology and forest history*. CABI Publishing, Wallingford: Oxon.

Vera, F. W. M. (2002) The dynamic European forest. *Arboricultural Journal*, **26**, 179-211.

White, J. (1998) *Estimating the age of large and veteran trees in Britain*. Forestry Commission Information Note 12, Edinburgh.

Yalden, D. (1999) *The History of British Mammals*. T & A D Poyser Ltd., London, UK.

Worldviews in Transition: The Impact of Exotic Plants and Animals on Iron Age/Romano-British landscapes

Naomi Sykes
University of Nottingham

Abstract

Cultural geographers have long accepted that plants and animals play an important role in the construction and perception of landscape but such beliefs are yet to be embraced by landscape archaeologists who seldom give consideration to bioarchaeological data beyond the occasional economic or environmental reconstruction. In an attempt to highlight the value of plant and animal remains for landscape research this paper examines the Iron Age/Romano-British transition from a bioarchaeological perspective, focusing on the landscape change brought by the exotic species introduced around AD 43. I argue that the establishment of new plants and animals altered patterns of landscape organisation by introducing horticultural spaces – gardens, orchards, vineyards – and wild animal reserves - *vivaria* and *leporaria* - all of which were unknown before the Conquest. In itself, the use of bioarchaeological data to highlight the widespread existence of Roman horticultural spaces and game reserves is important since these have received little attention from landscape archaeologists due to the difficulties of their detection. Beyond this, however, I propose that the arrival of these species and spaces impacted on the way that people engaged with, traversed and experienced their world. Indeed, the very concept of 'wild animal enclosure' indicates a Roman worldview fundamentally different to that seen in the Iron Age period, when people seemingly negotiated with the wilderness and wild things rather than feeling they had the right to bring them to order.

Introduction

Plants and animals are, and always have been, central to the creation, use and perception of landscape. Their importance is well recognised by cultural geographers who accept that plants and animals have agency and that, by acting together with humans, they give shape and meaning to the world. Human-animal-plant interactions are the architects of the physical landscape, responsible for the form and location of settlements, roads, enclosures, woodland and fields. Plants and animals, however, also play a more psychological role in transforming space into place. Whether as living organisms or as 'products' (grain, bread, wood, meat, bones, artefacts), the behaviour and properties of plants and animals – how they look, sound, smell, feel – are important ingredients for human cultural experience. They are bound up with notions of social reproduction, wealth and status, ideology and materiality. Our everyday interactions with plants and animals, whose lives are so inter-twined with our own, inform the way we think about and behave in our environments.

There is a voluminous literature on human-animal geographies (e.g. Wolch and Emel, 1998; Philo and Wilbert, 2000) and, although human-plant-landscape interactions have received less attention (e.g. Head and Atchinson, 2009 – but see Hitchings' (2003) excellent application of Actor Network Theory to English gardens), cultural geography has a floribunda of plant-based studies compared to the situation in landscape archaeology. Looking through past issues of the *Landscapes* journal, plants and animals are startlingly absent, aside from their occasional incorporation into environmental and economic reconstructions. The same is true of the wider literature on landscape archaeology, where non-human performers are seldom considered. This is particularly apparent in the illustrations which show maps, plans and photographs of pristine landscape features, all eerily devoid of the biota that inhabited them. Within the last few years archaeobotanists and zooarchaeologists have made attempts to contribute to landscape studies, (Pluskowski, 2007; Sykes *et al.*, 2006; Sykes, 2007; van der Veen, 2005; 2008; van der Veen *et al.*, 2008). These works have had some influence, as is evidenced by very recent publications by landscape archaeologists (see in particular Creighton, 2009). However, although providing a more nuanced social discussion of plants and animals in the landscape, these bioarchaeological studies have, with a few exceptions (e.g. Johnston, 2005), remained largely economic and environmental in their remit – there is scope for examining plants and animals in terms of landscape experience (Figure 1).

As a case-study to highlight the contribution that plant and animal studies can make to both landscape archaeology and period-based knowledge as a whole this paper will examine the Iron Age-Roman transition in southern Britain. Recent years have seen an upsurge in research concerning the landscapes of Iron Age and Roman Britain. Many of these studies (e.g. the work of Taylor, 1997; Petts, 1998; Willis, 2007; 2008; Rogers, 2007; 2008) have been theoretically-informed, advancing our understanding beyond the traditional, polarised interpretation of the Iron Age landscape as 'symbolic' and that of the Roman period as 'economic' (see Petts, 1998). They have emphasised the complexity of the cultural landscape, highlighting the importance of human experience for the creation of place. Moore (2007, 80) has argued that we can only begin to reach Iron Age perceptions of place if we examine landscape from its widest perspective and, in particular, give consideration to material culture – the theory being that 'objects' give a space meaning. I concur with Moore's view and would argue that the same case can

Figure 1. Space is turned into place by the interactions of plants, animals and people. Each actor gives the landscape texture and meaning.

be made, perhaps even more strongly, for plants and animals – living things which 'act back' in a way that static artefacts do not.

To appreciate the agency of the plants and animals represented on archaeological sites we need to recognise that their remains are more than economic or depositional 'end products' (although both these aspects may be significant for understanding perceptions of landscape). We may retrieve plant and animal remains from their final resting place but each specimen has back-history, or 'biography', of human inter-relationships, of varying duration and purpose, which would have been played out within, and would have given meaning to, the cultural landscape and environment.

This paper takes as it central tenet the idea that plants and animals (whether alive or as products/ foodstuffs), landscape, social structure and ideology are inter-connected to the point that a change in one will be reproduced in the others. That this inter-connectivity was acknowledged in the past, perhaps more than it is today, is intimated by classical texts. According to Roman origin myths, for instance, the boundaries of the city state of Rome were laid out by cattle and the position of the city's walls and gates were marked out by a bull. Indeed, the very name Italy was said to have been bestowed because of the number and beauty of its cattle, the name 'Italy' coming from the ancient Greek for cattle, '*itali*' (Schwabe, 1994, 46). In these few lines are articulated the fact that land, people and other non-human actors work together to create cultural landscape and cultural identity.

If it is accepted that landscape cannot be extrapolated from other ecological and socio-cultural factors, its study becomes a work of almost unwieldy magnitude. In order to streamline this paper into a manageable form, it will focus on one very specific aspect of plant-animal-human-landscape inter-relations; that is, the landscape change resulting from the exotic plant and animal species deliberately introduced to Britain around AD 43. Here discussion will centre on the rural landscape; for a more wide-ranging analysis which deals also with urban landscapes see Allen (in prep). Whilst this study is based primarily on my own zooarchaeological work, it benefits from the many excellent reviews of archaeological plants and animals that have recently been undertaken (Livarda, 2008; van der Veen, 2008; van der Veen *et al.*, 2008; Locker, 2007; Hambleton, 2008; Poole, 2010). I argue that plant and animal introductions can be examined not only in terms of biodiversity, economic change and dietary impact (all of which are important issues) but also as evidence for fundamental shifts in landscape organisation and experience, worldview and attitudes to nature.

Plants, animals and the Iron Age/Romano-British transition

Today, with the rise of global trade, plants and animals are finding it increasingly easy to transgress their natural ranges and become established in unfamiliar ecosystems. Concern over their ecological impact has motivated numerous researchers to study the effects of alien biota and these works have highlighted the dramatic effect that introduced plants and animals can have on landscape and environment (see Hobbs, 2000). This is something I appreciate well having recently introduced two free-ranging hens (a non-native species) into our back-garden (Figure 1). They have rapidly and increasingly transformed the space since their arrival: its look, smell and feel have changed – it is a different place. This is also reflected in the way that we now engage with the space – we spend more time in the back garden but our patterns of movement within it have also changed as we collect eggs, attempt to avoid the deep dust bowls and avoid or collect the genuinely awesome quantities of faeces produced by these small animals. If our hens are, in any way, representative of the domestic fowl whose populations became widely established in Roman Britain, I could believe that the arrival of the chicken had, for many people, a greater influence on the form and perception of landscape than the arrival of the Roman army itself.

But chickens were not the only species to be transported by the Romans, whose consumption of biodiversity is well known (Hughes, 2003; Whatmore and Thorne, 1998; Coates, 1998). Historical texts document the large quantities of plants and animals that were imported to the Mediterranean from where they were taken across the Empire, the scale of the trade often ecologically impoverishing the regions from where the biota was sourced: for instance north Africa is said to have been denuded of its populations of rhinoceros, zebra, hippopotamus, elephant and lion, and the area had become barren from the intensive agriculture that supplied Rome with its grain (Coates, 1998, 25, 38; Hughes, 2003, 26). The ecological impact of the Romans is also charted in the archaeological record, reflected by the substantial number of species found outside their natural range in Roman period contexts (Lepetz and Yvinec, 2002; Gardeisen, 2002; Livarda, 2008; van der Veen, 2008; van der Veen *et al.*, 2008). For Britain AD 43 brought not only the introduction of new species but also a change in the relationship between people and their locally-available native plants and animals. This shift is brought into relief only when viewed against the pre-Conquest situation, which will now be examined, admittedly in a rather broad-brush way.

The 'nature' of the Iron Age in southern Britain

Bioarchaeological assemblages from Iron Age sites are generally characterised by 'the domestic', the remains of cattle, sheep, pigs and crop plants being ubiquitous. Less apparent are those wild resources that must surely have been plentiful within the landscape: recent reviews of the archaeological data have highlighted the dearth of fish, marine molluscs and crustaceans, wildfowl, game mammals and wild plants in Iron Age assemblages, especially when compared to those of Roman date (Allen, forthcoming; Dobney and Ervynck, 2007; Hambleton, 2008; Locker, 2007; van der Veen, 2008; Willis, 2007). Whilst hunting, gathering, fowling and fishing clearly contributed little to the Iron Age diet, it should not be assumed that these activities and the resources they were used to crop were of little social importance, indeed the opposite was probably the case. Today, farming societies are seldom ambivalent to wild plants and animals – even where they are not exploited regularly they always carry social meaning and the relationships that people have with them often reflect wider social structure and ideology (e.g. Cartmill, 1993; Pieroni and Leimar Price, 2006).

The possibility that during the Iron Age wild animals had a social/symbolic significance far in excess of their nutritional value has been raised by several authors (e.g. Grant, 1984; King, 1991; Green, 1992) and is supported by the work of Hill (1995, 64, 104). Through detailed analysis of Iron Age disposal practices, Hill demonstrated that wild animals are significantly better represented in so-called 'special deposits' (or Associated Bone Groups – ABGs), than they are in other contexts: it should be noted however that wild animals are still rare, most ABGs comprising domestic animals (see Morris, 2008). Based on this disparity, Hill proposed that the hunting and consumption of wild animals were proscribed, only being undertaken on rare occasions of feasting and sacrifice. Such a scenario would certainly account for Caesar's account of the Britons, where he stated with incredulity that 'hare, fowl and geese they think it unlawful to eat' (V.12 – trans. Handford,

1982, 111). When combined with apparent avoidance of freshwater and marine resources as well as wild plants the evidence may, as Hill suggests, indicate a worldview in which domestic: wild or culture: nature oppositions were central. This is not to suggest that culture was seen as separate from nature, the two were probably intertwined to the point that neither existed as concepts (Green, 1992; 2004; Bell, 1995, 145). However, if it is accepted that interactions with plants and animals are formative to human experience and are key to the creation and perception of landscape, the lack of evidence for the exploitation of wild resources suggests that the environments in which fish, birds and game mammals dwelt were being engaged with, and so comprehended, in very particular ways.

In many pastoral societies, hunting landscapes are symbolically remote from the domestic world, belonging to a different temporality where the social rhythms of the everyday do not apply (Hamilakis, 2003, 240). To venture into the 'wilderness' is therefore to move within an unfamiliar, dangerous and usually sacred geography, where past and present and life and death are merged (Ingold, 2000, 84). Ability to mediate between the boundaries of these different worlds and time-cycles is often seen as a sign of power and those who do so are frequently conferred with a shamanic status or supernatural authority (Helms, 1993, 153–7, 211). Similarly, things derived from these remote realms also tend to be seen as powerful, carrying associations with ancestors and cultural heroes (Helms, 1993, 7). That the 'wildness' and wild things may have been viewed as sacred during the Iron Age is indicated not only by the ritual treatment of wild animals, which are occasionally deposited in association with human remains, but also by the iconography of the period in which human-animal hybrids are frequently depicted – this resonates with the cosmologies of non-western societies such as the Dogon of Mali, who believe that whilst in the wilderness humans may take the form of animals or exchange body parts with the spirits who dwell there (see for example Green, 2004, 150; Ingold, 2000, 84).

The possibility that the wilderness was seen as boundary or liminal space during the Iron Age is also indicated by the fact that votive offerings of coins and metalwork are frequently found at the edges of bogs, lakes, rivers, estuaries and the sea shore, areas in which settlement and day-to-day activities appear to have been limited during the period (Creighton, 1995, 298; Willis, 2007, 115; Rogers, 2008). Whilst watery places may have divided the world horizontally, vertical boundaries – sky and earth – also appear to have been symbolically important, indicated by the ritual deposition of birds and birds' wings, and the interment of comparatively high numbers of burrow-dwelling mammals: Hill (1995) has shown that of the wild mammals present in ABGs, foxes, badgers, stoats and martens are amongst the more common. Willis (2007, 118) has suggested that these deposits may have been attempts to manage and control nature at a time when agricultural production was becoming increasingly socially and politically important. This is a neat and attractive idea but if, as is the case in most non-western native cosmologies, there was no concept of 'nature', it may be that rather than trying to impose order on the wilderness, the deposits reflect a desire to come to terms with it (Ingold, 2000, 83). Taken together, the evidence suggests to me that the Iron Age landscape was composed of different spheres of influence, some (e.g. the domestic) under human care, others (the wild) more closely aligned with the divine but all part of the same interconnected world.

The 'nature' of Roman southern Britain

In many respects Roman perceptions of landscape appear to have been very similar to those of the Iron Age: culture, nature and the divine were not seen as separate entities but as inter-twined parts of the whole (Beagon, 1992, 32). There is evidence that watery places and their animals continued to hold religious significance (Willis, 2007; Rogers, 2008), that votive offerings were still made at boundary locations (Rogers, 2007), and that there was some continuity in the ritual deposition of wild animals (King, 2005, 363; Morris, 2008). However, evidence from the archaeobotanical and zooarchaeological record demonstrates that human-animal-plant-landscape interactions were changing.

Recent reviews of the archaeobotanical data demonstrate that very shortly after AD 43, and in some cases just before, new 'exotic' plant foods – e.g. figs, olives, grapes, lentils, mulberry and pine nuts – were imported to Britain and widely distributed (van der Veen, 2008; van der Veen *et al.*, 2008). Whilst these species were not grown in Britain, at least initially, there is clear evidence that other taxa – particularly plum, pear, walnut, box and probably domestic apple and cherry – did become established (van der Veen, 2008, 104; van der Veen *et al.*, 2008, 33). Similarly, the zooarchaeological record indicates that new animal species were introduced whilst Britain was under Roman occupation. For instance, although there are a few Iron Age records of domestic fowl, they become increasingly well represented after AD 43 and it seems likely that pheasants, peafowl and perhaps even rabbits were also introduced during the Roman period (Maltby, 1997; Yalden and Albarella, 2008; Poole, 2010; Sykes and Curl, 2010).

There is now conclusive proof that fallow deer, a species native to Anatolia, was established in Roman Britain (Figure 2). A substantial collection of fallow deer remains has been identified at Fishbourne Roman Palace in Sussex (Sykes *et al.*, 2006; M. Allen *pers. comm.*). From this assemblage two jaw bones were AMS dated – one to AD 60 ± 40 years (Beta-201535 2σ Cal BP 1990 to 1820), the other slightly later to about AD 90 ± 40 (Beta-201534 2σ Cal BP 1930 to 1740) – and their teeth were submitted for strontium isotope analysis, a geochemical provenancing technique. The methods and results of this study are presented in Sykes *et al.* (2006) but, in brief, the analyses demonstrated that the *c.* AD 60 individual was imported as a fawn to Fishbourne where it lived out the rest of its life. From where this animal was brought is currently uncertain but Italy or southern Gaul seems a plausible source given the apparent absence of fallow deer in the rest of northern Europe (Sykes, 2004). Results for the *c.* AD 90 individual indicate that the animal was born and raised at Fishbourne, and it is tempting to suggest that it descended from the earlier import. More recently another set of fallow deer remains, identified from the rural settlement at Monkton on the Isle of Thanet, Kent (Bendrey, 2003) have been AMS dated variously to between the first and third century AD, most returning second and third century dates (Sykes *et al.*, 2011). These specimens are currently undergoing ancient DNA analysis but preliminary results suggest a Mediterranean, possibly Italian, origin (*ibid*).

Whilst the Roman importation of fallow deer is indisputable, more complex is the issue concerning the hare. The mountain hare, *Lepus timidus*, is native to Britain but genetic evidence suggested that the brown hare, *L. europaeus*, is an introduced species (Yalden, 2010). The date at which the brown hare was brought to Britain is currently uncertain, obfuscated by the difficulties of separating the remains of the two species, but the 'received wisdom' is that it is a Roman import (Yalden, 1999, 127). Certainly Figures 3a and 3b show how the zooarchaeological representation of hare

Figure 2. Male fallow deer (*Dama dama*) © **Richard Ford, Digital Wildlife**

increases from the Iron Age into the Roman period, both in terms of the number of sites on which it is found and as a percentage of the overall animal bones assemblages. Regardless of whether this upsurge reflects the introduction of the brown hare or simply increased exploitation of an earlier-established population, it demonstrates a change in human-animal interactions co-incident with Roman occupation.

The Roman period saw a host of other plant and animal introductions and it seems unlikely that these, or any other materials brought from 'outside', would have been viewed in a neutral light (Helms, 1993, 3). Indeed, I would propose that the increased importation of exotic species may have instigated a re-calibration of Iron Age worldviews, with geographies expanding to incorporate those areas beyond the traditional boundaries of the 'wilderness'. In much the same way that the arrival of the European fur trade in Northwest America altered native cosmologies – whereby European goods (e.g. woollen blankets) took on ritual and ideological significance, even replacing the traditional animal skins in ceremonial activities (Helms, 1993, 156) – it may be envisaged that Roman-imported exotics, and the realms from which they came, began to replace the Iron Age 'wilderness' as the new sacred spheres. With this possibility in mind it is interesting to note that several scholars have highlighted the fact that exotic plants and animals are found in higher frequencies within Roman ritual contexts – human graves, temples, shrines and votive deposits – than they are in other deposit types (van der Veen et al., 2008; King, 2005; Morris, 2008).

If the boundaries to divine spheres were shifting, and the traditional wilderness was losing its sacred status, this may explain two of the changes that took place during the Roman period. First is the increased settlement of coastal areas and fenlands, which may indicate that it was now deemed acceptable for humans to inhabit these spaces, as well as being physically possible due to a combination of marine regression and the construction of drainage networks (Taylor, 2007, 65; Willis, 2007, 119). Second is the observed rise in the utilisation of native wild plants and animals, species that had previously been avoided (Locker, 2007; van der Veen, 2008; Willis, 2007). There is evidence to suggest that these wild species were still considered to be 'special' (e.g. Willis, 2007, 114; Morris, 2008, 152), so their sacred association may have remained, but their procurement and consumption was clearly no longer prohibited.

The act of consumption is important because it is perhaps the most potent act of engaging with the world, allowing whole landscapes to be incorporated into the human body in a single bite. But consumption does not require that plants and animals are eaten, they maybe 'consumed' through all the senses – touch, sight, smell and sound. As such, the observed shifts in the archaeobotanical and zooarchaeological record, in particular the appearance of new plants and animals, are likely to

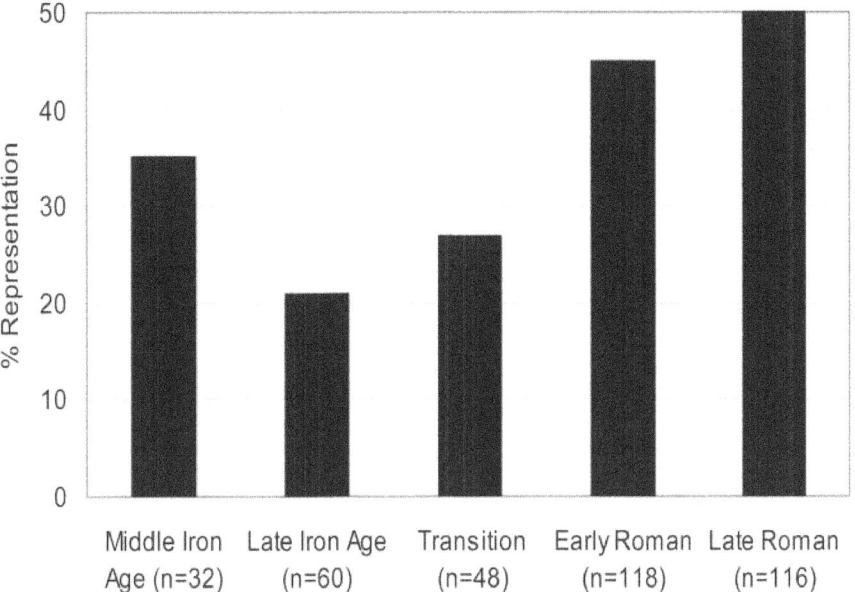

Figure 3a. Inter-period variation in the representation of hare – the number of sites on which hare are represented is here shown as a percentage of the total number of sites within the database (sample size is shown in parentheses). Source: Allen forthcoming. Date labels equate to the following: Middle Iron Age (fourth to second century BC), Late Iron Age (second century BC to mid-first century AD), Transition (mid-first to mid-second century AD), Early Roman (mid-first to mid-second century AD), Late Roman (mid-second to mid-fourth century AD).

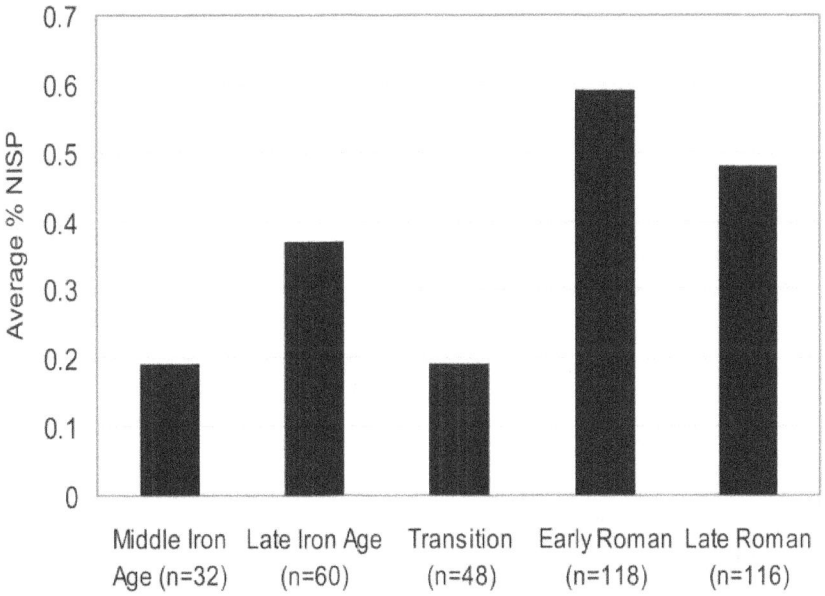

Figure 3b. Inter-period variation in the representation of hare according to NISP – shown here as a percentage of the total mammal assemblage. The number of assemblages for each date group is shown in parentheses. Source Allen forthcoming. See Figure 3a for explanations of date groups.

reflect changes in the way that people traversed and experienced their environments. In an attempt to explore this, I now turn to examine how these imported exotics were responsible for creating new landscapes, specifically the horticultural spaces and animal enclosures that were established for the first time in Roman Britain.

Vivaria, leporaria and *hortus*: new plant and animal geographies

Classical texts provide considerable detail about Roman gardens and parks in the Mediterranean, and in this region there is a tradition of investigating these landscape features from an archaeological perspective, especially where their remains are well preserved, as at Pompeii (Jashemski, 1981; 1987). Whilst literary studies have resulted in complex analyses of perceptions and attitudes to the Roman garden/park landscapes (e.g. Beagon, 1992; 1996; Purcell, 1987), archaeological investigations have been more restricted in scope, often limited to descriptions of garden features, boundaries and typology, with emphasis being placed on the methods of their detection, excavation and reconstruction (e.g. Cunliffe, 1981; Gleason, 1994; Farrar, 1996; 1998; Zeepvat, 1991). The actual meaning of these spaces has been largely overlooked, with Cunliffe (2000, 115) and Carroll (2003) being perhaps the only scholars who have attempted to raise the issue. The lack of investigation into Roman parks and gardens is particularly apparent in Britain where studies have been curtailed by both a lack of documentary evidence and the scarcity of preserved garden features, although fishponds and bedding trenches are known from several Roman sites (Cunliffe, 1981; Zeepvat, 1991). I would argue, however, that the detection and physical tracing of garden and park features are unnecessary; their presence can be ascertained and their significance understood through the study of plant and animal remains.

As has been shown by Van der Veen (2008; *et al.*, 2008), Iron Age to Roman shifts in the archaeobotanical record, in particular the evidence for the establishment of exotic fruit trees, are clear proxy indicators for the emergence of garden plots, orchards and even vineyards – spaces that are unknown in Iron Age Britain. Similarly the presence of fallow deer can be viewed as evidence for parks or vivaria, as it seems unlikely that exotic animals would have been transported great distances only to be released to roam freely (Sykes *et al.*, 2006). Whilst at Fishbourne it would have been necessary to create a physical boundary to restrict the movement of the herd, a slightly different situation is attested by the fallow deer remains from Monkton on the Isle of Thanet, which in the Roman period would have been a true island, a natural enclosure onto which deer could be released. Whilst the utilisation of islands as game parks is known from classical, and earlier, periods in the Mediterranean (Masseti, 2002), this is the first example of such a phenomenon in Roman northern Europe.

There is increasing evidence that hares may also have been emparked, perhaps adding credence to the idea that the species was a prized Roman import rather than being widely available. At Fishbourne Roman Palace, for instance, hare remains account for three per cent of the identified mammal assemblage, a figure far in excess of the national average (see Figure 3b, Allen forthcoming). Given that Fishbourne is an exceptional site and has already been identified as the location of a Roman park, the high frequency of hare in its assemblage may serve as a benchmark for the identification of parks, or rather *leporaria*, at other locations. With this in mind it is noteworthy that recent excavations at the Late Roman villa at Whitehall in Northamptonshire have yielded similarly large quantities of hare bones: their remains account for 2.8 per cent (123 of 4312 specimens) of the total mammal assemblage (Sykes *et al.*, 2011). Allen's (forthcoming) review of hare representation in Iron Age and Roman Britain highlights only two other sites where hare have been found in comparable frequencies: Caister-on-sea in Norfolk, where hare make up two per cent of the mammal assemblage, and Great Holts Farm in Essex (two and a half per cent). It is interesting to note that the wider biological assemblage from the villa at Great Holts Farm has been interpreted as reflecting a Mediterranean lifestyle, so the presence of a *leporarium* would certainly fit the character of the site (Murphy *et al.*, 2000; Locker, 2007, 150).

That it is possible to infer the presence of garden plots and parks in the absence of their physical remains appears something of methodological break-though; however, in reality, it is little more advanced than the traditional use of bioarchaeological evidence for environmental reconstruction – we need to consider the meaning of these spaces. Van der Veen with others (2008; *et al.*, 2008) has argued that that the emergence of horticulture should be seen as an economic and dietary innovation with implications for human nutrition and the way in which social and cultural identity were negotiated. A similar case has been made for the introduction and emparkment of fallow deer; that their ownership and consumption would have been symbols of social status (Sykes *et al.*, 2006; Sykes, 2010). Yet this concentration on plants and animals as 'products', 'nutrition' and 'symbols' is to overlook the inter-relationships that preceded these outcomes. It is important to remember that even where plants and animals were raised for only short periods (a few weeks or months) the majority of their associations with humans would have been played out whilst alive, the act of being processed and eaten representing a small, albeit intense, fraction of the total relationship. In situations where plants and animals were maintained for years it has to be expected that, as is found amongst most modern pastoral societies, bonds would have developed between them and the people with whom they dwelt (e.g Ingold, 2000). Indeed, it is the very process of dwelling that, according to

Ingold (2000, 208), constitutes landscape, and he argues that the temporality of dwelling needs to be considered if we are to understand the meaning of landscape. The study of plants and animals give us this perspective on time.

Wild animal enclosures and horticultural spaces, in particular orchards, have very specific temporalities, quite different from those of the fields beyond. Both deer parks and orchards are characterised by intense seasonality, where time is charted in a dramatic and highly sensory way by the annual cycle of development (leaves and blossom, antlers and the rut), bounty (fruit and fawns), colour change (autumn leaves and winter coats) and shedding (dropping leaves and casting of antlers). Whilst all temperate landscapes are seasonal, parks and gardens are set apart by the constancy of their constituent plants and animals: their life-spans are significantly longer than those of most domestic crops and livestock, allowing more complex relationships with humans to develop. For instance, ageing data for the Roman fallow deer indicate that, almost without exception, these animals were kept for many years before their eventual death and consumption. The rationale for their maintenance cannot have been secondary products because fallow deer provide none; even their antlers are unsuitable for bone working because the *compacta* is too thin, although they could feasibly have been powdered for medicine (a common use of antler in the Roman period). For this reason, it is clearly inappropriate to view parks simply as larders where venison was stored on-the-hoof; fallow deer were obviously appreciated for something other than their meat. We need to consider the possibility that fallow deer, and hence parks, were animals/spaces of life, valued for the emotional and sensory sustenance they provided. A similar case can be made for garden plots and orchards, especially since the latter take between 5–10 years to become productive (van der Veen *et al.*, 2008, 33). It seems unlikely that orchards would have been ignored until such time as they came of age; instead we may envisage that these places were appreciated in their own right, as landscapes of potential, filled with the different characters of their various trees and plants, all of which would have been performing hard to encourage people to look after them (Hitchins 2003). By the time they were productive, fruit trees would be embedded parts of the landscape, their branches already laden with meaning and memories.

These new animal enclosures and horticultural spaces would have been not only physically but also conceptually alien to the majority of the native population of Britain. At the most basic level their presence demonstrates that the socio-cultural groups responsible for their establishment perceived exotic plants and animals as being worth the expense of their upkeep – this itself is a cultural stance. Perhaps more importantly, however, the presence of *vivaria* and *leporaria* indicate that people believed they had the right to enclose wild animals. This is a key point which would seem to separate the ideologies of Iron Age and Roman society. Whilst both cultural groups saw nature and the wilderness as sacred, their beliefs appear to have manifested themselves in different ways. Archaeological and iconographic evidence indicate that the Iron Age population negotiated with the world around them, their cosmology reflected by the avoidance of wild resources and the ritual treatment of the animals derived from 'outside' (Green, 1992, 241; Aldhouse-Green, 2004). The Romans, on the other hand, saw it as their spiritual duty to bring the wilderness to order, investing their efforts in the paradox of domesticating the wild so that they might dwell, in the manner of their gods, in close proximity to the plants and animals that had been brought from beyond the shores of Britain (Coates, 1998, 27; Beagon, 1992, 55; 1996, 299; Purcell, 1987, 201; 1996).

Discussion and conclusion: plants and animals in the landscape

The ideological differences between the Iron Age and Roman population of Britain have long been recognised, so the argument presented here is hardly new. However, it does draw upon a source of data not traditionally embraced by landscape archaeologists – the evidence from plant and animal remains. I hope I have shown that bioarchaeological data have great potential to address questions beyond economic and environmental reconstruction. If viewed in the right way (as representing complex interactions with people and place) plant and animal remains can provide profitable insights into past cultural landscape, and therefore the cultures themselves. Here I have suggested that the Iron Age to Romano-British changes apparent in the bioarchaeological record are direct reflections of the way in which people engaged with, behaved in and thought about their environments. The introduction and establishment of new plants and animals during the Roman period was more significant than simply an increase in biodiversity or available nutrition; it would have brought new sights, sounds, smells and characters to the landscape. The management of these species, in particular the emparkment of exotic animals, would also have been a significant conceptual leap and, as proxy indicators for the presence of wild animal enclosures and horticultural spaces, the bioarchaeological data should be viewed as tangible evidence for a fundamental Iron Age to Romano-British shift in world view. Certainly the arrival of the exotic seems to have altered attitudes to the native, with an increase in wild plant gathering, fowling, fishing and hunting – activities through which people would have engaged with the elements and traversed the landscape in new ways, and probably at specific times.

The speed at which worldviews began to alter is currently uncertain and deserves further investigation; however, it is already apparent that some sites

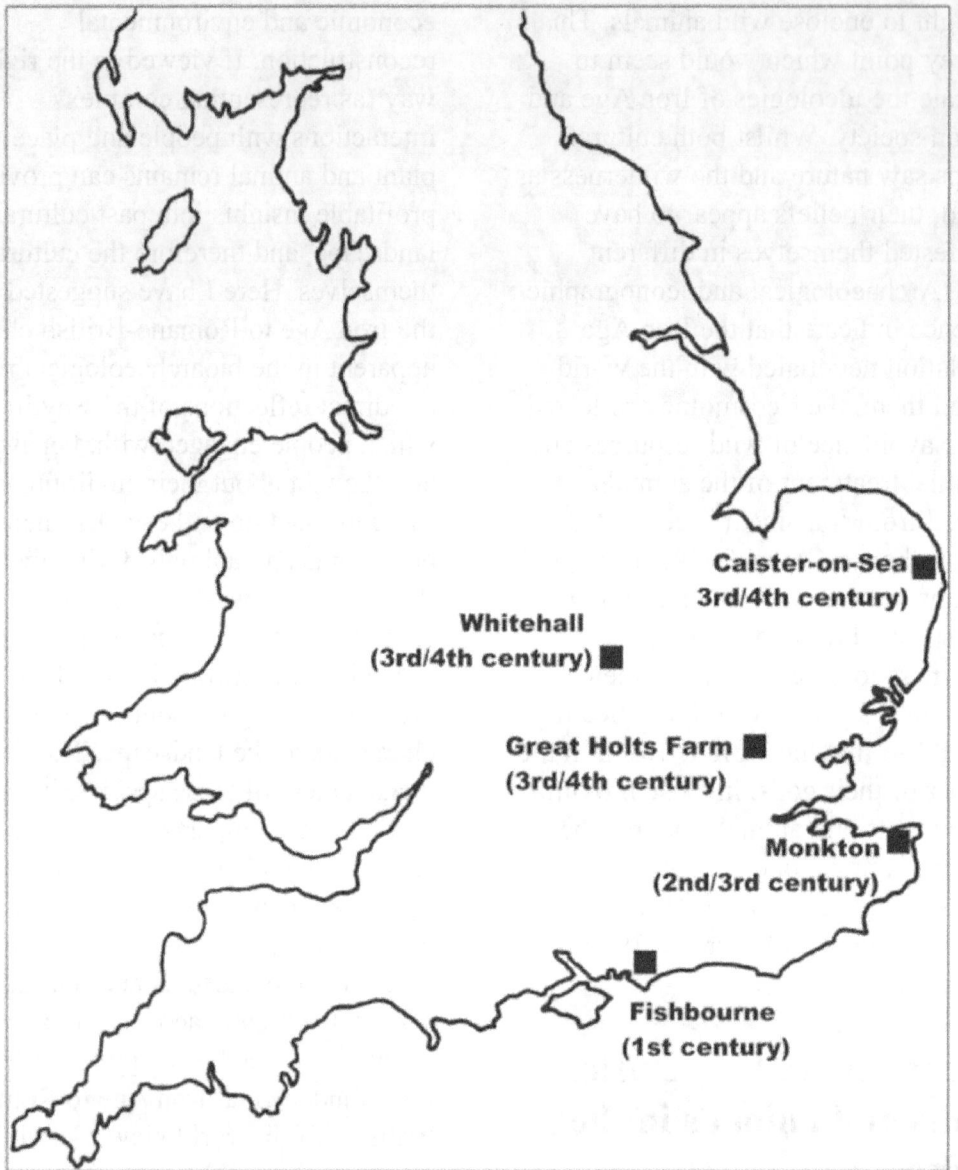

Figure 4. Location of possible Roman animal parks (vivaria/leporaria) identified using animal bone data.

indicate increased engagement with the wild before others. Fishbourne Palace is a good example. Here wild animals were being hunted and some exotic species (fallow deer and probably hares) were being emparked shortly after the Conquest, certainly by about AD 70. At less prestigious sites, emparkment seems to have been a much later phenomenon: for instance, the fallow deer remains from Monkton in Kent are most probably of late second or early third century date; the hare remains from Whitehall Roman villa in Northamptonshire are third to fourth century, and those from Caister-on-Sea in Norfolk and Great Holts Farm in Essex are late Roman (Figure 4). This suggests that AD 43 cannot be seen as a point at which the ideological polarity reversed – the situation was clearly more complex with new perspectives creeping in and merging with the old until, at some point, worldviews had gradually (and probably imperceptibly to those involved) been transformed. It would seem that the political elite, such as the owners of Fishbourne Palace, were quickest off the mark, consciously adopting Mediterranean attitudes to landscape and the natural order, perhaps, as Helms' (1993) work has highlighted, for the cosmological power that it would bestow upon them. But we should be wary of seeing landscape change as the preserve of the elite simply because there is more evidence for it. Maltby's (1997) study of the archaeological representation of domestic fowl demonstrated that these introduced birds were present at all site-types of Roman date. Admittedly, they are less abundant on low-status rural settlements but, as I have found in my own garden, just two birds can fundamentally change landscape and our perception of it.

The arrival and establishment of exotic plants and animals in Roman Britain would have been felt at all social levels, in different ways. Exotic species represent a small fraction of the human-animal-plant-landscape relationships experienced by people in Iron Age and Roman Britain. If studies are broadened out to examine a wider variety of relationships, and chronological periods, there is every reason to suspect that we can gain a fuller, more nuanced, vibrant and dynamic understanding of those past landscapes that people and other non-human actors worked together to create.

Acknowledgements

This paper was inspired by my galliform companions, Redwick and Marley; given the theme of this paper their contribution must be acknowledged. More practical help was provided by Martyn Allen, who kindly provided background data for the hare study and also read and commented upon an earlier version of the text. Steven Willis and Jim Morris also provided very useful feedback on the draft, for which I am very grateful. My thanks go also to the anonymous referee for their comments on the paper, to ORADS for funding the AMS dating of the fallow deer specimens from Monkton, and to both the University of Nottingham and the AHRC who supported the period of research leave in which this paper was written.

This paper first appeared in *Landscapes*, 2009 (2) and is published here with permission of the author and publisher (Oxbow).

References

Aldhouse-Green, M. (2004) *An Archaeology of Images: Iconology and cosmology in Iron Age Roman Europe*. Routledge, London.

Allen, M. (forthcoming) *Animalscapes and Empires: New Perspectives on the Iron Age/Romano-British transition*. Unpublished PhD University of Nottingham.

Beagon, M. (1992) *Roman Nature: The Thought of Pliny the Elder*. Clarendon Press, Oxford.

Beagon, M. (1996) *Nature and views of her landscapes in Pliny the Elder*. In: Salmon, J. and Shipley, G. (eds.) *Human Landscapes in Classical Antiquity: Environment and Culture*. Routledge, London, 284–309.

Bell, M. (1995) *People and nature in the Celtic world*. In: Green, M.J. (ed.) *The Celtic World*. Routledge, Oxford, 145–58.

Bendrey, R. (2003) *The identification of fallow deer (Dama dama) remains from Roman Monkton, the Isle of Thanet, Kent*. In: Riddler, I.D. (ed.) *Materials of Manufacture: The Choice of Materials in the Working of Bone and Antler in Northern and Central Europe During the First Millennium A.D.*. BAR International Series S1193, Oxford, 15–18.

Carroll, M. (2003) *Earthly Paradises: Ancient Gardens in History and Archaeology*. British Museum Press, London.

Coates, P. (1998) *Nature: Western Attitudes Since Ancient Times*. Polity Press, Cambridge.

Creighton, J. (1995) *Visions of power: imagery and symbols in Late Iron Age Britain*. Britannia, **26**, 285–301.

Creighton, O. (2009) *Designs Upon the Land: Elite Landscapes of the Middle Ages*. Boydell, Cambridge.

Cunliffe, B. (1981) *Roman gardens in Britain: a review of the evidence*. In: MacDougall, E.B. and Jashemski, W.F. (eds.) *Ancient Roman Gardens*. Dumbarton Oaks, Washinton, 95–108.

Cunliffe, B. (2000) *Landscapes with people*. In: Flint, K. and Morphy, H. (eds.) *Culture, Landscape and the Environment: The Linacre Lectures*. Oxford University Press, Oxford, 111–30.

Dobney, K. and Ervynck, A. (2007) *To fish or not to fish? Evidence for the possible avoidance of fish consumption during the Iron Age around the North Sea*. In: Haselgrove, C. and Moore, T. (eds.) *The Later Iron Age in Britain and Beyond*. Oxbow, Oxford, 403–18.

Farrar, L. (1996) *Gardens of Italy and the Western Roman Provinces of the Roman Empire from the 4th century BC to the 4th century A.D.*. BAR international series 650, Oxford.

Farrar, L. (1998) *Ancient Roman Gardens*. Sutton, Stroud.

Gardeisen, A. (ed.) (2002) *Mouvements ou Déplacements de Populations Animales en Méditerranée au cours de l'Holocène*. BAR International Series 1017, Oxford.

Gleason, K. L. (1994) *To bound and to cultivate: an introduction to the archaeology of gardens and fields*. In: Miller, N.F. and Gleason, K.L. (eds.) *The Archaeology of Garden and Field*. University of Pennsylvania Press, Philadelphia, 1–24.

Grant, A. (1984) *Animal husbandry Danebury: an Iron Age Hillfort*. In: Cunliffe, B. (ed.) *Hampshire. Volume 2. The Excavations 1969–1978: The Finds*. Council for British Archaeology Research Report 52, London, 102–19.

Green, M. (1992) *Animals in Celtic Life and Myth*. Routledge, London.

Hambleton, E. (2008) *Review of Middle Bronze Age to Late Iron Age Faunal Assemblages from Southern Britain*. English Heritage Research Report 71/2008.

Hamilakis, Y. (2003) *The sacred geography of hunting: wild animals, social power and gender in early farming societies*. In: Kotjabopoulou, E., Hamilakis, Y., Halstead, P., Gamble, C. and Elafanti, V. (eds.) *Zooarchaeology in Greece: Recent Advances*. British School at Athens, London, 239–47.

Handford, S.A. (1982) *Caesar: The Conquest of Gaul*. Penguin, London.

Head, L. and Atchinson, J. (2009) Cultural ecology: emerging human-plant geographies. *Progress in Human Geography*, **33(2)**, 236–45.

Helms, M. (1993) *Craft and the Kingly Ideal: Art Trade and Power*. University of Texas Press, Austin.

Hill, J.D. (1995) *Ritual and Rubbish in the Iron Age of Wessex: A Study on the Formation of a Specific Archaeological Record*. BAR British Series 242, Oxford.

Hitchings, R. (2003) People, plants and performance: on actor network theory and the material pleasures of the private garden. *Social and Cultural Geography*, **4(1)**, 99–113.

Hobbs, R.J. (2000) *Land-use changes and invasions*. In: Mooney, H.A. and Hobbs, R.J. (eds.) *Invasive Species in a Changing World*. Island Press, Washington D.C., 55–64.

Hughes, J.D. (2003) Europe as consumer of exotic biodiversity: Greek and Roman times. *Landscape Research*, **28(1)**, 21–31.

Ingold, T. (2000) *The Perception of the Environment: Essays in Livelihood, Dwelling and Skill*. Routledge, London.

Jashemski, W.F. (1981) *The Campanian peristyle garden*. In: MacDougall, E.B. and Jashemski, W.F. (eds.) *Ancient Roman Gardens*. Dumbarton Oaks, Washington, 29–48.

Jashemski, W.F. (1987) *Recently excavated gardens and cultivated land of the villa of Boscoreale and Oplontis*. In: MacDougall, E.B. (ed.) *Ancient Roman Villa Gardens*. Dumbarton Oaks, Washington D.C., 31–76.

Johnson, R. (2005) A social archaeology of garden plots in the Bronze Age of northern and western Britain. *World Archaeology*, **37(2)**, 211–23.

King, A. (1991) *Food production and consumption – meat*. In: Jones, R. *Britain in the Roman Period: Recent Trends*. J.R. Collis, Sheffield, 15–20.

King, A. (2005) Animal remains from temples in Roman Britain. *Britannia*, **36**, 329–69.

Lepetz S. and Yvinec J.-H. (2002) *Présence d'espèces animales d'origine méditerranéennes en France du nord aux périodes romaine et médiévale: actions anthropiques et mouvements naturels*. In: Gardeisen, A. (ed.) *Mouvements ou Déplacements de Populations Animales en Méditerranée au cours de l'Holocène*. BAR, International Series 1017, Oxford, 33–42.

Livarda, A. (2008) *New temptations? Olive, cherry and mulberry in Roman and Medieval Europe*. In: Baker, S., Allen, M., Middle, S. and Poole, K. (eds.) *Food and Drink in Archaeology 1*. Prospect Books, Totnes, 73–83.

Locker, A. (2007) In *piscibus diversis*; the bones evidence for fish consumption in Roman Britain. *Britannia*, **38**, 141–180.

Maltby, M. (1997) Domestic fowl on Romano-British sites; inter-site comparisons of abundance. *International Journal of Osteoarchaeology*, **7**, 402–14.

Masseti, M. (2002) *Island of Deer*. City of Rhodes Environment Organisation, Rhodes.

Moore, T. (2007) Perceiving communities: exchange, landscapes and social networks in the later Iron Age of Western Britain. *Oxford Journal of Archaeology*, **26(1)**, 79–102.

Morris, J.T. (2008) *Re-examining Associated Bone Groups from Southern England and Yorkshire, c.4000BC to A.D.1550*. unpublished PhD, University of Bournemouth, Bournemouth.

Murphy, P., Albarella, U., Germany, M. and Locker, A. (2000) Production, imports and status: biological remains from a Late Roman farm, Great Holts Farm, Boreham, Essex. *Environmental Archaeology*, **5**, 35–48.

Petts, D. (1998) *Landscape and cultural identity in Roman Britain*. In: Laurence, R. and Berry, J. (eds.) *Cultural Identity in the Roman Empire*. Routledge, London, 79–94.

Philo, C. and Wilbert, C. (2000) *Animal Spaces, Beastly Places: New Geographies of Human-Animal Relations*. Routledge, London.

Pieroni, A. and Leimar Price, L. (2006) *Eating and Healing: Traditional Food as Medicine*. Haworth Press, New York.

Pluskowski, A.G. (2007) *The social construction of medieval park ecosystems: an interdisciplinary perspective*. In: Liddiard, R. (ed.) *The Medieval Park: New Perspectives*. Windgather Press, Macclesfield, 63–78.

Poole, K. (2010) *Bird introductions*. In: O'Connor, T. and Sykes, N. (eds.) *Extinctions and Invasions: A Social History of British Fauna*. Windgather Press, Oxford, 156-165.

Purcell, N. (1987) *Town in country and country in town*. In: MacDougall, E.B. (ed.) *Ancient Roman Villa Gardens*. Dumbarton Oaks, Washington D.C., 185–204.

Purcell, N. (1996) *Rome and the management of water: environment, culture and power*. In: Salmon, J. and Shipley, G. (eds.) *Human Landscapes in Classical Antiquity: Environment and Culture*. Routledge, London, 180–212.

Rogers, A. (2007) *Beyond the economic in the Roman fenland; reconsidering land, water and religion*. In: Flemming, A. and Hingley, R. (eds.) *Prehistoric and Roman Landscapes*. Windgather Press, Macclesfield, 113–30.

Rogers, A.C. (2008) Religious place and its interaction with urbaniszation in the Roman era. *Journal of Social Archaeology*, **8**, 37–62.

Schwabe, C.W. (1994) *Animals in the ancient world*. In: Manning, A. and Serpell, J. (eds.) *Animals and Human Society: Changing Perspectives*. Routledge, London, 36–58.

Sykes, N.J. (2004) The introduction of fallow deer (*Dama dama*): a zooarchaeological perspective. *Environmental Archaeology*, **9**, 75–83.

Sykes, N.J. (2007) *Animal bones and animal parks*. In: Liddiard, R. (ed.) *The Medieval Deer Park: New Perspectives*. Windgather Press, Macclesfield, 49–62.

Sykes, N.J. (in prep) *Husbandry, Hares and Feasting: The Animal Remains from Whitehall Roman Villa, Northamptonshire*. unpublished Bioarchaeology Research Laboratory Report to CLASP.

Sykes, N.J., White, J., Hayes, T. and Palmer, M. (2006) Tracking animals using strontium isotopes in teeth: the role of fallow deer (*Dama dama*) in Roman Britain. *Antiquity*, **80**, 948–59.

Sykes, N.J. and Curl, J. (2010) *The rabbit*. In: O'Connor, T. and Sykes, N. (eds.) *Extinctions and Invasions: A Social History of British Fauna*. Windgather Press, Oxford, 116-2.

Sykes, N.J., Baker, K., Carden, R.F., Higham, T.F.G, Hoelzel, R. and Stevens, R.E. (2011) New evidence for the establishment and management of fallow deer (*Dama dama dama*) in Roman Europe with specific reference to Britain. *Journal of Archaeological Science*, **38(1)**, 156-65.

Taylor, J. (1997) *Space and place: some thoughts on Iron Age and Romano-British landscapes*. In: Gwilt, A. and Haselgrove, C. (eds.) *Reconstructing Iron Age Societies: New Approaches to the British Iron Age*. Oxbow Books, Oxford.

Taylor, J. (2007) *An Atlas of Roman Rural Settlement in England*. CBA Research Report 151, London.

Van der Veen, M. (2005) Gardens and fields: the intensity and scale of food production. *World Archaeology*, **37(2)**, 157–63.

Van der Veen, M. (2008) Food as embodied material culture: diversity and change in plant food consumption in Roman Britain. *Journal of Roman Archaeology*, **21**, 83–110.

Van der Veen, M., Livarda, A. and Hill, A. (2008) New plant foods in Roman Britain – dispersal and social access, *Environmental Archaeology*, **13(1)**, 11–35.

Whatmore, S. and Thorne, L. (1998) Wild(er)ness: reconfiguring the geographies of wildlife. *Transactions of the Institute of British Geographers*, **23(4)**, 435–54.

Willis, S. (2007) *Sea, coast, estuary, land and culture in Iron Age Britain*. In: Haselgrove, C. and Moore, T. (eds.) *The Later Iron Age in Britain and Beyond*, Oxbow, Oxford, 107–29.

Willis, S. (2008) *Roman towns, Roman landscapes: the cultural terrain of town and country in the Roman period*. In: Flemming, A. and Hingley, R. (eds.) *Prehistoric and Roman Landscapes*. Windgather Press, Macclesfield, 143–64.

Wolch, J. and Emel, J. (1998) *Animal Geographies: Place, Politics and identity in the Nature-Culture Borderlands*. Verso, London.

Yalden, D. (1999) *A History of British Mammals*. T. and A. Poyser, London.

Yalden, D. (2010) *Conclusion*. In: O'Connor, T. and Sykes, N. (eds.) *Extinctions and Invasions: A Social History of British Fauna*. Windgather Press, Oxford, 190-196.

Yalden, D. and Albarella, U. (2008) *The History of British Birds*. Oxford University Press, Oxford.

Zeepvat, R.J. (1991) *Roman gardens in Britain*. In: Brown, A.E. (ed.) *Garden Archaeology*. CBA Research Report 78, London, 53–59.

Integrating Trees into Modern Agriculture
Michael J. Townsend
Woodland Trust

A managed landscape

It is axiomatic that the British landscape is a managed landscape. Almost no part has avoided use or exploitation (Simmons, 2001). Much of what we now treasure and value is the emergent result of human struggle to wrest a living from the land, harnessing what nature provides and shaping it to our ends. Throughout much of history the view of the countryside has been a utilitarian one, harvesting what could be harvested and protecting 'nature' only insofar as it provided for our needs. We have seen value in use, and safeguarded that which provides value.

When our needs have changed or could be met in other ways we have abandoned what went before and adopted new approaches and management. There has been little nostalgic attachment to tradition where progress made life easier, and no time to waste on unprofitable labour. Trees have been part of the managed landscape and expected to pay their way.

Previous generations did not farm in order to protect trees and woods; they protected trees and woods for the use they provided or because they occupied places where farming was problematic. Trees and woodland had no teleological existence. Their conservation as an end in itself didn't fuel fires, make charcoal, shelter stock or provide timber – value came through use.

Nonetheless, the limitations of preindustrial agriculture meant that insofar as the landscape changed it changed more gradually or with fewer consequences for the nature it supported. As Rackham (1986) noted... 'much of England in 1945 would have been instantly recognisable by Sir Thomas More and some areas would have been recognised by the Emperor Claudius'.

Post war Britain

For the British countryside that changed after the Second World War. Urgent and (given the shock of two world wars) understandable support for increased production saw greater mechanisation, increasing field sizes, a loss of many mixed farms, and increased use of fertilisers and agrochemicals. A watershed moment in understanding some of the consequences of this rush to increased production came with the publication of Rachel Carson's *Silent Spring* (Carson, 1962). The concept of food chains and connected ecosystems was given meaning, and gave birth to much of modern environmentalism.

The period since the 1960s, has seen successive attempts to mitigate some of the worst impacts of modern agriculture on wildlife. In general these have taken the form of grants to encourage activities which, at the margins (quite literally in the case of some measures for arable fields), attempt to protect wildlife. Nature conservation seeks to protect that which remains of habitats, to insert conservation into farming, to limit its destructive power, and to create pockets and strips of safe haven for wildlife. These can be legitimate and important measures. They provide the source populations for conservation which we hope will lead to their survival, revival and expansion.

This approach sees agriculture and nature as opposing and contradictory forces. It is easy, at least in an audience of nature conservationists, to knock agriculture. But technology and its application to agriculture have brought huge benefits in terms of increased production. We want to see wildlife, but we also want guaranteed and cheap food. Whatever people say about a willingness to pay more for our food, not many exhibit the behaviours that reflect this stated preference (Carrigan and Attalla, 2001).

Food security and protecting nature

The narrative of food and farming is again on the move. Food security is gaining hegemonic status. An increasingly productivist language permeates discussions of agricultural policy. This is understandable; whether you believe the figures for the ultimate projected size of the world's population or not, there are more of us today than yesterday and there will be more again tomorrow. We are likely to want agriculture to produce more.

At the same time there is recognition that nature is important. Not just as a source of wonderment and delight, but as foundational to almost everything upon which we rely, and which we have come to label 'ecosystem services'. Importantly nature is of course foundational to agriculture; for healthy soil, pollinating insects and predators of pests, for regulating the climate, and the availability of plentiful and clean water.

Agriculture needs to find a way to increase production whilst also maintaining, or better still, improving, the condition of nature. Equally, if we want continued support for existing trees in the countryside and, critically, see future generations of trees which can provide the landscape and ecosystem functions which are of importance, then we need to find a way to integrate trees into farming systems which will simultaneously be trying to produce more food.

Integration of nature into the landscape is also apparent in *Making Space for Nature*, the review of England's protected areas (Lawton *et al.,* 2010). The review emphasises the need to protect and expand existing habitat and to generate connections and a network across the landscape, both to help wildlife respond to climate change, but also to...' provide a range of high quality ecosystem services today and in the future'.

Giving value to trees

An approach to these, at times, apparently paradoxical aims, is to give value to trees beyond that ascribed to conservation objectives alone and to make that value understood. To understand that integration should reflect not just nature conservation and landscape objectives, but should be seen to meet the needs of farming and of society, and thereby secure value in use.

Supporters of intrinsic value of nature as reason enough to ensure protection, may despair at the idea of nature being reduced to a utilitarian calculus. It would be possible to conduct a semantic debate about the intrinsic value of nature and whether this is important, but in the context of the British countryside this might seem rather redundant. Nature does not exist regardless of human activity in most of Britain; it exists despite it and alongside it. But importantly human existence cannot continue regardless of nature.

It is this interdependence, which is hardly a new concept, which has begun to be codified in the *UK National Ecosystem Assessment* (2011) and, in England, the *Natural Environment White Paper* (2011). Both documents stress the importance of trees and woods in the delivery of ecosystem services. Can ecosystem services become more than a rhetorical device and provide a framework for the proper integration of nature, and in this case trees in particular, into farming practice and the countryside?

Sustainable intensification and 'first mover' problems

'Sustainable intensification' of agriculture, which at first has the appearance of an oxymoron, may also be suggesting a similar approach; a need to reconcile greater production from agriculture with greater protection for the natural elements which support it and vice versa (Godfray *et al.*, 2010). If we fail to make this reconciliation then, aside from the possible dire long term consequences for agriculture, there are more immediate consequences for nature. Greater intensification of agriculture which does not recognise the interdependence on the natural world is likely to be destructive.

Each farming unit makes decisions based on a range of factors including current farming system, economic viability, security of income, tradition and knowledge base, and other motivational factors (Townsend, 2008). Decisions on nature conservation measures are, in large part, driven by the system of subsidies and cross compliance arrangements under the Common Agricultural Policy (CAP) and any national designed conservation schemes. These aim to reward farmers for environmental actions or compensate them for income foregone.

However, schemes for reward or compensation suffer from the 'first mover problem' (Bowers, 1997). First mover problems occur when changing circumstances make the income from conservation measures for biodiversity less than the income from farming. In a world of rising agricultural commodity prices, concerns over food security, and pressures on budgets, staying ahead of the game on conservation subsidies becomes increasingly parlous.

In order to be valued, conservation of trees or new planting (whether as woodland or more scattered trees in the landscape) must work with the grain productive agriculture and the motivations of individual landowners.

Notwithstanding the power of subsidies, Slee et al. (2006) identified a core of 'productivist' farmers who are uninterested in optional entry environmental enhancement schemes, even where there is income to be gained level. In order for these farmers to engage more fully with environmental enhancement schemes, such schemes need to be contributing to the 'symbolic capital', the social cultural and material items of value to farmers. As the narrative around food security strengthens, good husbandry will increasingly mean productive agriculture. Unless environmental measures are seen as contributing to this narrative then their adoption is likely to be poor or fail. On the other hand, where trees can be seen to support productive agriculture then they will promote adoption, possibly without the impetus of subsidies.

Conservation of trees and woods

The conservation of existing trees is important. Surviving ancient woodland within the agricultural landscape is recognised as valuable for wildlife. But a report to the Woodland Trust by Brown and Fisher (2009) also identified the value of trees outside woods (TOWS). The report found that while the communities associated with TOWs may be qualitatively different from those of woodland (Ozanne et al., 2000) they often contain a significant component of woodland specialist species.

Isolated ancient trees are often relics of former old-growth woodland and may constitute a distinct and important genetic resource which, in addition to their own importance, may harbour a rich and distinctive community of wood-decay invertebrates, fungi, lichens and epiphytes (Butler et al., 2001). Trees integrated into hedgerows can also be important for supporting invertebrates, including pollinating insects (Merckx, 2009, 2009a).

Any future agricultural landscape will need to protect and manage these trees as a resource which supplies at least some of the ecosystem services needed.

Increasing tree cover

There are however, a number of compelling reasons for farmers and landowners, and for wider society, to increase tree cover in the farmed landscape. In some cases measures will have a direct benefit to individual farms e.g. in the management of livestock or production of woodfuel, or may benefit the sector e.g. reduction in greenhouse gas emissions from agriculture. In other cases they may represent wider social benefits (public goods) e.g. improvements to water courses. Both the National Ecosystem Assessment and the Natural Environment White Paper made clear the value and importance of trees in the delivery of public goods, particularly in water management, but also in the provision of shade and shelter.

Climate change in particular creates a need for urgent action. Climate change is predicted to increase summer droughts particularly in the south and east, but with milder winter temperatures and higher winter rainfall especially in the west of the country (UKCIP, 2011, http://www.ukcip.org.uk/index.php?option=com_content&task=view&id=41&Itemid=142, accessed 6th July 2011). There is likely to be an increase in severe weather events including heat waves, higher intensity rainfall and storms. This will have consequences for both livestock and arable producers (Commission for the European Communities, 2009).

A 2009 survey showed that half of all farmers already believe they are being affected by climate change, and over 60% expect to be affected in the next ten years (Forum for the Future available at: http://www.forumforthefuture.org/node/3029, accessed 12th June 2011). The imperative to respond in some way is therefore, not an alien concept.

Pontbren Farmers

Pontbren Farmers in mid Wales, was formed in 1997 and grew to the current ten farms in 2001 (Pontbren Farmers, http://www.pontbrenfarmers.co.uk/env_work.html, accessed 6th July 2011). The group farm around 1,000 ha around a stream catchment in Powys. Increasing costs and an ill-suited subsidy system, led them to take measures into their own hands – designing and undertaking work which met their needs and then, if needed, seeking the funding support. Degradation of the tree cover on the farms had meant a loss of shelter for livestock and rainwater runoff from the fields which was affecting pasture fertility. By restoring hedges and increasing tree cover on the farms they have had a dramatic impact on runoff to streams, improving pasture growth, but also improving stream water quality and peak flows.

The increased shelter and a change to the sheep breed has permitted lambing outside, and careful siting of the shelter belts has allowed for sheep to be excluded from wet areas previously prone to encourage foot rot. Pasture growth and productivity has increased, but so has the level of care for existing trees and the overall tree cover on the farms. Over 120,000 trees have been planted and 16.5 miles of hedges restored, whilst making the management of the livestock easier and more productive.

This scheme is driven by the need to manage sheep and livestock, but the result is also increased tree cover and an increase in biodiversity and improved water management (Bird *et al.*, 2003; Chel *et al,* 2008). Whilst the farmers within this area are witness to the wildlife benefits their care for trees has yielded, they have managed their trees to help with their animal husbandry.

Shade and shelter

Rising summer temperatures and greater solar radiation will increase heat stress to both housed and outdoor livestock. Heat stress affects both animal welfare and production. For instance dairy cattle have reduced milk yields when subject to heat stress (Mayer *et al.*, 1999). In countries already facing higher temperatures and heat stress for dairy cattle and other livestock, integrated provision of shade is already considered. Trees reduce direct solar radiation on livestock and also reduce ambient air temperature through latent heat absorbed during transpiration (Escobedo and Zipperer, 2009).

In Australia advice is available on the integration of trees into dairy farms (Dairy Australia, http://www.coolcows.com.au/Infrastructure/Paddocks%20and%20laneways/trees-for-shade-case-study.htm, accessed 6th June 2011). New Zealand dairy farmers are also encouraged to plant trees as a cost effective way to provide shade (Farm Forestry New Zealand, http://www.nzffa.org.nz/farm-forestry-model/resource-centre/tree-grower-articles/tree-grower-february-2009/in-summer-shade-rules-the-science-behind-why-trees-help-maintain-dairy-productivity/, accessed 6th July 2011).

Increasing in-field shade from trees is not necessarily in conflict with productivity of pasture, as the shelter effects can provide positive benefits by increasing water infiltration and reducing evapotranspiration loss from pasture (Macaulay Land Use Research Institute, 2009). In addition the trees can produce timber, fodder and bedding for housed livestock (Centre for Alternative Land Use, 2005). The latter can have cost advantages over straw bedding and has been shown to reduce the release of volatile nitrogen compounds into the air.

Greater frequency of storms increases the need for shelter for livestock. Shelter can have a positive impact on pasture growth and has been shown for instance to increase lambing percentage and yields of wool from sheep reared in sheltered pastures (Bird, 1988). Shelter also increases the food efficiency of other outdoor housed livestock through reduction in the chill factor (Slusher and Wallace, 1997).

Greenhouse gas emissions

Agriculture is responsible for around 7% of UK GHG emissions. Livestock farms make a significant contribution to emissions through methane emissions directly from livestock and their waste, but other parts of the farming system also contribute. The planting of trees on farms, for whatever purpose, will have some benefit in sequestering atmospheric carbon. In addition shelter for housing and buildings can reduce energy consumption and CO_2 emissions, as well as improving the feed conversion of livestock.

Trees can be used in a number of ways to mitigate pollution from farming. Livestock units, particularly intensive poultry and pig unit, emit ammonia. Trees located close to livestock units are able to intercept a part of these emissions through dry deposition on the leaf and bark surfaces of the trees (Theobald et al., 2001). The high leaf surface to ground area ratio of trees, electrostatically charged leaf surfaces and the three dimensional structure of trees makes them particularly effective and scavenging air borne pollutants. Trees located around farm building and livestock units can, in addition to the benefits of shelter and shade, contribute towards the mitigation of air borne pollutants.

Conclusions

The relationship between trees, man and animals is, inevitably, changing. It is part of a larger change in the relationship and understanding of the importance of 'nature' to the functioning of agriculture and other systems which provide the things we need. We are at one of those moments when the path divides. The pressures to increase agricultural production are likely to lead to calls for greater intensification of land use. An appeal to the model which separates nature into reserves seems likely to lead to further decline. We need to break from a dichotomous system which sees agricultural production as something separate from trees and woods, and something separate from nature conservation.

The National Ecosystem Assessment, the Natural Environment White Paper and '*Making Space for Nature*' all emphasise the need for and benefits from increased tree cover and other measures. But these appeals for action at a national level need also to address action at a farm scale, where decisions about land use are made.

We need to find ways to integrate nature, and in this case trees in particular, into agriculture in such a way that it supports both nature and production. Whether this is labelled as 'sustainable intensification' or some other appellation matters little as long as it is done. For agriculture there is the necessity of a healthy natural environment to support productivity, and for nature the necessity of an agricultural system that can help in creating cohesive networks.

References

Bird S.B., Emmett B.A., Sinclair F.L., Stevens P.A., Reynolds B., Nicholson S. and Jones T. (2003) *Pontbren: Effects of tree planting on agricultural soils and their functions*. Final Report, March 2003, available at: http://www.ceh.ac.uk/sections/bef/Pontbren_report.html, [accessed 6th July 2011)

Bird, P.R. (1988) *Financial gains of trees on farms through shelter, the international forestry conference for the Australian Bicentenary 1988*. Proceedings of papers contributed Volume II of V. Albury-Wodonga 25th April-1st May 1988

Bowers, J. (1997) *Suitability and Environmental Economics*. Pearson Education Limited, Harlow, p.211

Brown, N. and Fisher. R. (2009) *Trees outside woodlands – a report to the Woodland Trust*. December 2009, unpublished.

Butler, J.E., Rose, F. and Green, T.E. (2001) *Ancient trees: icons of our most important wooded landscaped in Europe*. In: Andersson, L., Marciau, R., Paltto, H., Tardy, B. and Read, H. (eds.) *Tools for Preserving Woodland Biodiversity*. pp. 20–26. Töreboda Tryckeri AB, Sweden.

Carrigan, M. and Attalla, A. (2001) The myth of the ethical consumer – do ethics matter in purchase behaviour? *Journal of Consumer Marketing*, **18 (7)**, 560 – 578.

Carson, R. (1962) *Silent Spring*. Houghton Miflin, Chicago.

Centre for Alternative Land Use (2005) *Woodchip for animal bedding and compost*. Technical Note, available at: http://www.calu.bangor.ac.uk/Technical%20leaflets/050104woodchipbeddingcompostrev3.pdf, [accessed 12th June 2011].

Chel, J., Francis, O., Frogbrook, Z., Jackson, B., Marshall, M., Mcintyre, N. Reynolds, B., Solloway, I. and Wheater, H. (2008) *Impacts of upland land management on flood risk: multi-scale modelling methodology and results from Pontbren experiment*. Flood Risk Management Research Consortium, Research Report UR16.

Commission for the European Communities (2009) *Adapting to climate change: the challenge for European agriculture and rural areas*. Commission Working Document, available at: http://www.uknlo.gov.uk/docs/DG%20Agri%20Working%20Document.doc, [accessed 12th June 2011].

Escobedo, F., Seitz, J.A. and Zipperer, W. (2009) *Air Pollution Removal and Temperature Reduction by Gainesville's Urban Forest*. University of Florida, Florida.

Godfray, H.C.J., Beddington, J.R., Crute, I.R., Haddad, L., Lawrence, D., Muir, J.F., Pretty, J., Robinson, S., Thomas, S.M. and Toulmin, C. (2010) Food Security: The Challenge of Feeding 9 Billion. *Science*, **327**, 812-818.

Lawton, J.H., Brotherton, P.N.M., Brown, V.K., Elphick, C., Fitter, A.H., Forshaw, J., Haddow, R.W., Hilborne, S., Leafe, R.N., Mace, G.M., Southgate, M.P., Sutherland, W.J., Tew, T.E., Varley, J. and Wynne, G.R. (2010) *Making Space for Nature: a review of England's wildlife sites and ecological network*. Report to Defra, London.

Macaulay Land Use Research Institute (2009) *Agroforestry Forum*. available at: http://www.macaulay.ac.uk/agfor_toolbox/manage.html, [accessed 12th June 2011].

Mayer, D.G., Davison, T.M., McGowan, M.R., Young, B.A., Goodwin, P.J., Jonsson, N.N., Gaughan, J.B. and Matschoss. A.L. (1999) Extent and economic effect of heat loads on dairy cattle production in Australia. *Australian Veterinary Journal*, **77 (12)**, 804–808.

Merckx, T., Feber, R.E., Dulieu, R.L., Townsend, M.C., Parsons, M.S., Bourn, N.A.D, Riordan, P. and MacDonald, D.W. (2009) Effect of field margins on moths depends on species mobility: field-based evidence for landscape-scale conservation. *Agriculture, Ecosystems and Environment*, **129**, 302-309.

Merckx, T., Feber, R.E., Riordan, P., Townsend, M.C., Bourn, N.A.D., Parsons, M.S. and Macdonald, D.W. (2009a) Optimising the gain from agri-environment schemes. *Agriculture, Ecosystems and Environment*, **130**, 177-182.

Natural Environment White Paper (2011) *Natural Choice – securing the value of nature*. DEFRA, HMSO, London.

Ozanne, C.M.P., Speight, M.R., Hambler, C. and Evans, H.F. (2000) Isolated trees and forest patches: Patterns in canopy arthropod abundance and diversity in *Pinus sylvestris* (Scots Pine). *Forest Ecology and Management*, **137**, 53-63.

Rackham, O. (1986) *A History of the Countryside*. Dent & Sons, London., p. 26

Simmons, I.G. (2001) *An environmental History of Great Britain*. Edinburgh University Press, Edinburgh, p. 8

Slee, W., Gibbon, D., and Taylor, J. (2006) *Habitus and style of farming in explaining the adoption of environmental sustainability-enhancing behaviour*. Final report, University of Gloucester Countryside and Community Research Unit.

Slusher, J.P. and Wallace, D. (1997) *Planning tree windbreaks in Missouri*. MU Guide G5900. University Extension, University of Missouri-Columbia, Columbia.

Theobald, M.R., Milford C., Hargreaves K.J., Sheppard L.J., Nemitz E., Tang Y.S., Phillips V.R., Sneath R., McCartney L., Harvey F.J., Leith I.D., Cape J.N., Fowler D. and Sutton M.A. (2001) *Potential for ammonia recapture by farm woodlands: design and application of a new experimental facility*. The Scientific World, downloaded at; http://www.cababstractsplus.org/abstracts/Abstract.aspx?AcNo=20023039112 .

Townsend, M. (2008) *Who owns land in the UK and why might they want to plant trees?* Woodland Trust, unpublished.

UK National Ecosystem Assessment (2011) *The UK National Ecosystem Assessment: Synthesis of the Key Findings*. UNEP-WCMC, Cambridge.

Can't see the trees for the forest
Frans Vera

Introduction

When it comes to trees, it seems that we can't see them for the forest. It is the forest that regenerates or returns, not the trees.

However, in the forest, many of the individual characteristics that a tree displays cannot develop. The restricted availability of, and the competition for, daylight leads to a uniformity in the shape of trees. They develop long branchless slender stems and small crowns. It is precisely because of the unrestricted availability of daylight outside the forest that the individual characteristics of a tree show to full advantage. There they develop a short thick stem and a low, large crown with thick curved branches. They attain such impressive grandeur and solidity that, despite their multiplicity, they can be recognized individually. Such trees become etched in the memory of local people and traditionally are used as beacons in the landscape.

The forest that impoverishes the shape of trees does exactly the same for biodiversity. It devours the natural ecosystem at the trophic level of large indigenous herbivores. They are either removed, like cattle and horse, or culled to such a low density, like deer, that they become almost invisible, and certainly non-functional, elements in the system. This "management" leads to a cascading effect, including the disappearance of light-demanding plants, such as the two species of oak that are indigenous to Western and Central Europe; as well as of all indigenous shrubs species - with the exception of Honeysuckle - and many species of grasses and herbs. A major shift occurs towards the system of a forest, characterized by the dominance of a few shade-tolerant tree species, such as beech, lime, hornbeam, elm, ash and field maple; which gives rise to a catastrophic shift in biodiversity.

What lies behind the removal of large herbivores' influence on the succession of the vegetation?

1. Linear succession in areas where the effect of large herbivores on vegetation has been eliminated to such an extent that a forest develops spontaneously.

2. Scientific definition of this forest as the baseline for the natural conditions.

3. Claims that large indigenous herbivores in high densities prevent the regeneration of the forest unnaturally, because under natural conditions there should be a forest.

I want to make clear that there is an ecosystem with densities of large herbivores that indeed prevent the regeneration of the forest, yet at the same time create the conditions for the successful regeneration of trees. This system is that of park-like wood-pasture. It is not – as is often scientifically stated - a high forest that has been degraded into a park-like landscape because large indigenous herbivores prevent regeneration of the forest. It is a well-functioning ecosystem in itself.

It consists of a kaleidoscope of grassland, fringe and mantle vegetation, open fully-grown trees, and groves (forests). Large herbivores, especially specialized indigenous grazers like horses and cattle, facilitate the regeneration of trees by creating the conditions for seedling survival through associational resistance. This enables palatable trees and shrubs to grow up under the protection of certain light-demanding so-called nurse species, that are able to establish in grassland grazed by those large herbivores. These nurse-species are shrubs and herbs that are unpalatable because they possess spines, thorns or toxic chemicals. Their effect is like barbed wire.

In this way single trees grow up, as well as groups which develop into groves that can be considered as analogues to a forest. The single trees become impressive open-grown trees with short stems and large crowns, while in the groves the trees are forest-grown, that is they have long slender branchless stems and small crowns. When open-grown trees in the grassland eventually die, only grassland is left. Meanwhile, large herbivores impede regeneration of trees in the grove (forest) so grassland can return there also. With this return a circle is closed, and the process of seedling survival through associational resistance can develop again in the grazed grassland, initiating a new succession from grassland to single trees and groves mediated by nurse species.

Large herbivores in this way modulate the system into a non-linear succession that starts in grassland, goes through a stage of shrubs, then solitary trees, and ends in grazed grassland again, where the cycle starts once more with the processes of associational resistance. It depends also on the fertility of the soil, which determines the densities of large herbivores, and so the area of grassland, the opportunity for nurse species to establish there, and the frequency of solitary trees and groves.

This non-linear succession mediated by large herbivores results in a kaleidoscope of vegetation types making wood-pasture a tree-scape with the greatest diversity of tree forms and the highest biodiversity of life forms.

References

Vera, F., Buissink, F. and Weidema, J. (2004) *Wildernis in Nederland*. Het verhaal van bossen en beesten, page 85. Tirion Uitgevers BV, Baarn.

Vera, F. (2007) The wood-pasture theory and the deer park: the grove – the origin of the deer park. *Landscape Archaeology and Ecology*, **6**, 107-112.

Yarncliff Wood at Hathersage: initial assessment of the impacts of sixty years of sheep exclosure on an upland Pennine ancient wood

Ondřej Vild [1,2,3] & Ian D. Rotherham[3]

[1] Institute of Botany, Department of Vegetation Ecology, Academy of Sciences of the Czech Republic, Lidická 25/27, Brno, 603 00, Czech Republic.
[2] Masaryk University, Department of Botany and Zoology, Kotlářská 2, Brno, 611 37, Czech Republic.
[3] Sheffield Hallam University, Faculty of Development & Society, Pond Street, Sheffield S1 1WB, United Kingdom

Introduction

Yarncliff Wood (or Padley Gorge) is located 53°18' N, 1°37' W, south-west of Sheffield and on the eastern edge of the Derbyshire Peak District in the UK. It is a southeast facing, upland ancient wood, dominated by oak (*Quercus petraea* agg.). At the end of the 1970s, there had been almost no tree regeneration at least since 1852 (Pigott, 1983). To find out if the regeneration was blocked by extreme climatic conditions or sheep grazing, a fence (1.12 ha) was constructed in 1955 to exclude sheep. Since then, the site has been surveyed several times (Jarvis, 1960; Earvey, 1977; Anderson, 1978; Pigott, 1983). In particular, Donald Pigott carried out detailed site surveys with students from the Department of Botany at the University of Sheffield, and then re-surveyed the site following a period of exclusion of grazing. This was written up and presented in Pigott (1983), and was a uniquely important contribution to the understanding of the ecological dynamics of upland oakwood ecology in Britain.

Moreover, following concerns over the adverse impacts of intensive sheep grazing on Peak District upland oakwoods, expressed by the Peak Park Wildlife Advisory Group, a larger area of the wood was enclosed to exclude sheep in the early 1980s. In both the smaller original enclosure, and in the larger and later enclosure, a significant vegetation change was observed. This change included vigorous tree and shrub regeneration and the re-appearance of 'ancient woodland indicators' and other herbaceous plants in the ground flora. These observations supported the suggestion of the significance of former sheep grazing. However, no systematic survey has been done since 1981. Penny Anderson described the ecology and vegetation of these woods in Anderson & Shimwell (1981) and this is a good starting point in understanding the ecology and management of these acidic upland oakwoods.

This present study aims to describe the situation as it has established in the past three decades. Furthermore, the ongoing work will place the Yarncliff Wood study into the emerging context of 'Shadow Woods' and of historic woodland management as highlighted by the *Woodland Heritage Manual* (2008).

Field survey

Altogether twenty-four plots (twelve, five and seven in the old enclosure, new enclosure and outside, respectively) were placed randomly within the study area. The plots were squares of 100-metre quadrats, where all vascular plant species were recorded and tree seedlings (below sixty cm) counted. Tree composition was studied in a smaller area (0.34 ha) within the old enclosure. These data were compared with the previous research of Pigott (1983). Two age categories were distinguished: (a) individuals younger ('seedlings') and (b) older than one year ('saplings' and 'trees'). Additionally, to indicate the age distribution of regenerating trees, height and girth 0.3 m above ground of all individuals (of girth < 500 cm and higher than sixty cm) were measured. In addition, individuals of a greater girth not recorded in 1981 were included.

Results and Discussion

The unenclosed part of the wood was characterised by the presence of species of open areas and disturbed stands (*Poa annua*, *Rumex acetosella*, *Galium saxatile*, *Luzula campestris* and *Rubus fruticosus*). Both old and new enclosures were dominated by *Vaccinium myrtillus* and *Dryopteris dilatata* and had distinctive woodland species such as *Carex pilulifera* and *Oxalis acetosella*. Climbing corydalis (*Corydalis claviculata*), greater stitchwort (*Stellaria holosteoides*), and bluebell (*Hyacinthoides non-scripta*), are all woodland indicator plants that have increased markedly since the 1980s enclosure. Whilst the two latter has not been found in the old enclosure area during the survey of the summer of 2011, they have been observed in the wood in areas from which they were previously absent, including parts of the 1980s enclosure. There was almost no difference between the old and new enclosures in terms of the plant species composition. In the new enclosure, there was a higher frequency of non-woodland or open woodland species: *Agrostis capilaris*, *Galium saxatile*, *Pteridium aquilinum*, which are probably a remnant of previous conditions and will probably reduce or disappear as the canopy closes.

The number of birch seedlings declined markedly over the period, whereas the numbers of oak, rowan and beech seedlings increased (Table 1). The inability of birch to germinate in shady conditions under a thick layer of litter was noted previously (Pigott, 1983). An obvious increase of both rowan and beech is probably related either to either or both, improving soil conditions or maturation of young trees in the area. The older trees may be producing a higher seed input than was happening under the earlier conditions. A distribution of height and girth values

Table 1: Number of individuals of four most abundant species found in 1981 and 2011.

	1981		2011	
	Seedlings	Saplings & Trees	Seedlings	Saplings & Trees
Oak	35	111	91	103
Birch	88	70	17	50
Rowan	8	11	45	47
Beech	3	4	74	15

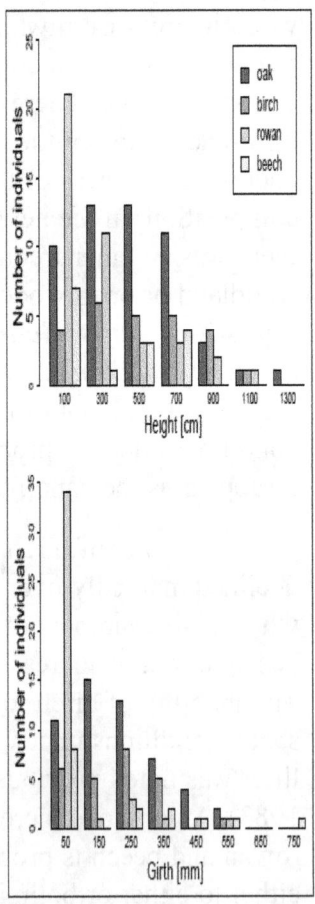

Figure 1: Histogram of distribution of height and girth values of selected tree species.

(Figure 1), demonstrates a gradual change in the tree species composition towards a more extensive admixture of rowan and beech and a slight decline of oak and birch.

Conclusions

Species composition of herbs in the enclosure is very stable. However, there is a strong difference between fenced and unfenced area of the wood as reported previously (Pigott, 1983; Anderson, 1978; Earvey, 1977). A gradual change in tree species composition from declining dominants of oak and birch towards increase of rowan and beech was observed.

References

Anderson, P. (1978) The Longshaw Estate, Hathersage. Ecological Survey. Unpublished technical report to the Peak Park Joint Planning Board and the National Trust, Aldern House, Bakewell.

Anderson, P. and Shimwell, D. (1981) *Wild Flowers and other Plants of the Peak District*. Moorland Publishing Co. Ltd., Ashbourne.

Jarvis, P.G. (1960) Growth and Regeneration of *Quercus petraea* (Matt.) Liebl. in the Sheffield Region. Unpublished Ph.D. Thesis, University of Sheffield, Sheffield.

Earvey, S. (1977) A preliminary study of site management at Padley Wood. Source unknown.

Pigott, C.D. (1983) Regeneration of oak-birch woodland following exclusion of sheep. *Journal of Ecology*, **71**, 629–646.

This volume of papers was published as part of a major event 'Animal, Man and Treescapes' conference organised by Professor Ian D. Rotherham and colleagues held in September 2011 at Sheffield Hallam University.

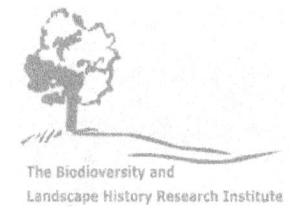

www.ingramcontent.com/pod-product-compliance
Lightning Source LLC
Chambersburg PA
CBHW080934300426
44115CB00017B/2817